# EDMUND BURKE

## THE PRACTICAL IMAGINATION

EDMUND BURKE, 1776

*Mezzotint engraving after a portrait by George Romney*
*Yale University Art Gallery, M. B. Garvan Collection*

# EDMUND BURKE

## THE PRACTICAL IMAGINATION

Gerald W. Chapman

HARVARD UNIVERSITY PRESS

Cambridge, Massachusetts

1967

Distributed in Great Britain by
Oxford University Press, London

Library of Congress Catalog Card Number 67-17305

Printed in the United States of America

TO RUTH, WHO ENDURED, AND TO
JACK, WHO WAITED

# Foreword

BURKE was a practical and imaginative thinker unpredictable in the range and depth of his insights. In his feats of language, in the kind of open and reflective sensibility which he carried into the world of fact, he was, as Coleridge said, "almost a poet." A useful approach to his thought, therefore, must look for "sense" instead of "system." The unity in Burke's thinking is to be sought in its latent character or spirit, in what I have called "practical imagination"—his power to experience the life of a thing in its "organic" complexity, to discriminate its relations, and to act upon (or reverence) its latent good.

Hence the form and method of this book. I have divided chapters to correspond with the five great issues or crises of his career—America, Ireland, Constitutional Reform, France, and India—not for the sake of geographical neatness, but because these were the great political crises in his lifetime, and not to admit them in the organization of the book would falsify things-as-Burke-encountered-them, the conscious horizons within which his thinking was carried out. Such was his fate, after he entered Parliament at age 36, that one crisis followed another, with steadily mounting weight and complexity, and I have wanted to preserve his sense of engagement with each, as well as with their interrelations. Accordingly, I have made an interpretive summary and analysis of his actual thinking about each crisis, more or less following the nature of the materials, striving at once to be as precise and as inclusive as possible, and trying to resist fixation upon any single drift of thinking to the exclusion of all others. I have wanted to express the unique quality emergent from the mutual bearings of his particular thoughts upon one another, to elucidate characteristic principles with as little loss as possible of their concrete envelope of feeling and unspoken intention.

In short, I wanted to "get inside" Burke's thinking, his sense of things, and to follow its development, while at the same time maintaining an "over the shoulders" distance and freedom of judgment. For this reason—as also because he is a writer of great beauty and force of intelligence—my method is heavily "quotative," to coin a word. I have allowed Burke to speak for himself as freely as I could, and I have relegated the most of general scholarship and criticism to the endnotes. Many of the quotations, I believe, are not well known, even to well-educated people; and many of the well-known quotations have appeared in misleading or, on occasion, openly false contexts. I have wanted to create a perpetual context which, while remaining readable in itself, would make the quotations yield a correct tone with correct implications. If the method fails, then it fails in a good cause, which was to search for some fresh way of dealing with prose values and of suggesting what happens, or should happen, in our transactions with a great prose writer. Burke has had a spirited revival since the end of World War II, and yet I confess to a considerable disappointment with some of the directions which the revival has taken, and the uses to which his presumed ideas have been put. There is danger lest his greatness be lost, once again, in partisan bickering, so that shortly he may cease to be read for the right reasons—for humane wisdom in the grand style. The remark of Matthew Arnold, who, almost a hundred years ago, was beset by a like anxiety, still seems to me relevant, though his choice of "stories" would have to be changed:

> Shakespeare and Milton we are all supposed to know something of; but of none of our prose classics, I think, if we leave stories out of the account, such as are the *Pilgrim's Progress* and the *Vicar of Wakefield,* are we expected to have a like knowledge. . . . Our grandfathers were bound to know their Addison, but for us the obligation has ceased; nor is that loss, indeed, a very serious matter. But to lose Swift and Burke out of our mind's circle of acquaintance is a loss indeed, and a loss for which no conversance

with contemporary prose literature can make up, any more than conversance with contemporary poetry could make up to us for unacquaintance with Shakespeare and Milton.

My method is really unmethodical; the result, a hybrid of biography and history of ideas, neither quite one nor the other, but akin to each insofar as they are both arts of characterizing the actual. To invent a term, the result might be called ideo-biography. In Chapter I, and off and on throughout the book, I have discussed some of the background from which Burke's thought emerged, especially the relation of his thought to the tradition of English philosophic empiricism and to the new organic premise gradually dawning in the eighteenth century. But I am only too aware of the limitations and possible traps in such a discussion. When history is reduced to intellectual environments, the historian risks forgetting that ideas also are individual activities which a man "moves" on his own as surely as if they were parliamentary resolutions or proposals of marriage; that ideas are practical and characteristic; that an idea has quite as much of its "meaning" in the puzzled and frail dynamism of a man living along uniquely, as in its implications to a supposedly objective logic or in its approximate repetition of ideas previous or later. Expository critics risk inventing an "intellectual man" quite as arbitrary as "economic man" in classical economics or "political man" in classical utilitarianism. With a hope therefore of doing some justice to the actual spirit and character of Burke's thought (and, in passing, of hitting upon a better technique *préciser et nuancer*), I have tried to remember that his ideas were the finite activities of a man who, day by day, like other men, felt the weight of his own existence, and exerted his thought as he could to lighten the weight, grope for the ideal ground where truth and practice meet; who comprehended some matters well, perhaps better than anyone else in his day or since, but saw others in the twisted lights and dark glass of his passion; who drew upon inspirations of many unrelated kinds; who embodied much of his best thinking in a happy phrase as often as in a logical deduction. Whether such an empirical essay on *dem Burkes Geist* really solves anything, others must decide. I have taken consolation from Burke's own youthful conclusion to the preface of *The Sublime and the Beautiful:*

I am satisfied I have done but little by these observations considered in themselves; and I never should have taken the pains to digest them, much less should I have ever ventured to publish them, if I was not convinced that nothing tends more to the corruption of science than to suffer it to stagnate. These waters must be troubled, before they can exert their virtues. A man who works beyond the surface of things, though he may be wrong himself, yet he clears the way for others, and may chance to make even his errors subservient to the cause of truth.

A preface, by convention, is not only a confession of limits, but also an acknowledgment of debts; yet I would like to thank so many people encountered along the way, obliged as I am to so many, that I despair of naming them all. I thank them dearly and with a paradox—singly *en masse*. I must specify my thanks, however, to the Henry P. Kendall Fund for its generous and timely help. My wife, the silent partner, helped heave the lead every inch of way I made. By his careful reading of the manuscript, John Bullitt prevented many errors and gaucheries, at the same time sharing his knowledge and communicating his enthusiasm for eighteenth-century studies. Without the friendship of Herschel Baker and the late Hyder Rollins, I could never have studied at all. My greatest immediate debts, however, are to Walter Jackson Bate, whose open, manly, and brilliant spirit, whose humanity and whose humor and eloquence, are beyond my thanking. I cannot decide that I am indebted to him for any single thing more than another. Perhaps he would be most pleased to hear, what is true and to me especially important, that "he may be said to have formed my mind and to have brushed off from it a deal of rubbish."

G. W. C.

*Denver, Colorado*
*November 10, 1966*

# CONTENTS

# EDMUND BURKE

## THE PRACTICAL IMAGINATION

# I

# The Organic Premise

BURKE means many things to many men. His prelacy in conservatism is commonly recognized; yet, as Harold Laski says, Burke also gives "deep comfort to men of liberal temper." [1] He is neoclassic, but also romantic; he is a nationalistic citizen of the world and a Tory Whig, a throwback to the seventeenth century and a seminal thinker for the nineteenth, an Irishman who reveals much that is best in the English mind, a busy-buzzing M.P. whom at least three respectable judges—Hazlitt, Arnold, and Leslie Stephen—have called the greatest prose writer in English literature. He is one of those great amphibious Englishmen, not quite liberal, not quite conservative, poetically open in his thinking, broadly practical in his poetry, whose diffuse and many-mansioned thought seems always implicit with a coherent and synthetic system which, however, is never achieved. Laski, after a cautious sizing-up from an opposing camp, pronounced Burke the greatest figure in the history of English politics, and sensed in his writings the latent but obscure presence of "a system which, even in its unfinished implications, is hardly less gigantic than that of Hobbes or Bentham." [2] Observing that Burke's emphasis on expediency is not, to his mind, a real "release from metaphysical inquiry," Laski went on to suggest "that what was needed in Burke's philosophy was the clear avowal of the metaphysic it implied." [3] One might like to agree, and to announce that at last, after a century and a half of mellowing, the metaphysical system is ready to be avowed, that one can drag it out of obscurity into the limelight and the applause of the world. But no. Pin Burke down at one point, and he dances away at another, in what Hazlitt called admiringly, his "circumgyrations." His thought is a master-solvent of antinomies—metaphysics and common sense, poetry and practicality, liberalism and conservatism, neoclassicism and romanticism, Christianity and pragmatism, to name but a few. Every digging after "Burke's system" to date has come up with a something bleached of the full meaning and value of the context—"Burke's sense." One is reminded of nothing so much as the affectionate frustration of a modern interpreter of Hooker:

> He is both a Humanist and a Protestant, both a Thomist and an Augustinian, both a rationalist and a traditionalist; he believed both in authority and freedom, both in consent and obligation, both in law and sovereignty, both in uniformity and toleration, both in Church and State, both in human nature and in the Fall.[4]

Something there seems to be about the characteristically English mind which is a living paradox. Possibly, somewhere in the depths of Burke's "experienced benignity" may have lain, or may lie, a system. To ignore a latent coherency and rational dependence in his *ad hoc* propositions is surely to miss a principal feature in his thought and a source of his quality. But the possibility of abstracting a system is small. One may suspect that dying in 1897, or in 1997, Burke would have bequeathed the same character of splendidly unfinished thought, and that for future as for present readers he will remain a living paradox.

More than any other single figure, he typifies the union, in his own thinking, of what are perhaps the two greatest achievements of English culture to date—its literary imagination, and its success in practical politics.

Certain specific drifts of his thought are, of course, evident. Burke is a key—if not the first great—exemplar of the *geschictlichen Sinn* in one of its forms—a mode of imaginative sensibility to the past, and to the present as continuous with the past, which has added a new dimension to human experience. It has not gone unappreciated. Coleridge perceived, and learned from Burke's historical sense. The strange and passionate Novalis remarked of the *Reflections:* "Burke has written a revolutionary book against the Revolution." [5] Later in the century Lord Acton, then only twenty-four, perceived the amazing subtlety and novelty of Burke's penetration of history even in the youthful *Essay Towards an Abridgement of English History,* which Burke turned off at twenty-eight. As there is very little doubt, he said, that "Burke was our greatest statesman," so if he had persisted, he "would have been the first of our historians." Acton admired Burke's freedom from pedantry, capacity for scholarship, vigor of experience —and his intelligent appreciation of the medieval:

> Several generations of men were still to follow, who were to derive their knowledge of the Middle Ages from the Introduction to Robertson's *Charles V,* to study ecclesiastical history in the pages of Gibbon, and to admire Hume as the prince of historians. At the age of thirty [*sic*], Burke proved himself superior to that system of prejudice and ignorance which was then universal, and which is not yet completely dissipated.[6]

Burke had the imagination to seize a contemplative order of history which was imperfectly conscious, obscurely felt, in the cultural life of his period, and which the life of his period sorely required. Clinging to his theory that romanticism and the recovery of medieval sympathies among Protestants were intimately related, Acton concluded, in a note near the end of his life: "History issues from the Romantic School. Piecing together what the Rev[olution] snapped. It hails from Burke, as Education from Helvetius, or Emancipation from the Quakers." [7] Accepting Acton's view, Herbert Butterfield could state as late as 1955 that Burke—instead of Sir Walter Scott—"exerted the presiding influence over the historical movement of the nineteenth century." [8] Certainly one cannot turn to Burke from the cunning succinctness of Hume, or the erudite analyses and massive ironic portraiture of Gibbon, without sensing that one is present somehow in a new world —superficially familiar, yet at bottom strangely altered and intense.

Burke is hardly a romantic medievalist, however. To understand his thought with reference to political developments in early nineteenth-century Germany, where his influence was enormous, is almost inevitably to short-change its neoclassic, eighteenth-century, practical, and characteristically English, spirit. Conservative followers in Germany—his friend Brandes, Rehburg and Möser—admired Burke's sense of living in history, and what appeared to them his aristocratic responsibility and attack upon natural law; romantic organicists—Novalis, Adam Müller, and Stein—abstracted from him an idealization of the medieval state to accommodate their own admiration of the ancient Holy Roman Empire. The common denominator of all, as of the publicist Gentz, was that they used Burke's name, example, and ideas to express their hatred of the French Revolution. Much of the dust raised by these men has settled upon Burke's reputation and obscured his full quality. As Reinhold Aris justly remarks: "When Burke praised the age of chivalry he was using a historic flourish to strengthen his position, but he would have been horrified at the idea that someone would use his arguments in order to revive feudalism." [9] In spirit, Burke is really more comparable with the half-romanticist, half-classicist Goethe, who called himself a "moderate liberal"—one who "tries, with the means at his command, to do as much good as ever he can, but is cautious of wishing to destroy immediately by fire and sword faults which are often inevitable. He endeavours by intelligent progress gradually to suppress public wrongs, without simultaneously spoiling just as much that is good by taking violent measures. He contents himself, in this always imperfect world, with what is good, until time and circumstances favour the attainment of something better." [10]

Burke approaches politics in a hardheaded and present-minded fashion, as well as with that quality of imagination which might be called romantic and historical; he turns upon hard fact, wherever it is to be met, a contemplative subtlety and concrete appreciativeness. He is committed to a *practical* approach to politics, and those features in his thought which link with the romantic and the medieval rise, as it were, as by-products of other and, one may think, equally significant features—his old-fashioned love of liberty, his classical discipline; his humanitarianism; his prosaic duties as an M.P.; his lawyer's respect for process, negotiation, and specific reason; his confidence that the natural law persists; his play of satire and concern for decorum; his confidence in common sense. As G. M. Young observes, classical criticism of every kind is "a form of public service," whose interest is not "to expatiate on the result, but to show how it was brought about, because by studying that you may be able to produce something like the same result yourself." [11] It asks "how to do it." Confronted with a novel occasion, Burke searches its texture of necessities, its correlation of component factors, for the course of action latently most effective, and for the "principles" or fruitful generalities which may be applied in future occasions to produce, or avoid, like effects, or which at least increase one's intelligence of probabilities. Hence his emphasis upon "common sense." Unwilling to jump with each fashionable evolution of opinion, Burke suspends commitment until the rear dimensions of experience and old partiality, various, multiform, and intricate, are brought up to be compared critically and, if possible, reconciled. He applies new knowledge wherever it throws a clear light, but would apply it in moderation—that is, intelligently—with due regard to its ascertained limits within the context of the familiar and the past. He tries not to be one of those whose accurate and logical reasonings bring them up against an impasse, or who, being too exquisite in their conjectures of the future, can only bring to the gross emergences of actuality an immense surprise. Common sense, restrained by the actual, is often blind to hypothetical goods and obstinate within the familiar, but it is also capable of great delicacy of adjustment to novel occasions. Unburdened with the vanity of hypostatized systems, it is more natively responsive to main events. It is the particular stage of intelligence in which the relation of imagined probabilities to a factual situation is clearly descried. There is much truth in Laski's conclusion that Burke "is destined doubtless to live rather as the author of some maxims that few statesmen will dare to forget than as the creator of a system"; [12] he will live by the example of his moral elevation and by the perpetual relevance of his thought "in that middle ground between the facts and speculation [where] his supremacy is unapproached." [13] A man in politics, Burke said, must seek "the exactest detail of circumstances, guided by the surest general principles that are necessary to direct experiment and inquiry, in order again from those details to elicit principles, firm and luminous general principles, to direct a practical legislative proceeding." [14]

Even at those moments when, one feels, the vast seething stability of the organic commonwealth looms hauntingly in his imagination, Burke is less interested in painting his fancy of it, or in spinning a theory about it, than in deciding how, in all common sense, one had best behave, and in keeping his generalizations "useful" or "expedient." He is intent upon abstracting *axioms of practical method,* whose spirit W. E. H. Lecky has caught in so brilliant an epitome that one can do no better than to quote him at length:

Government is obliged to discharge the most various functions, to aim at many distinct and sometimes inconsistent ends. It is the trustee and the guardian of the multifarious, complicated, fluctuating, and often conflicting interests of a highly composite and artificial society. The principle that tends towards one set of advantages impairs another. The remedies which apply to one set of dangers would, if not partially counteracted, produce another. The institutions which are admirably adapted to protect one class of interests, may be detrimental to another. It is only by constant adjustments, by checks and counterchecks, by various contrivances adapted to various needs, by compromises between competing interests, by continual modifications applied to changing circumstances, that a system is slowly formed which corresponds to the requirements and conditions of the country, discharges the greatest number of useful functions, and favours in their due proportion and degree the greatest number of distinct and often diverging interests. The comparative prominence of different interests, tendencies, and dangers, must continually occupy the legislator, and he will often have to provide limitations and obstacles to the very tendency which he wishes to make the strongest in his legislation.[15]

Furthermore, though in his attacks upon "metapoliticians," upon natural rights, *raison,* and conventional contract theory, Burke seems, at times, as German romanticists thought, to desert natural law for a philosophy of organic process, yet the fact remains that every effort to draw his implicit assumptions into an organic focus sooner or later, after every partial success, will confront the obstinate and opaque presence of Nature.[16] View it from what perspective you will, Nature will not yield, will not take its place in the system. At point after point, Burke's magnificent intellect pushes beyond and shatters that Nature which had become a platitude of the salon, and that Nature which only named a comfortable emotion and was idolized either as a set of propositions or as a mythic image. One thinks of his grasp of American character and growth; his awareness of the mutual relatedness and interpenetrative correspondence of elements in the empire, in the constitution, in the "commonwealth" of Europe; his reaching out into the uniqueness of Indian life; his watching, horrified, the "unfolding of the Germ of Jacobinism." [17] Time after time, guided as it were by some intuitive navigation, his thinking breaks upon the mystery of organic process. Yet only to retract on other occasions. When all is said, an older idea of nature remains essential in his thought, a clear and distinct concept of "law" accessible to reason, including that "eternal, immutable law in which will and reason are the same." [18] His search for practical principles, for example, implies belief in a human nature more or less recurrent within actual political occasions, no matter how cautious he is about predicting the limits of its possibilities.

The whole tradition of English empiricism (not to mention Christian humanism) lies behind him; and in many ways, what was happening to English empiricism, generally speaking, explains the status of Nature in his thought.

Bacon, to take a representative figure, is an example of English empiricism in a dramatic early stage. His imagination is still active about first principles, still charged with grateful vision and jealous of its purity. He is busied with originating new strategy to solve the age-old conflicts of permanence and change. Bacon is dedicated to changing the world by learning the "causes," the limitations of possibility, of change in nature. His metaphysics pushes him constantly into the realm of hard fact and practical suggestion, but always in behalf of the larger aim—the "interpretation" of nature. The Nature that emerges in his thinking is significant of things to come in the way that the child is father of the man. A vision of things melts into subtle crevices of the mind and silently motivates thinking. Visions are causes in history. The Nature which Bacon isolates for thought, however exquisitely subtle and beautiful its movements, amounts in the end to a uniform texture of causes, fixed in a static eternity of relation. True, "in nature nothing really exists beside individual bodies," but within *the acts and changes* of individual bodies there is a "latent process" which is "perfectly continuous" though invisible in its causal texture, and this causal texture "embraces the unity of nature in substances the most unlike." [19] Thus, the causal texture (rational unity) of concrete change is the true object of philosophy, and hence the name "rational empiricism." Rational empiricism is the faith that all concrete particulars are generated by interlocking principles which, though very intricate and obscure, can nevertheless be inferred from their "effects." The empiricist always watches concrete "effects," discriminates abstract relations or connections among them, in hopes thereafter to direct his knowledge to the discovery, generation, or control of new "effects." This is true, for example, of Newton, who in the *Opticks* fatefully labels the up-and-down method "analysis" and "synthesis":

By this way of analysis we may proceed from compounds to ingredients, and from motions to the forces producing them; and in general, from effects to their causes, and from particular causes to more general ones, till the argument end in the most general. This is the method of analysis: and the synthesis consists in assuming the causes discovered, and established as principles, and by them explaining the phenomena proceeding from them.[20]

But later empiricists, turning their thought to politics, art, morals, history, and psychology, wade into unsuspected deeps of metaphysical darkness, from which, generally speaking, English empiricism only begins to emerge, in its theoretical foundations, in the twentieth century (for example, in the works of Whitehead and Russell) . For it is the paradox of rational empiricism, fully illustrated in Bacon's own arguments, that in shuttling back and forth between fact and law, selecting facts to form laws and forming laws to explain facts, it tends to complete itself in systems of greater and greater abstraction from the very "experience" it pronounces solely real. Later inheritors of empiricism, like Burke, faced the obstinate paradox that the more empirical they became the less rational, and the more rational the less empirical. They came to experience more than they could rationally account for. Thus they wrestled with insistent dualisms of permanence and change, unity and multeity, generality and particularity, abstraction and circumstance, ideality and fact. Facts had penumbras and fringe areas of meaning that defied classification and experimental rule, and unfolded vistas of startling complexity and nuance. One thinks of Montesquieu's idea of "spirit"; of Burke's response to the "great contexture of the mysterious whole"; of Sir Joshua Reynolds' trying to decide what "Idea" was; of Lord Kames' being haunted by "relations":

Cause and effect, contiguity in time or in place, high and low, prior and posterior, resemblance, contrast, and a thousand other relations connect things together without end. Not a single thing appears solitary and altogether devoid of connection: the only difference is, that some are intimately connected, some more slightly, some near, some at a distance.[21]

One may also remember that Kames goes on puzzling until he describes a work of art as like an "organic system" in which it is required that "its parts be orderly arranged and mutually connected, bearing each of them a relation to the whole, some more intimate, some less, according to their destination." [22]

Partly from this love quarrel of the rational and empirical faculties, whose marriage Bacon sang with such hope, something indeed like "organicism" is born. The texture of enduring causes too subtle for sense and *a priori* reason is a haunting certainty which must somehow be reconciled with fleeting fact and value. The practical empiricist, like Burke, discovers his need for a self-legislated restraint of reason in order to continue "empirical." He resists the threat of mental inflation; he stops the dangerous spiral of his thinking, so as not to break his moorings in experience and perish in the thin air of conceptual abstraction. Thus, though he may not escape believing in a universal order of causes, he shies from it with reverent caution. He is committed to the theory of a strict, overarching rational order, but also to an exploration of actual existence for its latent and emergent circumstances. Nature yields something to History, and the chain of causes is submerged in the chain of events. He may grow resentful of other empiricists, trenchant intellects who cling fast to rational systems, to "metaphysics," without staying open to the nuances of actuality and practice which have a vital bearing on the case at hand. He becomes suspicious of their "reason," though he may learn from it, and cultivates in himself an imaginative sagacity which, turning outward upon current or past events, and being nourished by his general power of experiencing, searches for "practical" principles—which, "feeling the effect" (a constant motif in Burke), then grasps discrete circumstances into a unity expressive of latent particular relations.

In this reaction from the Nature of mechanico-materialism and its "philosophy of death," [23] as Coleridge called it, Burke indeed approximated thinking of an "organic" character. A host of conditioning ideas like *continuity, the virtual, permanence* and *change, spirit, coalescence, interrelation,* and *vital character* threw open vistas of perception in his experience and suggested to him frequently that reality is like *this* and not like *that.* For example, it occurred to him as early as 1774, in the quiet of his notes, that the "real character" of the English parliament derived from its reconciliation of permanence and change, past and present: from the perpetuity of its actualization within novelties of the historical process.

> Nothing is more beautiful in the theory of parliaments than that principle of renovation, and union of permanence and change, that are happily mixed in their constitution:—that in all our changes we are never either wholly old or wholly new:—that there are enough of the old to preserve unbroken the traditionary chain of the maxims and policy of our ancestors, and the law and custom of parliament; and enough of the new to invigorate us and bring us to our true character, by being taken fresh from the mass of the people; and the whole, though mostly composed of the old members, have, notwithstanding, a new character, and may have the advantage of change without the imputation of inconstancy.[24]

The idea of *the organic* is implicit insofar as the term implies a recognition that reality presents itself as a fabric of actualizing possibilities requiring the human mind to make endless reconciliations of possession and emergence, each emergent as it is assimilated, modifying the whole tenor of the possessed, by an endless feeling attention to incursions of novelty, like showers of meteoric light within the atmosphere of the familiar. No example could seem clearer. Yet this reconciliation of permanence and change in English institutions Burke called "the pattern of nature." [25] The importance of this perpetual confrontation of tradition, law, or custom, with change, was that the more changes it withstood or negotiated, without loss of its essentials (principles, fundamentals), the more likely that its principles correspond with Nature, to which an empirical appeal is always open. Burke's organicism, therefore, is not thoroughgoing or exclusive; natural law is still a regulative notion; one has to do with an "organicism," so to speak, evolved and sustained on strictly empirical premises; one confronts another antinomy reconciled in practice when it might appear irreconcilable to logic.

Wherever one turns, the story is the same. There seems hardly a trend of Burke's thinking for which there is no countertrend almost equally essential, locked up in the mystery of his quality and not to be shaken out. Patterns of meaning break toward system, then stop, or fall away; ideas familiar enough at one point appear elsewhere suffused with uniqueness, in flickering degrees of intensity and in fresh relations; what is dark or tentative at one point is clarified at another, but rarely completed. Burke's organicism is a premise for experience, not a systematic philosophy of the kind which soared into fashion during the nineteenth century, after his death; it has affinities with Hooker instead of with Hegel, with Wordsworth instead of with Novalis, or in this century with Whitehead instead of, say, with Heidegger. It is practical and imaginatively open, and must be experienced manysidedly as a spirit of his thought within *ad hoc* occasions.

One must search his particular judgments, then, not for a system, but for a characteristic activity, of which they are *ad hoc* expressions. The unity in Burke's thought would seem to lie in the character of his intelligence as it operates upon the life of his time. It is a mode of imaginative practicality which has appeared in English culture within many very different and often cross theoretical positions—a peculiar fusion of poetic conception and literary brilliance, ethical awareness and religious reverence, preference for concrete inquiry and compromise, common sense and sense of duty, and what Fox called a "reverse of selfishness." Burke was at once, for his time, its exemplar, and in some measure, by rendering it conscious, its creator.

# II

# Burke and America

THE Americans, Burke felt, were justly alarmed by English politics in the postwar decade. He was alarmed himself by "the particular distemperature of our own air and season" [1]—a drift toward ultra-conservatism, especially among the new Tories with their "cabal of the closet and backstairs," [2] their Procrustean legalism, their confidence in Hessians and redcoats. He feared for the long-run subversion of English liberties from within:

> A system unfavourable to freedom may be so formed, as considerably to exalt the grandeur of the state; and men may find, in the pride and splendour of that prosperity, some sort of consolation for the loss of their solid privileges. Indeed the increase of the power of the state has often been urged by artful men, as a pretext for some abridgment of the public liberty. But the scheme of the junto under consideration, not only strikes a palsy into every nerve of our free constitution, but in the same degree benumbs and stupifies the whole executive power: rendering government in all its grand operations languid, uncertain, ineffective.[3]

In *Thoughts on the Cause of the Present Discontents* (1770) he spoke out, with courage and foresight, against the first stages of Georgian reaction at home; in the American debacle he watched, with incredulous horror, the fruits of reaction abroad. To Fox he pointed out "manifest marks of the resurrection of the Tory Party"—men of public spirit retiring in fatigued disgust, jingoism in the clergy, secretive complacence in ministers and Crown, and what worried him most perhaps, "a sort of heavy, lumpish acquiescence in government." [4] To Rockingham he expressed fears that the national character was changing, had changed within a few years.

> We seem no longer that eager, inquisitive, jealous, fiery people, which we have been formerly, and which we have been a very short time ago. The people look back, without pleasure or indignation; and forward, without hope or fear. No man commends the measures which have been pursued, or expects any good from those which are in preparation; but it is a cold, languid opinion, like what men discover in affairs that do not concern them. It excites to no passion; it prompts to no action.[5]

With apathy grew also a muddied, scoundrel patriotism. For example, Burke noticed that some of his Bristol constituents, merchants once in favor of peace, were snuffing "the cadaverous *haut gout* of lucrative war." [6] In postwar ministries, excepting the one-year Whig administration of 1766, Burke thought he saw doctrinairism, vacillation, and pretense—a spirit of littleness and fraud. And all this in a great nation which in victory, after the Peace of Paris (1763), had suddenly found itself responsible for an empire.

The situation called for great efforts of political intelligence. But a tide had set for turbulent repose. To be sure, the nation was wealthy and powerful; corruption and meanness, though greatly spread, were certainly not universal; many men in many parties kept their character; private life and people at large were disposed to good; and luxury, of course, when "well balanced and diffused, is only decency and convenience," nourishing emulation and in all ranks a "sense of personal value." [7] But an atmosphere of black reaction frightened Burke—a reaction which, ironically, in its later Francophobic stages would be linked by many historians with his name.

Against such a backdrop, Burke's spiritual achievement in

the American crisis stands out sharply. Perhaps he was too ready to see the *Götterdämmerung* of Whig power as national decadence. Burke had knit himself nearly with the Rockingham party and with the squadron of Old Whig families—"with the Saviles, the Dowdeswells, the Wentworths, the Bentincks; with the Lenoxes, the Manchesters, the Keppels, the Saunderses; with the temperate, permanent, hereditary virtue of the whole House of Cavendish." [8] The threats to what they represented in English life, which Lord David Cecil has brilliantly sketched,[9] filled him with anxious sadness. In crises he was only too likely, first, to judge of what these families were by what they ought to be, and then, having descried the generous limit, to suspend it over history like the Logos. His growing awareness of their insecurity adds a special and poignant and, in view of later developments, a seminal subplot to his American writings: the several Whig apologias scattered over a decade [10] foreshadow the later, more impassioned and explicit *Appeal from the New to the Old Whigs* (1791). Very likely much of Burke's fear for the national character was a fear for his own deeply-felt Whiggery. Partly for that reason, however, his achievement stands out. Despite an ominous train of conflicts and disappointments, ending in loss of empire, Burke made a serenity out of near despair, and came away counseling magnanimous realism, in an age, as he felt it, of violence and ideology. "I am aware that the age is not what we all wish. But I am sure, that the only means of checking its precipitate degeneracy, is heartily to concur with whatever is the best in our time." [11] It was an instance of practical imagination.

At some moment in 1777 Burke laid aside his pen with the pain of one who has lost something, and the dignity grimly decorous of one resolved not to repine. Throughout the crisis, as almost all critics admit, he had conducted himself with generosity, poise, and intelligent passion. His American writings have a special unity all their own, a spiral of awareness, from his early criticism of Grenville policies, through his alarmed pleas for sanity and reconciliation, to his wartime resignation and levelheaded acceptance of the facts. They are the fruits of ripeness, and they glow with the bitter innocence of manhood. Conservatives may draw from them a program, and liberals an armory of arguments. After 1777, when the war was still raging, Burke never again discoursed formally on America, and alluded to it only in the most casual, infrequent, and broken way, partly, as he told Fox, because his earnest and anxious perseverance had persuaded many people (including Samuel Johnson) that he was dishonest.[12] But partly, too, because it was no longer an issue to be acted upon. Instead of railing at the colonists for shattering the lovely mold of empire, Burke wished the new nation well. In almost all his references to "the dreadful schism" his sympathy and even admiration show through for the "quiet and rational people in the provinces . . . united with, and hurried away by, the violent; having indeed different dispositions, but a common interest." [13] Their outburst of rebelliousness, in which by force of events they had erected their own government, would have subsided of itself, he felt, but for the agitation of a few mutinous insolences and the cold-blooded blundering of blind, largely Tory misgovernment.

Burke had done all he could to show, and he promised that some day people would see, "this mass of weakness and violence" [14] in its true light. His last effort in 1777, following *A Letter to the Sheriffs of Bristol, on the Affairs of America,* came when a group led by the Duke of Richmond planned a walkout of American sympathizers in both Houses. For the occasion Burke prepared two petitionary addresses, one to the Crown, one to "the British Colonists in North America," summarizing the case for conciliation, and fixing blame squarely on misgovernment where Burke thought it belonged. They are not polemics, however, but open pleas, expository, luminous, and candid; they breathe the genuine simplicity of heart which he had told the Commons two years before, in a famous passage, was the only practical means of conciliation; they practice his earlier proposition:

The proposition is peace. Not peace through the medium of war; not peace to be hunted through the labyrinth of intricate and endless negotiations; not peace to arise out of universal discord, fomented from principle, in all parts of the empire; not peace to depend on the juridical determination of perplexing questions, or the precise marking the shadowy boundaries of a complex government. It is simple peace; sought in its natural course and in its ordinary haunts. . . . My idea is nothing more. Refined policy ever has been the parent of confusion—and ever will be so, as long as the world endures. Plain good intention, which is as easily discovered at the first view, as fraud is surely detected at last, is, let me say, of no mean force in the government of mankind. Genuine simplicity of heart is an healing and cementing principle.[15]

For some reason not clear, the plans were postponed as improperly timed, and finally dropped. Avoiding, then, the effete composure that ascribes no blame, but also the irritable malice that, once set in motion, cannot stop till it hangs a culprit, Burke turned his mind to other urgencies at home: "This we know with certainty, that, though we cannot reclaim them, we may reform ourselves." [16] Grieved as he was, a fine edge of contempt defended him against the defeatism and excess which he predicted would afflict "ingenuous and feeling minds" [17] in such an age. He looked down, as he told a Bristol gathering, upon the clamorous "trifling petulance, which the rage of party stirs up in little minds . . . just as you, gentlemen, when you enjoy the serene air on your lofty rocks, look down upon the gulls that skim the mud of your river, when it is exhausted of its tide." [18]

At this moment of practical poise, Burke had produced three major tracts on America—*Speech on American Taxation* (1774), *Speech on Moving His Resolutions for Conciliation with the Colonies* (1775), both extempore and later revised, and *A Letter to the Sheriffs of Bristol, on the Affairs of America* (1777). As a unit John Morley praises them as "the most perfect manual in our literature, or any literature, for one who approaches the study of public affairs, whether for knowledge or for practice." [19] No small reason is that they illustrate, in a multitude of subtle ways, a practical imagination, which may be defined, for what a definition is worth, as the power to experience the life of a thing in its concrete complexity, discriminate its relations, and act upon (or reverence) its latent good. Such an imagination as discerns answers to the questions, "How is it actually?" and "What is its meaningful relevance?" In retrospect they reveal a mind neither liberal nor conservative in any programmatic way. In the time of American troubles Burke was a self-consciously English moderate caught, in the prime of his forties, between two burgeoning extremes—reaction at home, international radicalism abroad—and thus forced to think freshly through his political experience as occasions for thought arose.

## II

In the midst of triumphant violence in 1777, Burke wrote his Bristol constituents a sad assurance: "I think I know America. If I do not, my ignorance is incurable, for I have spared no pains to understand it: and I do most solemnly assure those of my constituents who put any sort of confidence in my industry and integrity, that every thing that has been done there has arisen from a total misconception of the object." [20] His pains probably began when, as a young, ambitious Irishman, he itched to try his luck in the colonies (he backed out in obedience to his father). In 1757 he helped his cousin William patch up an *Account of the European Settlements in America,* a scholarly piece of journalism. When he entered the Commons in 1765 he was plunged immediately into current debates over the Stamp Act. Thereafter, in a tragic crescendo, America alerted some of his best energies. In 1770 he became agent for the New York Assembly.[21] Very likely he knew as much about the colonies as anyone else in England. He had contemplated with awe and admiration their growth, in less than a century, from "a little speck, scarce visible in the mass of the national interest, a small seminal principle," [22] into something very like "ancient nations" —wealthy, populous, and idiosyncratic. Population, trade, agriculture—in economic simplicities the growth was so obvious it almost daunted imagination; it was taken for granted. "Such is the strength with which population shoots in that part of the world, that state the numbers as high as we will, whilst the dispute continues, the exaggeration ends." [23] In 1772 English exports to America alone were nearly equal to the whole export trade of all England in 1704—a growth from about one twelfth to about one third of the whole, and that in the greatest trading nation in the world. Nor was the American trade, as some feared, "an unnatural protuberance, that has drawn the juices from the rest of the body"; rather it had "nourished every other part into its present magnitude." [24] At the beginning of the century some of the colonies had to import grain from England. Now, Burke pointed out, "for some time past, the Old World has been fed from the New." [25] American fisheries encircled the world. Something new and historically significant was transpiring in America (although even Burke underestimated what it was), and he cautioned against trying to understand it by *a priori* maxims, general theories of government, or historical analogies. "The object is wholly new in the world. It is singular; it is grown up to this magnitude and importance within the memory of man; nothing in history is parallel to it. All the reasonings about it, that are likely to be at all solid must be drawn from its actual circumstances." [26]

The wealth and stir of America was a postwar commonplace. Burke was exceptional in his three-dimensional grasp of the event, his sense of history, and his awareness that changes so obvious hid portentous energies not idly to be tampered with. The first colonial nationalism in modern times was coming to birth inside the English-speaking world. Burke groped for an understanding of it. Having no better terms, he spoke of "natural regards," "natural interests," and "natural feelings"; "through a wise and salutary neglect," he observed, "a generous nature has been suffered to take her own way to perfection." [27] In a freely metaphorical way, he inclined to view any national state and national character as a mysterious generation of "nature" and "Providence"—like a mammoth, aspiring plant. Nobody knows why it begins, though one may locate the time and place of its beginning; it springs upon a soil, and assimilates itself to landmarks and determinate peoples; it has its physical necessities and its transient circumstances. But its ultimate roots reach down into the fertile void that fills the interstices of history and from whose teeming seeds all novel existence is procreated.

Burke pleaded with Parliament to study the portent wisely, with a view to accommodation. "They who can read the political sky," he said with Biblical gravity, "will see a hurricane in a cloud no bigger than a hand at the very edge of the horizon, and will run into the first harbour." [28] As the American cloud grew and lowered, however, he felt that British policy, far from seeking a haven of repose and conciliation, kept the British state dangerously at sea; ministers, ignorant of the real circumstances, shook their fists at the storm, with a futile and impotent unreality. A new people, "numerous and mighty," had awakened to self-consciousness in a new world, though within the circuit of British dominion. They would not have their interests and feelings trifled with. Whoever governed them must understand their "true nature" and "peculiar circumstances" or be resigned not to govern long. Policy must tack with the times, or run the risk of being overwhelmed. Taking care not to be "blown about by every wind of fashionable doctrine," Burke sought to ballast his thought and conduct with the actual circumstances of colonial life and the whole history of British policy in America.[29]

Burke felt obliged to familiarize Parliament with "an object so remote from our eye, and so little connected with our immediate feelings," [30] to enliven the sympathy smothered by complacency or inattention. It was no longer necessary, since the Seven Years' War, to draw a map; the days had gone when a Duke of Newcastle, chief of the colonial Board of Trade 1724–1748, could suppose New England to be an island.[31] Yet what distinguished Burke's mind was not simply a learned control of facts, but the power to etherealize them in an almost poetic grasp. He sought, he would one day explain, "a large, liberal, and prospective view of the interests of states," though with some it might pass "for romance; and the principles that recommend it, for the wanderings of a disordered imagination." [32] He deprecated "the mischief of not having large and liberal ideas in the management of great affairs," and he blamed Tory officials for having "taken things by bits and scraps, some at one time and one pretence, and some at another, just as they pressed, without any sort of regard to their relations and dependencies." [33] With Burke, the neoclassic "prospect" or "view," derived in good part from Virgil and Milton, was generally more than a mere imagistic convention; it tended to take on special qualities of intellect and moral penetration, such as might be suggested by the present-day phrase "vision of life." Burke was a key figure in the gradual eighteenth-century development of the concept of imagination away from "the power of visualization"—the Addisonian "view"—toward "the power of evoking associations, especially emotive ones, the power of entering sympathetically into other peoples' feelings." [34] The imaginative "view" was manifest in his practice, but also in his admirations. For example: in 1757 Burke considered Montesquieu, the great eccentric theorist of English liberty and comparative history, "the greatest genius which has enlightened this age." [35] In later years he explained why: Montesquieu not only had a "penetrating, aquiline eye," judgment, industry, detachment, "herculean robustness of mind," circumstantiality in scholarship, but also was like the universal patriarch in Milton who had "drawn up before him in his poetic vision" whole generations.[36] The many purple passages in Burke, which some castigate as "rhetoric"—forgetting that rhetoric is only artifice with practical aims—are generally efforts to project such a vision or view and to elevate his audience to it. Burke argued himself inward, gradually shaping a thing as it concretely was, in its objective circumstances, relations, and dependencies, but generally with a view to some larger sense, persuasion, or practical sympathy.

Thus Burke painted his famous "view" of the American character and its driving force, to approximate the distant and inertly felt to Parliament's understanding—that is, to waken a sense of American practice as conditioned by ingrown values and principles, fixed, and lively, though more or less unconscious, and suspended in the dearest web of moral feelings. He shaped his view around the principle of liberty to stress a latent English community with America.

And pray, Sir, what in the world is equal to it? . . . look at the manner in which the people of New England have of late carried on the whale fishery. Whilst we follow them among the tumbling mountains of ice, and behold them penetrating into the deepest frozen recesses of Hudson's Bay and Davis's Straits, whilst we are looking for them beneath the arctic circle, we hear that they have pierced into the opposite region of polar cold, that they are at the antipodes, and engaged under the frozen serpent of the south. Falkland Island, which seemed too remote and romantic an object for the grasp of national ambition, is but a stage and resting-place in the progress of their victorious industry. . . . whilst some of them draw the line and strike the harpoon on the coast of Africa, others run the longitude, and pursue their gigantic game along the coast of Brazil. No sea but what is vexed by their fisheries. No climate that is not witness to their toils. Neither the perseverance of Holland, nor the activity of France, nor the dexterous and firm sagacity of English enterprise, ever carried this most perilous mode of hardy industry to the extent to which it has been pushed by this recent people; a people who are still, as it were, but in the gristle, and not yet hardened into the bone of manhood. When I contemplate these things; when I know that the colonies in general owe little or nothing to any care of ours, and that they are not squeezed into this happy form by the constraints of watchful and suspicious government, but that, through a wise and salutary neglect, a generous nature has been suffered to take her own way to perfection; when I reflect . . . I feel all the pride of power sink, and all presumption in the wisdom of human contrivances melt and die away within me. My rigour relents. I pardon something to the spirit of liberty.[37]

On land Burke pointed to a like inner-directed, aggressive, and pioneering energy, which could be tempered to British authority only by great delicacy. So far, success had been achieved not by the "hoarding of a royal wilderness," [38] but by lax grants and concessions: authority had followed and not constrained the energy; it had given a direction, a form, a technical dress, and a specific sanction to the colonists' self-willed adventures. "We have thrown each tract of land, as it was peopled, into districts, that the ruling power should never be wholly out of sight." [39] But such an energy, like adolescent pride,[40] could only be conciliated, it could not be possessed; if blocked, it would force legal channels with great violence. Suppose, for example, that royal grants should be stopped, as a measure of punishment or regulation?

> The people would occupy without grants. They have already so occupied in many places. You cannot station garrisons in every part of these deserts. If you drive the people from one place, they will carry on their annual tillage, and remove with their flocks and herds to another. Many of the people in the back settlements are already little attached to particular situations. Already they have topped the Appalachian mountains. From thence they behold before them an immense plain, one vast, rich, level meadow; a square of five hundred miles. Over this they would wander without a possibility of restraint; they would change their manners with the habits of their life; would soon forget a government by which they were disowned; would become hordes of English Tartars; and pouring down upon your unfortified frontiers a fierce and irresistible cavalry, become masters of your governors and your counsellors, your collectors and comptrollers, and of all the slaves that adhered to them.[41]

An impetuous liberty was instinct in the colonists' historical conditioning and perpetually renewed by a frontier wilderness, where barbarism was the alternative to governmental tact.

Now, Burke was speaking of American liberty in 1775, which—despite its grounding English affinities—had special traits. "Abstract liberty, like other mere abstractions, is not to be found." [42] Like a contextualist, he tried to imagine the concrete meaning of the idea in its living relations, and thus to prevent *liberty* from sliding into a mere icon (a "reverend abstraction," as Morley says) [43] or into a theoretical distinction (as, for example, a disjunctive of *necessity*).[44] Liberty in Burke's eyes amounted to a practical enjoyment within a historical community and therefore, at any given moment in history, it would be "like all other things in common life, . . . variously mixed and modified, enjoyed in very different degrees, and shaped into an infinite diversity of forms, according to the temper and circumstances of every community." [45] In England it had evolved one way; in classical slave-holding commonwealths it had existed in other modes, as in America or some future commonwealth it might exist in still other modes and degrees. In his opinion, liberty was at any time a good to be improved, "the vital spring and energy of the State itself, which has just so much life and vigour as there is liberty in it." [46] Yet like all else, it had to be limited to be enjoyed and no limits could be settled by the politician *a priori,* outside the exigencies of the historical moment. "If any ask me what a free government is, I answer, that, for any practical purpose, it is what the people think so; and that they, and not I, are the natural, lawful, and competent judges of this matter." [47] To which Johnson replied, "I will let the King of France govern me on those conditions, for it is to be governed just as I please." [48]

> If I were sure [Burke continued] the colonists had, at their leaving this country, sealed a regular compact of servitude; that they had solemnly abjured all the rights of citizens; that they had made a vow to renounce all ideas of liberty for them and their posterity to all generations; yet I should hold myself obliged to conform to the temper I found universally prevalent in my own day, and to govern two millions of men, impatient of servitude, on the principles of freedom.[49]

Abstract liberty is an extreme whose speculative perfection is its practical fault; it cannot exist except in practice. And once it relates to human affairs and is tinged with practicality, it becomes this or that liberty among this or that people at this or that time or place; it takes on the hues of actual circumstance.

Of the six circumstances which Burke chose to discuss in his conciliation speech—national descent, politics, religion, manners, education, and location—the foremost was the English heritage. Mixed and aberrant as the population was in

America, its civil liberties fundamentally resembled those of the first-settling English. Not only were colonials descended from Englishmen, most of them, but they had emigrated during great seventeenth-century libertarian movements. "They took this bias and direction the moment they parted from your hands. They are therefore not only devoted to liberty, but to liberty according to English ideas, and on English principles." [50] Burke gave an example of what he meant: the squabble over taxation only restated an ancient English squabble. "Liberty inheres in some sensible object; and every nation has formed to itself some favorite point, which by way of eminence becomes the criterion of their happiness." [51] In England the touchy point had been traditionally not franchise or patrician privilege, but taxation, and the conviction that the people, directly or indirectly, must grant their own money if they are to enjoy freedom. The colonies had imbibed the principle as with their lifeblood: "Liberty might be safe, or might be endangered, in twenty other particulars, without their being much pleased or alarmed. Here they felt its pulse; and as they found that beat, they thought themselves sick or sound." [52] Parliament would be absurd to combat one of the principles by which its own existence was upheld: "It is not easy, indeed, to make a monopoly of theorems and corollaries." [53] In profound, traditional ways, the colonials behaved like Englishmen abroad.

So in their political mores. All the colonies had legislative assemblies not unlike Parliaments in little, all democratic in degree and some purely so. The colonials shared in their ordinary governments and from this they were inspired with a lofty, self-valuing sentiment. Their image of themselves was fixed in political practice. True, the assemblies and their liberties had sprung from royal instructions or charters and had once resembled city corporations. "But nothing in progression can rest on its original plan. We may as well think of rocking a grown man in the cradle of an infant." [54] As the colonies flourished, the assemblies gradually and insensibly subtilized themselves in the variety of local needs, and accreted local favor. They grew every day more like parliaments in form, function, power, and respectability. At the same time, governed by the same historical necessities, not by systematic planning, Parliament itself expanded from locally English to imperial superintendency. A double legislature, imperial and colonial, each reciprocating and confirming the other, twined and grew strong out of "imperceptible habit, and old custom, the great support of all the governments in the world." [55] Even if it were desirable, history could not be rolled back.

As an example of how individual responsibility and a sulky civic pride suffused colonial politics, Burke pointed at the startling ease with which Massachusetts, when Parliament abrogated its charter in 1774, persisted in quiet and prosperous order, and therefore for all practical purposes formed a new government, "without the bustle of a revolution, or the troublesome formality of an election. Evident necessity, and tacit consent, have done the business in an instant. . . . This new government has originated directly from the people; and was not . . . a manufacture ready formed, and transmitted to them in that condition from England." [56] Those who argued (like Samuel Johnson) [57] that the very presage of anarchy would humble the colony ill understood the fertility of the actual. "The experiment was tried. A new, strange, unexpected face of things appeared. Anarchy is found tolerable. . . . Our late experience has taught us that many of those fundamental principles, formerly believed infallible, are either not of the importance they were imagined to be; or that we have not at all adverted to some other far more important and far more powerful principles, which entirely overrule those we had considered as omnipotent. I am much against any further experiments. . . ." [58] One motive for Burke's conservatism, when he talked conservatism, was his awareness that combinations of human behavior, though referable to a moral order, are yet infinite and unpredictable. He had shaken off the political provincialism which can talk "change" without really believing in its imminence or foreseeing its queer disregard of one's presumptions about reality.

The religion of the colonists, in "no way worn out or impaired," reinforced their libertarian politics. In the crazy-quilt of churches, creeds, codes, sects, and denominations scattered along the Atlantic coast, Burke discerned no common denominator of doctrine, but certainly one of behavior. The colonists agreed in "the communion of the spirit of liberty"—ironically enough, a secular value—which Burke analyzed as in this instance a rationalization of historical need (that is, "natural" liberty does not exist in the abstract). Unlike Roman Catholicism and the Anglican branch of Protestantism, whose history had happened to go hand in hand with political establishments, the dissenting interests had "sprung up in direct opposition to all the ordinary powers of the world; and could justify that opposition only on a strong claim to natural liberty. Their very existence depended on the powerful and unremitted assertion of that claim." [59] Even the most "cold and passive" Protestantism is a sort of dissent, Burke observed, but most of the colonists, especially in the northern provinces, professed "a refinement on the principle of resistance"; they were "the dissidence of dissent, and the Protestantism of the Protestant religion," [60] which later would horrify Matthew Arnold.[61] They were programmatic nonconformists, "the most adverse to all implicit submission of mind and opinion." [62] Engrained in their character was a high-spirited jealousy of "all that looks like absolute government," especially in the character of those who had emigrated, including "that stream of foreigners, which has been constantly flowing into these colonies," most of them dissenters from something or other, mixing "a temper and character far from alien" with that of the settled English.[63]

Although the Church of England, Burke's own profession, had a lively establishment in the south (for instance, Virginia and the Carolinas), the spirit of liberty there was not moderated, but made "still more high and haughty" by a local circumstance—slave-holding. Instead of the dissidence of dissent, liberty fused with a stubborn class-consciousness: "Those who are free, are by far the most proud and jealous of their freedom. Freedom is to them not only an enjoyment, but a kind of rank and privilege. Not seeing there, that freedom, as in countries where it is a common blessing, and as broad and general as the air, may be united with much abject toil, with great misery, with all the exterior of servitude, liberty looks, amongst them, like something that is more noble and liberal. . . . such will be all masters of slaves, who are not slaves themselves." [64] Pride made liberty a "high aristocratic spirit" and by so much the more intractable.

From manners, Burke turned to colonial education, which he found dominated by the lawyer mind. "In no country perhaps in the world is the law so general a study" [65]—a subtle observation later confirmed by Lecky.[66] All who could read, and literacy was very high, obtained at least a smattering of law, and from that grew litigious. "This study renders men acute, inquisitive, dexterous, prompt in attack, ready in defence, full of resources. In other countries, the people, more simple, and of a less mercurial cast, judge of an ill principle in government only by an actual grievance; here they anticipate the evil, and judge of the pressure of the grievance by the badness of the principle. They augur misgovernment at a distance; and snuff the approach of tyranny in every tainted breeze." [67] Burke warned Parliament not to "be pushed by metaphysical process to the extreme lines, and argued out of your whole authority," but also not to push back "with too much logic and too little sense." [68] A "dangerous spirit of disquisition" was abroad, "not in the coolness of philosophical inquiry, but inflamed with all the passions of a haughty, resentful people, who thought themselves deeply injured, and that they were contending for everything that was valuable in the world." [69]

The sixth and last circumstance of American liberty which Burke singled out was "natural" instead of "moral." Three thousand miles of ocean lay between the colonies and England. "Seas roll, and months pass, between the order and the execution; and the want of a speedy explanation of a single point is enough to defeat a whole system." [70] The colonials had accustomed themselves to privileges, immunities, and responsibilities appropriate to their spot on the earth. The very quality of their liberty had varied with their remoteness from authority. "Nothing worse happens to you than does to all nations who have extensive empire; and it happens in all the forms into which empire can be thrown. In large bodies, the circulation of power must be less vigorous at the extremities. Nature has said it." [71]

Such was the American character which Burke laid before Parliament's imagination. "We stand where we have an immense view of what is, and what is past. Clouds, indeed, and darkness rest upon the future." [72] A "fierce spirit of liberty" was actual among the colonists. "I cannot alter the nature of man. The fact is so." [73] In the face of such a novel evolution, one might try to restrain or squelch it, or prosecute it as criminal ("I do not know the method of drawing up an indictment against a whole people"),[74] or comply with it as necessary. But it would remain a fact.

Burke chose compliance, and, as a principle illustrated in conduct, it is one of his more important contributions to political intelligence.[75] The spirit of American liberty would run its course; and wishful nostalgia for the old days, when political power in America seemed only an emanation from the British stock, was quite as impractical as its other extreme, a chortling admiration for liberty in the abstract:

> The question is, not whether their spirit deserves praise or blame, but—what, in the name of God, shall we do with it? [76]

It was the cry of an actualist and a conservative (or more accurately perhaps, a conservationist). History is always forcing up novel manners seeking political expression, but which bear the aspect of a *fait accompli* by the time anybody sees them in full. Therefore, in one of its fundamentals, government—and indeed most social thinking—is a kind of hindsight and acquiescence, and the question, "What, in the name of God, shall we do with it?" is the only one practicable. Opaque, long-hardened words like *govern,* with its complicated fringe of meaning, constantly reawaken in Burke and startle one back into familiarity with them. "People must be governed," Burke said, "in a manner agreeable to their temper and disposition; and men of free character and spirit must be ruled with, at least, some condescension to this spirit and this character." [77] Thus he argued that, like it or not, the practicing politician has ever forced upon him by the pulse of events a political actuality which, however changeful or distasteful it might be, he has to accept and conserve if he hopes to govern. More specifically, he has to reckon with character and circumstance in history, with the peculiar configuration of the public mind in both its permanent and transient features—the passing persuasions of a day or generation, but even more, the larger and more elusive *Grundsatz* of national character laid up in the infinite depth of fact and only to be confronted here and there in salient surfaces.

But compliance is not so easy as it may sound, as Burke realized. Self-control and a talent for creative expedients, rare as they are, will not suffice. The problem, as Burke made clear in the American crisis and in the whole string of crises that formed his political career, is to see or "imaginatively view" the object to be governed. The mind of a people, with all its other intricacies, is also, in part, a function of history, bafflingly subject to "silent and insensible revolution" whether for growth or decay or both. It is hard to grasp; facts are partly interpretation. In "the silent lapse of events," Burke observed, "as material alterations have been insensibly brought about in the policy and character of governments and nations, as those which have been marked by the tumult of public revolutions." [78] In the issue of decay, for example, Burke expressed his fears about England in this way: "A nation may slide down fair and softly from the highest point of grandeur and prosperity to the lowest state of imbecility and meanness, without any one's marking a particular period in this declension, without asking a question about it, or in the least speculating on any of the innumerable acts which have stolen in this silent and insensible revolution. Every event so prepares the subsequent, that, when it arrives, it produces no surprise, nor any extraordinary alarm." [79] The same latent, insensible, gradual change had been apparent to him in American growth. The effects of manners and events are felt

—enjoyed or endured—while their actual causes operating in behavior elude understanding. And a politician cannot comply with what he does not understand.

It is very rare indeed for men to be wrong in their feelings concerning public misconduct; as rare to be right in their speculation upon the cause of it. I have constantly observed that the generality of people are fifty years, at least, behind-hand in their politics. There are but very few, who are capable of comparing and digesting what passes before their eyes at different times and occasions, so as to form the whole into a distinct system. But in books everything is settled for them, without the exertion of any considerable diligence or sagacity. For which reason men are wise with but little reflection, and good with little self-denial, in the business of all times except their own. . . . Every age has its own manners, and its politics dependent upon them.[80]

The problem is to imagine the full depth of the *status quo,* which is at once an end in itself and yet at the same time a means working in complicated ways toward something else.

One meets the curious paradox that in his behavior during the American crisis, while turning to discover and accord with actual circumstances in a way that critics generally have called "liberal," Burke was really busying himself with, and urging conformity to, the *status quo.* The paradox is resolved by realizing his assumption that change, novelty, growth, is often part of the *status quo,* and indeed that the *status quo* itself is not made up primarily of "dead things" but of "principles" which are "living and productive." [81] The presupposition of conserving the American colonies was a liberal view of their character and circumstances: nothing better shows the futility of trying to ticket (and dispose of) Burke by some neat little tag—more especially if "conservative" is to be made antithetical to "liberal" and both terms sent crabwalking down history in a narrow and jealous dialectic of change and resistance. To imagine principles as they live in daily manners was his presupposition of compliant realism in government; and for that reason, if no other, persuasion of the sort Burke attempted for Parliament (and the "rhetoric" which accomplishes it) would seem to be of the profoundest utility.

Burke's conservatism is like deponent verbs: his superficially backward voice has active meanings.

The idea is to progress without destroying, to maintain the state as an equilibrium of values and arrangements reflecting common sense. "In effect, to follow, not to force, the public inclination; to give a direction, a form, a technical dress, and a specific sanction to the general sense of the community is the true end of legislature." [82] It is this perception which led many idealists like Hegel to construe the state as the bearer of civilization. But with Burke, only individuals and particular arrangements between them (of whatever complexity) are real, and therefore what "civilization" is must somehow be found in the ongoing lives of individuals as embodying their generally voluntary and common interests. It lives only in the generality of their habits, prejudices, customs, opinions, feelings, values, as these come practically to exist; and as these change, the politician who wishes to govern by complying has the problem perpetually of reaching out into the rich complication and mystery of fact, to ascertain what is practicable.

If one is to judge by Burke's practice, retaining a sense of mystery is sometimes the only practical, sure way of invading the facts. This is, of course, to be distinguished from a talent for mystification. The tendency of social and political thinking is to abstract neat doctrines, gathering the trends of many minds into the artifice of identity, piecing fragments into ideal molds; and in degree, there would seem to be no way around it. But such rarefied joinery usually oversimplifies, and what it leaves out may be as significant as what it includes. In dealing with individual men, it may leave out all-important nuances of commitment, hesitation, wonder, ambiguity, and balance. It tends to overlook situations in which a dumb question overhangs a man's mind and is more truly his "idea" than various doctrines measuring out uniform answers. What is commended in a novelist as honesty may be damned in the critic as obscurantism. And therefore to sum up Burke as a mere advocate for the *status quo* and nothing more than that would be gross, would be blind to the elementary first fact of his actual thought—his vividly felt, inquiring respect for the relations between change and continuity in history. Things enduring, things changing, things changing in order to endure—a sense of the mystery in these relations guides and keynotes his thinking. Ever freshly, it drives him to scrutinize "the silent lapse of events," that which has come to be and that which is becoming.

It required a special order of imagination which is easier to feel than to define.

## III

After the great seventeenth-century constitutional struggle, the idea became commonplace that liberty of a diffusive, stable kind distinguished English society and government.[83] Among Whig extremists, like Sir Edward Coke, the idea had hardened in bookish fancies which long survived: Burke laughed at the myth of an Anglo-Saxon liberty floating down time with archetypal purity and again at the "retrospective wisdom, and historical patriotism" of the "Whig on the business of an hundred years ago" who, "discharging all the splendid bile of his virtuous indignation on King John and King James," would then sit down "perfectly satisfied to the coarsest work and homeliest job of the day he lives in." [84] Such a "stern republican" lacked a sense of life; "gorging himself with a full feast of admiration of the Grecian commonwealths and of our true Saxon constitution," he was obtuse to the practical present, in which, to be sure, the past yet lived, but latently, in a filmy network of principles. On the other hand, Burke also attacked a liberty at the other extreme from such delusive phantasms. Imagination without practice was no worse, and perhaps more innocent, than practice without imagination. Principles, which "to men truly initiated and rightly taught" were all in all, sounded "wild and chimerical" to men with their eyes always on the ground: "to the profane herd of those vulgar and mechanical politicians who have no place among us; a sort of people who think that nothing exists but what is gross and material; and who therefore, far from being qualified to be directors of the great movement of empire, are not fit to turn a wheel in the machine." [85] In fits of dispossession, in whole generations, manners may slide away from principle, but the principle will persist independent like a lure. Under the pressure of crisis, Burke gathered himself for lofty, almost lyrical celebrations of a principle of liberty which he felt to be endangered from several sides. Perhaps liberty is most consciously a value in times just achieving or losing it, as is order or some like value at opposite times. Nobody worries about what he can take for granted. Certainly the idea of a spirit of liberty growing anew in America, on the general principles and within the bounds of English community, stands forward in Burke's American writings glowing with a bright tender excitement, as of something hallowed and freshly understood, something wonderful and urgent and ineffable. And precarious. Harshnesses are purged, in a thrill of vision—edged by anxiety.

*Liberty* is a curious plus word in Burke. At first reflection, one would suppose its meaning plain: liberty is the condition of doing as one pleases within certain limits, and these limits are the prevailing mode of justice. But the word often slips its legal formality and edges unannounced into a culture pattern. The abstract definition, whose worth is undisputed, presto robes itself in circumstances, without warning. The practical consequences of an idea grip his attention. As a politician, Burke is cautious about separating ideas from their envelope of suggestion, feeling, and intention, their unspoken relation to other ideas, their observable effects. Abstract essences splinter into existence and become moral essences, only to retract once more, as his thought moves, into abstraction. And the quick grace of his flight between abstraction and circumstance, definition and practice, idea and behavior, is sometimes deceptive, hard to follow. When he spoke of English liberty, he often confused conception and fact, and therefore he ended up with something like "cultural" liberty, broad and general as the air, a profound and present liberty which, long growing in a Whig-powered England, irradiated, as he hoped, all its dominions—a ruling and master principle latent in manners, habits, and old affections.

That is, liberty was only a salience of a larger community. Amid the din of shortsighted squabbles, the cries of arrogance or resentment, the crossfire of defiance and chop-logic, Burke struggled, sometimes with an almost mystical fervor, with glowing intellectual passion, to express his sense of a calm, silent depth of English community in which rebellionists and old-guardists alike, merchants, lawyers, and thieves, Whigs and Tories, were all upborne and carried along. It was, so to speak, a mysticism of the obvious. He spoke of the "spirit" of liberty in the "communion" of the country, and such a national communion, he believed, was a general and operative truth, apparent as day. It was general and operative in England.

> Do you imagine then, that it is the land tax act which raises your revenue? that it is the annual vote in the committee of supply which gives you your army? or that it is the mutiny bill which inspires it with bravery and discipline? No! surely no! It is the love of the people; it is their attachment to their government, from the sense of the deep stake they have . . . which gives you your army and your navy, and infuses into both that liberal obedience, without which your army would be a base rabble, and your navy nothing but rotten timber.[86]

And it was general and operative abroad. "We have invited the husbandman [in America] to look to authority for his title. We have taught him piously to believe in the mysterious virtue of wax and parchment." [87] But it was not paper chains —not registers, bonds, affidavits, sufferances, cockets, clearances, letters of office, instructions, certificates, warrants, or suspending clauses—which had long cemented, and could yet cement, the colonists within "the great contexture of the mysterious whole." [88]

> These things do not make your government. Dead instruments, passive tools as they are, it is the spirit of the English communion that gives all their life and efficacy to them. It is the spirit of the

English constitution, which, infused through the mighty mass, pervades, feeds. unites, invigorates, vivifies every part of the empire, even down to the minutest member.[89]

The idea of liberty had a positive content in communal behavior. And it was a marvelous thing to Burke that American behavior, despite its idiosyncrasy, was still in the spirit of the parent nation. *Spirit,* like *liberty,* is a favorite word of Burke's and difficult to pin down; in general it is always getting at the exquisitely subtle way in which the concrete in history becomes the receptacle of, and is structured or disciplined by, moral permanences. Upon such a community of permanences, ready-made in time and waiting to be accepted, Burke grounded his case for conciliation.

The Americans had been bound to the mother country by an "unsuspecting confidence," solid as family affection and continuous with it, by partialities so dear that they bore a resemblance to virtue. A "cement of reciprocal esteem and regard" united peoples who felt their latent sympathies, likenesses, and common interests.

My hold of the colonies is in the close affection which grows from common names, from kindred blood, from similar privileges, and equal protection. These are ties, which, though light as air, are as strong as links of iron. Let the colonies always keep the idea of their civil rights associated with your government;—they will cling and grapple to you; and no force under heaven will be of power to tear them from their allegiance. But let it be once understood, that your government may be one thing, and their privileges another; that these two things may exist without any mutual relation; the cement is gone; the cohesion is loosened; and everything hastens to decay and dissolution.[90]

The Americans, Burke felt, would listen to reason only so long as the fabric of their affection remained whole. But once bruise and embitter affection, once allow it to see the mother country in a hostile, resentful light, and nothing could persuade the Americans to be governed. The salt would lose its savor. Affection would seek other and worthier objects. In fact, Burke continued, with a remarkable and unintentional glimpse of the future, it would be better to grant Americans their independence outright, as a free gift, than to war over it. An English community would survive political separation; it was not so much English rule as the moral sentiments accompanying the rule, a deposit of affection and partiality, which it was most urgent to preserve.

> I have so much trust in the inclinations and prejudices of mankind, and so little in anything else, that I should expect ten times more benefit to this kingdom from the affection of America, though under a separate establishment, than from her perfect submission to the crown and parliament, accompanied with her terror, disgust, and abhorrence. Bodies tied together by so unnatural bond of union as mutual hatred, are only connected to their ruin.[91]

More than all else, Burke dreaded the poisoning of "affection"—permanent moral sentiments. Nothing could restore it if ever it slipped away. Though the very foundation and enabling means of civil life, it was delicate and contingent. Its very tenacity was its risk, for once altered, it would be as irrecoverable as time.

The incalculable frailty of such "permanences" is not likely to dawn upon anybody until they begin sliding out of use, or suffer threat, and then it dawns most intensely upon people aware of the subtlety of decay, and the awful waste and suffering in all cultural change. Perhaps the genuine conservative (and Burke is surely talking conservation here) is always someone adjusting to the shock of history—all those cultures, all that life evaporated. Time past, silently, slowly, irreversibly settling and unsettling its foundations, and time present—but time present in a world to act in, to be responsible for. Burke could only look on the American war as a willful, wasteful flying in the teeth of time, as an imprudent sacrifice of what history (or Providence) had brought into being. People little conceived how uncivilizing a civil war would be—and a civil war, as he felt, far from inevitable.

One should remember what Burke was doing. He was not

blind to serious conflicts between England and the colonies, or indeed between England and all parts of its empire. He blurred over numerous shades of which he was aware. For example, though he attributed a vehement love of liberty to New Englanders, he was also aware of their Puritan backgrounds of theocracy and persecution.[92] He was not writing a history text either *en philosophe* or *bloss sagen wie es eigentlich gewesen,* though he fused some of the features of each technique. Rather, the American character and English community which he opened before Parliament was a practical upshot of history—something which he thought a general and operative truth. Burke groped on the invisible air, he took the pulse of the living present during a crisis, because, as he told Parliament with a tingle of impatience, "we are strongly urged to determine something" [93]—something which, if acted upon, would work, harmonize struggling interests, comply with latent necessities, and subdue them to use. The empire, he reasoned, could exist only in virtue of a latent common interest actual and apparent *in practice,* and he set out to demonstrate it.

I am, and ever have been, deeply sensible of the difficulty of reconciling the strong presiding power, that is so useful towards the conservation of a vast, disconnected, infinitely diversified empire, with that liberty and safety of the provinces which they must enjoy, (in opinion and practice at least) or they will not be provinces at all. . . . Of one thing I am perfectly clear, that it is not by deciding the suit, but by compromising the difference, that peace can be restored or kept. They who would put an end to such quarrels, by declaring roundly in favour of the whole demands of either party, have mistaken in my humble opinion, the office of a mediator.[94]

It was a practical problem of equity, compromise, and conservation.

From discussions of American character and the larger English community embracing it, Burke carried his thought still higher, with like generality, fervor, and, as it were, mystical practicality, to discussions of empire, and he sketched his idea of what the empire of a free country must be like if it is to last. Empire was not solely an ambition but, like American growth, a plain fact of 1775 that had to be lived with. "To be a good member of Parliament," Burke reminded his constituents, "is, let me tell you, no easy task."

We [Burke and his co-electee] are now members for a rich commercial *city;* this *city,* however, is but a part of a rich commercial *nation,* the interests of which are various, multiform, and intricate. We are members for that great nation, which however is itself but part of a great *empire,* extended by our virtue and our fortune to the farthest limits of the east and of the west. All these wide-spread interests must be considered; must be compared; must be reconciled, if possible. We are members for a *free* country; and surely we all know, that the machine of a free constitution is no simple thing; but as intricate and as delicate as it is valuable. We are members in a great and ancient *monarchy;* and we must preserve religiously the true legal rights of the sovereign, which form the key-stone that binds together the noble and well-constructed arch of our empire and our constitution. A constitution made up of balanced powers must ever be a critical thing.[95]

Whatever arrangement was made to conciliate America must also keep in mind the whole of imperial interests among which America, and England itself, and Scotland, Ireland, the West Indies, British India, and other dominions, were all only parts. And since the colonies as such had been founded for trade, obviously "the spirit of an extensive, and intricate, and trading interest" would pervade the whole, "always qualifying, and often controlling, every general idea of constitution and government." [96]

Our measures *must be healing.* Such a degree of strength must be communicated to all the members of the state, as may enable them to defend themselves, and to co-operate in the defence of the whole. Their temper too must be managed, and their good affections cultivated. They may then be disposed to bear the load with cheerfulness, as a contribution towards what may be called with truth and propriety, and not by an empty form of words, *a common cause*. Too little dependence cannot be had, at this time of day, on names and prejudices. The eyes of mankind are opened; and communities must be held together by an evident and solid interest.[97]

Warning that a "great empire and little minds go ill together," [98] Burke urged a liberality of legislative reason to find the unity latent in the whole. He argued "the absolute necessity of keeping up the concord of this empire by a unity of spirit, though in a diversity of operations." [99]

Yet it was characteristic of Burke's thinking to resist tendentious arguments about the unity of empire at the very moment he pleaded for it. He sought a unity in spirit, not a Procrustean "state-bed of uniformity." [100] Compulsory equality of the parts and exact definition of powers seemed to him nigglingly unwise "in the complicated economy of great kingdoms, and immense revenues, which in a length of time, and by a variety of accidents, have coalesced into a sort of body."

The old building stands well enough, though part Gothic, part Grecian, and part Chinese, until an attempt is made to square it into uniformity. Then it may come down upon our heads together, in much uniformity of ruin; and great will be the fall thereof.[101]

His office as mediator, he conceived, was to reconcile, not to impose; at different stages of conflict to pursue different methods of reconciliation; [102] and in the spirit of philosophic analogy to keep the unity of his end by varying his means. To be sure, "government and legislation are matters of reason and judgment, and not of inclination," [103] but government is also "a practical thing, made for the happiness of mankind, and not to furnish out a spectacle of uniformity, to gratify the schemes of visionary politicians." [104] He was not wild enough to conceive that "the natives of Hindostan and those of Virginia could be ordered in the same manner; or that the Cutchery court and the grand jury of Salem could be regulated on a similar plan." [105]

By contrast, Burke envisioned an empire founded upon affections in full vigor, mutual benefits, and *ad hoc* arrangements materializing principles at work for the common interest.

Truly, Mr. Speaker, I do not know what this unity means; nor has it ever been heard of, that I know, in the constitutional policy of this country. The very idea of subordination of parts, excludes this notion of simple and undivided unity. England is the head; but she is not the head and the members too. Ireland has ever had from the beginning a separate, but not an independent, legislature; which, far from distracting, promoted the union of the whole. Everything was sweetly and harmoniously disposed through both islands for the conservation of English dominion, and the communication of English liberties. I do not see that the same principle might not be carried into twenty islands, and with the same good effect. This is my model with regard to America, as far as the internal circumstances of the two countries are the same. I know no other unity of this empire, than I can draw from its example during these periods, when it seemed to my poor understanding more united than it is now.[106]

The authority of the head must somehow be reconciled concretely with the freedom of the many parts to determine themselves. Imperial government must conform itself, within the limits of a "general good, resulting from the general reason of the whole," [107] to the particular needs and demands of particular peoples. "Perhaps, Sir, I am mistaken in my idea of an empire, as distinguished from a single state or kingdom. But my idea of it is this; that an empire is the aggregate of many states under one common head; whether this head be a monarch, or a presiding republic. It does, in such constitutions, frequently happen (and nothing but the dismal, cold, dead uniformity of servitude can prevent its happening) that the subordinate parts have many local privileges and immunities." [108] A provident and beneficent Parliament, "as from the throne of heaven," would superintend all the subordinate legislatures (coordinate to each other), guide and harmonize conflicts within the whole system without annihilating any of the parts, or enforcing a false character upon them.[109]

Hegel observes acutely, and with distaste, that the English

constitution has been by tradition "a complex of mere *particular Rights* and particular privileges," and he summarizes its leading features as follows:

Each particular Church, parochial district, county, society, takes care of itself, so that the Government, strictly speaking, has nowhere less to do than in England. This is the leading feature of what Englishmen call their Liberty. . . . the common interest is concrete, and particular interests are taken cognizance of and determined in view of that common interest. These arrangements, based on particular interests, render a general system impossible. Consequently, abstract and general principles have no attraction for Englishmen. . . . The *Parliament governs.* . . . The material existence of England is based on commerce and industry, and the English have undertaken the weighty responsibility of being the missionaries of civilization to the world.[110]

Synoptically and with allowances, this is Burke's view, on both the local and imperial scales; for in his vision of "a great political union of communities," [111] centering on the Atlantic but with global interests and ties, he sought to internationalize, as far as possible, the principles of constitutional government evolved locally in England over five centuries.

The very strength of an English constitution, and, as he hoped, of an English empire, was that without sacrificing the advantages of order, made, as Burke believed, to the people's needs and wishes as the people were made to it, it provided also for the assimilation of disorderly novelties like America, each in the peculiar manner and for the peculiar merits of its necessity. It struck its giant glimmering piles in the green depth of history, stable amidst mischief, because of, not in spite of its reconciling particulars that had come to be with particulars that were becoming. The drift of Burke's thinking, in the broadest light, was towards that which reconciles, that which *practically* unifies, that which establishes community among the various and particular. He never wanted or pretended a *theoretical* consistency or abstract system for its own sake. Reason was a means, whose subject was life as it came to hand and whose purpose was a practical concrete good—the harmonious coexistence of contrasts. "Liberty" was at once the product and the means of English community in time.

IV

In the American revolution, Burke confronted the first grave challenge (others were to follow) in settling the concrete arrangements of empire. When analyzing American liberty and character, without blinking their qualifying uniquenesses, he had groped for a communal bond, and he had discerned a long-lived-with community latent in the blind obvious. But what particular arrangements were most fitting to the colonies? What arrangements would accommodate the new without losing continuity with the old—sweep up the values and commitments of a rich solid past to temper them with the urgent moment? Burke immersed himself in the technicalities of imperial authority and its administration. As Chauncey Goodrich noticed,[112] the speech *On American Taxation* views the crisis from the point of view of England and the abuse of English authority, the speech *On Conciliation With the Colonies* from the point of view of America and the promise of American liberty. Burke threw his mind into the spirit and details of both sides; he wanted "patiently [to] go round and round the subject, and survey it minutely in every possible aspect" [113]—for his overriding purpose, as he said in a campaign speech at Bristol, was "to reconcile British superiority with American liberty" [114] by preserving each entire, just as history had shaped it. Rhetorically, the "reconciliation" of "liberty" and "superiority" (or "authority") became with him a kind of shorthand statement of the problem: the contrast of "liberty" and "authority" weaves frieze-like across the portico of envisioned empire—a rococo dialectic restraining a straight-lined solid reality in precise, slightly florid ornament.

English authority, Burke told Parliament, had faced four examples of a similar dispute—Ireland, Wales, Chester, and Durham—and in each precedent, after a period of anarchy and oppression ("The march of the human mind is slow"),[115] the dispute was resolved by political representation. "It was not English arms, but the English constitution, that conquered Ireland." [116] "Freedom, and not servitude, is the cure of anarchy; as religion, and not atheism, is the true remedy of superstition." [117] Yet direct representation in Parliament, which might have been the most satisfying and, in time, approximating bond, seemed unworkable in transcontinental government: *opposuit natura;* Burke lived before the communications revolution. "As I meddle with no theory, I do not absolutely assert the impracticability of such a representation. But I do not see my way to it." [118] Striving for a practical understanding of government by shipboard—that is, to use Whitehead's phrase, striving for an "imaginative perception of experiences, which, if they occurred, would be coherent with . . . actual experiences" [119]—Burke painted a comic picture of delay, frustration, and capricious circumstances. Writs of election would arrive at different times in different provinces. Vessels would be lost, or late in getting seaworthy. Newly-elected members would dock late to find business far advanced, or else Parliament freakily dissolved, whence back they must ride on the high seas, airing themselves and never serving. Disputed candidates would troop to the bar of Commons dragging "their train of attorneys, solicitors, mayors, selectmen, provost-marshals, about five hundred or a thousand witnesses." Perhaps a war would break out, and "our constitutional fleet" would be captured. The prospect was ridiculous. On the other hand, the "virtual" representation advocated by many Tories (including Samuel Johnson) [120] seemed to Burke unsafe, and more appropriate to England alone.

However, Burke continued, there were often several means to the same end. "When we cannot give the benefit as we would wish, let us not refuse it altogether." [121] The problem, simply put, was to find another arrangement to admit colonists to an interest in the constitution—that is, in the spirit of precedents. Hence Burke's advocacy of "the system of 1766," the Whig program which acknowledged an already-established tradition in America of local self-government and self-taxation, coexisting with an already-established tradition of imperial power. For better than a century the Navigation Acts, a purely commercial policy, had regulated colonial affairs by complicated restraints. It imposed a virtual monopoly, a mercantilism which Burke attacked as narrow and self-defeating, by obliging colonists to trade and purchase goods within the circuit of English interests. Nevertheless, before 1763, Burke thought, when the Tories meddled with the evolving scheme of things, the Americans had been "confirmed in obedience." [122] The commercial system "grew with their growth, and strengthened with their strength." [123] They scarcely remembered a time when they were not subject to its authority. Men do not dispute what is molded into their innermost fiber, what is indeed their practical nature. Furthermore, their monopolist happened to be the richest man in the world, and they had borne commercial servitude to enjoy the growth that English capital, and that alone, allowed them. By this capital, employed primarily for England's benefit, not theirs, they were enabled to develop their fisheries, their agriculture, their shipbuilding, and within limits, their trade, "in such a manner as got far the start of the slow, languid operations of unassisted nature. This capital was a hot-bed to them. Nothing in the history of mankind is like their progress." [124] But they had been a free people in all internal affairs; they had got "the image of the British constitution." [125] They had blended commercial servitude and civil liberty; and though not perfect freedom, "it was a happy and liberal condition" which Parliament should strive to improve, not to antagonize. So long as their customary, legitimate, and homegrown interests were satisfied, the colonies, self-governing, would roll in the English orbit.

Throughout this period, Parliament had possessed an unlimited legislative "right," but, in taxation, had doubted the propriety of exercising it. Taxation for revenue had been by free grant from the colonial assemblies. "In the midst of that happy enjoyment, they [the colonists] never thought of critically settling the exact limits of a power, which was necessary to their union, their safety, their equality, and even their liberty. Thus the two very difficult points, superiority in the presiding state, and freedom in the subordinate, were on the whole sufficiently, that is, practically, reconciled; without agitating those vexatious questions which in truth rather belong to metaphysics than politics." [126] Such power had a prescriptive title, acknowledged by both sides; with affection, the colonists saw their privileges protected by it; such a power should stand then, as it had always stood, a boundless reserve unexercised in most cases, but to be called into act and energy if ever, in the wisdom of time, it should be needed. For example, in one of his remarkable prophecies not often mentioned, Burke warned the colonists that their new nation might one day break up in a civil war if British "equipoise" were cast off.

That very liberty. which you so justly prize above all things, originated here: and it may be very doubtful whether, without being constantly fed from the original fountain, it can be at all perpetuated or preserved in its native purity and perfection. . . . We apprehend you are not now, nor for ages are likely to be, capable of that form of constitution in an independent state. Besides, let us suggest to you our apprehensions that your present union (in which we rejoice, and which we wish long to subsist) cannot always subsist without the authority and weight of this great and long-respected body, to equipoise, and to preserve you amongst yourselves in a just and fair equality. It may not even be impossible that a long course of war with the administration of this country may be but a prelude to a series of wars and contentions among yourselves, to end, at length, (as such scenes have too often ended,) in a species of humiliating repose, which nothing but the preceding calamities would reconcile to the dispirited few who survived them.[127]

Burke envisioned the power structure of the British constitution as overarching and progressively accommodating itself to history. Some of its powers were actual, some nominal or amortized, some deposited yet in the dim depth of the future. No limits would wisely be placed upon such power except prudence and conformity to circumstances.

Parliament's error had been to push its "right" to tax imprudently against the wish and custom of the governed. It had confused right and power, forgetting that it had no right except as the general sense of the community acknowledged it as such. "It is not only the invidious branch of taxation that will be resisted, but . . . no other given part of legislative rights can be exercised, without regard to the general opinion of those who are to be governed. That general opinion is the vehicle and organ of legislative omnipotence." [128] As an example, reminding Parliament of its complete legislative power in England, Burke pointed out that, since it had once made and repealed the High Commission Court and the Star Chamber, it still had the abstract power to revive them if it should decide on such unwisdom. Similarly, Parliament had three or four times altered the religious establishment of the country, and therefore still retained the abstract power to do so, though to exercise its power in 1777 would be impracticable. Furthermore, the king had power to negative any bill he pleased, but wisely he forebore to use it. "Its repose may be the preservation of its existence; and its existence may be the means of saving the constitution itself, on an occasion worthy of bringing it forth." [129] The Convocation of the Clergy, once a busy authority, now had only a legal existence; it met to pay "some polite ecclesiastical compliments to the king," then it retired; but it remained part of the constitution and could be resuscitated "whenever there is occasion; and whenever those, who conjure up that spirit, will choose to abide the consequences." [130] In the same way, Burke continued, Parliament should retain its ancient and boundless legislative power over the colonies; otherwise it would be imperial only in name. But it should exercise its power with great reserve, never intruding where the colonies by themselves "are equal to the common ends of their institution." [131] It should use its power only for provident and beneficent superintendence. In this manner, without internecine niggling over rights, a boundless authority would be reconciled with a practical liberty—"whether to serve a refining speculatist or a factious demagogue, I know not; but enough surely for the ease and happiness of man." [132] "The question with me is, not whether you have a right to render your people miserable; but whether it is not your interest to make them happy."[133]

As wrangling thickened into war, Burke changed his position, varying his means to keep his end. A limited good is better than a positive evil. He moved for "mutilating" authority with a fixed contract, observing that nevertheless all contracts spring from jealousy and distrust.[134] The British constitution had been often amended and its principles new-applied to insurgent changes. The growth of colonies and the threat of their alienation was such a pressing change, and Burke, in a last plea, urged both sides to pool their intelligence in contriving a revision permanently satisfying to both, even if precedents had to be made obsolete.

> Public troubles have often called upon this country to look into its constitution. It has ever been bettered by such a revision. . . . our happy and luxuriant increase of dominion, and our diffused population, have outgrown the limits of a constitution made for a contracted object. . . . If we set about this great work, on both sides, with the same conciliatory turn of mind, we may now, as in former times, owe even to our mutual mistakes, contentions, and animosities, the lasting concord, freedom, happiness, and glory of this empire.[135]

Burke interpreted constitutional power liberally, not as a set scheme, but as an instrument of practical goods; he was no partisan of the formalism which makes technique an end in itself.

Reviewing the behavior of those who wielded authority after 1763, when the innovation of taxing had begun, Burke stressed three things—illiberal vision, willingness to use force, and ideological blindness—which had abused authority and brought on the war, which indeed had sacrificed ends to technical trivia.

First, not contenting himself with dry analyses but holding as always to the concrete and actual, Burke turned to the characters of individual ministers, whom he considered illiberal, as he had turned to the American character. "Constitute government how you please," he had told the House years earlier, "infinitely the greater part of it must depend upon the exercise of the powers which are left at large to the prudence and uprightness of ministers of state."[136] Governmental power is executed by men, and stamped in the execution with their characters; the constitution "on paper is one thing, and in fact and experience is another."[137] With rich light irony and comic pathos (in his *Speech on American Taxation*), Burke mingled serious criticism in his characterizations of Grenville, Pitt, and Townshend, as he felt their private failings had influenced public affairs.

Grenville (1763–1765), whose high-serious ministry spun the first Stamp Act, Burke painted as a busy bureaucrat blinded by forms and convinced naively of the omnicompetence of legislation. Burke contemplated him by the metaphor of a jealous husband, in danger of being cuckolded. When he left law school with little experience of the human scene, Grenville married himself exclusively to public business, but his passion was soberly fixed upon forms and idealities. The idol of his cave was the Navigation Act, and "rather too detached," he mistook restraints for the whole of legitimate commerce. Thus the unaccountable fertility in American commerce baffled and amazed him, and as it swelled to his admiration again and again, he fell into a passion of anxiety. Overjealous of contraband, he multiplied perplexing and indiscriminate rules, regulation upon regulation, until he so straitened the bonds of intercourse that America was on the point of enjoying none at all, either contraband or legitimate. His rigidity provoked "the passions of a haughty, resentful people, who thought themselves deeply injured," especially by the Stamp Act, his "grand manoeuvre" to enforce a stricter monopoly. Restraint, Burke commented, is "well understood," but when it is suffered to run the full length of its principle, and is not changed and modified according to the change of times and the fluctuation of circumstances, it must do great mischief, and frequently even defeat its own purpose."[138] All is disputed where everything is enforced.

Chatham, the elder Pitt (1767), was obtuse in another fashion. A proud, eloquent giant in decline, the Great Commoner had lost his earlier vigor and, after accepting a peerage, some of his popularity. He accepted power in the vanity and influence of old age, and plotted a one-man rule of the ship of state. Into his administration he loaded old cronies and enemies alike.

He made an administration, so checkered and speckled; he put together a piece of joinery, so crossly indented and whimsically dove-tailed; a cabinet so variously inlaid; such a piece of diversified Mosaic; such a tesselated pavement without cement; here a bit of black stone, and there a bit of white; patriots and courtiers, king's friends and republicans; whigs and tories; treacherous friends and open enemies; that it was indeed a very curious show; but utterly unsafe to touch, and unsure to stand on. The colleagues whom he had assorted at the same boards, stared at each other, and were obliged to ask, "Sir, your name?—Sir you have the advantage of me—Mr. Such-a-one—I beg a thousand pardons—" I venture to say, it did so happen, that persons had a single office divided between them, who had never spoke to each other in their lives, until they found themselves, they knew not how, pigging together, heads and points, in the same truckle-bed.

As prime minister, Pitt sank out of control; if the old man fell into a fit of gout, principles not his own were sure to rule. "His whole system was on a wide sea, without chart or compass." If his sunlike face was hidden but for a moment, hangers-on and yes-men were "whirled about, the sport of every gust, and easily driven into any port." [139] Artful enemies seized control from within, and turning the vessel wholly from its course, pressed for American revenue (Pitt virtually retired in 1767, the year of the Townshend Acts).

Before such "a splendid orb was entirely set," Burke taunted, " and while the western horizon was in a blaze," Townshend, Pitt's Chancellor of the Exchequer, arose in the opposite quarter of the heavens. Townshend Burke painted as a charming *poseur* and rhetorician, "the delight and ornament of this House." Ardent for fame, "he worshipped that goddess wheresoever she appeared; but he paid his particular devotions to her in her favourite habitation, in her chosen temple, the House of Commons." Pointed in wit, fastidious, lucid, he struggled to please universally, and he flattered the preconceived opinions and present temper of his gaping audience in exchange for applause. "He was truly the child of the House. He never thought, did, or said anything, but with a view to you. He every day adapted himself to your disposition; and adjusted himself before it as at a looking-glass." Fickle, fashionable, he withheld his part in debate until the last dramatic moment so that all eyes would fix on him. "While the House hung in this uncertainty, now the *hear-hims* rose from this side—now they rebellowed from the other; and that party, to whom they fell at length from their tremulous and dancing balance, always received them in a tempest of applause." He delighted in the clouds of incense, "which daily rose about him from the prodigal superstition of innumerable admirers." Hence, Burke continued, the "fine-spun scheme" of 1767, which "had the usual fate of all exquisite policy":

> To render the tax palatable to the partisans of American revenue, he had a preamble stating the necessity of such a revenue. To close with the American distinction, this revenue was *external* or port duty; but again, to soften it to the other party, it was a duty of *supply*. To gratify the colonists, it was laid on British manufactures; to satisfy the *merchants of Britain,* the duty was trivial. . . . To counterwork the American contraband, the duty on tea was reduced from a shilling to three-pence. But to secure the favour of those who would tax America, the scene of collection was changed, and, with the rest, it was levied in the colonies. What need I say more? [140]

The characters, the specific shapes and active peculiarities of things, broke into Burke's field of vision wherever he turned. Anxious constraint, confusion, and mincing littleness added up to illiberality, staining the white radiance of power. Though he centered his criticism on men, it was the Tories as a group, however, who came in for general blame. In reviving taxation in 1767, they had "proudly strutted" into difficulties from which later they tried "meanly to sneak out." [141]

Short-sighted, chicaning, at one moment they had cried treason to American complaints and had threatened force, but shortly afterward they had circulated in colonial assemblies, without counsel of Parliament, a confidential letter of soothing hypocrisy, which swore in the name of His Majesty that "faction," not Tory politics, had brought on the taxation and that the Tories would seek repeal. The repeal went through when Lord North became minister (1770), but it was partial and loaded; the tea tax was left in force on a paltry pretense of "commercial principles" but actually to legitimize the abstract right of Parliament to tax when it would. The Tories, Burke complained, "blustered like tragic tyrants here; and then went mumping with a sore leg in America, canting and whining, and complaining of faction." [142] Then, "all the old mercenary Swiss of state" [143] had the temerity to argue, with the same petty and selfish cunning, that concessions would lead to an insolent clamoring for more. The Americans filled "with new jealousy, and all sorts of apprehensions" had begun to dispute not just the tax but "all the parts of your legislative power"; ten million pounds of tea lay rotting in the warehouses of the distressed East India Company; general commerce slowed to near bankruptcy; and as smuggling increased, enemy nations would get the profits of colonial trade. But the Tories would preserve the tea tax and the preamble of the bill to save face and the "phantom" of abstract right, even at the loss of empire. Thus "so insignificant an article as tea in the eyes of a philosopher" threatened to shake "the pillars of a commercial empire that circled the whole globe." [144]

Secondly, such behavior, bringing on its own confusion, would resort to force, which even in victory must produce all the evil effects of a national defeat. "America, gentlemen say, is a noble object. It is an object well worth fighting for. Certainly it is, if fighting a people be the best way of gaining them." [145] Force, Burke said, is temporary: "It may subdue for a moment; but it does not remove the necessity of subduing again; and a nation is not governed, which is perpetually to be conquered." [146] "You have the ground you encamp on; and you have no more." [147] Again, force is uncertain. Not even Burke expected the colonists to win the war, but all along he admitted the possibility. "An armament is not a victory. If you do not succeed, you are without resource; for, conciliation failing, force remains; but force failing, no further hope of reconciliation is left." [148] Force impairs the object: "The thing you fought for is not the thing which you recover; but depreciated, sunk, wasted, and consumed in the contest. Nothing less will content me, than *whole America.*" [149] To break the American spirit would be absurd, since "it is the spirit that has made the country." [150] Finally, experience was against force: the growth and utility of the colonies had been owing to wise indulgence. In respect to taxation, for example, the colonists had willingly given far more than was expected of them; a million in grants had probably been lost since the paltry Stamp Act was enforced. The colonists, Burke argued, would not exercise their power of refusal, except in extreme emergencies, if Parliament likewise would not exercise its power to coerce. From a consequent sense of dignity and security which freedom gives, they would prosper and want to pay. "Tyranny is a poor provider. It knows neither how to accumulate, nor how to extract." [151]

What is the soil or climate where experience has not uniformly proved, that the voluntary flow of heaped-up plenty, bursting from the weight of its own rich luxuriance, has ever run with a more copious stream of revenue, than could be squeezed from the dry husks of oppressed indigence, by the straining of all the politic machinery in the world.[152]

Finally, and with special urgency, Burke deplored a formalism and ideological word-blindness which stirred bad blood and enlarged confusion on both sides. It was a theme which would loom even larger in his criticism during the years to follow. As will be apparent, a steady, at times wearied and exacerbated, opposition of the abstract and circumstantial runs through all of Burke's major thinking, like the design in a carpet. Constantly he would return to the psychological deception whereby words or forms take the place of actualities, dislocate and estrange the mind in a false and cloudy medium, so that actualities are jostled out of sight and honest men can no longer communicate with them or with each other. There were many versions of it. In polemics it might show up as great, sounding platitudes, as irrelevant as they were easy: "so much rubble to fill up the spaces between the regular masonry." [153] In practice it might show up as a flimsy framework of speculation, smelling of the study: "One of his projects depends for success upon another project, and this upon a third, all of them equally visionary. His finance is like the Indian philosophy; his earth is poised on the horns of a bull, his bull stands upon an elephant, his elephant is supported by a tortoise; and so on for ever." [154] It was even worse when accompanied by conscious dishonesty, when it showed up as pretexts: the Grenville ministry attributed its unpopularity to "faction"; American complaints against the Stamp Act were "insurrection"; the Stamp Act was revived on the pretext of "commercial principles." Or most generally, the deception might grow, with bland corruption, in the very mores of officialdom:

> Men too much conversant in office are rarely minds of remarkable enlargement. Their habits of office are apt to give them a turn to think the substance of business not to be much more important than the forms in which it is conducted. These forms are adapted to ordinary occasions; and therefore persons who are nurtured in office do admirably well as long as things go on in their common order; but when the high roads are broken up, and the waters out, when a new and troubled scene is opened, and the file affords no precedent, then it is that a greater knowledge of mankind, and a far more extensive comprehension of things, is requisite, then ever office gave, or than office can ever give.[155]

Most bitterly of all, however, Burke attacked the subtler misplacing of concreteness in metaphysical or pseudo-metaphysical abstraction. For example, he attacked the claims of both sides to metaphysical "rights," Parliament urging an "odious and suspicious *summum jus*" [156]—a legal point—the colonists arguing the rights of Nature—a rationalization of very old, inflammable feelings. The former had forgotten that "politics ought to be adjusted, not to human reasonings, but to human nature; of which the reason is but a part, and by no means the greatest part." [157] The latter, learning to call every government tyranny which was not formed on their fancies, had forgotten that civil freedom bears no "resemblance to those propositions in geometry and metaphysics which admit no medium."

> [Civil freedom] is not, as many have endeavored to persuade you, a thing that lies hid in the depth of abstruse science. It is a blessing and a benefit, not an abstract speculation; and all the just reasoning that can be upon it is of so coarse a texture, as perfectly to suit the ordinary capacities of those who are to enjoy, and of those who are to defend it.[158]

Burke held his ears against a liberty and authority "parcelled out by argumentative distinctions," [159] against "suspicions, conjectures, divinations, formed in defiance of fact and experience." [160]

> I do not enter into these metaphysical distinctions; I hate the very sound of them. Leave the Americans as they anciently stood, and these distinctions, born of our unhappy contest, will die along with it. . . . [Leave metaphysical distinctions] to the schools; for there only they may be discussed with safety. But if, intemperately, unwisely, fatally, you sophisticate and poison the very source of government, by urging subtle deductions, and consequences odious to those you govern, from the unlimited and illimitable nature of supreme sovereignty, you will teach them by these means to call that sovereignty itself in question. When you drive him hard, the boar will surely turn upon the hunters. If that sovereignty and their freedom cannot be reconciled, which will they take? They will cast your sovereignty in your face. Nobody will be argued into slavery.[161]

Such distinctions "arising from claims, which pride would permit neither party to abandon" [162] would end in a resort to force, as a way out of an impasse. To indulge metaphysical abstraction—or its sour cousins, pretexts, slogans, labels—in practical affairs overreaches the moral order; it risks losing a sense of reality and letting loose a train of unmanageable and destructive consequences.

Human practice, Burke asserted, is circumstantial—linked in community by innumerable compromises—not metaphysical. "Man acts from adequate motives relative to his interest; and not on metaphysical speculations. Aristotle, the great master of reasoning, cautions us, and with great weight and propriety, against this species of delusive geometrical accuracy in moral arguments, as the most fallacious of all sophistry."[163] It followed that any attempt to systematize and square off practical community would be tendentious; it would push metaphysical arguments in the service of hidden motives and interests. Burke hated metaphysical speculation, as he called it, because he saw that a litigious logic setting out to dissect the vitals of long-established community would most certainly make a case, would discover what it wanted to find in the guise of logical contradictions, logical discords, logical absurdities, logical irreconcilables. At its most innocent, it would violate the delicate texture of fact; it would sink in a great Serbonian bog of static and rigid abstractions. Since the texture of human community is not woven of abstractions, no reconciliation could take place in abstraction. It is woven of compromises, and grievances are allayed by further compromises, not by ignoring those already made.

> It is . . . a very great mistake to imagine, that mankind follow up practically any speculative principle, either of government or of freedom, as far as it will go in argument and logical illation. We Englishmen stop very short of the principles upon which we support any given part of our constitution; or even the whole of it together. . . . All government, indeed every human benefit and enjoyment, every virtue, and every prudent act, is founded on compromise and barter. We balance inconveniences; we give and take; we remit some rights that we may enjoy others; and we choose rather to be happy citizens than subtle disputants.[164]

Burke did not condemn speculative inquiries outright as they may tend to clear doubtful points, and possibly may lead, as they have often done, to real improvements. But he objected to their pretense to practicality and fact, their premature or headstrong eruption in practice. He wished the truth of political argument, as for example over "rights," to be referred to a practical end and judged relative to the amount of felt life saturating it.

In reviewing the maze of miswielded power, therefore, Burke arraigned the private feelings of leaders, and a general violence and arrogant logic. In opposition he held out prudent compromise and gradual achievement of goods within a prescriptive community. He sought to reconcile American liberty and British authority by recovering their "true centre of gravity, and natural point of repose," [165] their tested, long-ingrown, and viable unity in prescription: "My advice is this; when you have recovered your old, your strong, your tenable position, then face about—stop short—do nothing more—reason not at all—oppose the ancient policy and practice of the empire, as a rampart against the speculations of innovators on both sides of the question; and you will stand on great, manly, and sure ground. On this solid basis fix your machines, and they will draw worlds towards you." [166] Burke envisioned a practical reconciliation, only possible because ready-made by prescription and waiting to be accepted. Contenders had only to stop tormenting each other, in fact and argument, to will each other's ease, and in a twinkling the reconciliation would come to pass. Primarily, his American writings express the politics of crisis and of threatened civil war, not of reform, for no reform was generally possible except on a basis of concord, and no concord was possible apart from the behavioral depth of prescriptive agreement. The destruction of concord, if it came about, would make all technical arrangements, or rearrangements, unreal; and for this reason he urged authority before it was too late to fall back upon ancient limits and to consider technicalities solely as means to restoring concord. The same order of prudence which guided his discussions of American liberty and character applied also to British authority, a prudence within historical necessities and for historical goods.

In all politics, behavior reflects the ends it will bring to pass, and likewise, purposed ends, no matter what metaphysical independence they enjoy, can only be realized consistently with behavior. For example: a pogrom, no matter what its justifying purpose, could not produce a pacific liberty; it could only make organized murder "traditional," pursued on principle. But also a pacific liberty, no matter how glowingly it sits in the mind, could not come to pass apart from "prejudices" existing in the long behavior of those to be pacified and freed. The attempt to bludgeon prejudice—prescriptive practice—into submission, even in behalf of a good, is only a subtler form of pogrom, an ideological pogrom, not less vicious because difficult to see. Burke struck out at those who attempt violently to bend other people to their theories of subjection. It is quite as vitiating in the act as its opposite—a prejudice so inert that it fixates neurotically upon the transient and blindly accustomed until, in the widening split between profession and behavior, it loses all sense of reality in the good. The partisans of both errors—and Burke found such partisans on both the English and colonial sides—are blind to the actual consequences flowing from their conduct. One carrying thought beyond the prejudices and passions of a moment presumes also that he can act without passion and prejudice: this is the overreaching of *amor intellectus*. "We carry on a poor unequal conflict," Burke wrote the historian William Robertson in 1777, "with the passions and prejudices of our day, perhaps with no better weapons than other passions and prejudices of our own." [167] The other partisan bowing his mind to a static order presumes to regard himself as the culminating end of endless centuries, and therefore gradually his human dignity leaks away: this is the overreaching of *amor patriae*. The middle ground, which Burke sought, would be occupied by one actively committed to ideal goods but also aware of his own and of others' indissoluble roots in the historical process—and therefore, one seeking, by patience, compromise, and persuasion, and self-watchfulness, to elicit his ends from harmonies latent in actual necessities.

## V

As the colonies slid further and further beyond recovery, Burke turned with alarm to shocking prodigies at home, among them a nasty, febrile, piddling patriotism. The same measures and the same spirit which, as he felt, threatened to subvert liberties in America threatened England also. In fact, reconciliation failing, he preferred that the colonies win their independence: if they should lose, he reasoned, England itself would sink into a military despotism.[168] The constitutional crisis of 1780–1782 was gathering slowly to a head, and Burke turned in anticipation.

It cannot too often be repeated: Burke concerned himself with the relation of concrete values to practice, with motives which "must be in possession, not in expectancy, and must co-exist with every moment of our action." [169] Thus surveying a train of legal acts motivated, as he felt, by hate—the Boston Port, the Massachusetts Charter, the Military Bill, and finally, what frightened him into earnest remonstrance, the partial suspension of *Habeas Corpus* in 1777—he warned against the secret ambush, the reflexive consequence, that awaits those who pervert the legislative spirit.

> We have made war on our colonies, not by arms only, but by laws. As hostility and law are not very concordant ideas, every step we have taken in this business has been made by trampling on some maxim of justice, or some capital principle of wise government. . . . Had the principles of any of these acts been first exerted on English ground, they would probably have expired as soon as they touched it. But by being removed from our persons, they have rooted in our laws, and the latest posterity will taste the fruits of them.[170]

Parliament outlawed the colonists "for the mere new-created offense of exercising trade," [171] then with a cruel and insulting trick pronounced them "pirates"; it revived an *ad hoc* law of Henry VIII and twisted it to improper ends. Deviating from "the old, cool-headed, general law," [172] it based justice upon formal technicalities instead of "the moral qualities of human action."[173] Burke scorned legalism blind to the spirit of the law: "Lawyers, I know, cannot make the distinction for which I contend; because they have their strict rule to go by. But legislators ought to do what lawyers cannot; for they have no other rules to bind them, but the great principles of reason and equity, and the general sense of mankind. These they are bound to obey and follow; and rather to enlarge and enlighten law by the liberality of legislative reason, than to fetter and bind their higher capacity by the narrow constructions of subordinate, artificial justice."[174] Whatever it professed, he thought, Parliament *acted* as if everything against America were necessarily in behalf of England, and as if enlarged moderation were a sort of treason. Possessed by such a demon, it was no wonder, Burke reflected, that ministers struggled to shuffle off the possession of indefinite power.[175]

The partial suspension, for the first time in modern British history, of the Common Law and of the statute *Habeas Corpus* provoked Burke to a classic exposition of the way liberty "is nibbled away, for expedients, and by parts" in periods of public danger and alarm. People admit the entrance of injustices of which they are not immediate victims, and from apathy, malice, or panic, allow the proscription of minorities —not seeing that it is "the obnoxious and the suspected who want the protection of law." Universal suspension of civil rights "would operate as a sort of *Call of the nation,*" alerting everyone; such measures "are marked with too strong lines to slide into use."[176] But by a partial suspension, "a line is drawn, which may be advanced farther and farther at pleasure, on the same argument of mere expedience, on which it was first described."[177]

> Liberty, if I understand it at all, is a *general* principle, and the clear right of all the subjects within the realm, or of none. Partial freedom seems to me a most invidious mode of slavery. But, unfortunately, it is the kind of slavery the most easily admitted in times of civil discord; for parties are but too apt to forget their own future safety in their desire of sacrificing their enemies. . . . nothing is security to any individual but the common interest of all.[178]

Other laws may injure the community, but the suspension of civil rights dissolves it. Burke hoped that gross evils would result immediately to dramatize what was at stake.

It is by lying dormant a long time, or being at first very rarely exercised, that arbitrary power steals upon a people. On the next unconstitutional act, all the fashionable world will be ready to say—Your prophecies are ridiculous, your fears are vain, you see how little of the mischiefs which you formerly foreboded are come to pass. Thus, by degrees, that artful softening of all arbitrary power, the alleged infrequency or narrow extent of its operation, will be received as a sort of aphorism—and Mr. *Hume* will not be singular in telling us that the felicity of mankind is no more disturbed by it, than by earthquakes or thunder, or the other more unusual accidents of nature.[179]

Burke added that if by chance the Americans should be conquered militarily—in line with the insane policy of conquering what was already possessed—they would hardly be made obedient by such "judicial slaughter." The peace would be only "a sullen pause from arms"; the hostile mind would continue in a worse form, meditating revenge and festering into new rancor.[180]

But worst of all, the hybris of lawmakers was every day more instinct in public manners. "Whilst *manners* remain entire, they will correct the vices of law, and soften it at length to their own temper." [181] But as he looked around him, Burke observed hardened hearts puffed up with pride and arrogance, a blind frenzy of contention, a noisy multitude hallooing and heartening to doubtful and dangerous courses, violent men seized with a dogma of unconditional surrender, a war party summoning the nation to unite ("Delusion and weakness produce not one mischief the less because they are universal"),[182] profiteering, inflammatory propaganda (especially by the court gazette whose battle cry, ironically, was the "dignity" of the nation), cries that the Americans were cowards, exultation in the feats of German mercenaries. A war fever had hit, and combining with other causes long operating, it was working a change in the national character. In

1774 Burke worried about public passivity: "Any remarkable highway robbery at Hounslow-heath would make more conversation than all the disturbances of America." [183] By 1777 passivity had borne its natural fruit—an obverse lust for violence.

A familiar type stood out: the war zealots, those unhappy people to whom war was an insane joy, a kind of deliverance from themselves:

> I cannot conceive any existence under heaven, (which, in the depths of its wisdom, tolerates all sorts of things,) that is more truly odious and disgusting, than an impotent, helpless creature, without civil wisdom or military skill, without a consciousness of any other qualification for power but his servility to it, bloated with pride and arrogance, calling for battles which he is not to fight, contending for a violent dominion which he can never exercise, and satisfied to be himself mean and miserable, in order to render others contemptible and wretched. . . . The addressers offer their own persons, and they are satisfied with hiring Germans. They promise their private fortunes, and they mortgage their country. They have all the merit of volunteers, without risk of person or charge of contribution; and when the unfeeling arm of a foreign soldiery pours out their kindred blood like water, they exult and triumph as if they themselves had performed some notable exploit.[184]

Burke grieved as casualty reports rolled in, and one Sunday when Philadelphia was captured, he turned away bitterly from a "wild tumult of joy." [185] Fellow citizens urging moderation and peace drew down as much rage as the enemy—not an ordinary rage, Burke observed, but the nasty, vacillating rage of people secretly aware of and unwilling to admit their own contradictions.[186] It was no excuse for presumptuous ignorance that it was directed by insolent passion.[187] "Civil wars," he reflected, "strike deepest of all into the manners of the people. They vitiate their politics; they corrupt their morals; they pervert even the natural taste and relish of equity and justice. By teaching us to consider our fellow-citizens in a hostile light, the whole body of our nation becomes gradually less dear to us. The very names of affection and kindred, which were the bond of charity whilst we agreed, become new incentives to hatred and rage, when the communion of our country is dissolved." [188] Of course, the tide of colonial affection which once had set for England would flow irrecoverably in the opposite direction.[189] Burke observed that the Declaration of Independence complained in most of its articles against the spirit of hostility manifest in English acts, and if such hostility were real, he reflected, and endemic, then the Americans would be justified in revolution.[190]

In such a stale and vitiating atmosphere, when the nation was divided, Burke was tempted to despair, like many other Whig leaders. He spoke, wrote, and advised; he lay awake restless nights; he had no power to halt the grind of events. Yet in despair he recognized and fought against the worst of enemies—more especially the despair which befogs itself with speculations about "inevitability." [191] He cautioned the Duke of Richmond against it, and against blaming the people at large.[192] He urged to Rockingham the wisdom of hope in action, knowing that action has sanative consequences which alter the face of the worst defeats, soften *must* to *may,* clarify, and hearten to further action. The problem was gradually and persistently to regenerate Whig reputation among the people, to focus the scattered resentment of ministry, and to hope for reform. "All direction of public humour and opinion must originate in a few. Perhaps a good deal of that humour and opinion must be owing to such direction. Events supply materials; times furnish dispositions; but conduct alone can bring them to bear to any useful purpose. I never yet knew an instance of any general temper in the nation, that might not have been tolerably well traced to some particular persons." [193]

As a first step to healing dispositions of the times, Burke anatomized a general despair, a spineless brooding into which many public-spirited people had fallen, embittered by the triumph of political reaction. They consoled themselves with the cynicism that in an age so decadent, all politicians are corrupt. Behavior has consequences, Burke warned, and inaction from despair would "lead to practical passive obedience far better than all the doctrines which the pliant accommodation of theology to power has ever produced." [194] For if all men who come to political power must be corrupt, there remains no motive for change or resistance. Flatly to despair of honor because one has been duped or misled by mountebanks is practically to support them in power, and not less to dupe oneself.

A conscientious person would rather doubt his own judgment, than condemn his species. He would say, I have observed without attention, or judged upon erroneous maxims; I trusted to profession, when I ought to have attended to conduct. Such a man will grow wise, not malignant, by his acquaintance with the world. But he that accuses all mankind of corruption, ought to remember that he is sure to convict only one. In truth, I should much rather admit those, whom at any time I have disrelished the most, to be patterns of perfection, than seek a consolation to my own unworthiness, in a general communion of depravity with all about me.[195]

Typically, Burke forged public arguments out of corrective self-observation.

The reason Burke so often deflected analysis into manners was his assumption that whatever the objective merit of an idea, its practical consequences were sure to bear some relation to the men conceiving it. (Practicality of this order, however, should not be taken in a plain plebeian way.) He asked how far an idea or value was to be pushed, in assessing its "truth," and with what quality of concrete awareness—with what delicacy or tact, what zeal, what malice, what self-control, what prejudice. In countering the hatred and despair which had crept into English political life, Burke tried to break beneath surface pretexts to practical motives in behalf of the conciliatory mind. He wrote therefore on a premise of innocence. To gaze steadily upon facts, to see things as they are, is, more often than not, an act of innocence, a freedom from "sordid, selfish interest," "wanton caprice," or "arbitrary will." It is awareness of this hidden ground of innocence which has led humanists so often to equate reason and virtue, or in more Burkian terms sagacity and temper, and sentimentalists to minimize the significance of reason at all.

During the period of reaction, and especially in the aftermath of the American schism, Burke relied for reform in English life upon constitutional inheritances, which, if they lay idle in one generation, might be revitalized in the next, provided that a small group constantly bore witness to them and kept them viable. This historical role belonged, he felt, to the Whig family-aristocracies, around whom a body of discontent might grow. "If once we are able to find, and can prevail on ourselves to strengthen, an union of such men, [then] whatever accidentally becomes indisposed to ill-exercised power, even by the ordinary operation of human passions, must join with that society, and cannot long be joined without in some degree assimilating to it. Virtue will catch as well as vice by contact; and the public stock of manly, honest principle will daily accumulate. We are not too nicely to scrutinize motives as long as action is irreproachable." [196] That is, Burke reposed his hopes on a party attachment solid at center and flexibly assimilative, which would work like yeast in public opinion. Seen in such perspective, Burke's "aristocracy-worship," which his biographer Sir Philip Magnus puts in a severely unflattering and exaggerated light,[197] looks less like an inferiority complex and more like political realism. Certainly the heroic (or if one prefers heroicized) modesty with which Burke contemplated the Whig destinies ought not to be separated from his anxious, practical-minded assessment of the state of the nation. He preferred party alignments, but if party should fail, landed families, he reasoned, must keep the continuity of active principles. "Decorum, firmness, consistency, courage, patient, manly perseverance,—these are the virtues of despair," Burke wrote the Duke of Richmond.

Persons in your station of life ought to have long views. You people of great families and hereditary trusts and fortunes, are not like such as I am, who, whatever we may be, by the rapidity of our growth, and even by the fruit we bear, and flatter ourselves that, while we creep on the ground, we belly into melons that are exquisite for size and flavour, yet still are but annual plants, that perish with our season, and leave no sort of traces behind us. You, if you are what you ought to be, are in my eye the great oaks that shade a country, and perpetuate your benefits from generation to generation. The immediate power of a Duke of Richmond, or a Marquis of Rockingham, is not so much of moment; but if their conduct and example hand down their principles to their successors, then their houses become the public repositories and offices of record for the constitution; not like the Tower, or Rollschapel, where it is searched for and sometimes in vain, in rotten parchments under dripping and perishing walls, but in full vigour, and acting with vital energy and power, in the character of the leading men and natural interests of the country. . . . I do not look upon your time or lives lost, if, in this sliding away from the genuine spirit of the country, certain parties, if possible, if not the heads of certain families, should make it their business, by the whole course of their lives, principally by their example, to mould into the very vital stamina of their descendants, those principles which ought to be transmitted pure and unmixed to posterity. . . . This I say to comfort myself, and possibly your grace, in the present melancholy view of our affairs.[198]

That which is "in full vigour, and acting with vital energy and power, in the character" of something, Burke called a "principle," and his loyalty to the Whig party, which he might profitably have deserted many times, grew from his conviction that, for his time, it best approximated his principles in living conduct. Burke's ultimate obligation in politics was to principles, by which he meant, he said, "morality enlarged." [199] Principles preceded the partial Whig witness:

The principles that guide in public and in private, as they are not of our devising, but moulded into the nature and essence of things, will endure with the sun and moon,–long, very long after whig and tory, Stuart and Brunswick, and all such miserable bubbles and playthings of the hour, are vanished from existence and from memory. My friends and myself sink into errors, and even into considerable faults; but I trust that these principles will buoy us up again, so that we shall have something to set against our imperfections, and stand with the world, at least, not as the worst men or the worst citizens of our day.[200]

His Whig-aristocratic tie, which because he was Edmund Burke he could not help subliming, is simply, consistently, and honorably explained, for those who wish it explained, on practical grounds:

Never expecting to find perfection in men, and not looking for Divine attributes in created beings, in my commerce with my contemporaries, I have found much human virtue. I have seen not a little public spirit; a real subordination of interest to duty; and a decent and regulated sensibility to honest fame and reputation. The age unquestionably produces (whether in a greater or less number than former times, I know not) daring profligates, and insidious hypocrites. What then? Am I not to avail myself of whatever good is to be found in the world, because of the mixture of evil that will always be in it? [201]

Burke was no Candide, though, as a matter of fact (and possibly of fate), he was experimenting, during this very period, with the cultivation of garden cabbages.

# III

# Burke and Ireland

THE arrival of America, Burke saw, had generated by 1782 a new world situation, tending no man knew where: the appearance of "a new state, of a new species, in a new part of the globe" altered "all the relations, and balances, and gravitations of power" as if a new planet had swung into the solar system.[1] Its consequences irradiated the whole of English life with a tumult of uncertainty. Ancient bigotries were confronted with historic crisis, ancient benefits were mistaken for crimes. Burke was gentler and more respectful in his view of the new arrival than he was to be a decade later in his view of France, another "new power of a new species," whose revolution, he would argue, was of a different character and intention. America he considered another of the tribes of Europe, and he admired the new nation for not having destroyed "all traces of manners, laws, opinions, and usages, which she drew from Europe" in sacrifice to "Jacobinism." [2] Yet he was not laggard in facing the peril of a changed international climate. English society all along the line was undergoing a defensive readjustment. His only thought, Burke told his Bristol constituents, was how best to conform to the new situation, which must be conformed to whether one liked it or not, in such a manner as to unite what remained of the empire in prosperity and affection.[3] When a gambler had lost much, by a wrong management of the cards, "it was right for him to make the most of the game as it then stood and to take care that he did not lose more." [4]

Burke was a modern statesman, forced, in pursuit of a local office, to study the conditions and data of unseen lands and to commit himself to specific decisions concerning them. While he dissected the motives of foxhunters like the Duke of Richmond, weighed his own election chances at Bristol, and worried about the price of carrots in the Covent Garden market, he was also perusing appropriations for the forts in Senegambia (Africa) and about to throw himself into the gruelling technicalities of India. The image of one world, as a practical fact, lay well over the horizon, in a later day, but it began shaping up in the eighteenth century, not least in England whose trading empire enforced a practical attention to details abroad. A public writer in 1791 could mention "the important influence of commerce in liberalizing the modern world" without pretending to say anything new.[5] One side of Burke's character is shaped by his having to winnow and assimilate inert masses of detail, rumor, summary, history, statistics, pouring in from quarters of the world he never saw. One irony in Burke's life is that in the greatest crises of his career —America, India, France—he was driven to apply his principle that "political thinking must be concrete" within the semiabstract vacuum which distance imposes.

This was partially true even with Ireland, his birthplace, whose ferment Burke had to construct in imagination from a reflective distance, as one revolutionizing change followed another. Again and again, when his advice was sought, he apologized for having lost "the true practical notion of the country, and of what may or may not be done in it," [6] "the actual map of the country." [7] His guilt of remoteness is one source of his quality, since it excited him into trying to feel the impossibly complex relatedness of actual life as familiarly as he could whenever he came to reason. Thus he tended to reason dramatically. As with distance of place, so with time, which, as Hobbes once remarked, is like a distance in its effects. Burke turned a historical imagination upon the present.

The colonial war had scarcely begun before its reverberations were felt in Ireland. As in the case of America, Burke had urged a liberal reform long before it was forced by events; and he had further warned that, since the multiform parts of empire were vitally interwoven, the separation of America "would tear to pieces the contexture of the whole; and if not entirely destroy, would very much depreciate the value of all the parts." [8] And so it came to pass. The pressure of war, the need for troops, taxes, trade, and tranquillity, and especially the entry of France on the American side, made some sort of concession to Irish discontents inevitable. Burke pointed out the irony of Ireland's situation: the country was called upon to fight an enemy with many of whose grievances she sympathized, in a war brought upon her by councils in which she had no share:

> She suffered from an attempt to subdue to *your* obedience countries whose very commerce was not open to her. America was to be conquered, in order that Ireland should *not* trade thither; whilst the miserable trade which she is permitted to carry on to other places has been torn to pieces in the struggle.[9]

The only alternative to relief would be another war of rebellion.

The controlling ideas in Burke's view of Irish trade and government were substantially the same as those which he laid down in his discussion of America, modified, of course, by local circumstances. He regarded Ireland as part of the empire and therefore subject to imperial restraints, and legatee of imperial privileges. The goal which he held consistently before him was not the improvement of Ireland at any cost, but an integrated improvement—an improvement of the general good resulting from the general reason of the whole. Though his sympathies led him into association, on specific issues, with nationalists like Henry Grattan, whom he admired, he was not himself an Irish nationalist. He reprobated and ridiculed any notion that Ireland might go it alone. He felt for Ireland, to be sure, "a dearness of instinct more than I can justify to reason." [10]

When I came into this parliament, just fourteen years ago,—into this parliament, then, in vulgar opinion at least, the presiding council of the greatest empire existing, (and perhaps, all things considered, that ever did exist,) obscure and a stranger as I was,—I considered myself as raised to the highest dignity to which a creature of our species could aspire. In that opinion, one of the chief pleasures in my situation, what was first and uppermost in my thoughts, was the hope, without injury to this country, to be somewhat useful to the place of my birth and education, which, in many respects, internal and external, I thought ill and impolitically governed.[11]

Yet people who expected him to act as a sort of special agent and loyalist—and Burke had frequently to counteract the notion—received his favorite answer that of course he was "a true Irishman," as he told the nationalist Thomas Keogh, for he was a true Englishman, and he conceived that the interest of one was properly the interest of the other. "I was an Irishman in the Irish business, just as much as I was an American, when, on the same principles, I wished you to concede to America . . . and not to wait the well-chosen hour of defeat. . . . I am a Royalist, I blushed for this degradation of the crown. I am a Whig, I blushed for the dishonour of parliament. I am a true Englishman, I felt to the quick for the disgrace of England. I am a man, I felt for the melancholy reverse of human affairs, in the fall of the first power in the world." [12]

When a group of grateful Irish Catholics took up a collection to reward him for his service in pushing the Savile Act of 1778, Burke politely refused on grounds of disinterestedness; his reward was to be only his "share in the general prosperity of the whole."

My principles make it my first, indeed almost my only earnest wish, to see every part of this empire, and every denomination of men in it, happy and contented, and united on one common bottom of equality and justice. If that settlement were once made, I assure you I should feel very indifferent about my particular portion, or my particular situation, in so well-constituted a community. It was my wish that the objects of such a settlement should be much more extensive, and have gone not only beyond the Irish sea, but beyond the Atlantic ocean. But since it has happened otherwise, I hope we shall be wise enough to make the most of what is left.[13]

What Burke struggled generously to preserve in Ireland as in America, the overarching practical end which governed his ideas, was "the principle of *common naturalization* which runs through this whole empire." [14] He wished the principle secured as it stood so that it might work even larger benefits in time. His idea was that by a constitutional policy continuous with the past, and grounding mutual dependence in mutual benefits, peoples of varied customs and climes would be molded insensibly together, into a just and rich community. England would naturally be the head.

If it be true that the several bodies which make up this complicated mass are to be preserved as one empire, an authority sufficient to preserve that unity, and by its equal weight and pressure to consolidate the various parts that compose it, must reside somewhere; that somewhere can only be in England. Possibly any one member, distinctly taken, might decide in favour of that residence within itself; but certainly no member would give its voice for any other except this. So that I look upon the residence of the supreme power to be settled here; not by force, or tyranny, or even by mere long usage, but by the very nature of things, and the joint consent of the whole body. . . . then without question this country must have the sole right to the imperial legislation: by which I mean that law which regulates the polity and economy of the several parts, as they relate to one another and to the whole.[15]

With this in mind, Burke had opposed, and in a large measure had engineered the defeat of a bill put forward in 1773 by the Irish House of Commons to tax the estate of absentee landlords by ten per cent if they lived more than half the year in England. Though "a citizen of Dublin who looks no further than his counter" might imagine that forcing the landowners to reside at home would increase "the circulation of money that may be laid out in the purchase of claret or groceries" [16] in his store, yet the fact was that he stood to damage a circulation of travelers, politicians, schoolboys, careerists (like Burke himself), heiresses, peers, which in the long run certainly and often in the short run returned to Ireland as much in culture and services "unforced and unbought" [17] as it took away in guineas. Such a tax, amounting practically to a tariff, virtually would declare England a foreign country, and its principle was to penalize free communication of any kind. As no local legislature by oblique means should favor itself over the welfare of the whole, so no local community of the empire should discourage a "discretionary residence" in the capital community.

Burke knew as well as anyone else the real grievance which the bill aimed to relieve, but he reasoned that if "this country [England], in many instances, is mistaken enough to treat you as foreigners, and draws away your money by absentees, without suffering you to enjoy your natural advantages in trade in commerce," [18] nevertheless you ought not to injure yourself even more by retaliation. The solution was not to obstruct but to increase the circulation of property and talent, by reforming the long-standing mercantilist restrictions upon Irish manufactures and commerce. If the principle of the tax were established in imperial laws (Burke observed in a *reductio*), a man with property in Jamaica and in North America as well as in England and Ireland, a "poor distracted citizen of the whole empire," would endure such a "*ricochet* cross-firing of so many opposite batteries of police and regulation" that if he attempted to comply by "a flying camp," he would find himself "a citizen of the Atlantic Ocean and the Irish Sea." [19] Burke's idea was not to legislate provincialism so that a "gentleman of New York, or Barbadoes, will be as much gazed at as a strange animal from Nova Zembla or Otaheite; and those rogues the travellers will tell us what stories they please about poor old Ireland," [20] but to encourage an interpenetration among peoples, which was mutually enriching and assimilating. "We shall be barbarized on both sides of the water if we do not see one another now and then. *We* shall sink into surly brutish Johns, and *you* will degenerate into wild Irish." [21]

As a step towards common naturalization, he attached himself most particularly, he said, "to fix *the principle* of a free trade in all the ports of these islands, as founded in justice, and beneficial to the whole; but principally to this, the seat of the supreme power." [22] Just as subordinate political communities had particular modes of government, so they had particular economies: "They raise their supplies in different ways, in different proportions, and under different authorities; yet none of them are for this reason curtailed of their natural rights; but they carry on trade and manufactures with perfect equality. In some way or other the true balance is found, and all of them are properly poised and harmonized." [23] This seems to forecast some kind of "automatic" harmony, but not certainly; by speaking of free trade as only a principle, Burke implied there was to be no wholesale casting off of restraints; each part of the empire would proceed in step towards a "natural" harmony with regard to relative emergent circumstances. But as matters stood, the same mercantilist restrictions had suffocated Irish trade as had irritated America, and were kept in force by shortsighted and self-interested merchants in England who were unable to see that "the superfluities of a rich nation furnish a better object of trade than the necessities of a poor one. It is the interest of the commercial world that wealth should be found everywhere." [24]

Burke wished to leave Ireland to cultivate her "natural faculties," and argued that whatever progress Ireland had made in the past had been "chiefly owing to her own natural advantages, and her own efforts, which, after a long time, and by slow degrees, have prevailed in some measure over the mischievous systems which have been adopted." [25] As an example of nature cramped by restrictions, Burke pointed to the woollen manufactures of Ireland—a "natural staple" of the kingdom—which had been almost obliterated. If men "are suffered freely to cultivate their natural advantages," he continued, "a virtual equality of contribution will come in its own time, and will flow by an easy descent through its own proper and natural channels." [26] The governing ideas here are vestigial Aristotelianism—"perfection" (completeness of development), "utmost prosperity" [27] and "harmony" (happy interdependence). His idea was not to "consider those as rivals, whom we ought to regard as fellow-labourers in a common cause," [28] but to pursue "*every* means of prosperity" for the whole.[29]

I know, that it is but too natural for us to see our own certain ruin in the *possible* prosperity of other people. It is hard to persuade us, that everything which is *got* by another is not *taken* from ourselves . . . as if the objects of mutual demand and consumption could not stretch beyond the bounds of our jealousies.[30]

Burke pointed to the example of Scotland whose participation in free trade with England had augmented the wealth of both: even "the partnership of poverty" was enriching. And were it not so, even if Scottish trade had encroached on the English, still, "we should be gainers, not losers, by acquiring the hearty cooperation of an active, intelligent people, towards the increase of the common stock; instead of our being employed in watching and counteracting them, and their being employed in watching and counteracting us, with the peevish and churlish jealousy of rivals and enemies on both sides." [31]

A common naturalization meant a diffusion in all the parts of the empire of English wealth as well as English liberty, law, and culture. Naturally, England itself, as the metropolis and counterpoise, would have a centralizing influence on the whole, and thus, in time, would absorb even more of what it already had, a cultivated superiority—in manners, in fame and public affection, in depth of capital, in aggregation of talent, in accessibility of funded tradition. But a *common* naturalization would mean to be cultivated in depth everywhere, and not less with the equitable opulence that a cooperation, so to speak, with history and Providence could produce: "not a scanty, but a most liberal, provision for them all." [32] Burke could walk the streets and bye-lanes of London and see shopwindows swollen with goods, bursting to the streets; he could see the Thames crowded with ships; and he could meet an Armenian or a Gentoo and welcome the variety. He rose to the vision of a comparable wealth and cosmopolitanism, duly modified by local circumstances, growing in all English dominions.

Not until 1778 was Burke presented with an opportunity to press his views on Irish trade. "In every measure of moral and political prudence," he said, "it is the choice of the moment which renders the measure serviceable or useless, noxious or salutary." [33] The general dissension and depression of the Whigs made a concerted plan impracticable, he wrote to Fox, and though he knew "the heresy of depending on contingencies," [34] still there was no choice, and the Whigs would be lucky "if, keeping ourselves attentive and alert, we can contrive to profit of the occasions as they arise." [35] The Tories might by some chance "be brought to do more than they intend. If they could be got to take the lead, we [Whigs] might fall in, and something may be done. It is in this course only that I have now any hope." [36] An opportunity presented itself in 1778 at last. A Tory bill of relief was entered, which Burke described privately as frivolous, a mere sop to keep Ireland from rebellion, not to cure its ills. The Whigs, somewhat surprised, set to work to support and enlarge the bill, not in concert, Burke noted, but individually, by "the operation of our known liberal principles, in government, in commerce, in religion, in everything." [37] While the bill was being agitated in the House, a number of "the trading towns and manufactures of various kinds" [38] took alarm—persuaded that whatever was got by another must be taken from themselves—and deluging the House with petitions, frightened Lord North from what Burke considered "the most considerable part" of the bill.

In 1779 another bill was brought forth "extremely raw and undigested" but, as Lord North absented himself, it had a free debate which ended in adoption. At this point, the trading towns (including Burke's own Bristol) once more set Lord North under fire, and once again he backed down. Irish impatience then broke loose: the Irish Parliament demanded free trade with arms in their hands. In a series of measures, they stopped all commerce, refused to raise taxes, shortened the credit of the Crown from two years to six months, and, unofficially, raised a 40,000-man citizen army, the Irish Volunteers, professedly a national guard to protect against possible invasion by the French, but in reality a weapon of political threat. The portent was clear, and the trade restrictions were repealed at a stroke. It was a "universal surrender," Burke said: "No reserve; no exception; no debate; no discussion. . . . No town in England presumed to have a prejudice; or dared to mutter a petition." [39]

Burke felt ambiguously. The army was "not under the authority of law, most certainly; but it derived from an authority still higher; and as they say of faith, that it is not contrary to reason, but above it; so this army did not so much contradict the spirit of the law, as supersede it." [40] The Irish Parliament acted illegally, yet its action was "above all praise." "By your proceeding with regard to the supplies, you revived the grand use and characteristic benefit of parliament, which was on the point of being entirely lost amongst us." [41] The consequences of repeal were most desirable; it was "that liberality in the commercial system" [42] for which he had pleaded all along, and had predicted must come. Yet he was humiliated that concessions to Ireland should have to be extorted by organized force, as if they were claims recovered against a struggling litigant.[43] In applying to the Crown for their relief, the Irish had *ipso facto* bypassed Parliament, where alone English (and Irish) liberty could be preserved. The liberty of England "might now and then jar, and strike a discord with that of Ireland. The thing is possible, but still the instruments might play in concert. But if ours be unstrung, yours will be hung up on a peg; and both will be mute for ever. Your new military force may give you confidence ["the confidence natural to recent and untried power"], and it serves well for a turn; but you and I know that it has not root. It is not perennial, and would prove but a poor shelter for your liberty, when this nation, having no interest in its own, could look upon yours with the eye of envy and disgust." [44] After the success of the action, Irish gratitude turned away, ironically, from the Whigs, who were their liberal, long-run supporters and in "a honeymoon of fondness" focussed on Lord North who, Burke protested bitterly, "succeeded to all their slappings and scratchings." [45] The volunteer army, he warned, though adequate to the purpose, had no root, and could not provide a lasting shelter for liberty.[46]

Burke's conduct had been typical throughout the affair. When he had seen the earlier bills "mangled and stripped of the parts which were necessary to make out their just correspondence and connexion in trade," [47] he had nevertheless supported them as aiming at a right principle: "as preparatory to better things, and as a means of showing, experimentally, that justice to others is not always folly to ourselves." [48] He had submitted to the restraint to appease prejudice, and had accepted the enlargement, so far as it went, as the result of reason and sound policy.[49] It was his settled rule, he said, "to make the most of my *actual situation* and not to refuse to do a proper thing, because there is something else more proper, which I am not able to do." [50] Knowing that the bill was an offspring of fear, he had detested among the Tories "the awkward and nauseous parade of debate without opposition, the flimsy device of tricking out necessity, and disguising it in the habit of choice, the shallow stratagem of defending by argument what all the world must perceive is yielded to force." [51] Yet he had endured the hypocrisy and the slashed, grudging concessions in behalf of the practical end, "in hopes that we might obtain, gradually and by parts, what we might attempt at once and in the whole without success; that one concession would lead to another; and that the people of England, discovering by a progressive experience that none of the concessions actually made were followed by the consequences they had dreaded, their fears from what they were yet to yield would considerably diminish." [52]

In his assumptions about Irish trade and self-determination, as in economics generally, Burke seems to drive (as nearly as he can be classified) toward old-fashioned Whig *laissez-faire* capitalism, which was a liberal and liberalizing force in a time when economies were still largely agricultural, and which still has a residue of relevance, for example, in its vision of interdependent society whose general wealth is produced by developing all the means of prosperity within its particular parts. Generally speaking, Burke premises a market self-regulated by "natural" laws and therefore susceptible to cycles; he assumes that means of production are to be owned by individuals who are justified in making as much profit as possible "without fraud or violence"; "property" is inviolate; there will necessarily be a rich few and a multitude of the less prosperous, by degrees trailing off into a corps of the downright poor who must be exhorted to "patience, labour, sobriety, frugality, and religion," and provided for by "charity": "Let compassion be shown in action, the more the better, according to every man's ability; but let there be no lamentation of their condition." [53] He attacks "the zealots of the sect of regulation," [54] firmly convinced that "to provide for us in our necessities is not in the power of government," which can "prevent much evil" but can "do very little positive good in this, or perhaps in anything else." [55] For he sees the bluntness of human reason, which, in juggling the counters of *labor, capital,* etc. blots out the subtleties of life; he distrusts "laws prescribing, or magistrates exercising, a very stiff and often inapplicable rule, or a blind and rash discretion." [56] He is unable to forget that individual men are individual men, with individual characters, circumstances, and possibilities, and therefore he consistently refuses to divorce economic and moral relations in the state, considering both as simply aspects of the "practical." And therefore he has to conclude that "interest, habit, and tacit convention, that arise from a thousand nameless circumstances, produce a *tact* that regulates without difficulty, what laws and magistrates cannot regulate at all." [57] This is comparable to, though not the same as, the tact which he saw at work in the history of the English constitution, and his objection to regulation in the market is akin to, and perhaps derived from, his dislike for theory in the body politic. An order adequate to all the purposes for which human society exists must unfold itself substantially from within. In economics as in politics, he assumes it to emerge undesigned, without foregone theory, from the labors of men who have the liberty to pursue their private interests, with as little interference as possible with the liberties of other men. Hence the importance of liberty as the product of ethical restraint. "Men are never in a state of *total* independence of each other. It is not the condition of our nature: nor is it conceivable how any man can pursue a considerable course of action without its having some effect upon others; or, of course, without producing some degree of responsibility for his conduct. The *situations* in which men relatively stand produce the rules and principles of that responsibility, and afford directions to prudence in exacting it." [58] Burke did not live to see the day of industrialism when his prudence might have shown him—in my opinion, would have shown him—cases where interference with many men's liberties was so grossly implicit in the distribution of property that government regulation of some kind in the economy could become as ethically urgent as its regulation of other conduct.

However, quite apart from principles general in the system as a system, there is also a superflux of principle peculiar to Burke himself, in reading whom we have more commonly than not to reckon with aspects of sensibility and to be satisfied with a quality of vision instead of with a tight package of historically-determined propositions. If, as seems most convenient, the drift of Burke's economics is to be associated with Adam Smith, who was a supporter and admirer of Burke, it is still necessary to keep in mind the distinction which Burke himself drew between the statesman and the professor in a university:

> A statesman differs from a professor in an university; the latter has only the general view of society; the former, the statesman, has a number of circumstances to combine with those general ideas, and to take into his consideration. Circumstances are infinite, are infinitely combined; are variable and transient; he who does not take them into consideration is not erroneous, but stark mad,—*dat operam ut cum ratione insaniat,*—he is metaphysically mad. A statesman, never losing sight of principles, is to be guided by circumstances; and, judging contrary to the exigencies of the moment, he may ruin his country for ever.[59]

Because he allows for a perpetual recasting of thought in the light of freshly encountered circumstances, Burke may be found feeling along the surface of possibilities which a man of the study might miss. Though he spoke of "the laws of commerce, which are the laws of nature, and consequently the laws of God," [60] he spoke also of economics as an infant science; he left open avenues for the expansion of theory: "Legislative acts attempting to regulate this part of economy do, at least as much as any other, require the exactest detail of circumstances, guided by the surest general principles that are necessary to direct experiment and inquiry, in order again from those details to elicit principles, firm and luminous general principles, to direct a practical legislative proceeding." [61] He seized one of the conclusions of modern growth-economics —that economic "laws" are functions of long-evolved manners of life, and they work only in that context: "If, as I suspect, modern letters owe more than they are always willing to own to ancient manners, so do other interests which we value full as much as they are worth. Even commerce, and trade, and manufacture, the gods of our economical politicians, are themselves perhaps but creatures; are themselves but effects, which, as first causes, we choose to worship. They certainly grew under the same shade in which learning flourished. They too may decay with their natural protecting principles." [62] Burke had studied political economy when both he and it were young, even before, to his knowledge, it employed the thoughts of speculative men in other parts of Europe; and apparently he worked out his opinions pretty much on his own: according to Smith, Burke was the only man he had ever met who independently had arrived at the same conclusions as himself.[63] *Laissez-faire* was the English liberalism of the hour, and Burke, among other Whigs, was applying something like free-trade arguments in Parliament well before *The Wealth of Nations* was published. Burke escaped, however, one major error among natural-harmony economists—less really an error than a constipation, a brain-blockage of optimism—the folly of imagining that the removal of a few unjust restraints would result in a joy forever. Burke did not propose *laissez-faire* as a system unmodifiable, although like Smith he arrived at his understanding of it by the conceptual passageway of "nature." Instead, *laissez-faire* was a policy, a plateau in the much longer quest for "moderation, prudence, and equity." Burke felt responsibility to "the living economy of the age." [64]

The empiricist in Burke was constantly liberalizing the patrician.

II

But the issue in Ireland which occupied Burke's attention longest and most brilliantly was more religious than economic (though he could talk about both and about their mutual relation).

The whole of Burke's thinking breathes the spirit of a hard-headed Anglican charity. He is not a self-righteous sectarian. He shies away from niceties of dogma. "When religion is brought into a question of civil and political arrangement," he said, "it must be considered more politically than theologically, at least by us who are nothing more than mere laymen." [65] To act with prudence, moderation, fortitude, and justice—and with a fifth cardinal virtue that the English have almost made their own, toleration—a politician need not linger for the end of "scholastic disputes" which are "carried on *aequo Marte* by controvertists" able and learned on all sides.[66] "For the Protestant religion, nor (I speak it with reverence, I am sure,) the truth of our common Christianity, is not so clear as this proposition; that all men, at least the majority of men in the society, ought to enjoy the common advantages of it." [67] His job is at every moment to buoy up "the moral, civil, and political good" of the country under equitable laws, and since the very substance of law contradicts its use as an ideological weapon, he disregards "speculative" opinions, no matter how bitterly he regrets them, nor how backward or eccentric they seem, unless and until they fester into crimes. As for when religious behavior is criminal, each case must be adjudicated individually:

As no moral questions are ever abstract questions, this, before I judge upon any abstract proposition, must be embodied in circumstances; for since things are right or wrong, morally speaking, only by their relation and connexion with other things, this very question of what it is politically right to grant depends upon this relation to its effects. It is the direct office of wisdom to look to the consequences of the acts we do; if it be not this, it is worth nothing, it is out of place and of function; and a downright fool is as capable of government as Charles Fox.[68]

Fetichistic headhunters are obviously outlaws—because they are murderers, not because they are fetichists. On the other hand, toleration, which is "a part of moral and political prudence, ought to be tender and large." "A tolerant government ought not to be too scrupulous in its investigations; but may bear without blame, not only very ill-grounded doctrines, but even many things that are positively vices, where they are *adulta et praevalida.* The good of the commonwealth is the rule which rides over the rest; and to this every other must completely submit." [69]

Burke agreed with the latitudinarians that toleration touches "the best part of Christianity." [70] The case may arise where the state ought in prudence to proceeed against religious opinions, if they threaten its subversion, but the "coercive authority of the state is limited to what is necessary for its existence." [71]

Factions are formed upon opinions; which factions become in effect bodies corporate in the state;—nay, factions generate opinions in order to become a centre of union, and to furnish watchwords to parties; and this may make it expedient for government to forbid things in themselves innocent and neutral.[72]

"The whole question is on the *reality* of the danger." [73] Burke would only add the caution, "There are ways and means by which a good man would not even save the commonwealth."

All things founded on the idea of danger ought in a great degree to be temporary. All policy is very suspicious that sacrifices any part to the ideal good of the whole. The object of the state is (as far as may be) the happiness of the whole. Whatever makes multitudes of men utterly miserable can never answer that object;

indeed, it contradicts it wholly and entirely; and the happiness or misery of mankind, estimated by their feelings and sentiments, and not by any theories of their rights, is, and ought to be, the standard for the conduct of legislators towards the people.[74]

A practicing Anglican, Burke described himself, to his son, as "no more than a common layman, commonly informed in controversies, leading only a very common life, and having only a common citizen's interest in the church, or in the state." [75] He subscribed to the existence in England of a Christian commonwealth in which the Anglican communion—"with modest splendour and unassuming state, with mild majesty and sober pomp" [76]—is established by law; and "in a Christian commonwealth" he would like to believe "the church and the state are one and the same thing, being different integral parts of the same whole." [77] Not that any human authority, as, for example, a legislature, should try to enforce allegiance—what is today called heteronomy.[78] A religion "to have any force over men's understandings, indeed to exist at all, must be supposed paramount to laws, and independent for its substance upon human institution. Else it would be the absurdest thing in the world; an acknowledged cheat." [79] An established religion "is not believed because the laws have established it; but it is established because the leading part of the community have previously believed it to be true." [80] The distinctive English achievement of government-by-consent applies, in Burke's conviction, to religion as well as to politics; "the consent is the origin of the whole." [81] On these grounds, to tolerate is not to be indifferent.

Equal neglect is not impartial kindness. The species of benevolence, which arises from contempt, is no true charity. There are in England abundance of men who tolerate in the true spirit of toleration. They think the dogmas of religion, though in different degrees, are all of moment: and that amongst them there is, as amongst all things of value, a just ground of preference. They favour, therefore, and they tolerate. They tolerate, not because they despise opinions, but because they respect justice. They would reverently and affectionately protect all religions, because they love and venerate the great principle upon which they all agree, and the great object to which they are all directed.[82]

To tolerate is to prefer with justice to all. The kind of toleration Burke admired was that of Catholics who fought in the army of William of Orange, to preserve the English people from a "Popish prince" they did not want.[83]

His toleration is therefore not equality. Although in effect he argued for freedom of religion, Burke was not accustomed to think of religious freedom under the schema of the *laissez-faire* marketplace, each sect competing against every other while the state stands apart a stern, impersonal referee. He was not a pluralist, though a kind of qualified pluralism was implicit in his thinking. He said:

> I would give a full civil protection, in which I include an immunity from all disturbance of their public religious worship, and a power of teaching in schools as well as temples, to Jews, Mahometans, and even Pagans; especially if they are already possessed of those advantages by long and prescriptive usage, which is as sacred in this exercise of rights, as in any others. . . . I can never think any man a heretic, or schismatic, by *education*. It must be, as I conceive, by an act, in which his *own choice* (influenced by blamable passions) is more concerned than it can be by his early prejudices, and his being aggregated to bodies, for whom men naturally form a great degree of reverence and affection. This is my opinion, and my conduct has been conformable to it. Another age will see it more general. . . . But toleration does not exclude national preference, either as to mode or opinions, and all the lawful and honest means which may be used for the support of that preference.[84]

Toleration was simply another way of providing in the state "for the several parts according to the various and diversified necessities of the heterogeneous nature of the mass." [85]

In Burke's view, religion, abstractedly speaking, "is the basis of civil society." [86] His faith was that the will of God lures and sometimes invades the transient finitude which is history and, since the will of God is the perfection of human nature, whatever proves necessary to that perfection is also

His will. Therefore, a state of civil society is His will.[87] It would take only a short train of deductions to arrive at the premise that the particular state into which one happens to find oneself born, or which one consents to adopt—say, England—is by presumption divine until proven otherwise, and that, for this reason, it is sacrilegious to plot its destruction except as a last necessity—"a necessity that is not chosen, but chooses, a necessity paramount to deliberation, that admits no discussion, and demands no evidence," [88]—and a sacred duty to revere whatever good it accomplishes and can dutifully be brought to accomplish. Therefore, it is a sacred duty to acquiese and to improve. On the grounds of a piety this general, the sanctification of the state would apply to any state of any kind anywhere at any time, without precluding evolutionary changes within it. Burke assumed, he said, that the proper norm of social responsibility—a social conscience—is "a disposition *to take the state in the condition in which it is found*"—that is, to acquiesce in what has to be because it is—"and to improve it *in that state* to the best advantage" [89]—that is, not (because there is a reality out of one's control) to lay aside all dignity of private reason and ethical commitment. In this light, to acquiesce in established Anglicanism, the reality delivered to him in the mystery of time, and to work for the conservation of its benefits, seemed to Burke only mature common sense. For a Christian, who conceived that to promote a concrete human community was half his ethics, it became a part of duty too.

Such a position drew Joseph Priestley's criticism, which has never lost its popularity, that Burke was a "lay divine," restating an old high-church Toryism of passive obedience and nonresistance.[90] But this is nugatory: it only accuses Burke of not being a Unitarian. On Burke's premises, if he had found Unitarianism established, he would have worked for its security as well, no matter what his own beliefs. Since the Anglican establishment derived from prescription, from long usage, consent, and public preference, its title, abstractly speaking, was no better than that of any other religion already in possession. An establishment persecuting another religion in possession would contradict the principles of its own foundation, and *vice versa.* But no abstract reasoning could ever settle what religion ought to be established in a country: it was a matter of historical growth. To Lord North's fear that a generous toleration would end in a "promiscuous establishment," Burke answered:

> Presbytery was established in Scotland. It became no reason either for its religious or civil establishment here. In New England the Independent congregational churches had an established legal maintenance; whilst that country continued part of the British empire, no argument in favour of Independency was adduced from the practice of New England. Government itself lately thought fit to establish the Roman Catholic religion in Canada; but they would not suffer an argument of analogy to be used for its establishment anywhere else. These things were governed, as all things of that nature are governed, not by general maxims, but their own local and peculiar circumstances.[91]

As a constitution is only "the civil means of getting at the natural" [92] so a church establishment he considered politically as only a formal projection of the national sense and will, the underlying unity of affection, belief, value, and inclination.

Against such a background of enlightenment and toleration in a Christian commonwealth, Burke sketched in a kind of ideal paradigm of national preference—"ideal" not in the sense of "what it would be nice to have" but in the sense of "that towards which actuality intends," its nature.

The state was consecrated by an ecclesiastical establishment, according with the real sense of the English people, first of all, as an "oblation" of a whole particular culture, a "worthy offering on the high altar of universal praise" to be performed "as all public, solemn acts are performed, in buildings, in music, in decoration, in speech, in the dignity of persons, according to the customs of mankind taught by their nature." [93] Therefore, the nation worshipped "not only as individuals in the sanctuary of the heart" but also "in their corporate character." The commonwealth, by definition, was not and never had been secular. To draw a modern distinction, it intended a theonomy, but not a theocracy. The Anglican establishment was thus a finite cultural expression or reception of the infinite, a particular mode, disclaiming infallibility—able to "alter her laws without changing her identity" [94] —but holding fast to "a partnership not only between those who are living, but between those who are dead, and those who are to be born." It sanctified in the state "a partnership in all science, a partnership in all art, a partnership in every virtue and in all perfection," obtainable only in a succession of generations.[95] The criticism of Dissenters like Priestley, who looked askance at tradition, wealth, and ornament in the establishment, Burke considered as "the *patois* of fraud, in the cant and gibberish of hypocrisy."

The people of England must think so [too], when these praters affect to carry back the clergy to that primitive, evangelic poverty, which, in the spirit, ought always to exist in them, (and in us too, however we may like it,) but in the thing must be varied, when the relation of that body to the state is altered; when manners, when modes of life, when indeed the whole order of human affairs, has undergone a total revolution. We shall believe those reformers then to be honest enthusiasts, not, as now we think them, cheats and deceivers, when we see them throwing their own goods into common, and submitting their own persons to the austere discipline of the early church.[96]

Until such an unlikely event, the idea was to preserve the "spirit" of Christianity amidst all the possible accessions of history and combinations of national character, not to fixate upon the conditioning of one accidental epoch. A second reason for consecrating the state, however, was to prevent an "unprincipled facility of changing the state as often, and as much, and in as many ways, as there are floating fancies or fashions," for otherwise "the whole chain and continuity of the commonwealth would be broken; no one generation could link with the other; men would become little better than the flies of a summer." [97] Without this "wise prejudice," Burke feared that "the commonwealth itself would, in a few generations, crumble away, be disconnected into the dust and powder of individuality, and at length dispersed to all the winds of heaven." [98]

In addition to national homage and continuity, a third reason for the church establishment was ethical—expiation, both of governors and of governed.

This consecration is made, that all who administer in the government of men, in which they stand in the person of God Himself, should have high and worthy notions of their function and destination; that their hope should be full of immortality; that they should not look to the paltry pelf of the moment, nor to the temporary and transient praise of the vulgar, but to a solid, permanent existence, in the permanent part of their nature, and to a permanent fame and glory, in the example they leave as a rich inheritance to the world.[99]

An establishment, Burke felt, was necessary to revive continually and to confirm such "sublime principles" as a kind of ethos of English leadership, a "wholesome awe" operating to impress all who have power "with an idea that they act in trust: and that they are to account for their conduct in that trust to the one great Master, Author, and Founder of society." [100] For to be free, men must enjoy a portion of power, and power must perpetually be "purged from all the impurities of fraud, and violence, and injustice, and tyranny." [101] The same applies to the citizenry at large.

When the people have emptied themselves of all the lust of selfish will, which without religion it is utterly impossible they ever should, when they are conscious that they exercise, and exercise perhaps in a higher link of the order of delegation, the power, which to be legitimate must be according to that eternal, immutable law, in which will and reason are the same, they will be more careful how they place power in base and incapable hands. In their nomination to office, they will not appoint to the exercise of authority, as to a pitiful job, but as to a holy function; not according to their sordid, selfish interest, nor to their wanton caprice, nor to their arbitrary will; but they will confer that power (which any man may well tremble to give or to receive) on those only, in whom they may discern that predominant proportion of active virtue and wisdom, taken together and fitted to the charge, such, as in the great and inevitable mixed mass of human imperfections and infirmities, is to be found.[102]

In short, a nation in Burke's view was a "moral essence"—a cultural personality persisting in time—and the Anglican establishment was only the political outworks, the outward and visible sign, of the English people's mode of religious sense—a product of their "moral imagination, which the heart owns and the understanding ratifies." It was their particular way of receiving their religion, Christianity, not the only way. "The body of all true religion consists, to be sure, in obedience to the will of the Sovereign of the world; in a confidence in his declarations; and in imitation of his perfections. The rest is our own. It may be prejudicial to the great end; it may be auxiliary." [103] On these grounds, he thought, the nation could reconcile commitment with toleration—without bigotry in the one or cold insipidity in the other.

Toleration, the national preference, is the opposite of persecution; and no persecution, Burke said, is just; all politics which admit persecution are "rotten and hollow at bottom"; there is no exception to plead. Persecution may present itself, however, in specious lights. If a new religious sect tries to persecute one long in possession, it of course appears to be the monster it is, "because, in the very instant in which it takes a liberty of change, it does not leave to you even a liberty of perseverance." [104] But if an anciently established religion persecutes an innovation—a "preventive persecution" to stop its growth—its wickedness may be harder to see, for an establishment can count on having all the prejudices and presumptions of time on its side, and "commanding to constancy, it does nothing but that of which it sets an example itself." [105] The injustice is likely to be concealed by mists of veneration, but there is no difference, Burke said, to a mind saturated with "the tolerating maxims of the gospel." [106] Burke would not release upon humanity, miserable enough at its best, all the blind and passionate fanaticisms of the demon dark—whether new or old.

Partly for this humanitarian reason, Burke abhorred the "spirit of atheistical fanaticism" [107] abroad in the eighteenth century whose comprehensive scheme of negativism or "malignant charity" left a "black and savage atrocity" [108] in its wake, a desperate suffering, a hard and intransigent spirit, full of resentment and aggressive superficiality. The one flaw in Burke's toleration was "the atheist." Needless to say perhaps, like many other polemicists in the eighteenth century, Burke used the term *atheism* very loosely, almost impressionistically. Believing that all good proceeds from God, Burke was only too likely to consider demonic the energy of the secularist who must find the sole meaning of his existence, as it were, horizontally, in the unceasing succession of anxiety and satisfaction, or, as Hobbes says in a famous chapter, "a perpetual and restless desire of power after power, that ceaseth only in death." [109] A man without actual religious belief, therefore, or at least without a kind of vestigial reverence impressed by early training, figured in Burke's mind, at bottom, as a moral desperado, and therefore not only unfit to serve the commonwealth by holding power but only saved from himself by breathing in a moral atmosphere he cannot see. "Let no one judge of them by what he has conceived of them, when they were not incorporated, and had no lead. They were then only passengers in a common vehicle. They were then carried along with the general motion of religion in the community, and, without being aware of it, partook of its influence. In that situation, at worst, their nature was left free to counterwork their principles. They despaired of giving any very general currency to their opinions. They considered them as a reserved privilege for the chosen few." [110] But power would discover the true character of "the atheist," which was to persecute, in various hypocritical guises. "They who do not love religion, hate it. The rebels to God perfectly abhor the Author of their being. They hate him with all their heart, with all their mind, with all their soul, and with all their strength. He never presents himself to their thoughts, but to menace and alarm them. They cannot strike the sun out of heaven, but they are able to raise a smouldering smoke that obscures him from their own eyes. Not being able to revenge themselves on God, they have a delight in vicariously defacing, degrading, torturing, and tearing in pieces, his image of man." [111] One reason for an establishment was to insure that "the general motion of religion in the community" would always be in existence to leaven, protect, and silently civilize those who without it would menace both themselves and the civil rights of others.

People who persecute or perpetually harass a man for his religion little imagine what they do. A man, Burke said, is a religious animal, and if in any way his spiritual life is plundered—as distinct from resettled or redirected—he suffers horribly, and is likely to revert to savage compensations. "Men must believe their religion upon some principle or other, whether of education, habit, theory, or authority. When men are driven from any of those principles on which they have received religion, without embracing with the same assurance and cordiality some other system, a dreadful void is left in their minds, and a terrible shock is given to their morals. They lose their guide, their comfort, their hope." [112] An angry irrationality bursts to the surface in complacent fury, and reacting with the remnants of honor, they suffer the nasty stagnation of broken candor. Therefore, Burke felt that any positive piety which has the assent of a serious mind, even if human reason alone is its origin,[113] ought to be respected, for the "body and substance of religion"—the broadly "ethical" principles upon which he felt they could agree—is more important politically and psychologically than the forms and dogmas of particular sects.[114] "I speak for myself: I do not wish any man to be converted from his sect. The distinctions which we have reformed from animosity to emulation may be even useful to the cause of religion. By some moderate contention they keep alive zeal. Whereas people who change, except under strong conviction, (a thing now rather rare,) the religion of their early prejudices, especially if the conversion is brought by any political machine, are very apt to degenerate into indifference, laxity, and often downright atheism." [115] Among such common principles are charity and justice,[116] neither of which, he said, speaking of the Dublin Castle administration, can motivate the passionate pride and deluded zeal which never shows any wonderful heat but when it afflicts and mortifies its neighbor.[117] It is not genuine zeal and conscience, Burke said, which motivates persecution, so far as he had seen it, but "evil dispositions" [118] as in demonology—pride, arrogance, a spirit of domination.

> I am sure I have known those who have oppressed Papists in their civil rights, exceedingly indulgent to them in their religious ceremonies, and who really wished them to continue Catholics, in order to furnish pretenses for oppression. These persons never saw a man (by converting) escape out of their power, but with grudging and regret. I have known men, to whom I am not uncharitable in saying, (though they are dead,) that they would have become Papists in order to oppress Protestants; if, being Protestants, it was not in their power to oppress Papists.[119]

A charitable and just view would realize that it is not in a man's moral power to evacuate his religion when his or somebody else's convenience requires it, and furthermore that no dogma is so indisputably sure that it entitles men, by a positive action, to cram it down their fellows' throats.

## III

It is against a background of these general attitudes—his personal commitment, his grasp of concrete ethical values, and the scope of his toleration—that one can best understand Burke's position in regard to the Irish Catholics. For, considering them more politically than theologically, more as fellow-citizens and men than as rival ideologists, he wished to cut across doctrinal ties in order to cultivate "the locality of patriotism," the community of vicinity, to make the whole nation "one family, one body, one heart and soul" in accord with "the grand social principle, that unites all men, in all descriptions, under the shadow of equal and impartial justice." [120] Following a *via media,* he wished to see all religions in the state—Catholic as well as Dissenter—find an objective meeting-ground in the common good, and thereby improve to the best advantage the condition of things which had come to be. He would never "sport with a singular opportunity which offered for the union of every description of men amongst us, in support of the common interest of the whole." [121]

Sometime as a young man, before he entered Parliament, Burke drafted a fragmentary Tract on the Popery Laws, which by a variety of arguments set out to prove that the treatment of Catholics was a plain persecution "unjust, impolitic, and inefficacious," and that it could only be stopped by abolishing the laws. The Irish Catholics, Burke said, received their faith "on as good a footing as they can receive your laws and your legislative authority, because it was handed down to them from their ancestors. The opinion may be erroneous, but the principle is undoubtedly right." [122] It is simply untrue, what many have supposed, that Burke so much feared making a wrong move in legislation—because he was aware of the extreme complexity of arrangements which make up society and government, and of the peril in tampering—that he virtually argued himself into a timid acceptance of anything centuries old. This, the first specifically political tract he ever wrote, belies the accusation, and his opinion never changed before his death (as it happens, his very last political writing also concerns the relief of Irish Catholics).

For thirty years, off and on, Burke labored by public tract and backstage persuasion to disburden Roman Catholics of a "system of penalty and incapacity" [123] dating back to the time of Queen Elizabeth and progressively revised to such a "vicious perfection" that justice, he said, could only find "refuge in those holes and corners which had escaped the sagacity and inquisition of the legislator." [124] The laws rationalized very deep-seated fears and hatreds actual in many parts of England since the Reformation, and though their barbarities were softened by neglect, the laws still deprived Catholics of civil rights. Their general effect was to suspend common law in the acquisition and inheritance of property (and therefore of votes, state offices, service on grand juries, or entry into the legal profession), in self-defense and privacy of home, in establishment of schools or attendance abroad, and in free exercise of religious ceremonies. "If a man is satisfied to be a slave," Burke said, "he may be a Papist with perfect impunity." [125]

A spirit of toleration—"a late ripe fruit in the best climates" [126]—had long been gaining ground all over Europe, Burke saw, and he exerted himself to keep it alive in England and English dominions. "Tarnished as the glory of this nation is, and far as it has waded into the shades of an eclipse, some beams of its former illumination still play upon its surface; and what is done in England is still looked to, as argument and as example." [127] As a devout Anglican, he held a view of history with a distinctly Protestant coloring; and he especially hoped to see the repeal or, at the very least, the reform of Popery laws and the toleration of Catholics to issue gratis from Anglican hands. After the Reformation, "one of the greatest periods of human improvement," had subverted a "vast structure of superstition and tyranny, which had been for ages in rearing," the Protestants themselves, Burke argued, became infected with worldly interests and worldly passions. A persecuting spirit, sprung up in the bitterness of retaliation and fear, directed sometimes against "new sects" of Protestantism, always against the Catholics, threw a poisonous gloom over politics.[128] This spirit, he went on, originated the long succession of Popery laws, and in various shades of passion, malice, and indifference, permitted their refinement. Expressed in propaganda, it "tended to drive all religion from our own minds, and to fill them with nothing but a violent hatred of the religion of other people, and, of course, with a hatred of their persons." [129] The Reformation "is not complete," in his view, until "the spirit of true piety and true wisdom, involved in the principles of the Reformation" is depurated from "the dregs and feculence of the contention with which it was carried through." [130]

Thus, in Burke's analysis, the struggle of Reformation and Counter-Reformation had the long-run effect of polluting law and manners in some sectors of English society. "Europe was for a long time divided into two great factions, under the name of Catholic and Protestant, which not only often alienated state from state, but also divided almost every state within itself. The warm parties in each state were more affectionately attached to those of their own doctrinal interest in some other country, than to their fellow-citizens, or to their natural government, when they or either of them happened to be of a different persuasion. These factions, wherever they prevailed, if they did not absolutely destroy, at least weakened and distracted, the locality of patriotism." [131] The Popery laws thus survived from centuries when political sympathies were generally overborne by religious ones. Vagabond hatreds and suspicions still haunted the late partisans on both sides. There were still Protestants, Burke said, who could express the tenderest horror at the persecution of Huguenots under Louis XIV at the very moment that, without a sting of compassion, they persecuted their individual Catholic neighbors with a misery quite as intense and possibly more degrading. Their charity ran to foreign horizons, and admired (or proscribed) men by denominations, memberships, leagues. It was such a complete derangement of the whole system of human duties, he complained, "to transfer humanity from its natural basis, our legitimate and homebred connexions; to lose all feeling for those who have grown up by our side, in our eyes, of the benefit of whose care and labours we have partaken from our birth, and meretriciously to hunt abroad after foreign affections . . . that I do not know whether benevolence so displaced is not almost the same thing as destroyed, or what effect bigotry could have produced that is more fatal to society." [132] Thus the effect of the Popery laws in Ireland was to create a rigidly exclusive class structure, dividing "the nation into two distinct bodies, without common interest, sympathy, or connexion. One of these bodies was to possess *all* the franchises, *all* the property, *all* the education: the other was to be composed of drawers of water and cutters of turf for them." [133]

The dominant Protestant power presumed to regard itself as a sort of "colonial garrison," [134] subjecting natives of a remote outpost to Great Britain, and to regard the natives themselves as "enemies to God and man; and, indeed, as a race of bigoted savages who were a disgrace to human nature itself." [135] The very names "Irish and Papist" shut up the hearts of everyone against them. Manners had methodized furious transient passions of the past and perpetuated them as malignant fictions of imagination. Even in 1795, Burke could remark that if some poverty-stricken wretches "raise a riot about tithes, there are these gentlemen ready to cry out that this is an overt act of a treasonable conspiracy. Here the bulls, and the pardons, and the crusade, and the pope, and the thunders of the Vatican, are everywhere at work. There is a plot to bring in a foreign power to destroy the church. Alas! it is not about popes, but about potatoes, that the minds of this unhappy people are agitated. It is not from the spirit of zeal, but the spirit of whiskey, that these wretches act." [136] Even if there had been a conspiracy, Burke (advocating punishment) would still have recommended calm, individual justice, and leniency, as he did a few years later regarding the Gordon rioters: "Men, who see their lives respected and thought of value by others, come to respect that gift of God themselves. To have compassion for oneself, or to care, more or less, for one's own life, is a lesson to be learned just as every other; and I believe it will be found, that conspiracies have been most common and most desperate where their punishment has been most extensive and most severe.[137]

But all views of conspiracy were historically mad, Burke felt, in an age when Reformation and Counter-Reformation had long ceased to plot international invasions or subversions, "in an age when men are infinitely more disposed to heat themselves with political than religious controversies," [138] and a similitude of religion no longer, as long ago it had, "made a sort of country for a man." [139] Images of that "commodious bugbear" the Pope, in company with the Cardinal of York and the king of France, invading Ireland to force the freeborn naked feet of the people into the wooden shoes of absolute monarchy—such images were so fantastic that many a person vulgarized by them would not dare to make them public or even to shape them clearly in his own mind, but he would disguise them in a fog of ill-explained doubts, surmises, and apprehensions, where they would appear to have some size and would make an impression.[140] Other gentlemen less vulgarly bigoted would wish to enforce an "irreversible outlawry" but to disguise it in "bland and civil forms" of officialdom without knowing why. Most people in England, on the other hand, were too ignorant of Ireland to mean any ill; they knew only a faint "humming that remains on their ears of the burden of the old song about Popery." [141]

Burke, who had to endure false accusations of being a Jesuit and of being educated at St. Omer, knew the effects of recrudescent bigotry at first hand. His mother had been a Roman Catholic; he had grown up in full view of the sick humors afloat in the Irish countryside. He saw their brutalizing effects upon persecutor and persecuted alike. "To have any respect for the character and person of a Popish priest there—oh! 'tis an uphill work indeed." [142] As for the Catholic layman, his "jail-distemper" was so severely degraded below "that assured and liberal state of mind, which alone can make us what we ought to be," and so contagious, that, for his part, Burke vowed to God he had rather put the man to death and be done than "to keep him above ground an animated mass of putrefaction, corrupted himself, and corrupting all about him." [143] In the heart of the country was "a bank of discontent, every hour accumulating, upon which every description of seditious men may draw at pleasure." [144] As so often happens in civil slavery, effects were taken for causes: a large body of Protestants attributed the Catholic suffering not to those laws whose cruelties lurked unexamined in lawbook jargon and whose operations in the courtroom or in men's hearts went on "in a sort of comparative silence and obscurity," [145] and of course not to their own hard, habitual arrogance—which, since it came so easily to them, they found easy to ignore—but instead, to an inherent Catholic laziness, or superstition, or stupidity, or fear of liberty, or lack of virtue. Other Protestants, conditioned to surface judgments and hearsay, consented to hate what they knew nothing about. Thousands of people in Ireland, Burke said, had never conversed with a Roman Catholic in their lives unless they happened to talk with their gardener's workmen, or ask their way when they had lost it in their sports, and yet were so averse to have Catholics near their persons that they would not employ them even in the stable, or as a blacksmith.[146]

But the situation was even more complicated than sectarian disputes and all their long history of conditioned hatred and suspicion could make it. Since Catholics constituted a majority of the people, in the neighborhood of two million, the Protestants at large possessed something of the power and learned many of the manners befitting a "master cast[e]." [147] They controlled all offices and three-quarters of the landed property in the state; they were a vested interest but not along lines simply of class or wealth. Protestant tradesmen, servants, and workers—the "plebeian member" of the state—could also exercise an insulting and vexatious superiority in manners, and a monopoly in preferments. "The Protestants in Ireland," Burke said, "are not *alone* sufficiently the people to form a democracy; and they are *too numerous* to answer the ends and purposes of an *aristocracy*." [148] Thus they tended toward that "monster" among states—a plebeian oligarchy—and "that worst of all oppressions, the persecution of private society and private manners." [149] The web of political power was as tightly drawn. The Irish Parliament was wholly Protestant and subordinate to the English Privy Council; the Crown appointed a lord-lieutenant, over whose militantly anti-Catholic administration, located at Dublin Castle, the Parliament had no control. The largest power bloc since the Whig Revolution of '88 consisted of Anglo-Irish landlords, many absentee in England. It was simple and plain exclusion of the body of the Irish people from their civil rights in order to empower a caste—Protestant, white, nationalistic—and, as usually happens, exclusion led to exploitation and jobbery. Thus, whatever bigotry or conscientious fear existed in Ireland was intermingled with, and even bottomed upon, the material prejudices of the rich, the proud, and the powerful.[150]

The analogy with Negro slavery in the American South has already been drawn by John Morley.[151]

Burke added that natural goodness in many persons made exceptions;[152] and there is always to be found "that virtue, which shoots up in the full force by the native vigour of the seminal principle, in spite of the adverse soil and climate that it grows in."[153] Yet the energy of hatred which was always latent and which exploded periodically in riots or ground away in the silence of custom can be guessed by the mighty historical forces that were required to budge it, and which failed to destroy it, even by the twentieth century. One of the worst effects was to "waste the vigour" of the country.[154]

There were innumerable "corollary oppressions" flowing from the laws. A Catholic in litigation with a Protestant before a Protestant jury was ruined from the start. Any misdemeanors, such as are common among an oppressed populace—riots, or "nocturnal assemblies for the purpose of pulling down hedges, making breaches in park walls, firing barns, maiming cattle"—could very plausibly be twisted into conspiracies against the government; witnesses could be dug up to prove them plots of high treason; and thus the rioters could be believed to be only the troops of leaders higher up—"men of proprietary landed estates, substantial renters, opulent merchants, physicians, and titular bishops"—whose respectability of course was only a front.[155] Thus it would always be, Burke said, "by paroxysms," so long as Catholics carried the stigma of defenseless half-citizens.[156] The family, which Burke, along with most political theorists since Aristotle, revered as the primary test-unit and building block of society, was subjected to disintegrating pressures. The *pater familias* or an elder heir was emptied of all incentive to improve his rented property—"that laudable avarice which every wise state has cherished as one of the first principles of its greatness"[157]—and was encouraged to lead "a thoughtless, loitering, and dissipated life." His children had to learn their letters, Burke said, from the charity of enemies. He was burdened by special taxes. He was prey to "mercenary informers"—"the worst and most unmerciful men"—who could claim what he had. His wife or his children or near relations might at any moment rob him by a timely conversion.

To be sure, Burke noted, a persecution by law never works: "Ireland, after almost a century of persecution, is at this hour full of penalties and full of Papists." [158] The very reaction to a destructive policy, as the Jewish history shows, is often a long-run power of resistance and a search for compensations. For example, many Catholics driven from the land pushed their way in business and trade:

The system of laws which, by a perversion of all legal principles, and by various contrivances of vexation, had screwed the Roman Catholics out of their landed property, and in the same process broken the spirit of their gentry, has forced a commercial interest to grow up in its place, and (the former generation passing away) has drawn up with it a race of men who have escaped the toils of law. They have no longer the minds and qualities of men hunted into obscurity, and sinking into indigence by a daily impoverishment. What was once a landed interest, is now converted into a commercial interest; and the men who compose it feel something of the elevation, and possess the energy, which accompanies growing circumstances in those who feel that their fortune is due to their own vigour.[159]

Yet this disjunction of the landed and trading interests—a fault which Burke would later find with the *ancien régime* in France—prevented profits earned in trade from being regorged permanently on the land, and lost "the bold and liberal spirit of improvement, which persons bred to trade have often exerted on their land-purchases." [160] The Catholics were reduced to a knot of self-made urban businessmen and an army of common people, many of them hut-dwellers, without a stake in society. And the laws amounted to an express injunction, "Thou shalt not improve." [161]

One argument for the Popery laws pretended their enlightened benefits to the future: that is, Protestantism, which the laws sought to insure, was "beneficial to the whole community"; though harsh in operation, the laws would be pleasant in the end, for they were "only a discipline to bring over a deluded people to their real interest." Therefore, Burke said (in the 1760's, before Marxism was ever heard of), they would incur "a certain mischief for an advantage which is comparatively problematical," they would "suspend the rights of [human] nature, in order to an approved system for the protection of them"—that is, they have a "reversionary benevolence" which promises "the remote good of a late posterity" at the very moment it sacrifices "the present enjoyment which every honest man must have in the happiness of his contemporaries." [162] But true charity answers the perpetual claim of the concrete. "It is not permitted to us to sacrifice the temporal good of any body of men to our own ideas of the truth and falsehood of any religious opinions. By making men miserable in this life they counteract one of the great ends of charity; which is, inasmuch as in us lies, to make men happy in every period of their existence, and most in what most depends upon us." [163] Nothing is defensible which renders miserable millions of the race coexistent with oneself.[164] "I am perfectly indifferent," Burke said, in one of his most characteristic statements, "concerning the pretexts upon which we torment one another; or whether it be for the constitution of the church of England, or for the constitution of the state of England, that people choose to make their fellow-creatures wretched." [165]

On like grounds, Burke blasted the popular phrase "Protestant ascendancy" as only another pretext—an antiquated verbal fetish "hung about the necks of the unhappy, not to heal, but to communicate disease." [166] Ascendency meant "neither more nor less than the resolution of one set of people in Ireland to consider themselves as the sole citizens in the commonwealth." [167] In plain English it signified nothing more than *"pride and dominion* on the one part of the relation, and on the other *subserviency and contempt."* [168] Adding Protestant to it was no improvement; in fact, he said resentfully, it was a still "deeper evil" since it reduced *Protestant* to no more than "the name of a persecuting faction, with a relation of some sort of theological hostility to others, but without any sort of ascertained tenets of its own." [169] In actuality, there is no such thing, he said, as the Protestant religion; there are only Protestant churches, each with its peculiar confession of faith and settled discipline,[170] each sharing with the Roman Catholics a "positive part" of Christianity which Burke considered "infinitely the most valuable and essential." [171] Partisans of Protestant ascendency defined *Protestant* "as Cowley defines wit, not by what it is, but by what it is not." [172] London might be "the metropolis of the Protestant world"; [173] but Protestant*ism* had never been established in England or anywhere else; it was only a word hiding the kind of negativism or vengeful malignity that Burke usually claimed to find among "atheists." "The word Protestant is the charm that locks up in the dungeon of servitude three millions of your people." [174]

Indeed, to do justice to Catholics seemed even more urgent to Burke in his last years owing to the French Revolution. In the face of anti-clericalism ballooning over from France, Burke argued that all positive churches must secure their common basis, that they had nothing to gain and everything to lose by warring among themselves. "I think we may dispute, rail, persecute, and provoke the Catholics out of their prejudices; but it is not in ours they will take refuge." [175] Into the void of ousted prejudice would rush not some hypothetical Protestantism, but "that sort of active, proselytizing, and persecuting atheism, which is the disgrace and calamity of our time." [176] "If mere dissent from the Church of Rome be a merit, he that dissents the most perfectly is the most meritorious"; [177] and therefore "whatever ill humours are afloat in the state . . . will be sure to discharge themselves in a mingled torrent in the *cloaca maxima* of Jacobinism." [178] The "prejudices" of Catholics, it seemed to Burke, stood as one of the soundest dikes against "prejudices" of the new Church of Paris, so much so that he predicted "that if the Catholic religion is destroyed by the infidels, it is a most contemptible and absurd idea, that this, or any Protestant church, can survive that event." [179]

On still another pretext, again resisting the claims of concrete community with individuals, other persecutors argued that property was endangered by the tornadic succession of rebellion and confiscation in Irish history.

Whilst, say they, the Papists of this kingdom were possessed of landed property, and of the influence consequent to such property, their allegiance to the Crown of Great Britain was ever insecure; the public peace was ever liable to be broken; and Protestants never could be a moment secure either of their properties or of their lives. Indulgence only made them arrogant, and power daring; confidence only excited and enabled them to exert their inherent treachery; and the times which they generally selected for their most wicked and desperate rebellions were those in which they enjoyed the greatest ease and the most perfect tranquility.[180]

"Oblivion," Burke countered, "is the only remedy for irreparable wrongs," [181] assuming that the wrongs had occurred. But he also charged that modish accounts of Ireland, such as Sir William Temple's and the Earl of Clarendon's, were infected with party, spreading the opinion that Irish Catholics had rebelled against just governments instead of against "attempts to reduce the natives to the state to which they are now reduced." [182] To see a good history of Ireland was one of Burke's lifelong hopes; he encouraged several to undertake it, and himself gathered and consulted original records.[183] But no matter what history discloses, it is quixotic to joust against the vices of dead men. The real danger in every government is that it may irritate its living subjects into being vicious.

The majority of men are in no persuasion bigots; they are not willing to sacrifice, on every vain imagination that superstition or enthusiasm holds forth, or that even zeal and piety recommend, the certain possession of their temporal happiness. And if such a spirit has been at any time roused in a society, after it has had its paroxysm it commonly subsides and is quiet, and is even the weaker for the violence of its first exertion; security and ease are its mortal enemies. . . . if anything can tend to revive and keep it up, it is to keep alive the passisons of men by ill usage. This is enough to irritate even those who have not a spark of bigotry in their constitution to the most desperate enterprises; it certainly will inflame, darken, and render more dangerous the spirit of bigotry in those who are possessed by it.[184]

Fanatic Catholicism was not the danger, but fanaticism itself, which cannot be cured by fanatical provocation. It was a delusion, in order to make room for the vices of Papists, to clear the house of all the vices of men.[185] As long as men on either side of the fence "hold charity and justice to be essential integral parts of religion, there can be little danger from a strong attachment to particular tenets in faith." [186] "History records many things which ought to make us hate evil actions; but neither history, nor morals, nor policy can teach us to punish innocent men on that account. What lesson does the iniquity of prevalent factions read to us? It ought to lesson us into an abhorrence of the abuse of our own power in our own day; when we hate its excesses so much in other persons and in other times." [187] It was with this kind of ethical awareness that Burke called upon "prescription" as a cure. For wishing "to let Time draw his oblivious veil over the unplesant modes by which lordships and demesnes have been acquired," to permit "the sacred name of possession to stand in the place of the melancholy and unpleasant title of grantees of confiscation," [188] Burke has been mistaken to say that whatever is, is right. But this is not so. "The situation of every man," he said, "who comes in upon the ruin of another—his succeeding, under this circumstance [of confiscation] is *tristis et luctuosa successio.*" [189] After the passage of long time and generations, however, there is simply no just remedy, certainly not in counter-confiscations. The question becomes this: "Are we to make the best of this situation which we cannot alter? The question is—shall the condition of the body of the people be alleviated in other things?" [190] In this case, the question of prescription is whether charity and justice are to have an actual life henceforward in the moving present, or to be lost again in a struggle of factions—"those shocking retaliations which never suffer dissensions to subside." [191] In this situation, a coming together under the aegis of the prescriptive national state, without regard to theological differences, seemed to Burke an expedient solution. He wished to extend to Irish Catholics full privileges (and responsibilities) of citizenship, to be held under the law as individuals. Thus freed from a wholesale stigma, he felt, Catholic individuals would gradually blur into society, each on his own merits.

This way of *proscribing the citizens by denominations and general descriptions,* dignified by the name of reason of state, and security for constitutions and commonwealths, is nothing better at bottom, than the miserable invention of an ungenerous ambition, which would fain hold the sacred trust of power, without any of the virtues or any of the energies that give a title to it: a receipt of policy, made up of a detestable compound of malice, cowardice, and sloth. . . . Crimes are the acts of individuals, and not of denominations; and therefore arbitrarily to class men under general descriptions, in order to proscribe and punish them in the lump for a presumed delinquency, of which perhaps but a part, perhaps none at all, are guilty, is indeed a compendious method, and saves a world of trouble about proof; but such a method, instead of being law, is an act of unnatural rebellion against the legal dominion of reason and justice; and this vice, in any constitution that entertains it, at one time or other will certainly bring on its ruin.[192]

As an ultimate ground for reform and individuation, Burke reverted to the first principles of justice—in which the names of Protestant and Papist could make no change [193]—not, he said, "from a superfluous, vain parade of displaying general and uncontroverted maxims," but because there is no other recourse when irrationality is methodized in law and the manners supporting law. "Men want to be reminded," he said, in one of his most Johnsonian statements, "who do not want to be taught; because those original ideas of rectitude, to which the mind is compelled to assent when they are proposed, are not always as present to it as they ought to be." [194] A man may go into "a sort of oblivion," amounting in time more or less to denial, of fundamentals on which, in his more clearheaded hours, he acknowledges his own welfare, and perhaps the welfare of all mankind, most valuably and essentially to depend. And then he possesses them feebly as only "barren speculations" instead of "practical motives for conduct." [195] This self-split situation may be simply personal; or, more broadly, it may be the special burden of a whole generation or century. In either case, the remedy is once more "to offer them to the understanding," to repossess them in concrete perception—which may mean modifying them—with a view to their stable actuality in fact and practice. And so the conservative, of the Burkian brand, who ought to be an open and unashamed moral critic, is born. "Reason is never inconvenient but when it comes to be applied. Mere general truths interfere very little with the passions. They can, until they are roused by a troublesome application, rest in great tranquillity side by side with tempers and proceedings the most directly opposite to them." [196] What applies to private actions applies also to law, which is only a more generalized "mode of human action respecting society." [197]

The positivism advanced by Hobbes, that the rule of justice is to be taken from the constitutions of commonwealths and that laws derive their authority "from their institution merely and independent of the quality of the subject-matter," [198] Burke rejected "not only as unworthy of a philosopher, but of an illiterate peasant." Implicitly, Burke distinguished between validity and justice. To be valid, a law must have the *consent* of the people, "for in all forms of government the people is the true legislator." [199] This raised a difficulty which Burke does not pause to solve, that is, the fine line between consent and acquiescence. "The people, indeed, are presumed to consent to whatever the legislature ordains for their benefit; and they are to acquiesce in it, though they do not clearly see into the propriety of the means by which they are conducted to that desirable end. This they owe as an act of homage and just deference to a reason which the necessity of government had made superior to their own." [200] His only answer for the moment is that though the Catholics must acquiesce in the laws, they cannot be presumed to consent to their exclusion from the "common advantages of society," and therefore, since they are the majority, the laws are not properly valid; they have no "civil existence." The other criterion of validity is a constituted power sufficient to declare and enforce a law.

But validity is not justice: neither the constituted legislature nor the people themselves can justly "make a law prejudicial to the whole community, even though the delinquents in making such an act should be themselves the chief sufferers by it." [201] Law is not justified by majority consent or by prevalence of power. There are two, and only two, foundations of law—*equity* and *utility*. The first, equity, grows out of "the great rule of equality, which is grounded upon our common nature, and which Philo, with propriety and beauty, calls the Mother of Justice." [202] It is the moral law, "the will of Him who gave us our nature, and in giving impressed an invariable law upon it." [203] Human laws, properly speaking, are only declaratory: "they may alter the mode and application, but have no power over the substance of original justice." [204] In the same way, it may be recalled, Burke considered the Anglican establishment only a mode and application of Christianity, without alteration of its original substance. No arguments of "policy, reason of state, or preservation of the constitution" can be pleaded in favor of "statutes, which create an artificial difference between men, as the laws before us do, in order to induce a consequential inequality in the distribution of justice." [205] "Partiality and law are contradictory terms," and arguments based on any other principle, no matter how large a party they privilege, will hold equally well for a smaller party. "And thus we shall go on, narrowing the bottom of public right, until step by step we arrive, though after no very long or very forced deduction, at what one of our poets [Pope, whom Burke frequently quoted] calls the *enormous faith;* the faith of the many, created for the advantage of a single person." [206]

The other foundation of law, utility (or as Burke sometimes calls it, expediency), must be understood as "general and public utility, connected in the same manner with, and derived directly from, our rational nature." [207] Any other utility may be Machiavellian; it may be the utility of a robber, a tyrant, a bigot, or a sensualist, but not the utility of a citizen. The real interest of no part of the community can be separated from the happiness of the rest, but even if it could, a law made against one in behalf of the other would be "repugnant to the essence of law," which requires that it be made as much as possible *pro communi bono*.[208] True, no legislators "can regard the *minima* of equity," and therefore "a law may in some instances be a just subject of censure, without being at all an object of repeal." [209] There is an ineradicable infirmity in all human institutions; not even the finest and most delicate gauze of statutes can "provide beneficially for every particular case, and thus fill, adequately to their intentions, the circle of universal justice." [210] In all systems of human law as in all human institutions one has to be content with a kind of lump justice which regards the possible generality of benefits, or the general run of situations, and the limited scope of finite human reason, without pretending to accommodate every freak of particularity which can ever arise. "All our loose ideas of justice, as it affects any individual, have in them something of comparison to the situation of others; and no systematic reasoning can wholly free us from such impressions." [211] Hence utility as a foundation of law—"general and public utility"—and hence, Burke would one day say, the science of jurisprudence, "the pride of the human intellect, which, with all its defects, redundancies, and errors, is the collected reason of ages, combining the principles of original justice with the infinite variety of human concerns." [212] Yet utility is not to be separated from equity in the composition of a just law. Whatever the past worth of the Popery laws, Burke felt, "in time of trouble," their utility had been lost, and "in time of profound peace" they had become "a scheme of tyranny." [213]

Closely connected with the principle of justice, and from one angle identifiable with it, is the principle of liberty, on which Burke also based his criticism. "I have no idea of a liberty unconnected with honesty and justice. . . . It is but too true, that the love, and even the very idea, of genuine liberty is extremely rare. It is but too true, that there are many, whose whole scheme of freedom is made up of pride, perverseness, and insolence. They feel themselves in a state of thraldom, they imagine that their souls are cooped and cabined in, unless they have some man, or some body of men, dependent upon their mercy." [214] It was a "new political chemistry" that was to extract liberty out of a system of oppression [215] or again to protect it by an open proscription. "It will be said, in that country some people are free—why this is the very description of despotism! *Partial freedom is privilege and prerogative, and not liberty*. Liberty, such as deserves the name, is an honest, equitable, diffusive, and impartial principle. It is a great and enlarged virtue, and not a sordid, selfish, and illiberal vice. It is the portion of the mass of the citizens; and not the haughty license of some potent individual, or some predominant faction." [216] To clarify the premise of liberty, by reference to justice, was especially crucial since Catholics were commonly alleged to be its enemies—that is, Burke said, equity was cast out in "pedigrees of guilt" whereby the "inquisitive genealogist of proscription" [217] punished individual Catholics for the presumed crimes of other people long dead. Whatever tastes a Catholic might have or acquire for a general liberty would surely sour if he saw himself persecuted by those who professed it. "He who aims at another's life, is not to be surprised if he flies into any sanctuary that will receive him." [218] "If you treat men as robbers, why, robbers sooner or later they will become." [219] Utility was perverted by the ancient axiom of tyranny—"the general good is inconsistent with my personal safety." [220]

Among downright bigots, of course, anti-Catholicism could border on hysteria: "We shall be murdered in our beds; we shall be driven out of our possessions; we shall have a popish state,—a popish religion; we will quit the country, etc. etc.—the perpetual burthen of the song." [221] A "lust of party power" was the liberty they thirsted for.[222] Amid the ranting anxiety of pampered prelates, pageantry and hypocrisy, ages of superstition and ignorance, heresy and idolatry, king-lovers, Jesuits, and priest-ridden slaves, they forgot that no liberty is safe that is not diffused under law, and that liberty is a product of responsibility, not of professions. "If legal ways are not found, illegal will be resorted to; and seditious clubs and confederacies, such as no man living holds in greater horror than I do, will grow and flourish in spite, I am afraid, of anything which can be done to prevent the evil. Lawful enjoyment is the surest method to prevent unlawful gratification. Where there is property, there will be less theft; where there is marriage, there will always be less fornication."[223] Therefore, where there is liberty, there will be less inclination to subvert it. "Surely," Burke reflected, "the state of Ireland ought forever to teach parties moderation in their victories. People crushed by law have no hopes but from power. If laws are their enemies, they will be enemies to laws; and those who have much to hope and nothing to lose will always be dangerous, more or less."[224]

But more common than hysteria was the urgent, soberly logical warning against creeping Popery.

If you give them real property, they will acquire political privileges; then they will acquire more property; and then they will get into corporations, and from corporations into parliament; from the civil to the military; from the law to the revenue; and then, by one great bound, there will be none but Papists, or at least a great majority, in the army, in the senate, in the civil administration; and then we shall have a popish Church, and popish State, and then there is an end of it; and thus the basket of rotten eggs becomes a foundation for the subversion of an empire.[225]

Burke agreed that such a neatly contrived system of exclusion as the Catholic code, which he attributed to perverted ingenuity, "was so constructed, that if there was once a breach in any essential part of it, the ruin of the whole, or nearly of the whole, was, at some time or other, a certainty."[226] But collapse of the code would not certainly issue in an opposite extreme. The fallacy of the creeping-popery argument was not only that it assumed a will to conspire, which Burke saw no evidence of, but that, even if such a long-term conspiracy were afoot, the "principle of the *'pedetentim progredientis'*" did not describe what really happens in normal politics (and morals) when depressed people are admitted to a community of justice and legal liberty. "It is a fallacy for this reason: because it supposes that the same jealousies, and the same opposition of interest, between those who are within, and those who are without the pale, those who are privileged and those who are not, subsist *after* the communication of the privileges, and after the confusion of the boundaries which subsisted *before* it; whereas it is the direct contrary. As the participation advances, the adversity declines, and both parties meet in a middle point." [227] Rival parties meet in a community of enjoyments which they find themselves unwilling to hazard for their differences, and in time, the differences themselves moderate into peaceful habits. "Old religious factions are volcanoes burnt out; on the lava, and ashes, and squalid scoriae of old eruptions grow the peaceful olive, the cheering vine, and the sustaining corn." [228] If he had held office 150 years before, Burke said, he would have felt as earnest and anxious as anybody else to require abjuration of the Pope, but living in his own day he felt "obliged to speculate forward instead of backward"—to explore the possibilities for concord among men actually existing, not to turn against fact with a rancorous *idée fixe*. One never knows who his next friend or his next enemy may be, and in such a plight, which is as eternal as change, to bear grudges is no safe plan.

On these grounds, of justice, liberty, and charity—primary ethical ends for which he believed states ought to be instituted—Burke wished to incorporate the Catholics into an Anglo-Irish society, to nationalize them, so to speak, by dissipating the selfish barriers erected between them and the rest of the community by centuries of hatred. Burke would have liked to see the system of laws growing from hatred unravelled in an instant, and predicted that "no evils, but much good would happen, if it were so unravelled." [229] He was not necessarily an approver of the slow: Parliament had deliberated eighty years, he said, in repealing a law (the 1699 act prohibiting mass and Catholic teaching) which ought not to have survived a second session.[230] Rather, he wished to move gradually, by stages, to move as slow or as fast as is consistent with the generality of common good defined by circumtances. "A *remote* and a *gradual* abolition," he said, "though they may be connected, are not the same thing." [231] On the other hand, he knew that the dense league of hatred, self-interest, suspicion, and indifference, supporting the system, would probably yield slowly, and that if a legislator were to have any lasting success, he would have to watch all the angles. For example, there was a danger he said, that before the temper of the nation was ripe for genuine repeal, a number of half-measures would appear, with the result that the black letter of the law, every day fading more and more into disuse, might be snapped up into a succinct vigor it lacked before.[232] The bill of 1782 tolerating religious ceremonies, he complained, really riveted a new bolt on other civil rights.[233] Burke also knew that instant emancipations, or the nearest approximations to them, are generally brought about by some "great event" which a legislator would not produce even if he could, a time when smaller spites are forgotten in the general tide of anxiety—for example, a time like the American War, which he admitted had hastened Catholic relief by many years.[234] But to throw justice on the hazard of catastrophes was abhorrent to Burke, who honestly wanted to call ethical actualities into existence without destroying that portion of them already achieved.

To stress these overarching ethical ends is necessary to counteract another prejudice which has often obscured Burke's quality—the prejudice, in Vernon Parrington's phrase, of his "Whiggish legalism," [235] by which is meant, I take it, a supposed unwillingness to see beyond inherited red tape. But surely there is a difference between legalism and respect for law. In the first place, Burke believed that "a legislative act has no reference to any rule but these two, original justice and discretionary application. . . . the law which binds all others does not and cannot bind the law-maker; he, and he alone, is above the law." Only a judge or attorney goes to justice and discretion "at second-hand, and through the medium of some superiors." [236] The difference between old and modern law in Burke's eyes was the difference between "antique rigour and over-done severity" and "the accommodation of human concerns for which rules were made, and not human concerns made to bend to them." [237] However, to act ethically, in Burke's terms, is to act on principle, with a regard not only to the ends, but also the real latency or presence of the ends in the means—in one's instruments and one's conduct. He wished to bring Irish Catholics within the community of the law, not to destroy the law itself, and this meant that he must pursue his ethical ends in an ethical way. A progress toward ethical actualities may be legalistic, or it may not, but always—if it is not self-defeating—it requires what Burke called a "reverence for the substance." [238] Warmly as he detested the plight of the Irish Catholics, he knew that "laws, like houses, lean on one another," [239] and therefore that to repeal them once they are interlocked in existence and operation is a work of patience and delicacy, if by a violence of justice one is not to run into the greatest of all injustice. "It is easy enough to say what shall be done: to cause it to be done,—*Hic labor, hoc opus.*" [240] There must be "an *executory* principle," and therefore there must be law and lawfulness. What the man of sentiment, with a swell of his great impatient heart, bullies through in the name of justice, or liberty, or charity, can turn out a practical inversion of all three. But Burke was unwilling to "say *vae victis,* and then throw the sword into the scale . . . as a make-weight in political reasoning," [241] aware that, as Menander has it in one of his fragments, the greatest source of human evils is excessive goodness.

For this reason, his Catholic tracts are sprinkled throughout with recurrent emphases upon prudence, caution, and conformity to situations, that stand alongside and moderate the acidity of his criticism and the depth of his sympathy. "What a sad thing it is," he exclaimed, "that the grand instructor, Time, has not yet been able to teach the grand lesson of his own value; and that, in every question of moral and political prudence, it is the choice of the moment which renders the measure serviceable or useless, noxious or salutary." [242] This was not a plea to go slow, but a censure and expression of disappointment, because at the time he wrote it (in 1795) Burke saw an opportunity in the juncture of affairs that Parliament had not taken. One of the most impressive qualities of his Anglicanism is its restraint, arising from a refusal to consider ethical values apart from disciplined reason. His peacefulness was hardheaded, aware of earth. Clearly as he understood how the Catholics felt, and anxious as in his later years he was to see them assimilated in the commonwealth to be protected from, and to protect against, Jacobinism, he kept his sense of particular reality, of what could and could not be done when, where, by whom, and how. He might sympathize like a saint, but he calculated like a politician.

# IV

# Burke and Constitutional Reform

DURING the interval between the American and French revolutions, reform sentiment flurried up in England among groups who differed on fundamentals or who met on particular issues without power to act. It was fitful, eccentric, and dissentious. The Tories under Lord North, who was quite as well-meaning and respectable as he was obstinate in mediocrity, blocked avenues of liberalization until they were forced open by events; whereas the Whigs, long out of power, had broken into splinter groups, a "strange distraction," Burke said, "not only in interests, but in views and plans of conduct." [1] Abroad, the years from 1778 to 1782 especially, the closing stages of the American war, brought a critical ebb in English affairs. The intervention of France on the American side, which Burke had predicted and feared, started up the global war of fifteen years before; Spain joined against England; natives revolted in India, and subjects in Ireland; English sea power was temporarily eclipsed; there was earnest and fearful talk of invasion. The light of reform which broke in, Burke complained, "broke in, not through well-contrived and well-disposed windows, but through flaws and breaches; through the yawning chasms of our ruin." [2] At home, flying the banner of false or hasty Reform, public discontents sometimes threatened a clumsy violence; to keep one's good sense and balance was hard.

Wild and savage insurrection quitted the woods, and prowled about our streets in the name of reform. Such was the distemper of the public mind, that there was no madman, in his maddest ideas, and maddest projects, who might not count upon numbers to support his principles and execute his designs. . . . There are who remember the blind fury of some, and the lamentable helplessness of others; here, a torpid confusion, from a panic fear of the danger; there, the same inaction from a stupid insensibility to it; here, well-wishers to the mischief; there, indifferent lookers-on.[3]

Yet in this stormy season were planted many permanent nineteenth-century reforms—for example, the extension and reorganization of the electoral base, the abolition of the slave trade, the liberalization of rule in India, the softening of penal laws; and several permanent reforms were practically matured, most notably in Catholic civil rights, economy and efficiency in government offices, libel laws, and the publication of Parliamentary debates. Burke had a leading hand or voice in bringing to pass every one except the first, the projected reform in representation and election, which, for reasons to be discussed, he reprehended as both rash and impracticable *at this time* (the italics are his).[4]

Several times Burke tried to account for the discomfiture of the Whig party, and variously he blamed the stranglehold of royal "influence," Tory propaganda, and the sins of past Whigs, "our political progenitors,"[5] who had dominated England during the reigns of George I and George II. Burke appreciated the political skill of Walpole, and accepted the maxim *quieta non movere:* that is, "to innovate as little as possible, upon speculation, in establishments," from which, as they stand, one experiences "no material inconvenience to the repose of the country."[6] But he was no quietist *à outrance.* "I am not of the opinion of those gentlemen who are against disturbing the public repose; I like a clamour whenever there is an abuse. The fire-bell at midnight disturbs your sleep, but it keeps you from being burned in your bed." [7] Still another cause was a postwar spirit of business-as-usual, a languid content which is always likely to settle on a victorious country whose middle class is strong. There are "errors," Burke warned, "which are natural only to prosperity," among them a "spirit of delusion" that measures its necessities by its inclinations.[8] When happiness is free, the relation of freedom to effort is obscured. "We had been so very powerful [after the Seven Years' War], and so very prosperous, that even the humblest of us . . . lost all measure between means and ends; and our headlong desires became our politics and our morals." [9]

All these causes were real and helped to shake Whig authority over the popular mind. But perhaps the profoundest cause of all, which Burke saw with ever sharper clarity after the American war, and which, in a decade, would crack his party ties, was simply the "strange distraction" itself—the multanimity among those who were nominally Whigs, latent from the beginning but speeded up and enfactioned toward the close of the century. So long as Lord Rockingham lived (he would die unexpectedly in 1782), Burke could rely on the Rockingham Whigs as a small nucleus of energetic moderation who, in his view, understood the principles of the constitutional settlement (as distinct from the Chatham Whigs, the Bedford Whigs, the remnant of Grenville Whigs, Independents, and Protestant Dissenters). But he was increasingly conscious, wary, and resentful of a new stamp of politician in the party.

The bane of the whigs [he wrote in 1780] has been the admission among them of the corps of *schemers,* who, in reality and at bottom, mean little more than to indulge themselves with speculations; but who do us infinite mischief by persuading many sober and well-meaning people that we have designs inconsistent with the constitution left us by our forefathers. You know how many are startled with the idea of innovation. Would to God it were in our power to keep things *where they are* in point of *form,* provided we were able to improve them in point of *substance.* The *machine itself* is well enough to answer any good purpose, provided the *materials* were sound. But what signifies the arrangement of rottenness? [10]

Burke fails to specify who the "schemers" were, but it is simple enough to get his meaning: he referred, rather impressionistically, to a type of sensibility and point of view which, gathering in activity before his pained eyes, would later draw down his not always discriminating wrath on individuals like Richard Price and Joseph Priestley, and which would be essential stuff in his brilliant political mythologizing of the Jacobins. A remark to Tom Paine several years later may symbolize what Burke was feeling. Just before the revolution in France, Paine urged Burke, whom he mistook for a republican, to introduce a "more enlarged system of liberty" into England, using reform in Parliament as his means, and Burke replied: "Do you really imagine, Mr. Paine, that the constitution of this kingdom requires such innovations, or could exist with them, or that any reflecting men would seriously engage in them? You are aware that I have all my life opposed such schemes of reform; of course, because I knew them not to be reform." [11] "To innovate," he would say one day, "is not to reform"; his reforms had risen partly from his hatred of innovation.[12] Yet in an opposite quarter from "schemers," among Whigs whom Burke admired as "the first men of their age and their country," he picked up disturbing signals of variance and willingness to innovate in hurried, even contradictory ways:

I will say nothing about that tail which draggles in the dirt, and which every party in every state *must* carry about it. *That* can only flirt a little of the mud in our faces now and then; it is no great matter: but some of our *capital* men entertain thoughts so very different from mine, that if I come into parliament, I must either fly in the face of the clearest lights of my own understanding, and the firmest conviction of my conscience, or I must oppose those for whom I have the highest value. The Duke of Richmond has *voluntarily proposed* to open the elections of England to all those, without exception, who have the qualification of being eighteen years old; and has swept away at one stroke all the privileges of freeholders, cities, and boroughs, throughout the kingdom; and sends every member of parliament, every year, to the judgment and discretion of such electors. Sir George Savile has *consented to adopt* the scheme of more *frequent elections,* as a remedy for disorders which, in my opinion, have a great part of their root in *elections themselves;* and while the Duke of Richmond proposes to annihilate the freeholders, Sir George Savile consents to a plan for a vast increase of their *power,* by choice of a hundred new knights of the shire. Which of these am I to adhere to? Or shall I put myself into the graceful situation of opposing both? [13]

The Whig party at the close of the eighteenth century was assimilating odd bedfellows and in its course was shedding much which could attract and hold the affection of a man like Burke.

What can be traced, in retrospect, is the gentle percolation in odd quarters of English life of liberal-democratic, humanitarian, and revolutionary ideas—"this new system of optimism" [14]—some of which came to Burke as easily as breathing, some of which terrified him with their vicious simplicity. The issue of parliamentary reform in the eighties was a miniature dress rehearsal for the French Revolution in the nineties. Destiny and conscience—but not enthusiasm—made Burke a reformer from the moment he entered politics. A methodology of reform is substantial in his political thought. Forged in distress, it was his answer to a revolutionary era, in many of whose watchcries he concurred—reason, social justice, freedom, progress, tolerance, individual dignity—but whose play of extremes and mounting confusion alternately baffled, grieved, and infuriated him. The presupposition of reform is a liberal value—the application of reason to alter something in society or government—but there are many ways of working out the application. Violence and "innovation" were abhorrent to Burke; and he would look back upon the period from 1778 to 1782, during which he tried desperately to find a constitutional medium—to reform in order to conserve, to conserve so that something will be left to reform—as a time of "dreadful fermentation," when quite as much was imperiled in the name of reform as was gained. If "the changes, by a great misnomer called parliamentary reforms" had gone through at this time, he believed, "not France, but England, would have had the honour of leading up the death-dance of democratic revolution." [15]

## II

Was Burke's position liberal or conservative?

A conservative may be defined as one who is anxious lest the latent good of inherited fundamentals be destroyed. And certainly anxiety for inherited fundamentals permeates Burke's thinking from his first years in Parliament, when he defended the achieved rights of Commons and the people against the centralizing ambitions of George III, to the last years of life, when he fulminated against the Jacobins, whose attacks upon Christianity, the past, and common manners, amounted in his eyes to a schism with the fundamentals of European civilization itself. Epitomizing his career in a revolutionary age, Burke said that, as an ultimate commitment, he had hoped for a day when he should "see the surest of all reforms, perhaps the only sure reform, the ceasing to do ill," but meanwhile, meeting in fact and in his time with "the greatest of all evils,—a blind and furious spirit of innovation, under the name of reform," he had found it necessary to exert all the faculties he had "in favour not of this or that man, of this or that system, but of the general, vital principle, that whilst it was in its vigour produced the state of things transmitted to us" and that, through a joint operation of abusive extremes, "may perish in our hands." [16] He exerted himself not for the *status quo,* but for its principle, its fundamentals; setting himself in opposition to one kind of reform, he meant to contrive proper reforms as alternatives.

Rage and phrensy will pull down more in half an hour, than prudence, deliberation, and foresight can build up in a hundred years. The errors and defects of old establishments are visible and palpable. It calls for little ability to point them out; and where absolute power is given, it requires but a word wholly to abolish the vice and the establishment together. . . . No difficulties occur in what has never been tried. Criticism is almost baffled in discovering the defects of what has not existed; and eager enthusiasm and cheating hope have all the wide field of imagination, in which they may expatiate with little or no opposition.

At once to preserve and to reform is quite another thing. When the useful parts of an old establishment are kept, and what is superadded is to be fitted to what is retained, a vigorous mind, steady, persevering attention, various powers of comparison and combination, and the resources of an understanding fruitful in expedients are to be exercised.[17]

Reforming conservatism like Burke's, critical and adaptive, is grounded in a classic prudence resisting the *hybris* of abusive extremes—prudence, however, which is not a narrow code, but a vigorous dialectic of experience and situation. Burke is "conservative" at one time about one thing (and not at another time), and "liberal" at the same time about another thing (and not at another time), depending on the relative situations in which he finds himself. The conservative emphasis in his thinking, which, however, is only an emphasis, comes from his finding himself in the last fifty years of the eighteenth century, when the meaning of inherited fundamentals, especially in politics but also in manners, tastes, and professional knowledges, was increasingly precarious.

A man in anxiety about fundamentals is likely to talk about *principles,* and to this extent, anxiety, or the *eros* related to it, issues in a critical act. Criticism becomes conservative when its inquiry is directed to the elucidation of inherited or achieved principles, as, for example, in a national culture. As Ross Hoffmann and Paul Levack rightly point out, *principle* is one of the key words in Burke. The principle of justice, of liberty, of compromise, of growth, of vanity, of prescription, of toleration, of equipoise in the British constitution, of free trade, of royal favoritism, of economy—"Burke's thought was a ceaseless search for the principles that enabled men to understand practically the social and political world and make sound judgments upon it." But he consistently distinguished *principle* from *theory:* "Always a principle meant an objective reality apprehended by the mind, but a theory was something manufactured by the mind—and usually by a presumptuous mind." [18] Burke used the word more unsystematically than this may sound; sometimes it was only a tic of rhetoric, as Jeremy Bentham thought.[19] But in general *principle* designated something objective and fundamental in the stuff of practical life. In considering this aspect of Burke, one may be reminded of Coleridge's definition of the educated man as one who searches out "the indwelling law, which is the true being of things, the sole solution of their modes of existence, and in the knowledge of which consists our dignity and our power." [20] But one should also remember another dictum of Coleridge's, by way of qualification, which praises "the expediency even in a moral sense of not carrying speculation above a certain height uninterruptedly; but there to descend to the practical uses of which it might be capable—like the Indian fig, which still at a given height declines its branches to earth and takes root anew, forms a new principle." [21] Regretting Burke's unwillingness to systematize his *principles*—his "want of congruity in the principles appealed to in different parts of the same work . . . [and] apparent versatility of the principle with the occasion" [22]—Coleridge nevertheless attributed Burke's greatness to his being a "metaphysician" and "almost a poet." [23] "No one [else] ever read history so philosophically as he seems to have done." [24] Wherever one turns, one will find Burke searching social and political achievements within the historical process for the indwelling "laws" of their existence, in varying degrees of inclusiveness and application, and these "laws," fundamentally shaping and sustaining anything in the texture of practical life, he called *principles.* What are the principles on which the British constitution has come to be and which perpetuate its benefits? What is the principle according to which the medieval heritage has been transmitted to the present moment? What is the Protestant principle? What does it mean to have liberty under law? What distinguishes the American character? What distinguishes the English mind? Insisting that he had never governed himself, as "no rational man ever did govern himself, by abstractions and universals," nevertheless, Burke went on to say, he would not "put abstract ideas wholly out of any question, because I well know that under that name I should dismiss principles; and that without the guide and light of sound, well-understood principles, all reasonings in politics, as in everything else, would be only a confused jumble of particular facts and details, without the means of drawing out any sort of theoretical or practical conclusion." [25] Any conservatism deriving itself from Burke must be first no ism at all, except a criticism, honest and fresh, after the mode of an ancient wonder.

There is a certain ambiguity in Burke's *principles.* Sometimes he spoke of them as if they were transcendent. Principles are part of "nature"—not nature, however, as a cold scheme of concepts, for Burke dissociated himself from "the metaphysicians of our times, who are the most foolish of men, and who, dealing in universals and essences, see no difference between more and less." [26] Rather, he saw "nature" as a substratum of history, knowable if at all by experience, hardly more than a regulative ideal. At other times, and this most often, principles were quite clearly contingent, tentative, particular—in the widest extent of the word *achieved* historical things. Burke, on one of his sides, is the exegete of immanent tradition; he refracts the common light of familiarity to discover the complex spectrum of its past; and principles—for example, the principle of prescription in the British constitution—denoted those latent bases of behavior, belief, and organization, persisting unobserved or but obscurely glimpsed by those who enact them.

Burke, however, did not know he was a "conservative," in the doctrinal sense; he talked the same language with many liberals in his day. One should not forget the grieved astonishment of Priestley during the 1790's, and the resentful irritation of Paine, at what they felt was his apostasy. Until that time, and his break with the Fox Whigs, he was reputed among friends and enemies alike as a reformer and libertarian, a temperamental but vastly talented star of liberal ideas in England. He had a notion of progress; [27] and to progress, duly qualified, should be added a long list of eighteenth-century liberal themes like happiness, government by consent, social justice, peace, liberty, the dignity of the individual, *carrières aux talents* (a legislator ought not by a "cold penury" to "blast the abilities of a nation, and stunt the growth of its active energies"), [28] broad toleration (Burke quotes with approval, of all people, Pierre Bayle!). Like Pope, he condemned "the idle and vulgar superstition" of the antiquary who trembles "to have his shield scoured, for fear it should be discovered to be no better than an old pot-lid," [29] but also "the superstition of the pretended philosophers of the hour." [30] He referred slightingly to the "rust of superstition" in religion "with which the accumulated absurdity of the human mind might have crusted it over in the course of ages." [31] He made fun of prelates who "loll at their ease in high dignities," and thus are hard to persuade "that there can be anything amiss in establishments, which by feeling experience they find to be so very comfortable." [32] (But also Burke said, "from the same selfish motives those who are struggling upwards are apt to find everything wrong and out of order.") He saw that "established public prejudice . . . always overrules and stifles the private sense of men." [33] He agreed, "there is a time when men will not suffer bad things because their ancestors have suffered worse." [34] Tyranny of any fashion elicited his passionate anger; the "horrible and impious system of servitude" imposed on Catholics in Ireland was calculated, he felt, to "render men patient under a deprivation of all the rights of human nature." [35] "The rights of *men*," Burke said, avoiding the cloudy idol *mankind*, ". . . are indeed sacred." [36] He called himself a "citizen of the world," and warned against losing "the general communion of mankind" or "natural sympathy, in local and accidental connections." [37] He acknowledged the sometime justice of revolution—as a last measure of grave and overruling necessity.[38] In the state he laughed at "difficult trifles and laborious fooleries, which serve no other purpose than to keep alive corrupt hope and servile dependence."

When the reason of old establishments is gone, it is absurd to preserve nothing but the burthen of them. This is superstitiously to embalm a carcass not worth an ounce of the gums that are used to preserve it. It is to burn precious oils in the tomb; it is to offer meat and drink to the dead,—not so much an honour to the deceased, as a disgrace to the survivors.[39]

Some gentlemen, he explained, argue against reforms on "the principles of a criminal prosecution": "It is enough for them to justify their adherence to a pernicious system, that it is not of their contrivance; that it is an inheritance of absurdity, derived to them from their ancestors; that they can make out a long and unbroken pedigree of mismanagers that have gone before them." [40] Those convinced that Burke was a mushy traditionalist have often quoted a famous statement as if it were axiomatic: "Veneration of antiquity is congenial to the human mind." But they have not listened to the edge of ambiguity and sarcasm in Burke's voice. Veneration is congenial because the *status quo* is so obviously flawed and illusion so easy: "it is in the nature of man rather to defer to the wisdom of times past, whose weakness is not before his eyes, than to the present, of whose imbecility he has daily experience." [41]

The historical conditions in the last half of the eighteenth century which prepared for the appearance of liberalism, and of rational, practical, political men of letters, with an interest in history and psychology and a gift for sarcasm, prepared also for Burke. And though to call him a peculiarly English brand of liberal would blur sound distinctions (the title is more appropriate to Fox or Priestley), it would be little less apt than the misty image propagated during the nineteenth century and still in circulation, that Burke was a nineteenth-century conservative.

As Leslie Stephen observed, and Harold Laski reaffirmed, "no English writer has received, or has deserved, more splendid panegyrics than Burke." [42] But it is equally true that few writers have been more distrusted, and even hated. Since he became, by a loose common-sense recognition, patriarch of English conservatism, Burke has certainly metamorphosed into prejudiced legend and caricature, and his twentieth-century student faces the same problem as a student of Johnson: how to discriminate the legend from the man without propagating something hagiographic; also, Burke's surface inconsistencies are quite as hard to deal with as Johnson's. Partisan (or analogical) imagination has been his Boswell, and the emergent images, whatever their partial truth, have steadily shrunk in this partisan steam until one can hardly guess what they once fit. Hostility and suspicion were widespread, intense, and distortive, even in his lifetime, and have passed on images cheapened, even vulgarized. A number of contemporary cartoons, especially the anti-Catholic ones, picture a bent, thin-legged, waspish figure who looks very much like Truman in a wig, with sharp nose and pinched spectacles; they call Burke a Jesuit in disguise.[43] The same quality of misunderstanding persists in the attacks of those who resent "political theologians, and theological politicians," to use Burke's resentful phrase, unaware of what Burke really said. Better informed, the tradition suggested by Paine and Blake, which has had a wide following among American scholars (even admirers among the genteel, like Lowell, who called him an "inspired snob"), has painted Burke, at his worst, as an Irishman of extravagant and self-interested loyalties, narrow, intense, dishonest, and a mystagogue, having a tradition-directed (and therefore presumably dark, crass) mind frightened of progress and busied with arming his devil-crew of snobs with persuasive sophistries. One is supposed to believe that Burke was a rancorous, red-headed Irishman who, having bullied his way to the top of English society, then spent his brilliant years defending gains in the *status quo*. Some critics have also suspected Burke of being a "proto-fascist," in a line leading from Hegel to Nietzsche to Naziism—an ideological legerdemain that is beneath contempt. In his own time Burke was justifiably angry and indignant with those who proceed in argument,

> as if all those who disapprove of their new abuses must of course be partisans of the old; that those who reprobate their crude and

violent schemes of liberty ought to be treated as advocates for servitude. I admit that their necessities do compel them to this base and contemptible fraud. Nothing can reconcile men to their proceedings and projects, but the supposition that there is no third option between them and some tyranny as odious as can be furnished by the records of history, or by the invention of poets. This prattling of theirs hardly deserves the name of sophistry. It is nothing but plain impudence. Have these gentlemen never heard, in the whole circle of the worlds of theory and practice, of anything between the despotism of the monarch and the despotism of the multitude? . . . Is it, then, a truth so universally acknowledged, that a pure democracy is the only tolerable form into which human society can be thrown, that a man is not permitted to hesitate about its merits, without the suspicion of being a friend to tyranny, that is, of being a foe to mankind? [44]

In the opposite camp, Burke has been idealized selectively, with a partisanship not always as open but hardly less intense. Starting with a portrait of him as the eighteenth-century Cicero, the stately and open-collared orator who became a kind of culture hero for prep-school texts, the image is cultivated urbanely into the aristocratic moralism which gratified the mind of Irving Babbitt.[45] The image shaped up in Burke's lifetime. Boswell asked, "Do you think, Sir, that Burke has read Cicero much?" And Johnson replied: "I do not believe it, Sir. Burke has great knowledge, great fluency of words, and great promptness of ideas, so that he can speak with great illustration on any subject that comes before him. He is neither like Cicero, nor like Demosthenes, nor like anyone else, but speaks as well as he can." [46] Not unrelated is the image of Burke, which Wordsworth had some feeling for, as spokesman for an older, richer Europe of time-hallowed law, custom, and ceremony, against the attacks of ugly modernists.[47] This has been an interesting image to anti-liberals and anti-democrats generally, and to others not actively hostile to democracy or science but, like Matthew Arnold, like Lecky, worried and saddened by the modern world.[48] The image reappears in the twentieth century, embittered and crusading, among American "neo-conservatives"—for example, in Russell Kirk's informative and valuable partisan calendar *The Conservative Mind.* Underplaying "liberal" elements in his thought, G. G. Butler located Burke in *The Tory Tradition,* just as Roman Catholic scholars generally have highlighted the derivation of his thought from "the moral law." [49]

Liberalism, conservatism—partisan terms are slippery. As Burke said, "A very great part of the mischiefs that vex the world arises from words. People soon forget the meaning, but the impression and the passion remain." [50] Names and slogans bleached of all concrete perception, or weighing upon the mind so as to distort perception, are a flirtation with a kind of mental death. They are the "fictions operating as realities" which Johnson described, in his great chapter 44 of *Rasselas,* as approaching the insane in direct proportion to their exclusive fixity. For, in extreme cases, they "mean" what the tainted desires of the heart, the impression and the passion, require them to mean. Neutral, potentially useful fictions in themselves, when estranged or, at the extreme, divorced, from their anchorage in concrete perception, they are likely to become, in Burke's language, "abstract" pretexts for vice, which, however, "are always found in some specious appearance of a real good." So much did this pathogenetic abstraction horrify Burke by its ugliness, prevalence, and finality, that at one time he could see it as almost the very secret of human suffering in political history. It is a key idea for picking up his thought, where it is stated from a variety of angles—an idea, as Irving Babbitt perceived, akin to *hybris.*[51] Burke said, in a passage that is reminiscent of Gibbon, as indeed of much of the best in neoclassical ethics: "History consists, for the greater part, of the miseries brought upon the world by pride, ambition, avarice, revenge, lust, sedition, hypocrisy, ungoverned zeal, and all the train of disorderly appetites, which shake the public. . . . These vices are the *causes* of those storms. Religion, morals, laws, prerogatives, privileges, liberties, rights of men, are the *pretexts.*" [52] He went on to say that miseries of this kind are not cured by rooting up and obliterating the pretexts, which would be to root up all that is valuable among men. This is the *hybris* of the extreme partisan. On the contrary, the presupposition of their cure, insofar as they are curable, is constantly to turn, or return, perception to the concrete.

> Wise men will apply their remedies to vices, not to names; to the causes of evil which are permanent, not to the occasional organs by which they act, and the transitory modes in which they appear. Otherwise you will be wise historically, a fool in practice. Seldom have two ages the same fashion in their pretexts and the same modes of mischief. Wickedness is a little more inventive. Whilst you are discussing fashion, the fashion is gone by. The very same vice assumes a new body. The spirit transmigrates; and, far from losing its principle of life by the change of its appearance, it is renovated in its new organs with a fresh vigour of a juvenile activity. It walks abroad, it continues its ravages, whilst you are gibbeting the carcass, or demolishing the tomb. You are terrifying yourselves with ghosts and apparitions, whilst your house is the haunt of robbers. It is thus with all those, who, attending only to the shell and husk of history, think they are waging war with intolerance, pride, and cruelty, whilst, under colour of abhorring the ill principles of antiquated parties, they are authorizing and feeding the same odious vices in different factions, and perhaps in worse.[53]

Accordingly, in Burke's classical ethics, the place of prudence and moderation (which—again—are not timid codes, but vigorous and assured dialectics of experience) is to restrain conduct and the voracious reason from mutual self-defeat, and the place of decorum generally is as a description of concrete rectitude.

In politics, where Burke smoked it out, this secret ambush of the abstract is especially common. Wickedness is in fact very inventive, and the partisan enslaved by his slogans and names, his pretexts, is likely to find himself, in time, driven by illusory projections of his own vice into actions that contradict his real wishes, into extropunitiveness, into an ignorant slaughter of those whom the restraint of charity might have shown to be his friends, and finally into a self-recrimination cut off from known means of escape. For the tragedy of the name-and-slogan-bound partisan is the loss, sometimes irretrievable, of a practical imagination—which, as I defined it before, is a power to experience a thing in its concrete complexity, to discriminate its relations, and to act upon or reverence its latent good. The pathology of pretexts leads liberals to disavow Burke without a practical imagination of what he stood for; leads conservatives to draw on his arguments for ammunition in the war against men whose circumstances and hopes Burke never saw or dreamed of. The conservative is irresponsible and impractical when he sets up Burke in the role he most would have hated—that of a dealer in nostrums—or hires him as a goon to assassinate a rival clique. The liberal is neither honest nor imaginative when he types Burke quickly in a surface glance, and thereafter coasts on the surface he has willed for himself.

## III

Burke neither advocated nor denounced any form of government, snipped from its context of practical life and existing needs, like a textbook paradigm. The *comitatus* or the Navajo council of elders would ill suit the twentieth-century United States, but also it would be idle to find fault with ancient tribal governments for having no Ways and Means Committee, no Department of Agriculture. Repeatedly he fended off charges that he was a partisan of aristocracy. "I am no friend to aristocracy, in the sense at least in which that word is usually understood. If it were not a bad habit to moot cases on the supposed ruin of the constitution, I should be free to declare, that if it must perish, I would rather by far see it resolved into any other form, than lost in that austere and insolent domination." [54] If aristocracy meant the Peers, he felt neither "vulgar admiration, nor any vulgar antipathy, towards them; I hold their order in cold and decent respect." If, however, aristocracy meant "an adherence to the rich and powerful against the poor and weak," then:

> If it should come to the last extremity, and to a contest of blood, God forbid! God forbid!—my part is taken; I would take my fate with the poor, and low, and feeble.[55]

He considered himself "in middle life, in the mass of citizens." At the same time, he said, it was "one sign of a liberal and benevolent mind to incline to [the nobility] with some sort of partial propensity." "It is a sour, malignant, envious disposition, without taste for the reality, or for any image or representation of virtue, that sees with joy the unmerited fall of what had long flourished in splendour and in honour. I do not like to see anything destroyed; any void produced in society; any ruin on the face of the land." [56] It is also true, he believed, that in any healthy constitution, a principle must work for the benefit of the whole to postpone "not the interest, but the judgment, of those who are *numero plures,* to those who are *virtute et honore majores.*" [57] That is, like Jefferson, he looked to the "natural aristoi" to perform the actual procedures of government, complicated as they always are, no matter what its form. "There is no qualification for government but virtue and wisdom, actual or presumptive. Wherever they are actually found, they have, in whatever state, condition, profession, or trade, the passport of Heaven to human place and honour. Woe to the country which would madly and impiously reject the service of the talents and virtues, civil, military, or religious, that are given to grace and to serve it." [58] The "natural aristocracy" might not be equivalent to an aristocracy artificially constituted. "I have known merchants with the sentiments and the abilities of great statesmen; and I have seen persons in the rank of statesmen, with the conceptions and characters of pedlars. Indeed, my observation has furnished me with nothing that is to be found in any habits of life or education, which tends wholly to disqualify men for the function of government." [59]

On the other hand, habits of life and education are a presumption of qualification, until shown otherwise. Burke was too much a realist to conceive the "natural" aristocracy as more than a principle which reaches a *practical* (and therefore, imperfect, variable, more and less successful) embodiment according with the received "state of habitual social discipline." [60] He held the "natural aristocracy" in no superstitious abstraction, as if talent were in itself and on any terms it set for itself qualified to govern; in fact he would later oppose "Jacobinism" as in part a conspiracy of intemperate, irresponsible, and, as it were, gipsy, talent—political romantics—against the rest of the state and in defiance of qualifications.

A true natural aristocracy is not a separate interest in the state, or separable from it. It is an essential integrant part of any large body rightly constituted. It is formed out of a class of legitimate presumptions, which taken as generalities, must be admitted for actual truths. To be bred in a place of estimation; to see nothing low and sordid from one's infancy; to be taught to respect one's self; to be habituated to the censorial inspection of the public eye; to look early to public opinion; to stand upon such elevated ground as to be enabled to take a large view of the wide-spread and infinitely diversified combinations of men and affairs in a large society; to have leisure to read, to reflect, to converse; to be enabled to draw the court and attention of the wise and learned wherever they are to be found;–to be habituated in armies to command and to obey; to be taught to despise danger in the pursuit of honour and duty; to be formed to the greatest degree of vigilance, foresight, and circumspection, in a state of things in which no fault is committed with impunity, and the slightest mistakes draw on the most ruinous consequences–to be led to a guarded and regulated conduct, from a sense that you are considered as an instructor of your fellow-citizens in their highest concerns, and that you act as a reconciler between God and man–to be employed as an administrator of law and justice, and to be thereby amongst the first benefactors to mankind—to be a professor of high science, or of liberal and ingenuous art–to be amongst rich traders, who from their success are presumed to have sharp and vigorous understandings, and to possess the virtues of diligence, order, constancy, and regularity, and to have cultivated a habitual regard to commutative justice–these are the circumstances of men that form what I should call a *natural* aristocracy, without which there is no nation.

The state of civil society, which necessarily generates this aristocracy, is a state of nature; and much more truly so than a savage and incoherent mode of life. For man is by nature reasonable; and he is never perfectly in his natural state, but when he is placed where reason may be best cultivated, and most predominates. Art is man's nature. We are as much, at least, in a state of nature in formed manhood, as in immature and helpless infancy. Men, qualified in the manner I have just described, form in nature, as she operates in the common modification of society, the leading, guiding, and governing part. It is the soul to the body, without which the man does not exist. To give therefore no more importance, in the social order, to such descriptions of men, than that of so many units, is a horrible usurpation.[61]

Thinking this, Burke could have little sympathy with the extreme democratic mystique—the idea glimmering in the minds of so many men great and small, as the eighteenth century drew to a close, that democracy-unqualified somehow transcends all exigencies of time, place, circumstance, and personality, or at least that it was a necessary wave of the future, and that every man walking has not only an equal quantity of political power but an equal right to exert it. He distrusted "absolute democracy," he said, as he distrusted absolute monarchy; a "perfect democracy" is "the most shameless thing in the world" if its people are "suffered to imagine that their will, any more than that of kings, is the standard of right and wrong." [62] "In a democracy, the majority of the citizens is capable of exercising the most cruel oppressions upon the minority, whenever strong divisions prevail in that kind of polity, as they often must." [63] On the other hand, he refused finally to reprobate any form of government "upon abstract principles. There may be situations in which the purely democratic form will become necessary. There may be some (very few, and very particularly circumstanced) where it would be clearly desirable." [64]

Burke took it as an axiom that to "govern according to the sense and agreeably to the interests of the people, is a great and glorious object of government" which cannot be obtained, "but through the medium of popular election." [65] He reverentially looked up to the opinion of the people with an awe almost superstitious.[66] He insisted that when the general wish and sense of the people is known, it must be made to prevail, even if it turns out badly; for as he said, hardly any choice the people could make would be as mischievous as a human power strong enough to resist it.[67]

I am not one of those who think that the people are never in the wrong. They have been so, frequently and outrageously, both in other countries and in this. But I do say, that in all disputes between them and their rulers, the presumption is at least upon a par in favour of the people. Experience may perhaps justify me in going further. When popular discontents have been very prevalent, it may well be affirmed and supported, that there has been generally something found amiss in the constitution, or in the conduct of government. The people have no interest in disorder. When they do wrong, it is their error, and not their crime. But with the governing part of the state, it is far otherwise. They certainly may act ill by design, as well as by mistake. *"Les révolutions qui arrivent dans les grands états ne sont point un effet du hazard, ni du caprice des peuples. Rien ne révolte 'les grands' d'un royaume comme 'un gouvernement foible et dérangé.' Pour la 'populace,' ce n'est jamais par envie d'attaquer qu'elle se soulève, mais par impatience de souffrir."* [68]

He had stated before, many times in many wordings, that "in all forms of government the people is the true legislator," [69] and that "a conservation and secure enjoyment of our natural rights is the great and ultimate purpose of civil society" wherefore "all forms whatsoever of government are only good as they are subservient to that purpose." [70] One could multiply such *ille dixit's* into a kind of democratic catalogue. But Burke was not an admirer of democracy set up in and for itself in glittering lights; if anything, the reverse.

Like most of the constitutional fathers in America, indeed like most of the political thinkers in Europe who took Aristotle seriously, Burke distrusted the "mob," and the very type-name *democracy* stank faintly in the nostrils. It called up associations of riots, vulgar ambition and demagoguery, blind unmeaning prejudice, minority oppression, violent passion, and, in consequence, as a pendulum swing of relief from *anarchy,* a superseding *tyranny* or dictatorship, modulating in time into *oligarchy,* and then into *democracy* once more, where the cycle comes full swing. The opinion was common in the eighteenth century that the mass of individuals to be found in any country are without capacity to govern themselves for their own benefit, although as Aristotle said, they are excellently fitted to be critics of a government's success.

The question of representation—which involves the fundamental question of government by consent—had focussed Burke's attention for years. He discriminated two kinds—virtual and actual. Virtual representation, he said, describing the exact opposite of the Catholic plight in Ireland,

> is that in which there is a communion of interests, and a sympathy in feelings and desires, between those who act in the name of any description of people, and the people in whose name they act, though the trustees are not actually chosen by them. . . . Such a representation I think to be, in many cases, even better than the actual. It possesses most of its advantages, and is free from many of its inconveniences; it corrects the irregularities in the literal representation, when the shifting current of human affairs, or the acting of public interests in different ways, carry it obliquely from its first line of direction. The people may err in their choice; but common interest and common sentiment are rarely mistaken.[71]

Burke observed what is obvious when one stops to think about it, that no complex government (or, for that matter, no nation) is kept going by referendums and mass interviews: what would be the choice of an individual citizen, or else what is his choice when he pauses to deliberate, is prosecuted daily by relative strangers whose names he may possibly never hear and who never ask his advice. Communities of tenuous character—sense, taste, responsibility, and interest—overleap all distances and barriers, including the distance of time and the barrier of individuality, criss-crossing within a nation like invisible and sinewy rays. When someone in the power of office acts in tendency as a remote and unknown citizen would wish him to act, he virtually represents the wish of that citizen. The nation, as distinct from the government, is a coexistence of virtual communities of many kinds—the family, the club, the neighborhood, the region, the town, religion, party, profession, language, interests, education, taste. And morally speaking, government itself is, by presumption, a kind of virtual representative of the nation in this way: "There never was, for any long time, a corrupt representative of a virtuous people; or a mean, sluggish, careless people that ever had a good government of any form. If it be true in any degree, that the governors form the people, I am certain it is as true that the people in their turn impart their character to their rulers. Such as you are, sooner or later, must parliament be." [72] Whence Burke often argued that if the people had the "disposition" to clean up the house of government, if they actually had the intellectual and moral strength, then they could do so at any time under the existing constitution, which had a machinery for correction, but if they were intellectually and morally inferior, then changing the form of the constitution itself would make no difference for the better: the corruption would simply take on a new and possibly worse coloring. Again, the House of Commons, since elective, exists "to bear some stamp of the actual disposition of the people at large"; [73] its peculiarly distinguishing principle "consists in its being the express image of the feelings of the nation." [74] Yet *virtually,* the king is a representative also—"a representative of the national dignity" [75]—and so are lords and judges: "They all are trustees for the people, as well as the Commons; because no power is given for the sole sake of the holder." [76] In many lights, a nation is a virtual thing, and an official of decision and consequence will often represent opinions too subtle for a ballot and sometimes too general even to be articulated.

Burke is criticized, by George Sabine for instance, for seriously confusing *state, government,* and *society,* for making inadequate distinctions between them and even identifying them. Sabine objects—what is or is not true, according to circumstances—that government may be changed without disrupting society at large, and that much in a national culture is merely tangential to the state. Failure to discriminate drives thought toward the Hegelian idealization of the state as the guardian and bearer of civilized values, and thence to fascism.[77] But this is ideological sleight-of-hand, founded on analogy. Some hypothetical somebody's thought may be driven towards a hypothetical fascism, but not Burke's thought about the actual workings of eighteenth-century English politics. Also, Burke himself objected to the lack of distinction: " 'State'—'Protestant'—'Revolution.' These are terms, which, if not well explained, may lead us into many errors. In the word *State* I conceive there is much ambiguity. The state is sometimes used to signify *the whole commonwealth,* comprehending all its orders, with the several privileges belonging to each. Sometimes it signifies only *the higher and ruling part* of the commonwealth; which we commonly call *the Government.*" [78] In the first sense, he said, to be under the state but not a part of it, is simply slavery; in the second sense, to be part of the state but under the government is simply "a lower or degraded state of citizenship" as in Venice where a hereditary aristocracy ruled exclusively. To be a part of both state and government, and under both, is full citizenship. Yet between the two extremes of total exclusion, as in a slave society, and a universal unmodified capacity, as in pure democracy, "there are many different degrees and stages, and a great variety of temperaments, upon which prudence may give full scope to its exertions. For you know that the decisions of prudence (contrary to the system of the insane reasoners) differ from those of judicature; and that almost all the former are determined on the more or the less, the earlier or the later, and on a balance of advantage and inconvenience of good and evil." [79]

In his reflections on virtual representation, Burke simply drew on his experience of what practically happened in the life of the commonwealth. The idea of the *virtual,* innocently taken, can go a long way to clarify much of Burke's quality. Distinct verbally from the *actual,* it was not meant to be so in truth; it only arose as a concept because of a prior commitment to the actual; it was the unacknowledged actual, a fringe area of practicality not taken into account by the mind in ordinary moods, slogging along in custom-fitted ideas, without the least suspicion in the world. Acknowledging the virtual was only a way of using one's common sense to see beyond machinery, to get at the spirit of a thing without being enslaved by the letter. It was a flexible idea for analyzing the English commonwealth, in whose history, as a matter of fact, state, society, and government have very often overlapped and even blurred into one another (without fascism). It led Burke to attack the court clique of George III which, without directly violating the letter of any law, worked virtually against the constitution. Yet it also led him to see how "aristocratic" achievements can be diffused through a whole society and be most of value to those who do not know the source and means of the benefit.

Still another kind of virtual representation seemed important to Burke. A representative once actually elected may be alert to a widely diffused wish or discontent, and therefore, may find himself acting in the general interest no matter who his particular electors are. This was the case, Burke felt, in his reform of the civil establishment. "The people are the masters. They have only to express their wants at large and in gross. We are the expert artists, we are the skillful workmen, to shape their desires into perfect form, and to fit the utensil to the use." [80] Therefore, the legislation which he brings forth, though technically his own device and possibly such as few or nobody among the people had thought of, or may ever think about, virtually enacts their will, their desire that legislation of this drift and tendency should be passed. The people, he said, "have neither enough of speculation in the closet nor of experience in business" to legislate actually, but virtually they legislate through someone who holds the power of legislation in trust.

What I have always thought of the matter is this—that the most poor, illiterate, and uninformed creatures upon earth are judges of a *practical* oppression. It is a matter of feeling; and as such persons generally have felt most of it, and are not of an overlively sensibility, they are the best judges of it. But for the *real cause,* or the *appropriate remedy,* they ought never to be called into council about the one or the other. They ought to be totally shut out; because their reason is weak; because, when once aroused. their passions are ungoverned; because they want information; because the smallness of the property, which individually they possess, renders them less attentive to the consequence of the measures they adopt in affairs of moment.[81]

Burke even distinguished a kind of virtual people within the actual people, a "natural representative" within the "legal constituent," or what might nowadays be called informed public opinion, whose wishes are virtually represented in government: "those of adult age, not declining in life, of tolerable leisure for such discussions, and of some means of information, more or less, and who are above menial dependence, (or what virtually is such) . . . [82] These Burke calculated in 1796 to number about 400,000 in all of Britain. "If men have the real benefit of a *sympathetic* representation," he believed, "none but those who are heated and intoxicated with theory will look for any other." [83]

A good representative, even if responsible directly to a body of local electors, cannot follow their best interests unless momentarily and on special issues he is free to take an enlarged view of the whole which may frustrate what they say they want. Burke told his audience at the Guildhall in Bristol, defending his unpopular stands on America and Ireland: "I am to look, indeed, to your opinions; but to such opinions as you and I *must* have five years hence. I was not to look to the flash of the day. I knew that you chose me, in my place, along with others, to be a pillar of the state, and not a weathercock on the top of the edifice, exalted for my levity and versatility, and of no use but to indicate the shiftings of every fashionable gale." [84] Virtual representation could then become only an acknowledged way of freeing a choice intelligence for a maximum play obedient to the common good. Partly on this account, a public office must be, literally, a prudential trust. Under any other conditions, representative government would dissolve in a petty and degrading scuffle among poll-takers and messenger boys.

As Burke expresses the idea, it has something of an aristocratic air (natural-aristocratic, government of the people, by the best available, in accordance with the general sense and consent of the people and the principles of their established form of government) ; and with the coming of the French Revolution as Burke grew older, the "aristocracy" sharpens in its detachment, elevation, and acerbity. Yet for reasons as many as human beings are imperfect, Burke knew and said that "this sort of virtual representation cannot have a long or sure existence if it has not a substratum in the actual." He was under no illusions about the effect of power on mortal men, including himself. "The member must have some relation to the constituent"; and he added, with a dry, knowing understatement of a man who had sweated out several elections: "Gratitude may not always have a very lasting power; but the frequent recurrence of an application for favours will revive and refresh it, and will necessarily produce some degree of mutual attention. It will produce, at least, acquaintance." [85]

Where actual representation is lacking, even if an elite official is competent, responsible, and honest, and the people vivid, neither of which is sure, a gulf widens between them, and in time, as among Irish Catholics and their Protestant overlords, the governors and the governed no longer see each other as they really are, but through hideous masks of alienation as if they were separate peoples or even separate species.[86] To take away a vote, Burke said, is to take away a shield.[87] So long as the Irish Catholics were half-citizens, without political leverage, they would remain as they were, surrounded by the hostile or the indifferent, the scapegoats of every malicious fancy. The same principle, that a representation purely virtual passes into oppression, had applied to America: "What! does the electric force of virtual representation more easily pass over the Atlantic, than pervade Wales, which lies in your neighbourhood?" [88] It applied also to George III's "system of favoritism," which Burke damned for its separation of representatives from their constituents.[89] It would apply to Jacobin France, which he said was only a pretense of representative democracy, in fact "an ignoble oligarchy," comprised of political adventurers and moneyed burghers who had seized power in defiance of "the instructions of the people by whom they were sent." [90]

The solution to such a dilemma, and to others like it which harass government at every turn, could never be engineered in theory, like a mathematical equation. Such a solution as was imminently possible—as distinct from a future one unknowable until it arrives—must reside in existing circumstances, which meant, Burke told Parliament, "the inestimable treasure we have"—an already-established, proved, and operating constitution, in which both kinds of representation were "a subject of prudent and honest use and thankful enjoyment, and not of captious criticism and rash experiment." [91] Much of the benefits of both virtual and actual representation, with as few as possible of the shortcomings of each, seemed to Burke achieved in the famous "mixed constitution" of England, neither wholly democratic, nor wholly aristocratic, nor wholly monarchical, but, as Montesquieu theorized, a "balance" among all three.

A caution is in order here, however: Burke's relation to Montesquieu has been misstated.

Surely Montesquieu was a man of this world, fallible, soft, and shrewd, and yet chastened by a kind of eighteenth-century faith—that the carnival dark of this world in its glut of particulars acquiesces latently in Law, a network of principles invisible and infinite, and yet for a wonder, present and near, breaking into mind, shooting their light into the practice of every man with Wit. This principled side and reverence for law appealed to Burke. He might find in Montesquieu both a generalizing breadth and a sense of finitude, and a tolerant sympathy with, and interest in, national differences. He could find the fruitful idea that if only one could see the ancient past with the eyes of ancients, in Burke's phrase with a "fresh concern and anxiety" for the event,[92] ancient behavior would be intelligible. Montesquieu praised moderation, responded to the complexity of human society and the value of custom. *L'Esprit des Lois* (1748) especially, like Burke's own writing, is chockful of terse sayings and *aperçus,* many of which were doubtless helpful in shaping Burke's thought. One can imagine the young Burke writing "good" in the margin. Also, Burke's terminology is often like Montesquieu's (but this proves nothing). The intellectual escapism of the *philosophes,* the flight from ennui into theory, is nowhere more temperate and winning than in Montesquieu, with his glow of gentle conviction, his foppish fervor and serpent-wisdom charm. *L'Esprit des Lois* is a thin scheme imposed upon a giant mass of erudition (which Burke praised), aphorism, and coxcombry—a *cadre* holding in the heady brillance of a lifetime. Burke read it assimilatively, taking what he could use, over how many years it is impossible to tell. In the vigor of his old age, defending Whig forefathers (like Swift's admired Lord Somers) who off and on stood in his vision like ghostly guides, Burke mentioned Montesquieu with a similar admiration, especially for his cosmopolitanism—a Frenchman praising the British constitution.[93] Undoubtedly Montesquieu's world-famous analysis helped many Englishmen to sharpen their awareness of what they had.

But the one thing Burke most certainly did not do was to take over from Montesquieu a mean, mechanical rule of check and balance, or any other mechanical rule, as an explanation of the British constitution. And therefore, a statement like the one which follows, by Kingsley Martin, the historian of French liberalism, is the kind of partisan half-truth that obscures—and that makes it so hard for one trying to see Burke as he is not to obscure just as much by emphasizing only the other half:

> [For Montesquieu] to champion the British Constitution in the eighteenth century was to side with the party of reform. To explain, however, that the perfection of British institutions arose from the nice balance of forces and powers which they had miraculously achieved was to give Burke the opportunity of denouncing all reformers. Henceforward every suggestion of change, every denunciation of corruption or declaration that a rotten borough was in fact rotten, could be represented as an

effort to destroy the equilibrium of man's supreme architectural achievement. When Burke led the reaction against the Revolution he based his championship of the British Constitution upon the principles of Montesquieu.[94]

If Burke were a party-line robot, derivative and theory-ridden—that is, if there were only one color in the spectrum—one might believe this. But in the first place, Burke did not denounce all reformers; in the second place he discriminated, as Martin does not, between reform and revolution; and he did not talk about "balance" or assume it except in the most obvious, figurative way. Burke has written his own answer:

It were desirable that all hazardous theories concerning a balance of rights and privileges (a mode of expression wholly foreign to parliamentary usage) might have been forborne. His Majesty's faithful Commons are well instructed in their own rights and privileges, which they are determined to maintain on the footing upon which they were handed down from their ancestors: they are not unacquainted with the rights and privileges of the House of Peers; and they know and respect the lawful prerogatives of the crown: but they do not think it safe to admit anything concerning the existence of a balance of those rights, privileges, and prerogatives; nor are they able to discern to what object ministers would apply their fiction of balance; nor what they would consider as a just one. These unauthorized doctrines have a tendency to stir improper discussions; and to lead to mischievous innovations in the constitution.[95]

It would be preposterous, Burke said, "a perfect confusion of ideas, to take the theories which learned and speculative men have made from that government, and then, supposing it made on those theories, which were made from it, to accuse the government as not corresponding with them." [96] Burke went out and looked at the British constitution freshly—"a living, active, effective constitution" which he carefully discriminated from "a scheme upon paper." [97] For this reason the problem of securing a representation of the public sense and consent in government struck him as so much more complicated in fact than vote-counting, and the problem of distributing power effectively, with minimal harm to anybody, so much more subtle than occupying a mechanical balance or extending a mechanical franchise.

Now, what in all likelihood Montesquieu (although why not Voltaire?) may have set Burke on the track of grasping was the idea of the nation as a complex "moral essence," [98] a particular mode of human nature, whose particularity is a function, and often acts as a practical limit, of every aspect of historical behavior and contrivance—that is, the idea of a national culture.

In setting himself to investigate the *spirit* of a nation's law, instead of the laws themselves, Montesquieu was trying to formulate a simple moral essence inhering in the totality of relations which the laws bore "to each other, as also to their origin, to the intent of the legislator, and to the order of things on which they are established." [99] For example, as everybody knows, the English constitution, to his mind, was a nearly perfect elaboration of the spirit of liberty. The "infinite diversity of laws and manners" among mankind, he felt, are not "solely conducted by the caprice of fancy"; [100] there is a reason for them, which is to be sought in the character of the people by and for whom they are produced and the totality of circumstances which they are devised to accommodate. There are original relations of justice—that is, "relations of possible justice" transcending the particular laws by which these relations are actualized [101]—which it is the role of judicial reason to grasp; but the laws of every people ought to be an application of original justice to their conditions. Therefore, though law in general is human reason, the laws of each nation ought to be only the particular cases in which human reason is applied, and so:

They should be adapted in such a manner to the people for whom they are framed that it should be a great chance if those of one nation suit another.

They should be in relation to the nature and principle of each government; whether they form it, as may be said of politic laws; or whether they support it, as in the case of civil institutions.

They should be in relation to the climate of each country, to the quality of its soil, to its situation and extent, to the principal occupation of its natives, whether husbandmen, huntsmen, or shepherds: they should have relation to the degree of liberty which the constitution will bear; to the religion of the inhabitants, to their inclinations, riches, numbers, commerce, manners, and customs.[102]

His professed purpose was to help mankind recover from "whatever renders them ignorant of themselves," [103] and to show that the best government, meaning "the government most conformable to Nature," is that which "best agrees with the humour and dispositions of the people in whose favour it is established." [104]

Montesquieu's grasp of this tremendous idea is fumbling, but he has the merit of the better empiricists, of which Johnson and Burke are supreme exemplars, that in his very lack of system, and even contempt for it, he is wonderfully various and suggestive. The aggregation of his remarks have a consistency of tone—a spirit, if you will—which itself is a functional statement about his ideas. It arises from the reason returning again and again to basic aesthetic intuitions which are so suffusive and fine that they resist being snapped up by any single commitment as in a kind of pouch. The empirical reason always presupposes an implicit naive experience that is prior—a realm of impression or tact—and for the individual empiricist, the question is whether he is perpetually to have the use of that experience, or whether, in what Burke called "metaphysical madness," his reason is to split off and act the despot over it, with the usual effect of despotism, to coarsen both the ruler and the ruled. Montesquieu slibberslobbered between the two: that is, Burke said, he was sometimes "carried by the sharpness of his wit into a subtilty hardly to be justified." [105] But his directive notion of looking for the latent moral character regulating the particular relations of laws, institutions, and other devices of practical reason, was, and is, fructifying. As Leslie Stephen said, Montesquieu "deserves his place, less by reason of any clear results, than by certain tendencies implicitly contained in his arguments . . . He opens, in short, fertile lines of investigation, though he has not the patience to adhere to his own method." [106]

What Montesquieu did not have, among other things, that Burke had, was a depth and variety of concrete experience of English life, character, government, and society. The supposition that Burke was dependent upon somebody else for what he knew best and at first hand is another ridiculous oversimplification in the history of ideas.

## IV

Proposals to reform the representation grew from a resentment of Crown influence in the House of Commons, which no one distrusted more intensely than Burke, who had broken one of his first lances upon it (*Thoughts on the Cause of the Present Discontents,* 1770). Some, like Fox and the younger Pitt, wanted to make Parliaments annual and to add new county members. Others spoke of triennial Parliaments and the reform of corrupt boroughs. As stated earlier, the Duke of Richmond would have gone so far as to extend the franchise to every citizen eighteen years of age. All in all, Burke said, there were two parties. One would popularize the vote, to make representatives directly responsible (on a theory of "natural rights"); the other, less dramatic, argued simply that the House of Commons had decayed, had declined from its perpendicular, and ought to be propped up (on a theory, like "the fiction of balance," of what the Constitution was supposed to be). Burke opposed both, because he thought them not reforms, but gross and premature experiments redolent of quackery.

As for the latter, arguing from the theory of its principles—as, for example, the principle of a popular election of representatives—Burke countered: "How do you know the principles but from the construction? and if that remains the same, the principles remain the same. It is true, that to say your constitution is what it has been is no sufficient defence for those who say it is a bad constitution. It is an answer to those who say it is a degenerate constitution. To those who say it is a bad one I answer, look to its effects." [107] Always in pursuit of principles, Burke resisted their expulsion from actual experience into an unqualified self-sufficiency. Not objecting to theoretical principles themselves, he insisted that in practical affairs, their truth was relative to practice. "This is the true touchstone of all theories which regard man and the affairs of men—does it suit his nature in general?—does it suit his nature as modified by his habits?" [108]

Election of representatives to the House of Commons—"the legal and constructive organ of expressing the people's sense" [109]—was indeed a principle of the British constitution, Burke said, not contrived on a foregone theory of representation by numbers or majority rule, but evolved from the experienced need of centuries for some kind of control in English government issuing immediately from the governed and stamped with an express image of their actual feelings. Taken by itself, the expedient of counting votes and abiding by majority rule seemed to Burke a crude convention which, however, might very well work in a particular context and among a particular people whose needs and character he could not pretend to judge—as a result of "a very particular and special convention, confirmed afterwards by long habits of obedience, by a sort of discipline in society, and by a strong hand, vested with stationary, permanent power, to enforce this sort of constructive general will." [110] But it had only a limited relevance to the reform of a commonwealth already existing with a long experience of "a growing liberty and growing prosperity for five hundred years," [111] and among a people already under a discipline conformable to their character. "We are so little affected by things which are habitual, that we consider this idea of the decision of a *majority* as if it were a law of our original nature: but such constructive whole, residing in a part only, is one of the most violent fictions of positive law, that ever has been or can be made on the principles of artificial incorporation. Out of civil society nature knows nothing of it; nor are men, even when arranged according to civil order, otherwise than by very long training, brought at all to submit to it." [112] As for numbers, the particular conventions of each nation also determine what it is that constitutes the people, so as to make their act the signification of the general will." [113] That is, the choice of representatives in Commons by those legally *entitled* to choose them was the principle of election in England, and the title or privilege was general. But it was not a principle that everybody had an equal title; constitutionally, the franchise was surrounded by qualifications, e.g., the freehold.

In Burke's eyes, these qualifications—particular and of different kinds—made for a wise and beneficent adjustment *generally speaking* to the actual situations of Englishmen. This was a way of accommodating government, in Montesquieu's phrase, to "the humour and dispositions of the people in whose favour it is established." One who has grown up under American democracy is likely, and on Burke's principles ought, in degree, to cherish a different convention. "In all moral machinery, the moral results are its test." [114] But to understand Burke's wisdom, the recognition that democratic conventions do not work, and may be malign, apart from a prepared context of character and history, is easy enough (consider the Weimar Republic) . Something can also be said for the familiar eighteenth-century "stake in society" argument which Burke assumed. No liberty can long exist for the benefit of anybody which is not hedged around with responsibility, and it is hard to keep in mind the responsibility, and therefore the value, of a vote submerged, as Burke darkly foresaw it would be,[115] in a sea of equals.

"Popular" election was a proven principle, Burke felt, of the British constitution, that is, a proven expedient to a valuable end; and yet the same experience which had found out its worth also found its flaws and dangers. Therefore, it was made one principle in the constitution for the good purposes it could effect, while other principles and other qualifying contrivances, cross-checking and cooperating, were instituted alongside for other conjoint purposes quite as worthy.

That man thinks much too highly, and therefore he thinks weakly and delusively, of any contrivance of human wisdom, who believes that it can make any sort of approach to perfection.

There is not, there never was, a principle of government under heaven, that does not, in the very pursuit of the good it proposes, naturally and inevitably lead into some inconvenience, which makes it absolutely necessary to counterwork and weaken the application of that first principle itself; and to abandon something of the extent of the advantage you proposed by it, in order to prevent also the inconveniences which have arisen from the instrument of all the good you had in view.[116]

Burke feared that a plan to abolish privileges, qualifications, and boroughs outright and baldly to redistribute seats would not have the effect hoped for, of making Commons a supple, honest register of the general sense and consent, but instead —"in the present state of the country, in the present state of our representation, in the present state of our rights and modes of electing, in the present state of the several prevalent interests, in the present state of the affairs and manners of this country" [117]—it would work like a cancer in the traditionary constitution and ultimately destroy its complex achievements.

Burke by no means objected to *"some* remedy to the present state of the representation." [118] Corrupt boroughs disgusted him because they were corrupt, not because they were boroughs. He led the fight against the "officious cruelty" of Crown influence, that "mercenary nurse, who, under pretence of tenderness, stifles us with our clothes, and plucks the pillow from our heads. *Injectu multae vestis opprimi senem jubet."* [119] Nobody had worked harder to preserve the independence and popularity of Commons. But he wished to proceed cautiously on "state principles." There was a disease in the state, he agreed, which was deep, complicated, and "full of contra-indicants"; [120] it ought to be treated, perhaps by surgery; but the remedy ought to suit the real disease, the present disease, and the whole disease.[121] A remedy ought to be "healing and mediatorial," [122] to distinguish symptoms and plaints from causes, and not to tamper with the essential good of the body in trying to rid it of an accidental evil.[123] Those who argued that the constitution had decayed from the theory on which it was instituted were, Burke said, "like the unhappy persons who live, if they can be said to live, in the statical chair; who are ever feeling their pulse, and who do not judge of health by the aptitude of the body to perform its functions, but by their ideas of what ought to be the true balance of the several secretions."[124] There was a state to conserve, however, as well as to reform.

For that which, taken singly and by itself, may appear to be wrong, when considered with relation to other things may be perfectly right; or at least such as ought to be patiently endured, as the means of preventing something that is worse. So far with regard to what at first view may appear a *distemper* in the constitution. As to the *remedy* of that distemper, an equal caution ought to be used; because this latter consideration is not single and separate, no more than the former. There are many things in reformation which would be proper to be done, if other things can be done along with them; but which, if they cannot be so accompanied, ought not to be done at all. I therefore wish, when any new matter of this deep nature is proposed to me, to have the whole scheme distinctly in my view, and full time to consider it. Please God, I will walk with caution whenever I am not able clearly to see my way before me.[125]

The object, he said, was "to preserve the constitution entire, and practically equal to all the great ends of its formation, not in one single part, but in all its parts,"[126] to revive its health and nourish it in temperate habits.

The biological and medical analogy or metaphor was a favorite with Burke, who used it flexibly and with great force. It premised a delicate, ingrown organization, not a "balance," in the commonwealth, which ought not to be cut into except in grave emergencies and then only by the wise and steady hand of the professional. It suggested that the commonwealth was a body in nature, but a nature characterized by an individual history, and therefore that diagnoses assumed upon textbook theories of what a commonwealth ought naturally to be, instead of on study of how it actually was and could be kept sound in the concrete, were hazardous and clumsy. It likened this history to a continuous process of development, experience, and assimilation. It prompted Burke, in contrast to the prudent physician who draws on the wealth of accumulated human knowledge but treats each case individually, to point to mere theorists as quack magicians who, in their irrationality and ignorance, would cut the constitution in pieces and put them in a kettle, with the puddle of their compounds, in hopes of boiling them into youth and vigor.[127]

However, as Cobban notices,[128] Burke pushed the analogy no further than it was helpful. He foresaw, with remarkable prescience, the Spenglerian determinism—the decadence-mongering—in whose service it might be pressed.

I am not of opinion that the race of men, and the commonwealths they create, like the bodies of individuals, grow effete and languid and bloodless, and ossify by the necessities of their own conformation, and the fatal operation of longevity and time. These analogies between bodies natural and politic, though they may sometimes illustrate arguments, furnish no argument of themselves. They are but too often used under the colour of a specious philosophy, to find apologies for the despair of laziness and pusillanimity, and to excuse the want of all manly efforts, when the exigencies of our country call for them the more loudly.[129]

Such a position was explicitly advanced early in the eighteenth century by the antiquary Walter Moyle; implied by Montesquieu in his *Grandeur et Décadence des Romains;* and toyed with indulgently by Gibbon.[130] The analogy also appears in Bolingbroke's *Patriot King,* and in Robertson.[131] In fact, as the work of Professor Wellek demonstrates, "organic" analogies of many sorts pop up with increasing regularity throughout the eighteenth century.[132] They are common in Burke, who insisted, however, that they "rather furnish similitudes to illustrate or to adorn, than supply analogies from whence to reason. The objects which are attempted to be forced into an analogy are not found in the same classes of existence."

Individuals are physical beings subject to laws universal and invariable. The immediate cause acting in these laws may be obscure; the general results are subjects of certain calculation. But commonwealths are not physical but moral essences. They are artificial combinations, and, in their proximate efficient cause, the arbitrary productions of the human mind. We are not yet acquainted with the laws which necessarily influence the stability of that kind of work made by that kind of agent. . . . I doubt whether the history of mankind is yet complete enough, if ever it can be so, to furnish grounds for a sure theory on the internal causes which necessarily affect the fortune of a state.[133]

The biological analogies and metaphors in Burke can be taken too seriously. "Mechanical" analogies and metaphors also are common. So are other kinds—for example, analogies of the state with castles, temples, and other edifices, with climate, religious ceremonies, lotteries and gaming-tables, islands, kettles, raying lights, harbors, tombs, and so on almost inexhaustibly. To the historian who, for his purposes, assumes that ideas have a life of their own, the biological analogies will evidence a culture shift from "mechanical" to "organic" ways of thinking. But to one who regards ideas as individual activities, the most significant thing about Burke's analogies will be what they actually mean relative to other ideas and to the whole of his thinking. In this light, Burke will be seen in fundamental disagreement with, and not tending toward, "organic philosophies" of the state during the nineteenth century which in both theory and practice aspire to be closed systems. Dialectical materialism, for example, or the Hegelian dialectic, or any like theory, would be on Burke's premises no more than "speculative and ingenious amusements," possibly helpful, productive of nuances, but as bases for governing, reforming, or conserving the commonwealth, mere quack magic. What is important about the organic analogies, besides their suggestiveness, is Burke's refusal to bind himself by them, or to draw a theory from them.

During the many years, whatever may have swum through the fertile sublevels of his fantasy life, Burke, significantly, never mapped out a treatise on "The Ideal Nation" or an essay on "The General Will in History," though in the debate over parliamentary reform he spoke casually and by rough implication of both. He inclined to the professorial study—for example, his early pre-parliamentary tracts, his unfulfilled plan to write a refutation of Berkeley and of Hume [134]—but at some vital level and checkpoint, his personality rebelled against the critical stance of universalizing in politics so frequent among French *philosophes* and later among German philosophic idealists. Burke opposed the theorist who assumed that he could reason about the British commonwealth —which in fact was a social personality capable of "changing its mind"—and he attacked anyone who was confident that it was regulated by fixed, universal laws of nature, and who believed, therefore, that once these laws were reasoned out they could be used to remodel the constitution into what it ought to be. In opposing these beliefs, Burke resisted the entry into living politics of a mechanical concept of "nature" transliterated from the reigning physical sciences. He argued there could be no universal laws about a social personality; there could be only a growing, complex experience of it and within it, enriched by whatever angular lights various theories might on particular occasions throw upon it. But as Hoffman and Levack point out, Burke at the same time was implicitly detaching himself from the main ground of a kind of theorizing which would haunt the nineteenth century in a new (though related) form:

> The nineteenth century was to abound with it in the various philosophies drawn from contemplation of the historical process. Comte, Hegel, Cousin, Gioberti, Friedrich Schlegel, Karl Marx, and many others gave expression to it by abstracting from universal or institutional history various rationalized generalizations. Thus philosophies of history became the ideological bases of revolutionary, or reactionary, political creeds and programmes; and certain theories of institutional development–of the British constitution, for example–became the criteria for reforming institutions, which were conceived as the progressive realization of metaphysical purposes rather than accumulations of habit and experience made by successive generations adapting their behaviour to circumstances.[135]

He was unwilling, he said, to call in the constitution like a delinquent to see if it "did or did not accord with a pre-conceived scheme in the minds of certain gentlemen," [136] no matter what the scheme should be.

As for the second party of theorists, arguing to change the representation, their arguments could only lead to direct personal representation, "because all *natural* rights must be the rights of individuals; as by *nature* there is no such thing as politic or corporate personality; all these ideas are mere fictions of law, they are creatures of voluntary institution; men as men are individuals, and nothing else." [137] This once admitted, it meant, for all practical purposes, a democratic revolution posing as reform and put forward on theoretical grounds. It would illegalize all offices in the state, all branches of government, all political power—kings, lords, judges, generals, admirals, bishops, priests, ministers, justices of peace [138] —not conferred by direct election. To cede to every man an absolute right to govern himself fully, against all others, or else, where he cannot go to send his plenipotentiary, meant simply to dissolve the corporate personality existing into the dust of "uncovenanted man." [139]

Burke has sometimes been misunderstood in his attacking universal rights—"the supposed rights of man as man"—in political argument. He was as far as anyone could be from wanting a government in which the individual—English citizen or not—is deprived of his reason, dignity, liberty, security, or prosperity. Furthermore, he said, "If there be a moral, a political equality, this is the *desideratum* in our constitution, and every constitution in the world." [140] An "original" justice overarches all human affairs, an eternal will to the full possible development of every individual in a community of all possible good. No arguments of policy, *raison d'état,* or preservation of the constitution itself, can justify a government whose drift is counter to the higher expedience—"that which is good for the community, and good for every individual in it" [141]—for it would thus contradict the end of all human society in which government is only functional. To grasp these ends is the role of the theorist. "It is the business of the speculative philosopher to mark the proper ends of government. It is the business of the politician, who is the philosopher in action, to find out proper means towards those ends, and to employ them with effect." [142] As a practicing politician, Burke slanted the majority of his statements to persuade Englishmen to action within the English state. But there can be no question of the universality in his idea of justice—from which any notion of rights must derive—its independence of any single institution, government, race or other "artificial" distinction. Justice for the individual universally was simply the will of God.[143]

The question, however, was not what ideally it would be nice for every man to have and be, for men are flesh-and-blood individuals with flesh-and-blood limitations, not theories in the brain. The question was how, with the materials at any moment existing. The question was not so much about the theoretical end as about the living means, not about the *desideratum,* but about the process and agency. Burke pursued the answer in practical politics, which is the study of human contrivances to secure human benefits from human community. His central admiration is not really the romanticized state, but that vast public and publicly verifiable utility, the commonwealth, which embodies and transmits, in complicated and various ways, the achievements of generations of flesh-and-blood men, on the principle of the higher expedience—a proven means, he felt, not just of prating about "natural rights" or declaiming against human suffering, but what is infinitely better, of securing a wealth of those rights in fact and progressively, and of relieving that suffering in fact and progressively. Burke obliged himself to the principle of "that which is good for the community and good for every individual in it" and to the Anglican commonwealth as the most successful embodiment in fact and promise that he knew about.

In attacking natural-right politicians, Burke attacked not their idea of universal equality, which theoretically considered, he said, was a juridical commonplace, a foundation of all law, but their bullying the idea into politics without respect to the other foundation of law which renders it humanly valuable—that is, utility. For what was the justice of promising rights without responsible experience of some means by which they could be enjoyed and secured? "Those who think themselves not likely to be encumbered with the performance of their promises, either from their known inability, or total indifference about the performance, never fail to entertain the most lofty ideas. They are certainly the most specious, and they cost them neither reflection to frame, nor pains to modify, nor management to support. The task is of another nature to those who mean to promise nothing that it is not in their intention, or may possibly be in their power, to perform." [144] And what could better criticize theories about the means of securing just enjoyments than the *immediately existing* constitution, the tested experience of millions of individual Englishmen living and dead who, whatever their limits and errors, had transmitted a machinery that *judged by its long-run and obvious successes* was *fundamentally* adjusted both to human nature in general, and more adequately still, by a presumption legitimate till proved wrong, to human nature modified, by the concrete, complex and moral habits of a nation?

Burke conceived himself to be in no way obscurantist—which "ought not to be endured for a moment," he said, "in a country whose being depends upon the certainty, clearness, and stability of institutions." [145] Nor was he throwing the English people upon the mercy of historical accident: the constitution consisted of clear and positive settlements "modelled according to the occasion" and which therefore could be remodelled according to other occasions. Speaking of English juries, he said, "I spare your patience, and I pay a compliment to your understanding, in not attempting to prove that anything so elaborate and artificial as a jury was not the work of *chance,* but a matter of institution brought to its present state by the joint efforts of legislative authority and juridical prudence." [146] Nor was he irrational: he wished to keep people from turning "a rational principle into an idle and vulgar superstition." [147] Burke thought he was talking about the plain and verifiable when he referred Englishmen to their "inheritance" which "furnishes a sure principle of conservation, and a sure principle of transmission; without at all excluding a principle of improvement. It leaves acquisition free; but it secures what it acquires."

By a constitutional policy, working after the pattern of nature, we receive, we hold, we transmit our government and our privileges, in the same manner in which we enjoy and transmit our property and our lives. The institutions of policy, the goods of fortune, the gifts of providence, are handed down to us, and from us, in the same course and order. Our political system is placed in a just correspondence and symmetry with the order of the world, and with the mode of existence decreed to a permanent body composed of transitory parts; wherein, by the disposition of a stupendous wisdom, moulding together the great mysterious incorporation of the human race, the whole, at one time, is never old, or middle-aged, or young, but, in a condition of unchangeable constancy, moves on through the varied tenor of perpetual decay, fall, renovation, and progression. Thus by preserving the method of nature in the conduct of the state, in what we improve, we are never wholly new; in what we retain, we are never wholly obsolete. By adhering in this manner and on those principles to our forefathers, we are guided, not by the superstition of antiquarians, but by the spirit of philosophic analogy.[148]

The constitution has a psychological nature corresponsive to the institutional, and this may not be equally plain to all eyes. It is a "wisdom without reflection, and above it" because it represents an achieved way of feeling and solving practical problems, a thought-through experience, so much a part of the national character and culture, so much kept alive in the spirit of its laws and devices, that it is not usually thought about, is taken for granted. This achieved national experience—which Burke sometimes calls the "moral basis"—had about the same relation to the formal constitution as has the artist's experience in Sir Joshua Reynolds' view to the formal work of art. It embodies a changeable, relatively integrated preconscious landscape of affection and judgment, something like a tact or *savoir faire,* an insight cumulative in habit and quietly funneling up its insights into practice—

unless the theorizing brain, splitting off from its natural function, turns upon its experience, chokes and pollutes the channel. In this residual sagacity,[149] no more "past" than the experience of an artist is "past" at the moment it guides his creative hand, Burke located much of the "real sense" of the people, the profoundest security for continuity in their values, and a natural part of that "consent" which government-by-consent must somehow tap continually.

Burke agreed with natural-righters that a national choice, a voluntary and rational consent, is a necessity of free government, but he disagreed that the adequacy of devices of representation and election, which are the particular parts of a constitution designed to register a momentary national choice and consent, could be judged without regard to all the other relations of parts in the constitution in which the sense of the people was also, and had for a long time been present and actual. If the constitution had faults, as Burke admitted it might have, then "those faults, when found, ought to be corrected." But "not everything which appears at first view to be faulty in such a complicated plan" is "determined to be so in reality. To enable us to correct the constitution, the whole constitution must be viewed together; and it must be compared with the actual state of the people, and the circumstances of the time." [150] He was resolute that "the deliberate sense of the kingdom" should be known and should prevail, and that nobody in Parliament should employ "the legal and constructive organ of expressing the people's sense against the sense which they do actually entertain." [151] But he was equally certain that "no precipitate resolution on a great change in the fundamental constitution of any country can ever be called the real sense of the people" [152] because the sense of every people includes as part of its essence a deposition of mixed experience that, connecting backward and forward with collaborative generations, persists as stable and verifiable habitudes in the present, and it is much too definitive of the people's character to change uniformly and all at once, and much too subtle and many-sided to be in the special custody of theorists.

This is noticeably "organic" thinking—but also noticeably, "organic" here only describes a willing ability to see a problem in as many of its perceptible relations as can possibly be found flowing from it, including "virtual" relations that hover at the edge of reality as defined by standardized ideas. It does not describe what "the organic," like any other concept applied to human affairs, may easily become, a slavish mold. Burke had no organic idea like a pair of ultraviolet goggles which he could don or doff as he pleased. He applies no organic idea omnipresently in his experience; every portion of experience has its own order, which he struggles to seize. The frequency with which he seizes the "organic" arises not from systematic precommitment, but from something else—apparently from the very character of his sensibility and intelligence in relation to the particular life-problems that moved into its orbit. Burke's attention seems to have been drawn almost instinctively to the "personality" or "character" of a thing in unity with the many circumstances fastening it in existence.

Those who knew Burke well in society, and admired him, were almost unanimous in their general impression of what his genius was like, though each phrased it after his own fashion. The judgmatical scholar Edmond Malone admitted that Burke would be positively disagreeable if his superiority were not so great; that tending to disregard the remarks of others, he "urges on whatever rises in his mind with an ardour peculiar to himself." [153] Lord Lyttleton spoke of "an intemperate vivacity of genius"; [154] and Gibbon, calling him "diffusive," pronounced Burke "the most eloquent and rational madman" that he ever knew.[155] He "winds into a subject like a serpent," Goldsmith added.[156] Even Fanny Burney may be allowed a chatty few words of witness (though she must be cut off, firmly): ". . . such Spirit, such Intelligence,—so much energy when serious, so much pleasantry when sportive,—so manly in his address, so animated in his conversation,—so eloquent in Argument, so exhilarating in trifling,—! O, I . . ." [157] But as one might expect, Johnson made the sharpest definition. Agreeing with others—"Burke *is* an extraordinary man. His stream of mind is perpetual" [158]—he went on to define Burke's peculiar quality as "copiousness and fertility of allusion; a power of diversifying his matter, by placing it in various relations." [159] This gets to the point. Burke's *métier* and special calling is his urgent, passionate, almost obsessive awareness of the interrelatedness of things in actual life, combined with the power to let all sectors of his knowledge freely intersect and cross-fructify, after a literary fashion, in the interest of a humane practicality. "Reading, and much reading, is good," Burke wrote his son; "but the power of diversifying the matter infinitely in your own mind, and of applying it to every occasion that arises, is far better, so don't suppress the *vivida vis.*" [160] It is this assimilative side of his intelligence which keeps resistance to theory from being merely negative. Burke fed upon theory and upon knowledge of all kinds as a plant upon light, taking what he could use, assimilating, transforming, while his main energies were engaged by the world of solid and growing actuality:

> The world of contingency and political combination is much larger than we are apt to imagine. We never can say what may or may not happen, without a view to all the actual circumstances. Experience, upon other data than those, is of all things the most delusive. Prudence in new cases can do nothing on grounds of retrospect. A constant vigilance and attention to the train of things as they successively emerge, and to act on what they direct, are the only sure courses. The physician that let blood, and by blood-letting cured one kind of plague, in the next added to its ravages.[161]

Not to theorize in any fashion would almost be, of course, to abandon the good of the intellect. Theory as system orders ideas; theory as speculation sensitizes the mind with fresh possibilities and enables it to slough off the effete, inert, or gross; theory as vision may be an end in itself. Though a strain of something like anti-intellectualism runs, paradoxically, through his thought, Burke claimed to be no enemy of theory *per se:* "I do not vilify theory and speculation—no, because that would be to vilify reason itself. *Neque decipitur ratio, neque decipit unquam.*" [162] When he spoke against theory, he said he meant its abuse, and its abusers—system-mongers, speculatists, and visionaries. System by dint of being itself tends to be exclusive, rigid, and insensitive to nuance; speculation, feeble, hasty, and ignorant; vision, dogmatic, subjective, and proud. The defect of political theory, when it is not simply a swindle, is inherent in abstraction, whose very nature, it would seem, is to be positive by exclusion. The vice of theory, the abuse, comes when it is applied to the practical (or actual) world, when to exclude may mean to destroy, and the very human taint of prejudice or gullibility, which in the study may be harmless and even charming, becomes in practice something like criminal neglect or persecution. "Reason," Burke observed, "is never inconvenient but when it comes to be applied." [163] The exclusions which in the study seem few and small because invisible, suddenly magnify into a giant chaos of solid, animated particulars; the theory shrinks and loses dazzle. The danger always is lest it shrink upon the theorist's mind, endungeon him, and close his eyes to all but his own self-generated light.

To such theory—"the presumptuous pride of didactic ignorance" [164]—against which nobody who theorizes is proof, certainly not the vanguards of eighteenth-century rationalism, Burke tried to oppose various analytical, practical, and imaginative checks, which freed his common sense and common feeling for rich adventures in the concrete. Or to say the same thing in another way: Burke's "empirical" corrective to runaway theory was always to be making something out of aggregative experience. This making, which is endless, restrains the intellect from flight into the self-determinacy of system (though it does not preclude order), and the intellect itself keeps experience from dissolving in its own acids and energizes in practical possession what would otherwise have lain forever in the chaos of the latent, ignored, and unrelated. As Leslie Stephen observed, who was generously endowed himself, the "most marked peculiarity" of Burke's mind is his "admirable combination of the generalizing faculty with a respect for concrete facts." [165] In his attempts to moderate "theory"—rigid ideology, narrow schemes, arrogant oversimplifications, easy labels, and paper plans—Burke often settled himself in that inexhaustibly creative realm of middle axioms called "the practical," where generalizing reason and concrete experience are never so very far apart that they cannot fructify each other. His resistance to theory implied a certain imaginative way of encountering and using experience: a direct facing of concreteness, even an eagerness and longing for it; a poetic openness to novel and contingent relations in the actual.

## V

The English commonwealth was not a collection of "vague, loose individuals" in one spot of the earth, not "an idea only of local extent, and individual momentary aggregation," but also "an idea of continuity, which extends in time as well as in numbers and in space." [166] Its constitutional arrangements, good or bad, were not *chosen* on any one day or by any one set of people, as, in a loose comparative manner of speaking, the constitution of the United States was "chosen," incorporated whole during one period by general mandate. Its arrangements—like much in the United States since that period—were corporate by prescription, elaborated piecemeal and gradually by men grappling with affairs in their time and contriving to steady government in the stream of practical necessities. It was throughout prescriptive; it included the principle that a direct choice by the people should be at work in the constitution, but it also prescribed the mode of choice and qualifications of the choosers. Its sole authority was that it had existed prescriptively time out of mind, and by presumption since the nation had "long existed and flourished under it," it had at most moments of its existence coincided with something "better than choice"—with a corresponsive "real sense of the people" inhabiting the nation, with the national experience in the developing succession of its shapes among individual people related by their fortunes, or, in Burke's terms, with "the peculiar circumstances, occasions, tempers, dispositions, and moral, civil, and social habitudes of the people, which disclose themselves only in a long space of time. It is a vestment, which accommodates itself to the body." [167]

The choice of the people at any discrete moment, Burke said, whenever it can come to act, is or ought to be irresistible, but he was confident that unless it were momentarily stirred up into a "tumultuary and giddy choice," it would act consistently with the choice of the people at other discrete moments, that is, consistently with the choice of the nation, in the perfect freedom of duty. Thus in opposing prescription to election—or more accurately, in making election derivative from prescription—Burke gave vent to the principle by which the past complements the present and in turn prepares a completer future: the principle of a traditionary constitution (and by implication of a whole nation) as an endlessly developing order whose meaning is relative to all time and among whose values, at any given moment, is freedom from "the dust and powder of individuality." [168] Apart from the principle of prescription, which Burke considered so fundamental in all human society (not just English) as almost to be an instinct of the species, the constitution could never have come to exist and could not continue: nothing could have passed on, he believed, from the labor of one generation to unite with the labor of another. "All titles," Burke said, "terminate in prescription; in which (differently from Time in the fabulous instances) the son devours the father, and the last prescription eats up all the former." [169]

As any close reader of Burke knows, *prescription* is an idea fertile of many meanings if you abstract his usages of it, juxtapose them, and try, at a second abstract remove, to sift out a middle result. It's a sensible thing to do; as Whitehead says, when a rough guide to action becomes a formula for criticizing other points of view, one is entitled to ask what it means.[170] Of course, the general fortune of Burke's idea of prescription has been just the reverse: readers are likely to assume what it means and forget that it was ever a rough guide to action—like "nature," a regulative notion which only "meant" what it seemed usefully to help express. Leslie Stephen discriminates two brackets of meaning which it is useful to recall. In a perversion, to which Burke sometimes inclines, from a certain earnest and anxious fervor of conviction and a fine excess of expression, prescription can sound like the schoolboy optimism that whatever is, is right. That is, it smacks of a Dr. Pangloss, but a Pangloss frightened out of innocence and whose dialectic is guided by a resentment of further discovery. But in a nobler and more radically Burkian sense, prescription is simply a recognition of "the fact that ninety-nine hundredths of men's thoughts and instincts are those which they have inherited from their fathers, and of the corresponding doctrine, that reform is impracticable in the sense of an abrupt reconstruction of society, and can only be understood as the gradual modification of a complex structure."[171] Prescription is only a legal phrase "for that continuity of past and present, and that solidarity between all parts of the political order, the perception of which is the essential condition of sound political reasoning."[172] This helpfully clarifies, and removes from charged phrasing, what Burke valued in "the chain of legitimate prejudices" which people had upon the authority of habit and could not always be disputing and shaming and calling in as delinquent without very grave consequences to themselves and to the whole social order—a self-splitting, vulgarizing action which later he would find in the French revolutionaries generally. "Prescription" also denotes the difficulty, sometimes perhaps the impossibility, of finding any exact beginning of the state in history, but lays it down that once the state is in process, the soundest rule of thumb is *amate, colite;* and therefore, it is likely to imply a "conservative" politics insofar as that means a brand of political reason which values the fundamental principles of the *status quo,* and which demands, as a moral obligation, that change proceed by benign degrees continuous and consistent with those principles. But on a level still more abstract, which, shearing away political overtones, perhaps gets closer to something like Burke's sensibility, prescription seems to imply—or is a notion which is most consistent with—a certain way of taking in human life, a mode of experiencing and value. Prescription makes everything it touches finite: it acknowledges a complexity of limitation, a practical necessity, in the character of a thing. Secondly, it directs attention to the actual or the practical. Thirdly, it implies continuity in time or place or state of mind, continuity of any mode—development, variation, degeneracy, obsolescence, persistence, identity, etc. Thus, prescription is the kind of idea which is likely to be most valued by one who habitually sees the character of anything as continuously itself, through all the relations of finite change which may enter into and modify its life career. It points toward a practical fusion of nature and history to form the realm of common life. Metaphysically (as Burke would never have brought himself to speak) it points toward a reconciliation of permanence and change. Whether or not this analysis is right, it seems to be consistent with other, more plainspoken ideas of Burke's. For example, he distinguished the principles of the constitution—meaning something like the objective, general, permanent, valuable ends for which the constitution exists, or else the machinery which by experience has been found adequate to such ends—from its circumstances, which are variable and transient and full of perplexing thwarts and defects, and even plain iniquities, and which yet are the very materials of life in which a familiar good must find its home or not at all. Prescription—as, for example, the basis for the existence of the House of Commons—authorizes its permanence as a principle in the constitution, but in continuity with the variable requirements of changing historical circumstances which make it at any discrete moment an actual, finite thing, not *the* but *a* House of Commons. Thus it makes the point that in all the depth of existence, past and present, there is no ground and sanction for any constitution or state except as by a prescriptive use it is found to be good.

In some ways, this is a disturbing perception about the historical process. A man who is concerned about the relations of permanence and change (or principle and circumstance, or nature and history) is really worried most about change and can hardly help seeing that it has a kind of basic and ineradicable challenge in it: the idea of something being permanent (instead of eternal) is defined by the certainty of its having to negotiate change. Then he may even come by the frightfully possible idea that in all the depth of existence nothing human is certain but change, and everything human is in danger of being spun away in its endless dissipation. Something like this idea seems to underlie Burke's genuine reverence for prescription as also a moral sanction for such continuity of achievement as human beings—more successfully, the English—in the finite course of reason, good luck, and mysterious Providence may be able corporately to manage and pass on. "Dark and inscrutable," Burke said, "are the ways by which we come into the world. The instincts which give rise to this mysterious process of nature are not of our making." But "out of physical causes, unknown to us, perhaps unknowable, arise moral duties," including the moral duty of reverencing the finite good of the actual order of things into which we find ourselves born—"the social ties and ligaments, spun out of those physical relations which are the elements of the commonwealth, [and which] in most cases begin, and always continue, independently of our will," though we are endowed with its benefits.[173] Otherwise, Burke said, condemning any definition of the people with respect to a theoretical and abstract nature, instead of with respect to their many actual and finite relations within a prescriptive state, there is no way of knowing "what form it is that our [theoretical] incantations are about to call up from darkness and the sleep of ages," [174] inviting change to wreak the full chaos of its creativity. Armed with such a perception, Burke gazed down, during the debate on parliamentary reform, at the earnest and smiling dissenters from prescription (like his friend Fox, like the gentlemanly Duke of Richmond, like the cold and calculating Pitt, like honest Mr. John Sawbridge who respectfully submitted the same bill every year) with the hilarious scorn of the last bard chased to the crags of Snowdon and condemned to the mad solitude of a dying music.

It is a testimony of the degree to which an awareness of history had crept into late-eighteenth-century experience that the problem of change should haunt Burke throughout his career, be central in his response, and constantly waken to his attention. The word *change* is a useful lever for picking up a cluster of attitudes and senses elicited in this thinking. The *locus classicus* is a passage in his "Letter to Sir Hercules Langrishe" (1792), supporting enfranchisement of Irish Roman Catholics:

We must all obey the great law of change. It is the most powerful law of nature, and the means perhaps of its conservation. All we can do, and that human wisdom can do. is to provide that the change shall proceed by insensible degrees. This has all the benefits which may be in change, without any of the inconveniences of mutation. Everything is provided for as it arrives. This mode will, on the one hand, prevent the *unfixing old interests at once: a thing which is apt to breed a black and sullen discontent in* those who are at once dispossessed of all their influence and consideration. This gradual course, on the other side, will prevent men, long under depression, from being intoxicated with a large draught of new power, which they always abuse with a licentious insolence. But wishing, as I do, the change to be gradual and cautious, I would, in my first steps, lean rather to the side of enlargement than restriction.[175]

A man who leans too far out, however, overbalances the wheel of time, and finds himself, often with surprise, revolved into the abyss. Burke affirmed the double truth that "power rarely reforms itself," [176] but also that "a spirit of innovation is generally the result of a selfish temper, and confined views." [177] His feeling for change was shaped by a plain, shrewd distrust of the variety in human contests for power.

But it was also shaped by a more awful distrust of the interplay of accidents in nature and history itself: in one moment a state exists and flourishes "in nature," and suddenly at another moment declines, or is lost wholly, and in its place another state exists and flourishes, for no discernible reason. *Tristis et luctuosa successio.* Such a change usually touched some profound emotional chord in Burke, a helpless faith or stern horror, a pity for destroyed values, and occasionally sarcastic resentment. He knew that "a state without the means of some change is without the means of its conservation"; [178] but the view of causation in history which came down to him, in all its urbane naivete, was so thoroughly empirical as almost at times to deny the possibility of knowing causes and therefore to remind him often how easily *change* can slide into *chance,* even to suggest to him an inscrutability at the base of time. Looking back at the parade of states and ages in history, Burke found the "interior" causes of change obscure; "a thousand accidents might have prevented the operation of what the most clear-sighted were not able to discern, nor the most provident to divine." And therefore the causes at work in a present change, he had to conclude, were equally precarious and their potentialities obscure.

It is often impossible, in these poltical inquiries, to find any proportion between the apparent force of any moral causes we may assign and their known operation. We are therefore obliged to deliver up that operation to mere chance, or, more piously, (perhaps more rationally,) to the occasional interposition and irresistible hand of the Great Disposer. We have seen states of considerable duration, which for ages have remained nearly as they have begun, and could hardly be said to ebb or flow. Some appear to have spent their vigour at their commencement. Some have blazed out in their glory a little before their extinction. The meridian of some has been the most splendid. Others, and they are the greatest number, have fluctuated, and experienced at different periods of their existence a great variety of fortune. At the very moment when some of them plunged in unfathomable abysses of disgrace and disaster, they have suddenly emerged. They have begun a new course and opened a new reckoning; and, even in the depths of their calamity, and on the very ruins of their country, have laid the foundations of a towering and durable greatness. All this has happened without any apparent previous change in the general circumstances which had brought on their distress. The death of a man at a critical juncture, his disgust, his retreat, his disgrace, have brought innumerable calamities on a whole nation. A common soldier, a child, a girl at the door of an inn, have changed the face of fortune, and almost of nature.[179]

Historical truth is concrete, but the concrete is a practical infinity of individuals, fading away in their relations beyond the grasp of any single mind. So if we may believe that the causes are there, and if we catch sight of them now and then in discrete and continuing revelations, we are little nearer to grasping them whole. Anything can happen. We may gain in experience gradually, but infer beyond it at hazard. We therefore obey "the great law of change," but in the wisdom of experience, we try to change "by insensible degrees" and to provide for everything as it arrives.

Ideologically speaking, Hume probably helped to crystallize his view,[180] for despite his contempt in later years for Hume's epicureanism, atheism, and Toryism, and the long coldness in their friendship, Burke as a young reader was more appreciative. Certainly in *An Enquiry Concerning Human Understanding* he would find an influential discussion of the "secret powers" and principles,[181] of the "secret mechanism or structure of parts" [182] in nature which determine what the effects of change will be, but which also are concealed from human certainty, locked up, along with the Deity, in the boundless "ocean of doubt." [183] Or he could have been influenced even by Locke. Coming to define the idea of *power* ("able to make, or able to receive, any change") Locke had worried about "a secret relation of the parts" in nature, eluding inquiry.[184] Locke had also fled "the vast ocean of being"—what Burke called "the infinite void of the conjectural world"—where Providence alone operates, premissing that, "Our business here is not to know all things, but those which concern our conduct." [185] Or in Burke's restatement, "our business is what is likely to be affected, for the better or the worse, by the wisdom or weakness of our plans." [186] For "when we go but one step beyond the immediate sensible qualities of things, we go out of our depth. All we do after is but a faint struggle, that shows we are in an element which does not belong to us." [187] As a young man Burke had read himself "deep in metaphysics," [188] (though he came to hate it) in a period he called his *furor logicus,*[189] and a knowledge of empiricists —Newton, Locke, Hume, Hutcheson, Montesquieu—is apparent in his early writing, especially in *The Sublime and the Beautiful*.[190] But it is not necessary to go source-hunting for a view sufficiently accounted for by the general ethos of one branch of empiricism in England, except to suggest that the rudiments of Burke's view were not spun out of his singularity. A conditioning of ideas in eighteenth-century England could help him arrive at the notion of a secret phalanx of causes operative in every change in the state, as indeed sustaining the state in history, and could therefore teach him to be cautious and watchful whenever power of any kind was to change hands, to view change in an honest philosophical squint.

"Individuals," Burke said, "pass like shadows," [191] and the difference to them of today and tomorrow is immense; but "the commonwealth is fixed and stable" beyond the lonely and pleasing fretful span of individuals enjoying their portion, their life-rental, and as swiftly gone. One would expect them therefore, in their way of doing, to join their labors for the common good, and their labors may now and then issue in profound changes. But one would also expect a consciousness of their situation and the duties arising from it, a diffident and searching awe almost like a timidity whenever they find themselves preferring their single wisdom to long-enduring principles and the actualities defined by them, upon whose continuance the happiness of both the living and the unborn may depend. "If circumspection and caution are a part of wisdom, when we work only upon inanimate matter, surely they become a part of duty too, when the subject of our demolition and construction is not brick and timber, but sentient beings, by the sudden alteration of whose state, condition, and habits, multitudes may be rendered miserable." [192]

"Very plausible schemes," Burke noticed, "with very pleasing commencements, have often shameful and lamentable conclusions."

In states there are often some obscure and almost latent causes, things which appear at first view of little moment on which a very great part of its prosperity or adversity may most essentially depend. The science of government being therefore so practical in itself, and intended for such practical purposes, a matter which requires experience, and even more experience than any person can gain in his whole life, however sagacious and observing he may be, it is with infinite caution that any man ought to venture upon pulling down an edifice, which has answered in any tolerable degree for ages the common purposes of society, or on building it up again, without having models and patterns of approved utility before his eyes.[193]

Justice such as it is possible to establish—and no one can say what the exact shape of that estabishment shall be—can only be evolved from existing social materials in a succession of generations. Thus, laws are not right because they are established; if the artificial difference they set between men issues in injustice, then they are unjust laws; but they are established because there is no other human method of getting at the right, and because justice without permanence is no justice at all. "It is from this view of things that the best legislators have been often satisfied with the establishment of some sure, solid, and ruling principle in government; a power like that which some of the philosophers have called a plastic nature; and having fixed the principle [as Burke had tried to fix the principle of free trade in Ireland], they have left it afterwards to its own operation." [194] Succeeding generations, having received the establishment and the principle at work in it, set about testing its justice and utility in their time. But of all this, prescription is the moral and legal cement: without it, a legislator would have "founded a commonwealth upon gaming, and infused this spirit into it as its vital breath," with the result of diverting "the whole of the hopes and fears of the people from their usual channels into the impulses, passions, and superstitions of those who live on chances." [195]

Burke perceived that an established arrangement and custom in the state, as indeed also an innovation, though its facade in the present may be plain and homely, has an essential part of its existence in a vast outworks of past experience (which may or may not be wise) . Without grave, possibly disastrous effect, an establishment cannot be pulled down, as a revolutionary might dream, like a slum tenement, and a brave new efficiency apartment erected on the spot. The analogy is false. A traditional establishment is not a slum in the "spirit"—the latent, actual character and relations—of man, but, for better or worse, is an essential projection of it, and as the spirit becomes, so an establishment can possibly become. Therefore, Burke said, when he "changed, it should be to preserve"; he would make any "reparation as nearly as possible in the style of the building." [196] For example, he admired both the Restoration and the Whig Revolution of 1688, for at these two critical periods, the "two principles of conservation and correction operated strongly"; "in both cases they regenerated the deficient part of the old constitution through the parts which were not impaired"; they acted "by the ancient organized states in the shape of their old organization, not by the organic *moleculae* of a disbanded people." [197] Changes of this kind, on "public principles and national grounds" [198] were not in Burke's language changes at all, but reforms; correcting a defect (in this instance, a relation of the public will to the monarchy), they conserved or recovered the substance of the historic establishment; accommodating newly arisen needs, they adhered to a functional sameness.

> [Change] alters the substance of the objects themselves; and gets rid of all their essential good, as well as of all the accidental evil, annexed to them. Change is novelty; and whether it is to operate any one of the effects of reformation at all, or whether it may not contradict the very principle upon which reformation is desired, cannot be certainly known before hand. Reform is, not a change in the substance, or in the primary modfication, of the object, but, a direct application of a remedy to the grievance complained of. So far as that is removed, all is sure. It stops there; and, if it fails, the substance which underwent the operation, at the very worst, is but where it was.[199]

The reformer, therefore, unlike the revolutionary, does not have always to be starting over, and he is also less likely to be victimized by his own mistakes or misfortunes, caught in a backwash of the unpredictable and unsuspected. It is possible for thoroughgoing changes to end ironically in a simple reproduction of the old evils in a new or worse combination; and therefore, Burke said, though the shortcomings of old establishments are usually obvious, the means of really supplying them is not. It is wise "to know how much of an evil ought to be tolerated; lest, by attempting a degree of purity impracticable in degenerate times and manners, instead of cutting off the subsisting ill-practices, new corruptions might be produced for the concealment and security of the old." [200]

On these grounds, Burke contrived his own reform of the economical and civil establishment, hoping to accomplish on the principles of a prescriptive constitution, without precarious innovations, that strengthening of Parliament and purgation of Crown influence which were professed good aims of democratic or democracy-minded theorists. As soon as one tries to analyze prescription, to ask what it assumes, *omnia exeunt in mysterium;* it leads outward, for example, into the eternal problem of perpetuating a just order in the acids of actuality. But Burke's idea of prescription is not the contrived concept of armchair or obscurantist mysticism, hard as it is not to make it sound so. A notion derived from English common law, it is nothing in Burke if not practical and specific. Burke was the friend of no "contrivances, which are used to free men from the servitude of their reason, and from the necessity of ordering their affairs according to their evident interests." [201] If prescription presupposes a very specialized sense of history, it presupposes also a looking at something exactly and hardheadedly. There is no better illustration than Burke's famous speech announcing his reform bill, which in addition to being a cogent statement of prescriptive principles, is also a satire on the abuses to which a prescriptive constitution is liable, and which necessitate sharply critical, present-minded legislators. In his imagery he particularly ridiculed vestiges of Gothic "feudality" in the constitution which his plan would retrench and replace with a uniform and rational system more proper to "the living economy of the age."

The principles of his reform bill consistently and plainly exemplify his idea of how the constitution had come to pass and of what at bottom it was: the successive applications of particular reason by legislators conforming to "the irresistible demands" [202] of their situation. The first consideration, Burke said, was "the absolute, urgent *necessity* there is that something of the kind should be done," [203] for " (on some person or other) every reform must operate as a sort of punishment" [204] and it signifies nothing "to turn abuses out of one door, if we are to let them in at another." [205]

It is necessary from our own political circumstances [the encroachment of Crown influence on Parliament]; it is necessary from the operations of the enemy [France]; it is necessary from the demands of the people, whose desires, when they do not militate with the stable and eternal rules of justice and reason, (rules which are above us and above them,) ought to be as a law to a House of Commons.[206]

The second consideration was that from beginning to end the plan of reform should be objectively rational in every particular, upon "state principles" not reflecting "the private opinions, tastes, or feelings, of the man who attempts to regulate," [207] not proceeding from malignity or envy,[208] not "frittering and crumbling down the attention by a blind, unsystematic observance of every trifle," [209] not running into that rigor which "as usual, defeats itself," or worst of all, into "that over-perfect kind of justice which has obtained, by its merits, the title of the opposite vice." [210] Thirdly, it must be practical: "Those things which are not practicable, are not desirable. There is nothing in the world really beneficial, that does not lie within the reach of informed understanding and a well-directed pursuit. There is nothing that God has judged good for us, that He has not given us the means to accomplish, both in the natural and the moral world. If we cry, like children, for the moon, like children, we must cry on." [211]

Burke wanted to methodize and proportion an "accumulated patchwork of occasional accommodation,"[212] to pull down completely a "whole ill-contrived scaffolding" of sinecures which, having lost its utility relative to objective necessities, now "obstructs, rather than forwards, our public works."[213] For example, the clutter of offices in the royal household—buttery, pantry, patent hereditary cook, and so on—came to pass legitimately in answer to feudal "manners and customs that have long since expired," for Burke said: "There was some reason in ancient necessities for these ancient customs. Protection was wanted; and the domestic tie, though not the highest, was the closest."[214] But in the resistless tide of history, the reason for the offices had been lost, along with the stateliness of antique manners, until there remained only "the cumbrous charge of a Gothic establishment . . . shrunk into the polished littleness of modern elegance and personal accommodation."[215] These expensive, superannuated, and top-heavy offices, inutile and open to corruption (since many of them carried a membership in Parliament), Burke would pare away. Yet he interpreted utility in a generous fashion, remembering his own wisdom that "many things in the constitution of establishments, which appear of little value on the first view," may "in a secondary and oblique manner, produce very material advantages."[216] Therefore he left untouched all officers attending on the person of the king—the court proper—whose splendor was more valuable than their cost. With similar caution, he left intact many life-pensions in the patent offices whose profits, he said, were abusive yet beyond the reach of a present reform, for being pensions for life, they were acknowledged under law as any other private property would be, and what the law respects must remain sacred short of some occasions "of public necessity, so vast, so clear, so evident, that they supersede all laws."[217] These, therefore, he would put under fixed salaries; and furthermore, acknowledging that royal pensions were open to abuse, he still would keep the principle: the commonwealth profited by a means of rewarding public labor and merit with the repose of a fixed settlement: "There is a time, when the weather-beaten vessels of the state ought to come into harbour." [218] In short, in his radical surgery, which was systematic and substantial, he cut away nothing but such as reason showed it impossible to keep, and he made sure that the systematic order he substituted would in the future provide for all the complicated ends of government which prescription had brought to pass. Burke "heaved the lead every inch of way" he made.[219]

Decorum was his regulative notion—decorum as putting the cardinal virtues into practice relative to the limits of nature and the deliverances of actual life. Burke assumed that a reformer of genuine decorum, one who meant to improve and not to obliterate the achieved, would be fearful of himself, would look steadily on the business before him, and would temper his reason to conform with the actual, multiple, and emergent needs of the situation. He would seek the relative best mode of acting (which implies more than the negative of restraint, though it may include that), a mode of accommodation which inheres "not in official formality, nor in airy speculation, but in real life, and in human nature, in what 'comes home' (as Bacon says) 'to the business and bosoms of men.' " [220] Lest he disable himself from doing any good in the long run, he withholds from doing what he sees immediately to be invidious. He conflicts with "opposite vices, with the obstinacy that rejects all improvement," and lays down a smokescreen of pretexts, and also with "the levity that is fatigued and disgusted with everything of which it is in possession" and that plans a "hot reformation." [221]

In hot reformations, in what men, more zealous than considerate, call *making clear work,* the whole is generally so crude, so harsh, so indigested; mixed with so much imprudence, and so much injustice; so contrary to the whole course of human nature and human institutions, that the very people who are most eager for it are among the first to grow disgusted at what they have done. Then some part of the abdicated grievance is recalled from its exile in order to become a corrective of the correction. Then the abuse assumes all the credit and popularity of a reform. The very idea of purity and disinterestedness in politics falls into disrepute, and is considered as a vision of hot and inexperienced men; and thus disorders become incurable, not by the virulence of their own quality, but by the unapt and violent nature of the remedies.[222]

The reformer of decorum negotiates the eternal gulf between the achieved and the undisclosed, between principle and circumstance, between the experienced and the emergent. He remembers that "human affairs and human actions" are "not of a metaphysical nature" but are "concrete, complex, and moral," and therefore "cannot be subjected (without exceptions which reduce it almost to nothing) to any certain rule." [223] Though the excellence of metaphysics or mathematics may be to have but one thing before you, "he forms the best judgment in all moral disquisitions, who has the greatest number and variety of considerations in one view before him, and can take them in with the best possible consideration of the middle results of all." [224]

That is, to determine such a decorum is the office of prudence—not "that little, selfish, pitiful, bastard thing, which sometimes goes by the name," but long-sighted, strong-nerved, "public and enlarged prudence," [225] weighing suffering against suffering, balancing goods and evils in their degrees, withholding "thoughts, not yet fully ripened," [226] staying open to the unguessed, and proceeding throughout upon "principles of research" to get information, on "principles of method to regulate it; and on principles in the human mind and in civil affairs to secure and perpetuate the operation." [227] Burke did not wish to be like "many who choose to chicane with their situation, rather than be instructed by it." [228] On the contrary, he said, "It is right to consider, to look about us, to examine the effect of what we have done—then we can proceed with confidence, because we can proceed with intelligence." [229] To enact such a decorum is the office of temperance. "As it is the interest of government that reformation should be early, it is the interest of the people that it should be temperate. It is their interest, because a temperate reform is permanent; and because it has a principle of growth. Whenever we improve, it is right to leave room for a further improvement." [230] For this reason he constructed his reform "to operate gradually; and some benefits will come at a nearer, some at a more remote period." Also, he added, "we must no more make haste to be rich by parsimony than by intemperate acquisition." He aimed at a final system in which not only corruption would be reduced (though he had no fatuous dream of eliminating it, vices in government will always be) but also its temptation lessened; and therefore, Burke added, even if many high officers should volunteer to serve without salary they ought not to be allowed:

Ordinary service must be secured by the motives to ordinary integrity. I do not hesitate to say, that that state, which lays its foundation in rare and heroic virtue, will be sure to have its superstructure in the basest profligacy and corruption. An honourable and fair profit is the best security against avarice and rapacity; as in all things else, a lawful and regulated enjoyment is the best security against debauchery and excess. For as wealth is power, so all power will infallibly draw wealth to itself by some means or other; and when men are left no way of ascertaining their profits but by their means of obtaining them, those means will be increased to infinity.[231]

And finally, restraining his reform, and shooting critical light upon it from every angle, should be justice: if he could not reform with equity, he would not reform at all.[232]

# V

# Burke and the French Revolution

IN his private war with the French Revolution, Burke was not the aggressor. Three weeks after the Bastille had fallen, he found himself like the most of England "gazing with astonishment at a French struggle for liberty, and not knowing whether to blame or to applaud."

> The thing, indeed, though I thought I saw something like it in progress for several years, has still somewhat in it paradoxical and mysterious. The spirit it is impossible not to admire; but the old Parisian ferocity has broken out in a shocking manner. It is true, that this may be no more than a sudden explosion; if so, no indication can be taken from it; but if it should be *character,* rather than accident, then that people are not fit for liberty, and must have [that is, end up in subjection to] a strong hand, like that of their former masters, to coerce them. . . . What will be the event, it is hard, I think, still to say. To form a solid constitution requires wisdom as well as spirit; and whether the French have wise heads among them, or if they possess such, whether they have authority equal to their wisdom, is yet to be seen.[1]

He busied himself collecting documents from every source he could, but a month later he was still unwilling to be "too ready in forming a positive opinion upon matters transacted in a country, with the correct political map of which I must be very imperfectly acquainted." [2] His suspicion had sharpened, however, that the proclaimers of liberty at Paris were not yet free from "the worst of all slavery,—that is, the despotism of their own blind and brutal passions." [3] According to Prior, he resolved to write out his thoughts about this time, and the *Reflections on the Revolution in France,* published a year later (November 1790) after more than a dozen revisions,[4] images the hesitant progress of his thinking during the year. An undoubted masterwork, by general consensus Burke's greatest single production, the *Reflections* is not, however, an exhaustive, or in several important respects, even a representative statement of what he perceived in the Revolution. The purely quantitative fact is that during the next seven years, until his death in 1797, Burke spun out more single tracts, on a variety of topics, than during any other decade of his life (the only rival being the 1770's) and that most of them dealt with the French Revolution. The *Reflections* is just what its title implies, a catalogue of second thoughts; their range and density is very much extended in the brilliant series of pamphlets and letters succeeding: *An Appeal from the New to the Old Whigs, Thoughts on French Affairs,* and *A Letter to a Member of the National Assembly,* all in 1791; *Heads for Consideration on the Present State of Affairs* (1792), culminating in the more explicit *Remarks on the Policy of the Allies with Respect to France* (1793); the *Preface to the Address of M. Brissot to his Constituents* (1794); the sparkling (and too little anthologized) *Letter to William Elliot* (1795); the *Letter to a Noble Lord* (1795), and, most important of all, the four *Letters on a Regicide Peace* (1795–1797). To these should be added a copious outside correspondence and many related passages in other pamphlets and letters concerning Ireland, Parliamentary and party affairs.

This is the perennial problem and pleasure in studying someone like Burke whose perceptions are always developing in relation to new experience: who looks now at one side, now at another, and yet is always moving forward; who digresses, circles back, inverts, strikes out anew, takes advantage of inchoate impressions, indulges rhetoric for the sake of latent intuitive relations which otherwise would escape notice, and, in short, accepts the practical implications—as Hume did not—of an empirical view of history and society, to be contingent, many-sided, and penetrative. A statement of his general principles will not fix the limits of his perceptions, which reappearing in familiar guise seem always edging toward something else. Burke's most complicated and imaginative perception about the Revolution—its religiosity and its portent for Europe—is not developed in the *Reflections* at all, though implicit in casual suggestion. The *Reflections,* however, states several themes and attitudes that are essential in his whole approach during the following seven years and that ought to be stated first with regard to the whole.

Burke had imagined the quality of life flowing from the social structure of pre-revolutionary France more ably than is sometimes assumed, though it is true that he had little patience with the revolutionary *mystique*. From a variety of causes, the state had ossified in rigid class interests generating envies and rival prides.[5] Not the least of these causes was a vast national debt and a superannuated tax system which Burke believed the most oppressive and justly resented part of the French government.[6] In 1769, only four years after entering Parliament, he had studied the French financial system with the amazing foresight that one should "look hourly for some extraordinary convulsion in that whole system; the effect of which on France, and even on all Europe, it is difficult to conjecture." [7] As chief agent of civil-list reform in England, Burke had learned what absurdities could accumulate in time. Twenty years later the convulsion came to pass, and to the tangled unreason of the economy he attributed a large share in the growth of vice-ridden factions. France, he knew, had never enjoyed a liberal Whig movement; and by a "fatal error" the newly apparent moneyed interests, the middle-class *nouveau riche,* had not been assimilated to the government, as they had been in England.[8] In consequence, Burke said:

The middle classes had swelled far beyond their former proportion. Like whatever is the most effectively rich and great in society, these classes became the seat of all the active politics. . . . There were all the talents which assert their pretensions, and are impatient of the place which settled society prescribes to them. These descriptions had got between the great and the populace; and influence on the lower classes was with them. The spirit of ambition had taken possession of this class as violently as ever it had done of any other. They felt the importance of this situation. The correspondence of the monied and the mercantile world, the literary intercourse of academies, but above all, the press, of which they had in a manner entire possession, made a kind of electric communication everywhere. The press in reality has made every government, in its spirit, almost democratic. Without it the great, the first movements in this Revolution could not, perhaps, have been given.[9]

Against these insurgent facts of history, the spirit of Louis XIV and ancient France continued uncompromising: the same splendor in letters and war, but also the same enfeeblement by one-man rule, persecution, legislative artifice, sycophancy, and ostentation: the same unwieldy and topheavy state which he had left as an inheritance, repressive and factious—the state which chased Voltaire all over Europe. Almost everyone agreed, Burke felt, that a severe, rigorous, and systematic reform was a clear and present necessity. But he would not admire "the change of one piece of barbarism for another, and a worse." [10] The French had to face up to their problems realistically; otherwise the ancient France—"its iron frontier; its spirit of ambition; it audacity of enterprise; its perplexing intrigue"—would return to haunt them.[11]

Burke hoped for a bloodless "revolution" comparable to that in England in 1688; part of his bitter sorrow in the real French Revolution grew from his disappointed comparison. To the end he believed in a missed opportunity, in the possibility in 1789 of reform in the British manner. Some "spirit of reform" had prevailed throughout the reign of Louis XVI,[12] and representatives of the *ancien régime* who met at Versailles in 1789, when for the first time in 175 years the king convoked the States-General, breathed a warm spirit of liberty. They were not Orsinis and Vitellis, Nayres, or Mamelukes, robbers sallying from their fortified dens.

Their privileges relative to contribution were voluntarily surrendered; as the king, from the beginning, surrendered all pretence to a right of taxation. Upon a free constitution there was but one opinion in France. The absolute monarchy was at an end. It breathed its last, without a groan, without struggle, without convulsion. All the struggle, all the dissension, arose afterwards upon the preference of a despotic democracy to a government of reciprocal control. The triumph of the victorious party was over the principles of a British constitution.[13]

Burke's opinion of the Revolution cannot be detached from his belief that the minds of Frenchmen had been prepared, that the time was ripe for intelligent and permanent reform. The general theme of the *Reflections* was a comparison of "the principles of the National Assembly" with those of the British constitution "as practically they exist." [14] "You possessed in some parts," he admonished the French, "the walls, and, in all, the foundations, of a noble and venerable castle. You might have repaired those walls; you might have built on those old foundations."

In your old states you possessed that variety of parts corresponding with the various descriptions of which your community was happily composed; you had all that combination, and all that opposition of interests, you had that action and counteraction, which, in the natural and in the political world, from the reciprocal struggle of discordant powers, draws out of the harmony of the universe. These opposed and conflicting interests . . . render deliberation a matter not of choice, but of necessity; they make all change a subject of *compromise,* which naturally begets moderation; they produce *temperaments.*[15]

The states of Christendom, Burke believed, with all their complicated classes, orders, and distinctions, had "grown up to their present magnitude in a great length of time, and by a great variety of accidents,"[16] without any regular plan or unity in design, from "the old Germanic or Gothic custumary, from the feudal institutions which must be considered as an emanation from that custumary; and the whole has been improved and digested into system and discipline by the Roman law."[17] With or without a monarchy intervening, they had been improved as separate nations with greater and lesser degrees of felicity and skill, but none of them directed "to any *peculiar* end," that is, none of them designed upon a theory of their purpose. "The objects [purposes] which they embrace are of the greatest possible variety, and have become in a manner infinite. In all these old countries, the state has been made to the people, and not the people conformed to the state." The British state pursued the greatest variety of ends and was "least disposed to sacrifice any one of them to another, or to the whole."[18] "We have always cautiously felt our way. The parts of our constitution have gradually, and almost insensibly, in a long course of time, accommodated themselves to each other, and to their common, as well as to their separate purposes. But this adaptation of contending parts, as it has not been in ours, so it can never be . . . in any country, the effect of a single instantaneous regulation."[19] It made some approach to "taking in the entire circle of human desires, and securing for them their fair enjoyment"; its legislature was more closely connected also with "individual feeling, and individual interest"; sometimes it felt "the perplexity of an immense body of balanced advantages, and of individual demands, and of some irregularity in the whole mass."[20] But throughout Europe Burke sensed a similitude of religion, laws, and manners, that at bottom was the same—"a commonwealth . . . virtually one great state, having the same basis of general law, with some diversity of provincial customs and local establishments."[21] A "system of manners and of education" similar in all countries "softened, blended, and harmonized the colours of the whole," in universities, in sciences and the "more liberal and elegant kinds of erudition," "in the whole form and fashion of life"; "no citizen of Europe could be altogether an exile in any part of it."[22]

Men are not tied to one another by papers and seals. They are led to associate by resemblances, by conformities, by sympathies. It is with nations as with individuals. Nothing is so strong a tie of amity between nation and nation as correspondence in laws, customs, manners, and habits of life. They have more than the force of treaties in themselves. They are obligations written in the heart. They approximate men to men, without their knowledge, and sometimes against their intentions. The secret, unseen, but irrefragable bond of habitual intercourse holds them together, even when their perverse and litigious nature sets them to equivocate, scuffle, and fight, about the terms of their written obligations.[23]

Assuming this prescriptive base in France, the "riches of convention" [24] and positive materials of European and latently classical-Christian culture, Burke assumed also the desirability of building upon it, of improving it further, as it had been improved in England, by a long-term realism:

Political arrangement, as it is a work for social ends, is to be only wrought by social means. There mind must conspire with mind. Time is required to produce that union of minds which alone can produce all the good we aim at. Our patience will achieve more than our force. . . . By a slow but well-sustained progress, the effect of each step is watched; the good or ill success of the first gives light to us in the second; and so, from light to light, we are conducted with safety through the whole series. We see that the parts of the system do not clash. The evils latent in the most promising contrivances are provided for as they arise. One advantage is as little as possible sacrificed to another. We compensate, we reconcile, we balance. We are enabled to unite into a consistent whole the various anomalies and contending principles that are found in the minds and affairs of men. From hence arises, not an excellence in simplicity, but one far superior, an excellence in composition. Where the great interests of mankind are concerned through a long succession of generations, that succession ought to be admitted into some share in the councils which are so deeply to affect them. If justice requires this, the work itself requires the aid of more minds than one age can furnish.[25]

Not that he expected the French "commonwealth" to model itself as a replica of the English. On the contrary, Burke said, a year before the *Reflections:*

> The same object may be attained in many ways, and perhaps in ways very different from those which we have followed in this country. If this real *practical* liberty, with a government powerful to protect, impotent to evade it, be established, or is in a fair train of being established in the democracy, or rather collection of democracies, which seem to be chosen for the future frame of society in France, it is not my having long enjoyed a sober share of freedom, under a qualified monarchy, that shall render me incapable of admiring and praising your system or republics. I should rejoice, even though England . . . should no longer retain her proud distinction, her monopoly of fame.[26]

Thus Burke's study of the old France convinced him that despite its palpable flaws it had also latent excellences which an intelligent reform would release and improve. The question, however, seemed to be not upon the vices of the old order, but upon its existence.[27]

Revolutionaries do not reform. Generally speaking, Burke said, the revolutionaries began by despising all that belonged to them, as if they could safely throw out history and begin anew, and they found their punishment in their success.[28] Instead of making the best of what they had, instead of shaping out gradually and laboriously the latent particular constitution that could go some way toward harmonizing all the various interests for the common good, the "alchemistical legislators" of the National Assembly confounded all men into "one homogeneous mass," then tried to reconstruct the state by an *a priori* logic. With "the metaphysics of an undergraduate" and "the arithmetic of an exciseman," they divided "their amalgama" into arbitrary departments and thus reduced living, various men, with living and various possibilities, to "loose counters, merely for the sake of simple telling." "The troll of their categorical table might have informed them that there was something else in the intellectual world besides *substance* and *quantity*"—that is, the rest of Aristotle's categories: quality, relation, place, time, action, affectivity, state or position. But they ran roughshod over actual circumstances of actual men, while the economist, "subliming himself into an airy metaphysician, was resolved to know nothing of his flocks but as men in general." [29] The excuse of "the geometrical policy" was that "all local ideas should be sunk, and that the people should be no longer Gascons, Picards, Bretons, Normans; but Frenchmen, with one country, one heart, and one Assembly." But Burke rightly distrusted a metaphysical nationalism forced from without; the reality of the particular cannot very long be overridden without an explosive recoil whose consequences are beyond imagination:

> No man ever was attached by a sense of pride, partiality, or real affection, to a description of square measurement. He never will glory in belonging to the Chequer No. 71, or to any other badge-ticket. We begin our public affections in our families. No cold relation is a zealous citizen. We pass on to our neighbourhoods, and our habitual provincial connections. These are inns and resting-places. Such divisions of our country as have been formed by habit, and not by a sudden jerk of authority, were so many little images of the great country in which the heart found something which it could fill. The love to the whole is not extinguished by this subordinate partiality. . . . the citizens are interested from old prejudices and unreasoned habits, and not on account of the geometric properties of its figure. The power and pre-eminence of Paris does certainly press down and hold these republics together as long as it lasts. But, for the reasons I have already given you, I think it cannot last very long.[30]

They would soon have no country, no "moral France"—only a theatricality of abstraction floating in a void of cynical *Realpolitik.*

The sort of civil gradualism which Burke held out to French study is shown by his discussion of a crime with which older English history was also spotted—the confiscation and destruction of monasteries. (Of course, Burke deplored it in England as well as in France: like a good Whig he detested Henry VIII as "one of the most decided tyrants in the rolls of history.") [31]

Conceding for the sake of argument that monasteries "savour of superstition" and "nourish it by a permanent and standing influence," [32] Burke pointed also to the positive worth in society of fifty thousand men whose revenues take a public direction in the accumulation of libraries, specimen collections, art objects, the repair and decoration of monuments and churches, and the cultivation of the soil; [33] who are "wholly set apart and dedicated to public purposes"; who have renounced personal wealth and "whose avarice is for some community"; [34] whom "the fictions of a pious imagination raise to dignity." [35] Their corporate dedication, discipline, habits, funds—"in vain shall a man look to the possibility of making such things when he wants them. The winds blow as they list. These institutions are the products of enthusiasm; they are the instruments of wisdom. Wisdom cannot create materials; they are the gifts of nature or of chance; her pride is in the use." [36] Such corporate bodies, Burke said, perennially existing, are susceptible of reform by a politician who understands his trade. To make any improvement in the state when it is needed, he looks for "a *power,* what our workmen call a *purchase,*" predisposed social materials equal and congenial to the specific public uses he contrives for them. Meditating "designs that require time in fashioning, and which propose duration when they are accomplished," he never thinks of destroying "any power growing wild from the rank productive force of the human mind," any more than he would destroy, if he could, the power of steam, or of electricity, or of magnetism. "These energies always existed in nature [or, in the case of monasteries, in European history], and they were always discernible. They seemed, some of them, unserviceable, some noxious, some no better than a sport to children; until contemplative ability, combining with practical skill, tamed their wild nature, subdued them to use, and rendered them at once the most powerful and the most tractable agents, in subservience to the great views and designs of men." [37] As for their superstition, Burke said: a statesman making use of "the general energies of nature" has also to deal with men just as he finds them, in the rankness of their mixed and parti-colored growth, with all their "concomitant excellencies" and all their imperfections.[38] If he were forced to an unhappy choice between "fond attachment and fierce antipathy," between "the ancient founders of monkish superstition, and the superstition of the pretended philosophers of the hour," as agitated by "the immoderate vulgar" on both sides, he inclined to favor the superstition that builds, adorns, restrains itself, and "disposes to mistaken beneficence," than that which demolishes, deforms, and plunders.[39]

You derive benefits from many dispositions and many passions of the human mind, which are of as doubtful a colour, in the moral eye, as superstition itself. It was your business to correct and mitigate everything which was noxious in this passion, as in all the passions. But is superstition the greatest of all possible vices? In its possible excess I think it becomes a very great evil. It is, however, a moral subject; and of course admits of all degrees and all modifications. Superstition is the religion of feeble minds; and they must be tolerated in an intermixture of it, in some trifling or some enthusiastic shape or other, else you will deprive weak minds of a resource found necessary to the strongest.[40]

Similarly, Burke protested abolition of the old local parliaments, which, needing alterations, "had particulars in their constitution, and those not a few, which deserved approbation from the wise. They possessed one fundamental excellence; they were independent. . . . They composed permanent bodies politic, constituted to resist arbitrary innovation; and from that corporate constitution, and from most of their forms, they were well calculated to afford both certainty and stability to the laws. They had been a safe asylum to secure those laws, in all the revolutions of humour and opinion. They had saved that sacred deposit of the country during the reigns of arbitrary princes, and the struggles of arbitrary factions. They kept alive the memory and record of the constitution." [41] On the same grounds, of reforming conservatism, Burke argued against demolition of the French nobility. Conceding the existence of vices which ought to be corrected, and frailties which ought to be discouraged, Burke observed also that a nobility "forms the chain that connects the ages of a nation," and it is one objection to all new-fabricated republics "that the *prejudice* of an old nobility is a thing that *cannot* be made. It may be improved, it may be corrected, it may be replenished: men may be taken from it or aggregated to it, but the *thing itself* is matter of *inveterate* opinion, and therefore *cannot* be matter of mere positive institution." [42] When the thing itself is eradicated, the benefits possible from it are eradicated too. And beyond recovery. "If anything is, one more than another, out of the power of man, it is to *create* a prejudice. Somebody has said that a king may make a nobleman, but he cannot make a gentleman." [43] The prejudice might be, and that in large measure, misdirected or ineffectual—Burke considered Spain "a nerveless country" because it "does not possess the use, it only suffers the abuse of a nobility" [44]—but again it is one thing to contrive a propriety of restraints and uses and quite another to slay the mind of a country,[45] to brutalize a country, by erasing the variety of ways of life generated within it. This is the objective perception which underlies, in the *Reflections,* the glowingly heroic, the notorious, and inevitably anthologized paean to Marie Antoinette:

It is now sixteen or seventeen years since I saw the Queen of France, then the dauphiness, at Versailles; and surely never lighted on this orb, which she hardly seemed to touch, a more delightful vision. I saw her just above the horizon, decorating and cheering the elevated sphere she just began to move in,–glittering like the morning star, full of life, and splendour, and joy. . . . little did I dream that I should have lived to see such disasters fallen upon her in a nation of gallant men, in a nation of men of honour, and of cavaliers. I thought ten thousand swords must have leaped from their scabbards to avenge even a look that threatened her with insult. But the age of chivalry is gone. That of sophisters, economists, and calculators, has succeeded; and the glory of Europe is extinguished for ever. Never, never more shall we behold that generous loyalty to rank and sex, that proud submission, that dignified obedience, that subordination of the heart, which kept alive, even in servitude itself, the spirit of an exalted freedom! The unbought grace of life, the cheap defence of nations, the nurse of manly sentiment and heroic enterprise, is gone! It is gone, that sensibility of principle, that chastity of honour, which felt a stain like a wound, which inspired courage whilst it mitigated ferocity, which ennobled whatever it touched, and under which vice itself lost half its evil, by losing all its grossness! [46]

To a private friend, Burke confessed to have wept while he wrote this section of the book,[47] and indeed the writing is heavily charged with sentiment; it is a model of propaganda become literature. Yet it is not merely a subjective, elegiac chant; and it is by no means an indiscriminate defense of the *ancien régime;* it has objective point. The fairy-tale queen is a polemic symbol of a "mixed system of opinion and sentiment" which, originating in "the ancient chivalry," and "varied in its appearance by the varying state of human affairs," subsisted *in principle* "through a long succession of generations," even until the eighteenth century, and distinguished the *character* of modern Europe, "under all its forms of government," from any other governments in human history.[48] That is, existing nobilities in Europe, whatever their defects and aberrations, helped to keep continuity with specific moral achievements of the European past—for example, with a body of manners and customary attitudes whose positive benefit to the French nation was literally incalculable, which "harmonized the different shades of life, and which, by a bland assimilation, incorporated into politics the sentiments which beautify and soften private society." How much these "superadded ideas of a moral imagination" contributed to the intellectual and practical happiness and progress of the nation, indeed of the world, "cannot possibly be estimated." Ironically enough, the "noble equality" which was handed down "through all the gradations" of French life (and helped to prepare the Revolution) derived historically from the attitudes of the aristocracy. All Burke could say with confidence was that, unless this "moral France" were kept intact, and the essential part of it conserved and diffused in public manners by the nobility, one of the fountains of life itself would be attacked, as by a palsy: [49] some kind of "barbarism" or dehumanization would succeed, in literature and art, in science, in law and politics, in all professions and trades. "Manners are of more importance than laws. Upon them, in a great measure, the laws depend. The law touches us but here and there, and now and then. Manners are what vex or soothe, corrupt or purify, exalt or debase, barbarize or refine us, by a constant, steady, uniform, insensible operation, like that of the air we breathe in. They give their whole form and colour to our lives. According to their quality, they aid morals, they supply them, or they totally destroy them." [50]

"There ought to be a system of manners in every nation," Burke believed, "which a well-formed mind would be disposed to relish. To make us love our country, our country ought to be lovely." But "that sort of reason which banishes the affections is incapable of filling their place." [51]

Therefore, in defending the French nobility (and monasteries and local parliaments and other "feudal" remains) Burke was holding by the general principle, which he felt to be illustrated most successfully in England: that European nations had improved, and endured because they were being improved, by a patient and endless reconciliation of their existing interests, each functioning in its peculiar and quasi-autonomous way, for the wealth of common actuality. The question, of course, hinged upon judgments of degree and relation. Burke could not bring himself to believe that the French nobility—hundreds of whom he knew and entertained at his own house—had sunk in such total depravity that its relation to French society as a whole was morbid beyond correction. If it were so depraved that it "disgraced, whilst it persecuted, human nature," then "too critical an inquiry might not be advisable into the means of freeing the world from such a nuisance." There might possibly come to pass, amid all the kaleidoscopic transformations of human misery, "the dreadful exigence" when morality would have to suspend its own rules in favor of its own principles.[52]

In blasting the National Assembly for confining the intellectual world to questions of substance and quantity, in his caustic taunts at sophisters, economists, and calculators, his Cassandra-cries of barbarism, and in turn his defense of clergy, nobility, and chivalric sensibility, Burke touched upon a contest of opposed doctrinairisms which would split open much of the nineteenth century and last into the twentieth, and which has delivered a false image of what he characteristically stood for. That is, the contest of exclusions between bulldozing metaphysicians and aesthetic gentlemen. It is one of the most difficult passages in Burke to keep in perspective and context, a touchstone of a reader's penetration. Burke, of course, was a humanist in politics (that is, one who refuses to divorce any political analysis from qualities of human will and character, and who sees political causes as terminating in these qualities as at their primary source of meaning). Generally speaking, he could not go along with the politics of metaphysical materialism which considers the moral and aesthetic achievements of particular men as only derivative surface, and political reality to lie in a conflict of impersonal forces to be grasped by the naked intellect and regulated from a systematic vantage. The Jacobins, Burke complained, "are always considering the formal distributions of power in a constitution: the moral basis they consider as nothing. Very different is my opinion: I consider the moral basis as everything; the formal arrangements, further than as they promote the moral principles of government, and the keeping desperately wicked persons as the subject of laws and not the makers of them, to be of little importance. What signifies the cutting and shuffling of cards, while the pack remains the same?" [53] Consequently, Burke usually arranged himself on the side of the moral and the aesthetic. It was this particular stand of his which led some circles to accept what is now the blind cliché verdict that he praised the plumage of European culture but forgot the dying bird (Paine's remark),[54] that he dearly loved a lord, Versailles, and the chivalry of fairy tales, and was blind to the facts of power. It is not true.

A glance at some praisers and detractors of the *Reflections* may suggest how the split between gentlemanly aesthetes and metaphysical rough-riders could shape up in Burke's own time. Praise often ran in a rut of misplaced, politically naive aestheticism, which anthologists perpetuate by focussing on the Marie Antoinette passage and its lofty pathos. Horace Walpole, for example, delectated by Burke's "wit and eloquence" and "enthusiasm," confessed an especial liking for his phrase "the swords leaping out of their scabbards." [55] It isn't a bad phrase. Richard Cumberland observed that when "he has roused us with the thunder of his eloquence, he can at once, Timotheus-like, choose a melancholy theme, and melt us into pity." [56] The Reverend Robert Hall, speaking of the "eulogium on the Queen of France," said that its images were so select, "so fraught with tenderness and so rich with colours 'dipt in heaven,' that he who can read it without rapture may have merit as a reasoner, but must resign all pretensions to taste and sensibility." [57] All this while Europe trembled on its axis. Burke's opponents, however, as he saw with horror, were almost invariably more trenchant, outfitted with arguments. Like Sir James Mackintosh, they accused Burke (wrongheadedly, but with a measure of truth) of arguing from "impressions" which "cannot be disputed, more especially when their grounds are not assigned"; [58] like Priestley, they accused him (wrongheadedly, but with a measure of truth) of more rhetoric than reason.[59] Burke grounded his "eloquent apology" for the French nobility and clergy, Mackintosh said, "purely on their *individual* and *moral character,"* which "is totally irrelative to the question." [60] Irrelative indeed! to one who has shut out the relations. Instead, Burke should have spoken of "their *political* and *collective* character" by which Mackintosh means "a body which it is politic to dissolve"—that is, instead of seeing it as it really was, Burke ought to have riveted his vision to an abstract idea of its malignity as a power structure. (The fact is that Burke does speak of the nobility, the monasteries, and others, as corporations and as powers, but the idea of *power* has relative and particularized meanings for him that it does not generally have for his opponents.) They all, Burke complained, liked to talk amorally about *power,* or some transmogrification of it like *liberty* ("liberty, when men act in bodies, is *power*," [61] Burke reminded them), "on a simple view of the object, as it stands stripped of every relation, in all the nakedness and solitude of metaphysical abstraction" [62]—especially power as tending in history. Mackintosh, for example, dropped the blanket hint that "Church power (unless some Revolution, auspicious to Priestcraft, should replunge Europe in ignorance) will certainly not survive the nineteenth century." [63] Priestley, balancing abstraction against abstraction, spoke broadcast of "the spirit of reformation, which is now gone forth" as *"another great power,* as well as the *existing systems* to be reformed by it; and it is a power which grows stronger as they grow weaker." [64] A widening split, between the moral-aesthetic and the metaphysical as exclusive categories of political judgment, reaches expression in a baffling multitude of ways, at points interlocking and breaking like lights in a fog, and the Marie Antoinette passage has become famous largely because, in a moment of passionate excess, it catches the spirit which the antithesis would assume in the next century, in brief and striking exaggeration.

But here as elsewhere, it violates the character of Burke's thought and sensibility to squeeze him out of his century—to see him, for example, as a precursor of nineteenth-century medievalism, without careful distinction of the narrow limits within which this is true. It is too easy to superimpose upon Burke an *ex post facto* contempt or admiration, to appropriate to him some one or another cluster of prejudices that really belong to Scott, or Newman, or DeMaistre, or Chateaubriand, or Ruskin, or T. S. Eliot, or any others who, each in his own peculiar fashion, have found themselves an exponent of the medieval or of some affiliated sympathy like "literary Catholicism," and at the same time an irritated enemy of one or another "barbarism" or "mechanic philosophy." (The quotation marks are not sneers: they indicate only that aesthetic attitudes of this character are defined by their relation to one another.) Not to deny the possibility of abstracting a likeness; the question will still remain to what degree the likeness is fundamental or essential and how it is modified by the presence of other practical sympathies and commitments. In the *Reflections* Burke deliberately, with rhetorical calculation, set out to highlight feudal elements in the eighteenth-century state in order to correct an excessive assumption that they were altogether and without discrimination malign or superannuated or valueless. A distempered climate of opinion gave him the materials of his rhetoric ready-conditioned: *feudal* (or Gothic), with all its erratic association of chivalry, aristocracy, religion, hierarchical society, and the past, was fixed in polar opposition to *enlightened,* with its clustered association of reason, modernity, philosophy, humanity, and natural rights. The opposition appears later, for example, in Marx,[65] and is still one of the fossils with which Communist propaganda wires up its monsters. Burke calculatedly set his tone and shaped his argument in favor of "feudality," as a decade earlier, in his speech on economical reform, he had taken an exactly opposite stance. He preferred neither and valued both. Ancient institutions, manners, and opinions, he said, are the supports of life, and if they are lost, "from that moment we have no compass to govern us; nor can we know distinctly to what port we steer"; [66] but, also, to preserve an establishment when its reason is lost is superstitiously to embalm a carcass not worth preserving.[67] In the reform speech, Burke had drawn satirical imagery from the palette of the "Dark Ages"—ghosts and shadows, superstition, original sin, scutcheons and knight-errantry, ballad-writing, legalism, *Preux Chevalier,* "foolish mystery," royal masquerade and punctilio, strolling players. A decade later, in the *Reflections,* he reversed himself rhetorically by making sardonic references to "the little glimmerings of reason which might break in upon the solid darkness of this enlightened age," [68] by praising the English constitution as a venerable castle and English liberty as an atmosphere dignified by armorial bearings,[69] and by referring contemptuously to the "aëronauts of France" and "their desperate flights." [70] It is easy to be deceived by his rhetorical tacking back and forth across an ideological chasm which it was one by-result of the revolutionary movement to crack open and establish. One ought not to mistake a rhetorical *modus vivendi,* written in hot tears to counter a vicious extreme, for an essential commitment to the opposite extreme. It was a mistake avoided by Gibbon, who, preferring to see "superstition" in Burke's reverence for the church establishment, was not so gross as to let it blind him to the spirit and context of the whole.[71] Significantly, the great historian of "barbarism and Christianity" agreed with Burke's analysis and condemnation of the French Revolution, and even pointed to *The Decline and Fall* as his own unintentional but corroborative commentary.[72] Burke was about as uncritically committed to the medieval as Gibbon was to the Age of the Antonines—that is, not at all; he had the warm, contingent appreciation of a man in the act of a tremendous intellectual recovery.

Burke was interested in the medieval as a practical, present legacy, of manners, principles, sentiments, laws, and institutions, which were part, but not all, of the given "powers" or moral materials which it was politic both to acknowledge, in all their cooperative degrees of good and ill, and to govern with a view to increasing their proportion of good.

To a man who acts under the influence of no passion, who has nothing in view in his projects but the public good, a great difference will immediately strike him between what policy would dictate on the original introduction of such institutions, and on a question of their total abolition, where they have cast their roots wide and deep, and where, by long habit, things more valuable than themselves are so adapted to them, and in a manner interwoven with them, that the one cannot be destroyed without notably impairing the other. He might be embarrassed if the case were really such as sophisters represent it in their paltry style of debating. But in this, as in most questions of state, there is a middle. There is something else than the mere alternative of absolute destruction, or unreformed existence. *Spartam nactus es; hanc exorna.*[73]

Instead of contemplating his country either metaphysically or romantically "as nothing but *carte blanche,* upon which he may scribble whatever he pleases," a competent politician "always considers how he shall make the most of the existing materials of his country. A disposition to preserve, and an ability to improve, taken together, would be my standard of a statesman. Everything else is vulgar in the conception, perilous in the execution." [74] Thus, Burke's "medievalism" is hardly more than a polemic emphasis against a crusading anti-medievalism. He may suggest someone like Scott or Newman mainly in his willingness to consider the "Middle Ages" seriously as part of the continuum of European civilization, whose depositions are essential to its character, not indiscriminately bad. His thinking, however, is hard against any kind of aestheticsm in politics that is basically a lust, the single-minded nostalgia for a lost past (or a lost church, or a lost nature), deaf to practical necessities and to the ordinary means of tranquillity that lie within sensible reach. He was at home in his century, though—like any sane person—objecting to abuses when he saw them. Burke may also suggest Scott or Newman in his sympathetic perception of the value, not just the picturesqueness, of a variety of local and national manners and customs, especially "interior" manners as embodying unique cultural achievements, which it is part of the fate, and may become the good fortune of a state or a civilization to contain and perpetuate, and which ought not to be destroyed. But even here, Burke has a kind of healthy, somehow eighteenth-century, good-natured, and worldly common sense, which is distinctive. Everybody knows the story (which is true) of the two unhappy Brahmins whom Burke found in London, estranged and embarrassed by their manners. Shocked by their having been snubbed, he asked them home as guests of the family, and gave them his greenhouse for a retreat where they could cook their special food and perform their strange ablutions and rites in privacy and as they pleased. As Augustine Birrell pointed out, it is hard in this instance to "fancy Cardinal Newman peeping through a window" with much pleasure.[75] But as Burke put it, "It was nothing more than the duty which one man owed to another." [76]

Burke was incapable of binding his perceptions and grounding his politics upon some species of romantic adulation of a former age or of former manners, indifferent to the actual and particular distribution, operation, and possibility, of power in relation to living manners. It is hard to find in his writing an exact refutation of something which was not to be full-blown (and gaseous) till after his death, but the whole drift of his career is against it. History, he said, is a liberalizing discipline, but it ought not to turn the understanding of a statesman "from the present exigencies of the world, to comparisons with former times, of which, after all, we can know very little and very imperfectly."

If a man with reasonably good parts and natural sagacity, and not in the leading-strings of any master, will look steadily on the business before him, without being diverted by retrospect and comparison, he may be capable of forming a reasonably good judgment of what is to be done.[77]

He ridiculed the "panegyrical declamations, in which some persons would persuade us that the crude institutions" of the remote past "had attained a height, which the united efforts of necessity, learning, inquiry, and experience, can hardly reach to in many ages." [78] He remarked the "vanity common to all nations" which leads them to invent "a very extravagant antiquity." [79] Commenting on the Magna Charta, which he considered an epochal but very limited historical document, Burke observed that one of the better results of its clauses was to prevent "the kingdom from degenerating into the worst imaginable government,—a feudal aristocracy." [80]

But he was equally incapable of admitting a politics split off from the moral and aesthetic and, with its metaphysical grapeshot, waging a frantic and obtuse war against them—for example, a politics armed with ideas of *power* and *rights* and *reason* and *liberty* and historical tendency, all in substantial and quantitative abstraction from quality, relation, place, time, action, affectivity, state or position.

The nature of man is intricate; the objects of society are of the greatest possible complexity: and therefore no simple disposition or direction of power can be suitable either to man's nature or to the quality of his affairs. When I hear the simplicity of contrivance aimed at and boasted of in any new political constitutions, I am at no loss to decide that the artificers are grossly ignorant of their trade, or totally negligent of their duty. The simple governments are fundamentally defective, to say no worse of them. If you were to contemplate society in but one point of view, all these simple modes of polity are infinitely captivating. In effect each would answer its single end much more perfectly than the more complex is able to attain all its complex purposes. But it is better that the whole should be imperfectly and anomalously answered, than that, while some parts are provided for with great exactness, others might be totally neglected, or perhaps materially injured, by the over-care of a favourite member.[81]

Burke was no enemy to metaphysics as such, nor to any of its derivations like *power*-analysis as such (*power* is a basic concept in most English philosophies—Bacon, Hobbes, Locke, Hume, Whitehead—for it is logically the matrix of *actuality,* the characteristic concern of English thinking, including Burke's). He knew that "a certain *quantum* of power must always exist in the community, in some hands, and under some appellation," [82] and also that since "it is not necessary to teach men to thirst after power," [83] the "due distribution" of power in a state is "a matter of the most delicate and complicated skill." [84]

Men love to hear of their power, but have an extreme disrelish to be told of their duty. This is of course; because every duty is a limitation of some power. Indeed, arbitrary power is so much to the depraved taste of the vulgar, of the vulgar of every description, that almost all the dissensions, which lacerate the commonwealth, are not concerning the manner in which it is to be exercised, but concerning the hands in which it is to be placed. Somewhere they are resolved to have it. Whether they desire it to be vested in the many or the few, depends with most men upon the chance which they imagine they themselves may have of partaking in the exercise of that arbitrary sway, in the one mode or in the other.[85]

What Burke objected to in the National Assembly was the intoxicating supposition that, having gathered power into their hands, presumably in behalf of "the people," they could then legislate a brave new world into existence, and if "necessary" by guillotining the former possessors of power. But this Burke argued is "attending only to the shell and husk of history."

> Those who will stand upon that elevation of reason, which places centuries under our eye, and brings things to the true point of comparison, which obscures little names, and effaces the colours of little parties, and to which nothing can ascend but the spirit and moral quality of human actions, will say to the teachers of Palais Royal,—The Cardinal of Lorraine was the murderer of the sixteenth century, you have the glory of being the murderers in the eighteenth; and this is the only difference between you. But history in the nineteenth century, better understood, and better employed, will, I trust, teach a civilized posterity to abhor the misdeeds of both these barbarous ages. . . . It will teach posterity not to make war upon either religion or philosophy, for the abuse which the hypocrites of both have made of the two most valuable blessings conferred upon us.[86]

Like the ablest critics, Burke realized that changes in the primary structure of power in society, as in the premises of a system of thought, have all-pervading consequences; they influence the whole aesthetic texture of conduct, taste, and opinion (though it does not necessarily follow, as Marx premised, that they create it). It is perfectly possible to dissolve a way of life by rooting up systematically the structure of power and principle upon which it rests; such "radical" changes, changes at the root, are perfectly adequate to disperse and disfigure (though not necessarily to eradicate). Burke disagreed, however, with the belief that their ramifications in fact can be controlled. It is not in human vision at once to set up a new power, operating on new principles, and also to know exactly what quality and way of life will flow from it. Everything good or bad must be referred to an actual context of particulars.

Obviously Burke saw feudal vestiges in France through very English spectacles. His avowed purpose was "to convey to a foreign people, not his own ideas, but the prevalent opinions and sentiments of a nation, renowned for wisdom, and celebrated in all ages for a well-understood and well-regulated love of freedom." [87] He knew himself that he had little concrete experience of French life in its whole spectrum; the principles he laid down were English principles; but they are not for this reason less wise, and applicable, nor was Burke less wise for stating them. It is not Burke's fault if the character and circumstances of the French people had decayed beyond the practicability of a political achievement like that in England. The *Reflections* is most important as a description of what the French Revolution was not, and therefore as a statement of what the principles growing out of the revolutionary era usually lack.

In his image of the English constitution which he held up for French instruction, Burke stressed, it is to be noticed, its "practical principles," its moral basis, deriving character from a persistent past, including but in no way contained by the medieval, and which is likely to escape the theorist's attention. He wanted especially to defend against shallow, schematic conceptions, popularized and *philosophiques,* of what English political achievements actually were like and of how they had come to pass, against what he called: "The counterfeit wares which some persons, by a double fraud, export to you in illicit bottoms, as raw commodities of British growth, though wholly alien to our soil, in order afterwards to smuggle them back again into this country, manufactured after the newest Paris fashion." [88] By the moral basis, he meant, most simply, the practical psyche—everything in the human mind (will, taste, affection, imagination, the virtues and vices, prejudice, feeling, national character) that is a qualifying relational context for human reason.

To begin with the least palpable and most indirect—taste and imaginative sympathies: James Russell Lowell was perhaps wiser than he intended to be when he indicted Burke for taking an aesthetic view of the state; [89] he was hasty in implying that any social and political allegiance—in its general contours, not in regard to a single judgment—can escape aesthetic conditioning. All political preference and perception transcending the merely tangible becomes ideal, and throws open vistas of indefiniteness which imagination, in the modes which custom and taste have familiarized, will in some degree qualify and fill. No reason is perfectly objective when turned upon human affairs: "There is nothing in the world so difficult as to put men in a state of judicial neutrality. A leaning there must ever be." [90] It is not surprising, for example, that the English constitution as Burke conceptualized it, in its arranged complexity of privilege and duty, should also have about it the elaborate symmetry of form which seems to have fascinated late eighteenth-century imagination. Burke is not, however, as Lowell wants to imply, a programmatic or tendentious aesthete; his politics is committed also to "objective" reason. He simply recognizes, in a commonsensical way, that taste, imagination, and ideal affection (or a dessication of it), are an essential part of human experience, and that in subtle ways they make up an atmosphere of the mind and character constantly selecting what experience will be available to reason about: they help "to regulate the human will and action." Therefore, though they are too personal and variable as a rule to be caught in the gross filter of law, and in a free country must always be, yet they enter into and define public manners, and often influence political perception and preference. "Taste and elegance, though they are reckoned only among the smaller and secondary morals, yet are of no mean importance in the regulation of life." [91] This is why a fruitful history of ideas, in politics or any other branch of human affairs, is relative to a history of taste, and the historiography relative to the taste of the historian. On analogous grounds, Burke thought it significant that in his own time, as "in the two last ages," the authors of "sound antiquity" were more generally read in England than on the continent.[92] On similar ground he attacked the influence of Rousseau, "the insane *Socrates* of the National Assembly"; [93] conceding that his writings (Burke refers to the *Confessions* and the *Nouvelle Éloise*) "contain observations which occasionally discover a considerable insight," [94] and that they are not "wholly destitute of just notions" as regards politics and education,

Burke yet concluded that "the *general spirit and tendency* of his works is mischievous." [95] They are without a "moral taste"; they are "indulgent to the peculiarities" of adolescents; [96] they are a handbook "in *the ethics of vanity*," [97] whose effect, transfused into the minds and manners of a reader, especially an immature reader who knows no better than to take Rousseau for a "moral hero," is to disguise "perfect depravity of sentiment" underneath "a style glowing, animated, enthusiastic" and sometimes "sublime," [98] to encourage a reader in principles whose practical drift is to make him "an artificial creature, with painted, theatric sentiments, fit to be seen by the glare of candle-light, and formed to be contemplated at a due distance." [99] And therefore these works present him with moral images of habits and sympathies—for example, as regards modes of courtship—which, *taken for models,* are more congenial to one train of political preference, perception, and reasoning, than to another. Sooner or later this makes a difference, especially in states where contrary models are feeble; and though taste, broadly conceived as an auxiliary part of morals, is very unlikely to *cause* a political opinion (the *post hoc, propter hoc* of the rigid censor), it is yet a factor, more important in one case than another, constantly at work, affecting human reason in politics as in all other human concerns. This is no reason for resisting everything that Rousseau has to say, and it does not justify persecution, which is never just, or an indiscriminate censorship (in Burke's eyes it justifies keeping Rousseau out of the hands of youth). It may justify an *ad hominem* (behavioral) criticism. Rousseau himself, Burke believed, would be "shocked at the practical phrensy" of his imitators.[100] Burke's censure assumes a relation of art and life that is not a necessary one, if there is such a thing as a necessary one, and that can be exaggerated (although does it not correspond with the way in which Rousseau was read? And is Burke not right in saying that "Rousseau is a moralist, or he is nothing"?).[101] Yet it illustrates the relation of probability, no less real for being indirect, secondary, and contingent, that he is willing to acknowledge as existing between taste—or "mental affinities, and elective affections"[102]—and political behavior. There is nothing mystical about all this: Burke was simply reapplying the old humanistic commonplace that example is the greatest instructor among men. For like reasons, he attacked the influence of libertine satirists of the *ancien régime* ("who would themselves be astonished if they were held to the letter of their own descriptions").

By listening only to these, your leaders regard all things only on the side of their vices and faults, and view those vices and faults under every colour of exaggeration. It is undoubtedly true, though it may seem paradoxical; but in general, those who are habitually employed in finding and displaying faults, are unqualified for the work of reformation: because their minds are not only unfurnished with patterns of the fair and good, but by habit they come to take no delight in the contemplation of those things. By hating vices too much, they come to love men too little.[103]

The general vulgarization of taste in France following 1789—the "shows and exhibitions, calculated to inflame and vitiate the imagination, and pervert the moral sense"—came to Burke as no surprise. "The whole drift of their [revolutionary] institution," he claimed, "is contrary to that of the wise legislators of all countries, who aimed at improving instincts into morals, and at grafting the virtues on the stock of the natural affections."[104] Casting off or polluting the graces to be gained from continuity with a long-cultivated past, whose advantages the common Englishman enjoyed, they ended by encouraging "an unfashioned, indelicate, sour, gloomy, ferocious medley of pedantry and lewdness; of metaphysical speculations blended with the coarsest sensuality."[105] They ended by worshipping, in the cathedral of Notre-Dame, under official state auspices, a prostitute dressed out in the tinsel finery of a Goddess of Reason.

A second part of the moral basis, more stable and determinate than taste and more direct in its political bearings, is old "prejudices," customs, and unreasoned habits. There is an element of freethinking cussedness in Burke's choice of the word "prejudice": he knew and disliked as much as anyone else the sick passions which can attach to *pseudodoxia epidemica*. One needs always to remember the context of polemics. As in his medievalism, so here also Burke was defending against an abusive extreme, a violent anti-Prejudice, a wild rejection under the phantasmic pretext of Prejudice of anything "irrational" that many of the revolutionaries, in the sweat of their philosophizing, happened not to like or to find an irritating obstacle to their systems and will. Here, as in the Marie Antoinette passage, is objective point, misted over slightly in wording, under the pressure of argument. Burke assumed that politics ought to be adjusted to human reason, but he argued that not everything in human behavior which appears at first glance to be unreasonable is determined to be so in practice: "because the real effects of moral causes are not always immediate; but that which in the first instance is prejudicial may be excellent in its remoter operation; and its excellence may arise even from the ill effects it produces in the beginning." [106]

Prejudices or "moral causes" of this sort can be particularized, of course, but to do so is an endless job: the particulars will vary from state to state, and from age to age within a state. In polemic heat Burke mentions fear of God, awe of kings, affection for parliaments, duty to magistrates, reverence for priests, respect for nobility [107]—and this is an adequate example so long as one remembers the revolutionary credo he is defending against. Such prejudices also would include, however, the preference for monogamy, the idea of a liberty inseparable from justice, and indeed the whole synergy of ideas, values, and predispositions operating silently at the base of human behavior in a particular society. Burke seems to have worked out something like the sociologist's idea of "culture," and in his defense of prejudice he was warning against the folly of overlooking, discounting, or rejecting those aspects of cultural behavior which do not slide neatly into a logical scheme.

Terms for describing these interpenetrative modes of psyche must be relative—prejudices, customs, habits: they are the "motives" which put a particular train of reasoning into action, and also the "affections" which give it permanence; [108] they are "inbred sentiments," [109] they are "the superadded ideas, furnished from the wardrobe of a moral imagination, which the heart owns, and the understanding ratifies"; [110] they are the "habits which are communicated by the circumstances of civil life." [111] They make up the whole formative and operating inheritance which "previously engages the mind in a steady course . . . and does not leave the man hesitating in the moment of decision, skeptical, puzzled, and unresolved." [112] *Prejudice* is a useful name for talking about them all.

Prejudice, however, is not just feeling: it is feeling in which a kind of reason is latent; it is the practical terminus of a train of reasoning, perhaps long and involved, which is not immediately evident. "Many of our men of speculation," Burke said, describing a type of English intellectual and scholar, "instead of exploding general prejudices, employ their sagacity to discover the latent wisdom which prevails in them," for in doing so they are making conscious and applicable in the present moment an essential derivation of experience from the past. "If they find what they seek, and they seldom fail, they think it more wise to continue the prejudice, with the reason involved, than to cast away the coat of prejudice, and to leave nothing but the naked reason" [113]—for in finding the reason they effected their purpose, which was not to destroy but to continue, integrate, and enrich, to make more effectively understood what in the fret of time is always tending to slip out of understanding. But a very great deal of this collective wisdom and virtue—or, as it may come to pass, absurdity and vice—must continue in the latency towards which it is always returning. It is simply a fact, whether one likes it or not, that large masses of judgment, partiality, attachment, and affection, have to operate without reflective analysis: nobody in politics or elsewhere can afford to epistemologize before the taking of every toast and tea. And in these masses of prejudged, settled, tentatively completed reasoning, along with much undoubted foolishness, is also to be found the actual springs of a political and social mechanism.

It is this refined perception, not a brash chauvinism, which moves Burke to panegyrize English character—that is, "the opinions and dispositions generally prevalent in England":

We still bear the stamp of our forefathers. We have not (as I conceive) lost the generosity and dignity of thinking of the fourteenth century; nor as yet have we subtilized ourselves into savages. . . . We have not been drawn and trussed, in order that we may be filled, like stuffed birds in a museum, with chaff and rags, and paltry blurred shreds of paper about the rights of man. We preserve the whole of our feelings still native and entire, unsophisticated by pedantry and infidelity. . . . You see, Sir, that in this enlightened age I am bold enough to confess, that we are generally men of untaught feelings; that instead of casting away all our old prejudices, we cherish them to a very considerable degree, and, to take more shame to ourselves, we cherish them because they are prejudices; and the longer they have lasted, and the more generally they have prevailed, the more we cherish them. We are afraid to put men to live and trade each on his own private stock of reason; because we suspect that this stock in each man is small, and that the individuals would do better to avail themselves of the general bank and capital of nations and ages. . . . Prejudice renders a man's virtue his habit, and not a series of unconnected acts. Through just prejudice his duty becomes a part of his nature.[114]

To give an example: one such prejudice was behind the church establishment. Institutional arrangements like the Anglican Church, which a human being grows up with, he may or may not conclude to be salutary, but he can hardly dismiss them as reasonless: they are implicitly ratiocinative; they embody prior efforts of judgment, grasp, and appropriation, which, although blurring out as the moments when they are conceived—1612, or 1801, or 2078—fade into history, continue nevertheless as *latent* explanations and causes for the institutions they build or conserve. The ratiocination may be awry or illusory, or being just at one time may ill suit the needs of another time, but reasoning it remains, and as reasoning it ought to be dealt with. So far Burke and the revolutionaries could agree. But Burke would go on to argue that such "institutional reason," though it can and ought to be corrected *in the particulars* of any inconvenience or vice obviously proceeding from it, is not easily to be judged in its fundamentals, because the experience out of which it grows, and against which the adequacy of its reason would have to be tested, is not to be had by a single man, and scarcely if at all by a whole generation: it accommodates a practical infinity of experiences which, in the probable course of affairs, no one man can even come close to acquiring, and therefore any fundamental change proceeds best as the pressure of particular reasons of particular men, drawing eventually and collectively on a comparable vastness of experience, shapes the change over generations. While this gigantic process of national learning and reflection upon experience—what Burke called "the process of nature" in the state—continues, individual men have little choice but also to experience and reflect in their limited measure, or (to phrase it less pejoratively) individual men who are "the temporary possessors and life-renters" [115] of the commonwealth have the privilege of drawing upon these preconscious funds of institutional life.

Therefore, in his apologia for the moral basis—that is, for conditioned and *conditional* experience—Burke conceived himself, paradoxical as it may sound, to be defending the "nature" of political man, against a reason drifting off and turning against it. One ought not to mistake this for the vulgar deception of the provincial who believes his little prejudices and manners a measure of universal truth: there is much more profundity in Burke's argument. In essence he argues that, no matter what the actual content of political and social arrangements in which a man finds himself cast adrift, in no matter what place or century, the proportionate (or practical) relations of reason to concrete experience are effectually the same. Thus the fallacy of all the purely rational Utopias: they have to premise a death to the "irrational" experience of men, as well as to the soft sift of time, change, and accident, in which that experience develops. These proportionate relations exist between theoretical right and the human condition, the nature of man, and hence Burke's protest that the revolutionaries ignored "the rankness of uncultivated nature": that "nothing is left to nature in their systems." [116] "All has been the result of design; all has been matter of institution. No mechanical means could be devised . . . that has not been employed." [117] But a mechanical reasoning is just what is most inept to cope with or to arrive at any understanding of a man in his practical *habitus*. And also if it sets itself up as a discipline aiming exclusively at the destruction of the prejudices, affections, and moral sentiments, which make up this *habitus,* its success must vulgarize a man by deadening the far greater part of what he has to live for, and the materials of his progress. Burke would have agreed with Whitehead that "civilization advances by extending the number of important operations which we can perform without thinking about them"; [118] and he would have added, that it is only reasonable, supposing many causes of present civilization to be latent in unreflective behavior, to be respectful of that behavior for perpetuating them.

It is not always easy to do: "Our complexion is such, that we are palled with enjoyment, and stimulated with hope; that we become less sensible to a long-possessed benefit, from the very circumstance that it is become habitual." And this Burke felt was the plight of France, for "from this temper, men and factions, and nations too, have sacrificed the good, of which they had been in assured possession, in favour of wild and irrational expectations." [119] Overshooting necessities (and possibilities) inherent in the concrete, they bring upon themselves tragic consequences.

All things considered, perhaps the most persistent attitude expressed in the *Reflections* is something like tragic irony—not an emotional dilation or *Weltschmerz,* not that illusory projection of self-pity sometimes called romantic irony—but a lucid intellectual realism that sees characteristic (and therefore potentially tragic) limits concretely as a built-in fact of human life and practice. To have any practical success in politics, the politician must work within the limits of the concrete, tempering the experienced with the emergent. This advice is stated in a letter to Mons. Dupont several months before the *Reflections*. Observing that a young Frenchman would have "now to live in a new order of things, under a plan of government of which no man can speak from experience," that the French state before obtaining a final form would probably pass "as one of our poets says, 'through many varieties of untried being,' " Burke cautioned him to remember that "nothing is good, but in proportion and with reference," and that during this period of indefinite crisis when a new state was in the making, "it is with man in the concrete; —it is with common human life, and human actions, you are to be concerned." [120] For this reason:

A positively vicious and abusive government ought to be changed, —and, if necessary, by violence—if it cannot be (as sometimes it is the case) reformed. But when the question is concerning the more or the less *perfection* in the organization of a government, the allowance to *means* is not of so much latitude. There is, by the essential fundamental constitution of things, a radical infirmity in all human contrivances; and the weakness is often so attached to the very perfection of our political mechanism, that some defect in it,—something that stops short of its principle,—something that controls, that mitigates, that moderates it,—becomes a necessary corrective to the evils that the theoretic perfection would produce.[121]

Possibly the defect may not be a corrective, but even so "an imperfect good is still a good," and it may be more prudent to tolerate the defect, in hopes of some future occasion of removing it, and therefore "to acquiesce in some qualified plan" than "to push for the more perfect, which cannot be attained without tearing to pieces the whole contexture."

In that case, combining the means and end, the less perfect is the more desirable. The *means* to any end being first in order, are *immediate* in their good or their evil;—they are always, in a manner, *certainties*. The *end* is doubly problematical; first, whether it is to be attained; then, whether, supposing it attained, we obtain the true object we sought for.[122]

Burke closed with the praise of moderation which "times and situations will clearly distinguish from the counterfeits of pusillanimity and indecision," which is the possession only of "superior minds," which requires "deep courage" and "reflection," and which has "a self-possessing and collected character, which, sooner or later, bids fair to attract every thing to it, as to a centre." [123]

There is a latent recoil mechanism in things, a sly continuous presence which enforces limits, and traps the heedless or the imperceptive, often without their ever guessing why their misery comes to pass. Thus one of Burke's motives in criticizing the Revolution was his hope of preventing (in the old double sense of anticipating and forestalling) the occasion of irreversible waste, of remorse without a possibility of restitution, of the horrified recognition that, now the existing achievements have been destroyed, the country is destitute of the means of progression and therefore without reason to hope. His conservative criticism purports to be a beneficent cunning of forestallment, a careful discrimination of limits, not for the limits' sake, but to protect, to free—to make safe the pursuit of novel and positive good without detriment to the pursuer or to the whole of that already-achieved good with which anything new must integrate if it is to deserve the title of a progression. His purpose is thus to be "practical"; but, Burke's version of the practical, far from being a Philistine niggling, would seem to be best defined as "that which nature allows without a reaction whose consequences are graver than the consequence of doing something else, and in many cases, of doing nothing." Such thinking may terminate in a defense of the *status quo,* but not *a priori;* it might urge change, but also not *a priori.* To defend the *status quo* is not necessarily to make an ism of defense, or even to like what cannot be helped. To be practical is to descry the inherent limits of a situation—limits which have to be acknowledged *if or unless;* and since there is a *hybris* of inaction and neglect, quite as common as the *hybris* of blind advance, these limits may include a catastrophe in standing still.

It is not hard to see, on these grounds, how Burke could

believe that over a period of many generations and even centuries of trial and error, struggle, and discovery, individual men could have come to understand the particular limits that persistently recur, and in turn to adapt their institutions with a fair degree of wisdom. To believe anything else would be to assume a fatuity in human behavior so enormous that it leaves one little hope for oneself. This is the thinking behind his famous dictum: "man is most unwise and a most wise being. The individual is foolish; the multitude, for the moment, is foolish, when they act without deliberation; but the species is wise, and, when time is given to it, as a species, it always acts right." [124]

If, then, in his idea of the moral basis Burke approximated the more modern-sounding idea of culture, he retained nevertheless a firm grasp upon the idea of an ethical propriety—or natural moral law—which transcends all cultural contexts. There are some ideas and principles "which were understood long before we were born, altogether as well as they will be after the grave has heaped its mould upon our presumption, and the silent tomb shall have imposed its law on our pert loquacity." [125] *Moral,* in Burke's usage, like *principle,* is a conscious equivoque, directing thought toward the inclusive unity of nature and history in the actualities of common life. It implies both an ethical norm and a contingent conditioning. Consider the following passage concerning the rights of man in a polity:

These metaphysic rights entering into common life, like rays of light which pierce into a dense medium, are, by the laws of nature, refracted from their straight line. Indeed in the gross and complicated mass of human passions and concerns, the primitive rights of men undergo such a variety of refractions and reflections, that it becomes absurd to talk of them as if they continued in the simplicity of their original direction. . . . The pretended rights of these theorists are all extremes: and in proportion as they are metaphysically true, they are morally and politically false. The rights of men in governments are their advantages; and these are often in balances between differences of good; and in compromises sometimes between good and evil, and sometimes between evil and evil. Political reason is a computing principle; adding, subtracting, multiplying, and dividing, morally and not metaphysically, or mathematically, true moral denominations.[126]

In this passage of characteristic brilliance, protesting the fallacy of misplaced concreteness among *philosophes,* Burke sees nothing abstruse about "nature," and therefore in modern retrospect may seem to commit the very fallacy he protests. However, once the historical context is understood, it can be seen that his argument is not, in fact, false. "Metaphysical" is contrasted with "moral," but the "moral" includes human nature as well as human affairs and circumstances; he is therefore referring to human nature qualified, or "human nature as it is found in the concrete"; both the ethically ideal and the historically conditioned are felt to be unified within the domain of common sense and common life; "human nature" in Burke's day was not felt to be abstraction.

More often than not, Burke's politics link backward with the classical-Christian humanism in the England of his own and earlier centuries: this seems to have contributed the ethical norm conceived as latently and continuously formative in the particular moral basis of English society and government. For example, the counters of moral judgment that were its stock-in-trade Burke took over bodily without any sense of their metaphysicalness. And this is why, avowing to be concrete, he consistently uses terms such as ambition, wisdom, virtue, prudence, liberty, envy, malice, sloth, and will, when making pronouncements about daily life. He measures living, concrete events against an order of ethical abstractions whose lineage would finally lead back through Cicero's *De officiis* to Aristotle's *Nicomachean Ethics,* and beyond. He presents the interesting predicament of a man who has begun to feel history move around him, whose sensibility responds, so to speak, existentially, but who feels obliged to interpret his new perceptions in traditionary concepts. It's as if, asked to arrest his subtlest sense of it in plain, honest, eighteenth-century language, Samuel Johnson were then handed *Dubliners.* For this reason, though he may cling superficially to old ideas, Burke has constantly to readjust their relevance, to wrench from them a dynamic suggestion they never had before—"at once to preserve and to reform." He is obliged, temperamentally and theoretically, to behold the moving present, in the full variety of its relations, as in itself a pathway to the real, as yielding to intrusive mind layer beyond layer of latent reality capable of persisting unobserved but actual. But at the same time he is obliged to stabilize and regulate the progress of his thinking with the wise weight of a traditionary ballast. Burke said he guided his judgment first by *mos majorum,* because "that point being fixed, and laying fast hold of a strong bottom, our speculations may swing in all directions, without public detriment, because they will ride with sure anchorage." [127]

II

Burke is a politician and a maker of speeches, and therefore on occasion not above theatricality, and of what appears to be cooked-up and even half-baked emotion. Long years of suffering the shocks of self-generated drama not only may scar a man's vigor but also harden him in a sort of cosmic egocentrism and vanity. As the French Revolution progressed, Burke came to write as if "the awful drama of Providence, now acting on the moral theatre of the world" [128] really were as transparent as he regarded it, or as if the peoples of Europe really had divided on a sudden into polar camps eternally irreconcilable, as if all who were not actively, and with decision and energy, against Jacobinism—a character in his play—were its partisans. He reminds us of the astronomer in *Rasselas* who thought himself secretly in control of the weather and was almost distraught with the terrible responsibility. This is the tone of the *Regicide Peace* letters—the capacity for dramatizing himself and the moment still there, but in exhaustion amounting almost to parody. The last of neoclassic giants survives his proper day; in heroic despair, testifies to wicked change. Everywhere the sarcasm, the tone like a mocking bow, everywhere the frantic fancies and acrimonious cartoons, party, obsession, and the anxiety (such as commonly troubles an old man who has lost, or is losing, his power) that sees historical change as conspiracy. We get an image, a gravely warning image, of self-satire in an old man—an old man pranked up in jewels and gesturing. We get an image of false heroics finally exhausted, and shrinking, alas, very much against his wish, in mock-heroic.

We get such an image, as a kind of miasmic smoke upon the style. But it is misleading. Without question, the *Letters on a Regicide Peace* are crisp, hard, analytical, flashing with anger and a grim intensity, but they are considerably more than the mere outlashings of rancor. Nobody should overlook the rancor and few are likely to be insensitive to the witchery (in a double sense) of the rhetoric. Tempting as it is, however, at times, to agree with many critics, including that master of passionate scoff Irving Babbitt,[129] that the generous, manly, and moral-imaginative Burke whom almost everybody admires in his American speeches had somehow "forgotten his own wisdom" in a decay of ego, one must remember that the *Regicide Peace* letters, and the kindred tracts written over eight years, are workmanlike, poised, and reasoned exposition—"a clear, positive, decided, long and maturely-reflected, and frequently declared, opinion." [130] One would err to suppose that in these dying years, broken in health (he was wasting with stomach cancer), grieved almost to despair by the deaths of his son, brother, and sister, cast off by the Fox Whigs, retired and indebted, Burke were really no more, in his own humiliated words, than "a dejected old man, buried in the anticipated grave of a feeble old age, forgetting, and forgotten." [131] It is true that the accents of indignant senility are to be pitied and controlled, not trusted. But a decently close reading will show far more than that—a Burke in the sharpest of faculties, and pleading as an independent citizen, with the riches of his whole experience and the full force of his literary genius, against what he felt was a persecuting and power-mad ideology threatening to demolish European civilization and return it to savagery—"the most craftily devised, the best combined, and the most extensive design, that ever was carried on, since the beginning of the world, against all property, all order, all religion, all law, and all real freedom." [132]

To the presence of this general moral and social movement, perhaps the profoundest undercurrent of his century, Burke had been acutely sensitive from his youth. His first formal work, *A Vindication of Natural Society* (1756),[133] had attacked the deist Bolingbroke on similar grounds. With mimicking (and to a large extent unrecognizable, and hence immature) irony Burke had maintained that the deist arguments against Christianity could be turned as well against the traditional state, that a natural society and "return to nature" was as sensible as a natural religion, and therefore, that the whole structure of European civilization might be cast off. What was intended, when Burke was about twenty-seven, as a *reductio* argument, became by the end of the century a serious program for revolutionaries. William Godwin, for example, accepted its propositions at face value (discounting the irony with wonder) and praised Burke for such graceful expression.[134] In every major speech and letter of his career Burke hammered away at some aspect of the movement, especially the vicious trust in ideology. In the very air, in *philosophes* like Voltaire, Diderot, Helvetius, in sentimentalists like Rousseau and Condorcet, in materialists like Baron D'Holbach and Priestley, and indeed in the Enlightenment at large on its skeptical, anti-clerical, and revolutionary side, Burke detected, amidst obvious achievements, what promised to be a barbarous schism with the past, and hence a betrayal of both present and future for whose sake the Enlightenment presumably existed. "It is a melancholy reflection, that the spirit of melioration which has been going on in that part of Europe, more or less during this century, and the various schemes very lately on foot for further advancement, are all put a stop to at once." [135]

The tendency was against reverence for existing materials, continuous growth, and the conciliating principle. By 1789 the tendency, in Burke's opinion, was more positively for anarchy and madness: extremists who surely would have horrified both Voltaire and Rousseau had armed themselves with pikes and flimsy abstractions and now planned to write off history, to make a clean slate of existing institutions, and then to construct society anew on secular and *a priori* grounds with "a general wild offer of liberty." Earnest moderates were swept along and destroyed. In the manners of all Burke came to see metaphysical speculations blended with the coarsest sensuality: a kind of schizophrenic morality which—having broken loose from its moorings in imaginative conscience—now threatened, with demoniac energy, to raze civilization. The blood-dimmed tide was loosed; and horrified by the Jacobin gaze, blank and pitiless as the sun, Burke marvelled what rough beast slouched toward Paris to be born.

As he wrote, however, Burke knew that he fell into exaggeration, and possibly rant, not on purpose, and not, he believed, from any disposition on his part to be intemperate, nor from a failure to sift information from every source he could—state documents, periodicals, *philosophie,* letters, confessions from the ousted like Brissot, interviews with refugees (hundreds of whom he received at Beaconsfield). Certainly not from a vulgar Francophobia; and certainly not from antipathy to the slogans (except as slogans) under which the revolution was carried out—liberty, philosophy, social justice, humanity, reason. One should not be deceived by his taunts at "the solid darkness of this enlightened age" or at the "short form of incantation—*'Philosophy, Light, Liberality, the Rights of Men.'* "[136] His feelings were more complicated than a blind, shut reaction. For one thing, he had to work fast in a race with death; sometimes, even in the expression of truth, there must be a compromise with circumstances:

> In this crisis I must hold my tongue, or I must speak with freedom. Falsehood and delusion are allowed in no case whatever: but, as in the exercise of all the virtues, there is an economy of truth. It is a sort of temperance, by which a man speaks truth with measure that he may speak it the longer. But as the same rules do not hold in all cases—what would be right for you, who may presume on a series of years before you, would have no

sense for me, who cannot, without absurdity, calculate on six months of life. What I say, I *must* say at once. Whatever I write is in its nature testamentary. It may have the weakness, but it has the sincerity, of a dying declaration.[137]

Also, he still remembered his distance from the scene, the secondhandedness of his information. To a member of the National Assembly he refused to speculate on particular remedies, because, he said:

I must see with mine own eyes, I must, in a manner, touch with my own hands, not only the fixed but the momentary circumstances, before I could venture to suggest any political project whatsoever. I must know the power and disposition to accept, to execute, to persevere. I must see all the aids, and all the obstacles. I must see the means of correcting the plan, where correctives would be wanted. I must see the things; I must see the men. . . . People at a distance must judge ill of men. They do not always answer to their reputation when you approach them. Nay, the perspective varies, and shows them quite otherwise than you thought them. At a distance, if we judge uncertainly of men, we must judge worse of *opportunities,* which continually vary their shapes and colours, and pass away like clouds.[138]

Burke knew that he must content himself with a virtual truth and criticism in generalized perspectives. Yet write he must. His urgency seemed at times to baffle Burke himself; his "exaggeration" had a peculiar quality. It was sprung from the abyss of his horror. He wrote like a man stunned, with a vision he could no more contain than he could escape, like the Ancient Mariner but without guilt, like Cassandra but with a possibility of persuasion, like Ahab enraged at the Jacobin whale, but modestly consecrated. In the profoundest depths his despair, Burke said there awakened "an impulse" which he had tried in vain to resist.[139] He spoke oddly of his "encounter" with France.[140] "Oppression," he observed, "makes wise men mad; but the distemper is still the madness of the wise, which is better than the sobriety of fools. The cry is the voice of sacred misery, exalted not into wild raving, but into the sanctified phrensy of prophecy and inspiration." [141]

Whatever one may wish to make or not to make of this prophetic "sacred misery"—and Burke himself was too busy being a man of his century to make much of it—it suggests the principle, the *epigigomenon ti,* of these later writings: as well as rhetorical persuasion and criticism earnest about fact, they are also a working out of a vision, an existential impression of something new in European history. In the way that one says the deepest quality of a work of art is the quality of mind of the producer, so in these writings one realizes that to get their true meaning one must work backward beyond logical relations to vision. One does not have to find the preterhuman in this: the basic equipment of the critic, a *sense* of fact, operates on numerous levels of generality and in greater and lesser degrees of complication.

Burke protested the evil of the new thing. "In the time I have lived to," he said, "I always seem to walk on enchanted ground. Everything is new, and, according to the fashionable phrase, revolutionary." [142] It made him perfectly thought-sick. He felt "condemned to see strange things; new systems of policy, new principles, and not only new men, but what might appear a new species of men. I believe that any person who was of age to take part in public affairs forty years ago, (if the intermediate space of time were expunged from his memory,) would hardly credit his senses." [143] The world after 1789 seemed out of joint, topsy-turvy, fraught with danger and ambiguity. "Oh the blindness of the greatest statesman," he mused, "to the infinite and unlooked-for combinations of things which lie hid in the dark prolific womb of futurity!" [144] New things in a new world! he saw "no hopes in the common tracks." [145] It was as if a new order were coming on, as if henceforth, by sudden fiat, sunlight would be greyish, dull as gun-metal.

Recurrently he compared what he feared, and hated because he feared, to a spectre, a spirit, a demonic essence, apparitional in time. "Out of the tomb of the murdered monarchy in France [he shuddered] has arisen a vast, tremendous, unformed spectre, in a far more terrific guise than any which ever yet have overpowered the imagination, and subdued the fortitude of man. Going straight forward to its end, unappalled by peril, unchecked by remorse, despising all common maxims and all common means, that hideous phantom overpowered those who could not believe it was possible she could at all exist." [146] The spectre aimed "to form an universal empire, by producing an universal revolution," meanwhile pretending to secure eternal peace and guaranteeing that its generosity and justice would grow with its power.[147] It laid down "metaphysic propositions which infer universal consequences," and then attempted "to limit logic by despotism." [148] It was like "the principle of evil himself, incorporeal, pure, unmixed, dephlegmated, defecated evil." [149]

The evil spirit possessed the body of France, informed it as a soul, expressed in its pernicious activity a characteristic mark.[150] No peace could be made with it, and the first struggle would be the last.

> It is a general evil. Where it least appears in action, it is still full of life. In its sleep it recruits its strength, and prepares its exertion. Its spirit lies deep in the corruption of our common nature. The social order which restrains it, feeds it. It exists in every country in Europe; and among all orders of men in every country, who look up to France as to a common head. The centre is there. The circumference is the world of Europe wherever the race of Europe may be settled. . . . In France is the bank of deposit, and the bank of circulation, of all the pernicious principles that are forming in every state.[151]

The evil lay in the heart of Europe and must, Burke cried, "be extirpated from that centre, or no part of the circumference can be free from the mischief which radiates from it, and which will spread circle beyond circle, in spite of all the little defensive precautions which can be employed against it." [152] For its power was "not so truly dangerous in its fortresses nor in its territories, as in its spirit and its principles." [153]

We have put Burke in a harsh perspective—as an irritable old man who sees the devil and like Luther has the urge to throw an inkpot at it—to dramatize the quality of his fury, which will impress some readers as comic-neurotic, others as sacred misery. Precisely what was he talking about?

Burke looked out in horror at a political movement international in scope, whose moving principle he sometimes described as "a certain intemperance of intellect [which] is the disease of the time, and the source of all its other diseases," [154] sometimes "atheism, the great political evil of the time," [155] and sometimes, depending on the relations in which for the moment he saw it, tyranny, nationalistic imperialism, rebellion of the unpropertied, disaffection of ambitious talents, and, as stated in the pitch of horror, a truly demonic eruption. His jeremiads had nothing to do *per se* with democracy or science, but grew from his primary perceptions of the quality, tendency, and already known results of the moral energies concretely at work in France—with "metaphysical madness," lust of the selfish will, persecution, military threat, mass murder, vulgarity in manners, and more particularly still, thought police,[156] lawless confiscations and "agrarian experiments" upon the estates confiscated,[157] people's courts,[158] and revolutionary tribunals,[159] surprise political arrests,[160] ration tickets for bread lines,[161] the closing down of churches, hostages taken to keep troops in the field,[162] something like brainwashing with steady propaganda,[163] the "dry rot" of fifth columns [164] who follow a party line,[165] an oligarchical clique financing political adventurers leading to domination of the country by a "handful of obscure ruffians," [166] ministers as spies,[167] family servants betraying the household to the state,[168] family members betraying each other,[169] Jacobin cells (clubs),[170] promiscuous executions after mock trial, the most meaningful of words (*the people, reason, liberty, philosophy, humanity,* etc.) debased into omnibus abstractions and used to justify crimes, rule "by the effects of fear alone," [171] "the operation of a system, which makes life without dignity, and death without hope," [172] a system in which "the people are absolutely slaves, in the fullest sense, in all affairs public and private, great and small, even down to the minutest and most recondite parts of their household concerns," [173] and in short, the general apparatus of what has come to be called the modern totalitarian state.

> Individuality is left out of their scheme of government. The state is all in all. Everything is referred to the production of force; afterwards, everything is trusted to the use of it. It is military in its principle, in its maxims, in its spirit, and in all its movements. The state has dominion and conquest for its sole objects: dominion over minds by proselytism, over bodies by arms. . . . France has, since the accomplishment of the Revolution, a complete unity in its direction. It has destroyed every resource of the state, which depends upon opinion and the good-will of individuals. The riches of convention disappear. . . . But unity in design, and perseverance and boldness in pursuit, have never wanted resources, and never will. We have not considered as we ought the dreadful energy of a state, in which the property has nothing to do with the government. Reflect, my dear Sir, reflect again and again, on a government in which the property is in complete subjection, and where nothing rules but the mind of desperate men.[174]

Constantly he urged the necessity of keeping precisely in view the "genius and character" or the "nature and character of the enemy." To render its character as it actually was under various woolly and seductive disguises was a major purpose of his French tracts of the late 1790's, for Burke was half-wild with the conviction that few of the British public imagined the malice and subtlety of what they had to live with. They had always been too inclined to shrink within the happy safety of their island, to appease.[175] He exhorted them to alertness, courage, and realism, which he foresaw they would soon need.

> Difficult indeed is our situation. In all situations of difficulty men will be influenced in the part they take, not only by the reason of the case, but by the peculiar turn of their own character. . . . Under misfortunes it often happens that the nerves of the understanding are so relaxed, the pressing peril of the hour so completely confounds all the faculties, that no future danger can be properly provided for, can be justly estimated, can be so much as fully seen. The eye of the mind is dazzled and vanquished.

An abject distrust of ourselves, an extravagant admiration of the enemy, present us with no hope but in a compromise with his pride, by a submission to his will. . . . The nature of courage is, without a question, to be conversant with danger; but in the palpable night of their terrors, men under consternation suppose, not that it is the danger, which, by a sure instinct calls out the courage to resist it, but that it is the courage which produces the danger. They therefore seek for a refuge from their fears in the fears themselves, and consider a temporizing meanness as the only source of safety.[176]

In the retrospect of beyond a century and a half, Burke's anxiety is intelligible. It was long before others saw the spectre. His horror was deepened by his loneliness. As late as 1794 he confessed to feeling strangely sometimes that he was "the only person in France or England who is aware of the extent of the danger with which we are threatened." [177] When war began, Pitt predicted that it would be short, ended certainly in "one or two campaigns," though Burke foresaw that, to the contrary, it would be long and dangerous,[178] and that all wars before it were comparatively but "the games of children." [179] The most striking common denominator among replies to the *Reflections*—for example, those of Major Scott, Capell Lofft, Joseph Priestley, and Sir James Mackintosh—is a complete insuspicion of what's coming, a joy of achievement, a feeling that, technicalities aside, the Revolution by 1791 had practically succeeded and that widening prospects open for mankind. Priestley's *Letters to Burke* has a noble, intelligent vision of a world without war, class oppression, and superstition, but he is completely deluded about the character of the Revolution itself; he sees it mistily through the spectacles of America. Mackintosh, as Hazlitt observed, sees through the spectacles of books,[180] as it were, in the generous comfort of a padded cell; he is one of those for whom the "burning, shining face" of raw fact comes as a vast surprise. In *Vindiciae Gallicae* his fine learning, candor, and method, are soaked in the vapid abstractionism which Burke saw gaining everywhere among contemporary Whigs—not abstraction militant and glaring enough to be "Jacobin," but abstraction sunk in the complex silence of will where it operates its consequences unseen and unsuspected, as a kind of bland sentiment.

No illustration will wholly suffice since abstractionism of this sort is cumulative and only to be experienced in the spirit of its thinking. Also, any illustration, since taken out of context, has to be unfair to Mackintosh's other, more cautious views. Citing Montesquieu's apprehension "that the spirit of increasing armies would terminate in converting Europe into an immense camp, in changing our artisans and cultivators into military savages, and reviving the age of Attila and Genghis," [181] Mackintosh disproves such nonsense by a theory of nature. Delighted by the defection of the French army to the revolutionists, he points the moral that when an army grows large enough, it is no longer a social danger; it becomes civic and popular. "If all citizens were compelled to become soldiers, all soldiers must of necessity adopt the feelings of citizens. . . . This is the barrier which nature has opposed to the increase of armies. They cannot be numerous enough to enslave a people, without becoming the people itself." [182] Therefore, Montesquieu, and Burke, and other testy old sophists and alarmists, err, having lost touch with "the progress of the human mind" since their youth and grown out of sympathy with "the people." [183] Absorbed by the see-saw jugglery of abstract *citizens* and abstract *soldiers,* all comprising the abstract *people* and regulated by the mechanical relations of an abstract *nature,* Mackintosh is blind to the spirit of real events, an exile from his own intelligence. Burke's answer would be that better a statesman had never learned to read if his understanding is diverted from the business before him, from the present exigencies of the world to rule-mongering. "There are some fundamental points in which nature never changes—but they are few and obvious, and belong rather to morals than to politics. But so far as regards political matter, the human mind and human affairs are susceptible of infinite modifications, and of combinations wholly new and unlooked for." [184] When Mackintosh says, "Every man that is added to the army is a new link that unites [the people] to the nation," he thinks "abstractly" of freedom, civic spirit, *la belle France,* the people, and a secret hostility in nature to despotism; he cannot hear, as Burke does, the adumbral tattoo of Napoleonic drums.[185] In this particular instance, which is only important for what it typifies, he is the practical dupe of a whole cluster of Enlightenment abstractions operating as a sentimental will to believe them exclusively true.

A will to believe and to proselytize, in different degrees of enthusiasm, is the common denominator among Burke's antagonists and a main cause of his alarm. Burke was probably the first man in history ever to grasp, certainly the first to give cogent expression to, the idea of revolutionary liberalism as a cultus (a view commonly recognized since).[186] Quixotically perhaps, he tried to combat the cultus single-handed, the whole ethos spreading into history, as it seemed to him, from a French source, like nerve gas. And he tried to combat it, impalpable as it was, at concrete points, in specific ideas and specific men, to discover and wherever possible to counteract every tentacle of the gas as it blew his way. Hence perhaps, in passages even of the most terrific anger, the peculiar diffuseness of the thinking and expression, which Burke himself was conscious of, even in the *Reflections.* Hence also his talking about spectres and spirits and other impalpables, against which, he admitted, there could be no real defense except a moral energy of equal or superior strength.[187] Hence his grim conviction, as he wrote, that "We must walk in new ways, or we can never encounter our enemy in his devious march. We are not at an end of our struggle, nor near it. Let us not deceive ourselves: we are at the beginning of great troubles." [188] Present times, opening upon "another Iliad of woes for Europe," [189] would forever decide its form and fate.[190] For example, all war hereafter, he predicted, would be total.[191] A revolution preparing in Germany was likely "to be more decisive upon the general fate of nations than that of France itself." [192]

A primary characteristic of the French Revolution was its pretension to legislate universally. Acknowledging the legitimacy of no traditional governments, it inferred also its right, if not mission, to subvert them, by force or intrigue. "We are at war with a system, which, by its essence, is inimical to all other governments, and which makes peace or war, as peace and war may best contribute to their subversion. It is with an *armed doctrine* that we are at war. It has, by its essence, a faction of opinion, and of interest, and of enthusiasm, in every country." [193] For an analogue truly cogent Burke had to desert political for religious history. Such a revolution, he said, of doctrine and theoretic dogma Europe had not witnessed since the Reformation,[194] and like the Reformation it could be expected to give a color, a character, and direction, to all the history of Europe succeeding. It would weaken, if not sometimes destroy, the long-evolved ethical bonds of neighborhood, dividing state against state and every state within itself according to doctrinal allegiances, as Catholic and Protestant had been divided, bloodily. Even as he participated in the first of them, Burke foresaw, as through a glass darkly, the host of violent controversies along doctrinal lines which has agitated social and ethical thinking in Europe since the French Revolution—the battles between science and humanism, materialism and Christianity, socialism and capitalism, liberalism and conservatism—even as the war between Catholicism and Protestantism had dominated practical thinking before.

Or again, in his favorite analogy, Burke described France as a "transatlantic Morocco," [195] and the adherents of the Revolution as a horde of militant proselytizers, shouting gibberish. Burke reflected upon the means "by which Mahomet and his tribes laid hold at once on the two most powerful empires of the world; beat one of them totally to the ground, broke to pieces the other, and, in no much longer space of time than I have lived, overturned governments, laws, manners, religion, and extended an empire from the Indus to the Pyrenees." [196] Even in peacetime, the armed doctrine would foment conspiracies and seditions in neighboring states so as to conquer them "if not to her dominion, to her resemblance." [197] Its position at the center of Europe further convinced Burke that its influence would be permanent if unchecked, even when "under the name of peace the war of intrigue begins."

It is not an enemy of accident that we have to deal with. Enmity to us and to all civilized nations is wrought into the very stamina of its constitution. It was made to pursue the purposes of that fundamental enmity. The design will go on regularly in every position and in every relation. Their hostility is to break us to their dominion: their amity is to debauch us to their principles.[198]

For in its universal dogmas and zeal to propagate, the armed doctrine was really religious in its substance, political in its scale and aspirations: "It must always have been discoverable by persons of reflection, but it is now obvious to the world, that a theory concerning government may become as much a cause of fanaticism as a *dogma* in religion. There is a boundary to men's passions when they act from feeling; none when they are under the influence of imagination." [199]

It was not just another party in the timeless parade of parties which diversify a healthy state, create and renew transient conflicts of particular opinions and particular interests: the armed doctrine exacted an ultimate, uncompromising loyalty. It made claims to the whole man:

They, who have made but superficial studies in the natural history of the human mind, have been taught to look on religious opinions as the only cause of enthusiastic zeal and sectarian propagation. But there is no doctrine whatever, on which men can warm, that is not capable of the very same effect. The social nature of man impels him to propagate his principles, as much as physical impulses urge him to propagate his kind. The passions give zeal and vehemence. The understanding bestows design and system. The whole man moves under the discipline of his opinions.[200]

Disciplined intellectuals (or in Burke's language, "philosophers") and politicians made up the sect, the first "going straight forward and openly," the second "by the surer mode of zigzag," to accomplish mutually supporting ends,[201] and with like devotion to "what LaFayette calls the *most sacred of all duties, that of insurrection.*" [202] Their behavior reflected a "ferocious indocility": "the little catechism of the rights of men is soon learned; and the inferences are in the passions." [203] The armed doctrine, once its tenets were implanted, luxuriated through the whole personality, like a spirit or tone; it entangled itself with "what at the bottom is the true character of any man," [204] swept up its vagrant ambitions and resentments, and organized them in the single-minded, desperate zeal of the proselyte—a "strutting and bullying insolence." [205]

Despondent but strong in the loneliness of his vision, Burke surveyed his acquaintances for men of strong nerves, "manly simplicity and a liberal openness of proceeding," [206] who could counter duty with duty, and zeal with zeal, overmatch the phantom piety of the revolutionaries, that vicious and distempered energy, with a piety more gracious, foreseeing, and firm. But he saw none; it was incredible. He cried, "I am alone. I have none to meet my enemies in the gate." [207] Resistance must start somewhere; perhaps in the heart of a single man. "Have we no such man amongst us?" Was it not possible, he said, that "one vigorous mind . . . confiding in the aid of God, and full of just reliance in his own fortitude, vigour, enterprise, and perseverance, would first draw to him some few like himself, and then that multitudes, hardly thought to be in existence, would appear, and troop about him"? "Novelty is not the only source of zeal. Why should not a Maccabeus and his brethren arise to assert the honour of the ancient law, and to defend the temple of their forefathers, with as ardent a spirit, as can inspire any innovator to destroy the monuments of the piety and the glory of ancient ages?" [208] Part of the fascination in Burke's horror proceeded from his suspicion that just possibly he himself, a tired and sick old man who had lost his son, might be called to the field, might be destined to make the first magnificent, lonely charge. "The storm has gone over me; and I lie like one of those old oaks which the late hurricane has scattered about me. I am stripped of all my honours, I am torn up by the roots, and lie prostrate on the earth!" [209] His only resources were his pen and his voice, his only arms.[210] If Providence had spared his son, his son would have shone forth the real leader, unconquerable in fortitude, clearheaded and honorable, though at times a little too easily discouraged with himself, yet always buoyed up again. His son had been a man for times like these.[211] But who shall fathom the ways of the Great Disposer? Gathering his griefs Job-like around his honor, Burke peered out upon the "monstrous tragi-comic scene" [212] with a bitter dedication. Baffled and frustrated as he was, and hurrying to "a timely grave," he resolved that, if any effect could be hoped from the meditations of his solitary closet, then most certainly would he "rake up the fire under all the ashes that oppress it." [213]

"The cure might come from the same source with the distemper." The same source, but not animated by the same principles or instinct with the same unscrupulous and vulgar intoxication with power. By what he called, confessing how paradoxical it sounded, "the true republican spirit," such as "we perhaps fondly conceive to have animated the distinguished heroes and patriots of old, who knew no mode of policy but religion and virtue," [214] by such a spirit spreading like fire in the hearts of private citizens, refusing "to shake off those moral riders which reason has appointed to govern every sort of rude power," submitting to the one "feudal tenure" which nobody can alter, "the dominion of prudence and of virtue"—such a spirit might vanquish "the infernal energies of talents set in action by vices and disorder": [215] "I would not wish to excite, or even to tolerate, that kind of evil spirit which invokes the powers of hell to rectify the disorders of the earth. No! I would add my voice with better, and I trust, more potent charms, to draw down justice, and wisdom, and fortitude from heaven, for the correction of human vice, and the recalling of human error from the devious ways into which it has been betrayed." [216] Burke knew that "mistaken or misapplied virtues, if they are not as pernicious as vice, frustrate at least their own natural tendencies." [217]

For example, one restraint should have been to remember that the conversion or seizure of the new revolutionary religion would be effectual in different degrees and for different reasons. Burke knew that many men of honest good will must undoubtedly have been drawn into the revolutionary whirlpool, and though his sympathy for them was acid and suspicious, diminished by his own emotional exhaustion, he tried to make distinctions. He could understand, he said, how a man rejoicing in the fall of an old system could put out of mind the suffering and ruin falling with it upon a million of individuals: "Because when people see a political object, which they ardently desire, but in one point of view, they are apt extremely to palliate, or underrate, the evils which may arise in obtaining it. This is no reflection on the humanity of those persons. Their good nature I am the last man in the world to dispute. It only shows that they are not sufficiently informed, or sufficiently considerate." [218] "Good men do not suspect that their destruction is attempted through their virtues." [219] Also, indulging "a sort of undefined hope," one may easily be deceived by fraudulent men: "There are cases in which a man would be ashamed not to have been imposed on." [220] But he had neither time nor means to investigate the phenomenon of disappointed or ruined enthusiasts; and if their leaning away from fundamentals of the European achievement was symptomatic of more than delusion, if it was historically significant, "if a new order is coming on, and all the political opinions must pass away as dreams, which our ancestors have worshipped as revelations," [221] then nothing he could say would stop it. He would state the evil as, in his opinion, it existed: the remedy he knew must lie where "power, wisdom, and information" were better "united with good intentions" than they ever could be with him. "If a great change is to be made in human affairs, the minds of men will be fitted to it, the general opinions and feelings will draw that way. Every fear, every hope, will forward it; and then they, who persist in opposing this mighty current in human affairs, will appear rather to resist the decrees of Providence itself, than the mere designs of men. They will not be resolute and firm, but perverse and obstinate." [222] But the future must take care of itself: "Perhaps the only moral trust with any certainty in our hands, is the care of our own time. With regard to futurity, we are to treat it like a ward. We are not so to attempt an improvement of his fortune, as to put the capital of his estate to any hazard." [223] Furthermore, no future that Burke could imagine would be worth having, hagridden, narrowed, and enslaved by the Jacobin spectre.

Jacobinism was Burke's name for the new political *religieux* in their general characteristics. He included by it "indiscriminately the Brissotins and the Maratists." [224] Burke contemplated the whole "rabble of systems" in France with disgust—"Fayetteism, Condorcetism, Monarchism, or Democratism, or Federalism," [225] and also "what they call the crime of *moderantism,* of which offence however few were guilty." [226] The succession of short-lived failures made up in his eyes one single monstrous and complicated failure. If he stopped to enumerate all the "alterations by which bungling practice corrects absurd theory," as the historian must do, he saw no end to his investigations:

> Because every day's past experience of impracticability has driven, and every day's future experience will drive, those men to new devices as exceptionable as the old; and which are no otherwise worthy of observation than as they give a daily proof of the delusion of their promises, and the falsehood of their professions. Had I followed all these changes, my letter would have been only a gazette of their wanderings; a journal of their march from error to error, through a dry dreary desert, unguided by the lights of heaven, or by the contrivance which wisdom has invented to supply their place.[227]

The reality of such political events lay in the practical character of the participants guided by the new dogmas; it lay in the whole ethos, not in the mistakes or misfortunes of parties. The ethos, the spirit, the essence, the spectre, the enemy, was Jacobinism. "The French Revolution did not cause it; it only discovered it, increased it, and gave fresh vigour to its operations." [228] Burke knew the differences between isms with fair accuracy, but writing as a moralist, not as a historian, he groped for the fundamental determinants of practice, and he needed a summary name. He referred to all the new converts, in their different shades of commitment, as Jacobins, with the same latitude of expression that one uses to talk about Christians.

The religion of the Jacobin was a religion of hostility, secular ambition, and "studied violence." [229] His moving spirit was to negate, to force, to obliterate resistance. First of all, he was hostile to the Christian church. *"It is a religious war.* It includes in its object undoubtedly every other interest of society as well as this; but this is the principal and leading feature. It is through this destruction of religion that our enemies propose the accomplishment of all their other views.[230] The "constitutional church" legitimized after the revolution was decked out, Burke said, as only a "temporary amusement to the people . . . until the time should come, when they might with safety cast off the very appearance of religion whatsoever, and persecute Christianity throughout Europe with fire and sword." [231] "Wearied out with incessant martyrdom, and the cries of a people hungering and thirsting for religion, they permit it only as a tolerated evil." [232] Atheism was one of its dogmas, "a regular church of avowed atheism, established by law," [233] which not only refused to acknowledge any God and persecuted those who did, but also substituted abstract deities in His place—Reason ("vitiated, perverted"), Virtue ("a theatrical, bombastic, windy phraseology of heroic virtue"),[234] Liberty (the "all-atoning name"),[235] and ruling over them all, the National State personified.[236] From the latter circumstance, Jacobinism had become a religion of hostility to all other states and patriotisms besides its own. Bloodthirsty nationalism of a totalitarian brand appeared first, in modern times, in revolutionary France, and in it, from the first, Burke detected an aggressive will to subject other countries and to dominate the world: "It is not France extending a foreign empire over other nations; it is a sect aiming at universal empire, and beginning with the conquest of France. The leaders of that sect secured the *centre of Europe;* and that secured, they knew, that whatever might be the event of battles and sieges, their *cause* was victorious." [237] The will to conquer and subvert was not a plan taken up "in the first intoxication of unexpected success," but "a standing maxim of national policy." [238] From this source came the striking hatred of England, the main obstacle to the plan.[239] Jacobinism required a whole code of hatreds—of Christianity, of nations, of monarchy and aristocracy, of the rich, of the feudal, of the established and traditional, of classes and titles. Altogether, Burke said, its "hostile amity can be obtained on no terms that do not imply an inability hereafter to resist its designs." [240] Its professions of a love of peace were only the "cold, formal, general" kind "which no power has ever refused to make; because they mean little, and cost nothing." [241]

But if hostility was the Jacobin's moving principle—aggressive malice, metaphysical in extension, and cynical in the abuse of power, volatile as spirit, but impenetrably hard and secular—his face and professional exterior was, often as not, a rollicking *bon ton* of good nature and sweet sentiment. Before the Revolution, Burke said, the Jacobins "seemed tame, and even caressing: They had nothing but *douce humanité* in their mouth. They could not bear the punishment of the mildest laws on the greatest criminals. The slightest severity of justice made their flesh creep. The very idea that war existed in the world disturbed their repose. Military glory was no more, with them, than a splendid infamy. Hardly would they hear of self-defence, which they reduced within such bounds, as to leave it no defence at all. All this while they meditated the confiscations and massacres we have seen." [242] After the Revolution was still to be heard "the tender, soothing strains, in the *affettuoso* of humanity, warbled from the throats of Reubel, Carnot, Tallien, and the whole chorus of confiscators, domiciliary visitors, committeemen of research, jurors and presidents of revolutionary tribunals, regicides, assassins, massacrers, and septembrisers." [243] It was a "homicide philanthropy," [244] which preened itself verbosely upon its integrity, humanity, courage, and patriotism, as a prelude to a blood bath.[245] From this basic hypocrisy of character proceeded the swindles of their propaganda: "The whole compass of the language is tried to find synonymes and circumlocutions for massacre and murder. Things are never called by their common names. Massacre is sometimes *agitation,* sometimes *effervescence,* sometimes *excess;* sometimes too continued an exercise of a *revolutionary power."* [246] From it proceded, in their perpetual purges of one another, the attempt to "cast their common crimes on the wickedness of their departed associates." [247] Never before, Burke said mockingly, "did a den of bravoes and banditti assume the garb and tone of an academy of philosophers." [248] In their new political religion, humility, "the basis of the Christian system," was replaced by the Rousseauan "ethics of vanity," in which to talk in powerful rhetoric about one's universal benevolence is an acceptable substitute for having even the rudiments of common feeling for individuals.[249]

The sparkling sarcasm of Burke's last years is surely some of the most brilliant in English prose, though at times almost too brilliant to be successful, "ungracefully gorgeous" as someone has remarked. It's as though he strained against the limits of language itself, as if he had abandoned all care for propriety in a desperate effort to shock his readers, or, more accurately perhaps, to shock his distraught vision into words —any words—as if words savage and strange enough might charm a savage, strange world into submission. *Genethliacon, dephlegmated, lixiviated, aulnager, exceptions, quadrimanous, psephismata, delation, provocatives of cantharides, stum, dulcify, boulimia, diachylon, compurgation, founderous, turbinating:* the language of his last years is thick with odd, hard diction (many words, according to the *New English Dictionary,* appear in Burke's late writings for the first time in English), with Gallicisms, with neologisms like *Frenchify* and *Jacobinize,* with odd compounds like *church mummy, constitution-fancier, spring-nailed, civil-creating, cannibal philosophers,* and *gaol pollution.* Burke's style, to be sure, like his intellect, had been distinguished from youth by its power to assimilate almost anything. He laid all history and literature tribute for allusions and out-of-the-way facts; he converted into metaphors the technical language of trade, law, war, music, painting, and architecture, theology, heraldry, shipping, indeed any subject that engaged him. But more important still, he fused such odd bits of phrase and fact in a style of luminous simplicity, of austere grace and exactness, in which their oddness merely forwarded the meaning or the playfulness of the fancy. The style of his writings on France continues all that was best and most powerful in earlier writings: the *Reflections,* for example, is majestic prose of lucid subtlety, building in power stage by stage, argument by argument, mood by mood, until, before it is finished, Burke has delivered an enlarged, feeling perception of his case as complete and intense as that of a good poem. Yet, taken as a whole, the French tracts of the 1790's are fraught with a special and bizarre rhetoric for which there is no fully developed precedent in Burke—especially the four *Letters on a Regicide Peace* (1795–1797), *A Letter to William Elliot, Esq.* (1795), and the little masterpiece *Letter to a Noble Lord* (1795). Some of the rhetoric, one must admit, is indefensibly tasteless, almost hysterical; what may be overlooked, however, is the artful consciousness with which most of it is constructed.

The later French tracts are Burke's *Dunciad,* or perhaps one should say *Philosophiad.* The longer he watched the "monstrous tragicomic scene" unfold before him, and the more his imagination was filled by it, the more self-consciously he drew upon the rhetoric and devices of early Augustan satire to express his disgust and his perception of incongruities. The image of a profane, mock-heroic procession, a farcical march of triumph upon the bastions of church and nobility, haunts the first third of even the *Reflections,* not to mention later works. His style comes to abound in paradoxes and functional puns, whose polarities are past and present, old and new, feudal and modern; in oxymorons like "pious violence," "homicide philanthropy," "lay divines," "malignant charity," "sovereign canaille," or in implicitly oxymoronic images like "the solid darkness of this enlightened age" and the "arch-pontiff of *the rights of men*" (juxtaposing *philosophie* with the Roman Catholicism toward which it was hostile). Such images, characterizing a thing by its opposite, often imply their virtual equivalence as extremes: they are the rhetoric of an unstated *via media* which, open to latent values in both, has been irritated into cursing both houses. In the same way, Burke's allusions—for example, to church history and the Scriptures, to Cicero, Virgil, Shakespeare, Milton—come to function, as in Pope's *Dunciad,* not as mere ornament, but as a self-conscious expression of anxiety about cultural uprootedness and discontinuity in a dangerous new world. They tend toward establishment of an impersonal standard, a standard of "wisdom" and "civilization," against which the cartoon-portraits of French revolutionaries—tailors, carpenters, hair-dressers, village notaries, tallow-chandlers—stand forth in farcical vulgarity. Burke mastered the trick, common in Augustan satire, of transmuting historic persons into burlesque emblems of anti-culture and *lèze-intelligence,* and of lodging them in a burlesque fantasy world of ugliness whose very existence pleads for its opposite; the fantasy, in no way believable, is so intertwined with facts and virtual truth that it shocks one into thinking. Much in Burke's diction which seems odd results from his playing off contrary idioms or levels of usage against one another—one of them "heroic," majestic, sententiously grave, the other "low," technical, outlandish, or obscene.

The *Letter to a Noble Lord,* for example, whose very title has a precedent in Pope, is carefully organized so as to juxtapose two orders of reality and value—the first, "close up," rational, honorable, centered in portraits "after the life"; the other, at a distance of minute exaggeration, inhuman, farcical-fantastic; one English, the other French; one traditional and sane, the other revolutionary and annihilative. The letter follows a simple outline: a politely ironical, stinging introduction, then Burke's *apologia* for his career, followed by analysis of grants to the Bedford family from Henry VIII (implicitly comparing past and present), fading into satire of the French revolutionaries with whom the present Duke of Bedford has flirted, and closing with an idealized portrait of Lord Keppel (Bedford's uncle). The real unity, however, is cumulative in a stream of metaphors, allusions, and images which establish contrasting worlds or orders of value. As in a

Popian satire—for example, "Epistle to Arbuthnot"—Reason is beleaguered by madness, Virtue by folly, Nature by the evilly monstrous.

With small exceptions, the revolutionaries figure as a multitude of destroyers, invading from without. Something lilliputian about them is defined by a bizarre particularity in Burke's descriptions. In contrast to the moral generality of language which surrounds Lord Keppel, we hear about the dry bones of the revolutionaries' diagrams and the soot of their furnaces, their experiments with mephitic gas, with mice in an air-pump, with insurrectionary nitre, with tallowing in the caul, with carving up rumps and sirloins and briskets. Or again, they are a national menagerie of tigers and hyenas, hunting down victims to prey on the carcasses; a comet threatening to collide with earth, and whirl it out of the highway of heaven; Indian savages which pour in the gates to sack and ravage; a dark storm menacing the ship; the harpies in Virgil's *Aeneid* (*III,* 214 ff.), sprung from the monster-breeding regions of hell in *Paradise Lost* (II, 625) and sousing down upon the table of Aeneas and his companions; a plague threatening to overspread the world; levelers with pickaxes, chopping at the dikes of civilization; invading Gauls; Nimrods hunting their proper game, the nobility; the bearded men with their dogs, cavalry, iron, and gunpowder, which poor invaded Mexicans did not know to exist in nature; butchers gleefully planning dissection of a helpless animal, locusts swarming from a rotten carcass to lay waste the fair world.

The images of convergent attack from outside by things savage, monstrous, even satanic, are a kaleidoscopic backdrop against which is defined a world of the natural and normal—an antithetical center within which move Burke himself, his son, the Rockingham Whigs (in a brief mention), the good people of England, and, finally, Lord Keppel, whose type-portrait as a paragon of the old school of statesmen rounds off the satire with a positive affirmation. The Duke of Bedford himself hovers shadowily between the two worlds. His animal *leit-motiv*—whale, bullock, mouse, ox, lamb—pulls downward against his putative role of English peer, landed gentleman, and nephew of Keppel.

Enveloping the whole is, so to speak, the *persona,* the self-portrait, of Burke himself. His general role as a gentleman insulted and defensive of his honor is deepened and defined by still another stream of metaphors, allusions, and images of a different kind—an old man dying in grief for his dead son, a shade prophesying disaster for those who will dig up his casket to make bullets from its lead, an old oak uprooted by a hurricane, a periwinkle cast up on a stormy beach, a heroic enemy of tyranny like the Hussite John Zisca, an accused man pleading his case in court, the physician of the state, Hamlet, Phaeton in Ovid's *Metamorphoses* falling in a great undertaking, the alien who must show his passport at every turnpike, a repentant Job with acid words for his neighbors. From the start of his career, one of Burke's chief ways of getting drama in his speeches and letters was to construct them around a thinking and feeling speaker, a kind of expository *persona,* who, though by no means divorced from Burke himself, was also more than a detached voice.

> Poetry and rhetoric do not succeed in exact description [he remarked as a young man] so well as painting does; their business is, to affect rather by sympathy than imitation; *to display rather the effect of things on the mind of the speaker,* or of others, than to present a clear idea of the things themselves. This is their most extensive province, and that in which they succeed the best.[250]

Burke had a gift for self-projection or self-rendition, for making himself a character in the drama of an occasion, so that to follow the workings of the "character's" mind is part of the experience of learning Burke's ideas: the intellectual and imaginative processes which we are made to feel at work in his speeches are a functional statement about his ideas. The unity, then, of *Letter to a Noble Lord* lies in a delicate weave of images and tonal contrasts within the language. A similar argument could be made for the more sprawling *Letters on a Regicide Peace;* what is sometimes dismissed as invective babble, a kind of diseased glossolalia, is in fact artful rhetoric based on long-established techniques of Augustan satire. Its quality of success is, of course, another question.

To unravel all the intricacies of such rhetoric, and to place it in the history of Burke's style, would require a book in itself, and is well beyond the purposes of this one. As Dryden remarks somewhere, "the corruption of a poet is the generation of a statesman"; and even "corrupt" poetry is not to be paraphrased. Suffice it to say that the sarcasm and invective of Burke's last years grew from his excited awareness of ironies which seemed to crowd in upon his imagination from all directions, contrast and incongruity piled upon contrast, insanity upon inanity. The Jacobins, slyly accusing others of their own deceits, were crying peace as they plotted conquest, enslaving millions in the name of the people, praising English liberty and hating England, crying up equality and enforcing the most absolute despotism of the few ever known on earth,[251] glorifying virtue and behaving like cannibals, apostatizing from apostasy. A world mad, a carnival of hypocrisy, where virtue is vulgar, and wisdom cunning, where the present renouncing the past in hate reproduces the very vice it professes to hate—such a world is imaged in the quality of sarcasm which Burke achieved, and perhaps, he felt, could be imaged in no other way.

# VI

# Burke and India

AS one commentator observes, it is a measure of Burke's stature that even "when his sole unassisted name is pitted against the outcome of centuries, and we say Burke and the French Revolution, we are not overwhelmed by any sense of obvious absurdity or incongruity." [1] Yet Burke himself—such are the illusions of human pride and of historical vantage—would have quarreled with his own fame. A year before he died, nearing seventy, surveying his career of strange and splendid failures, he valued himself most upon his efforts not for the Christian royalists of France, nor for Whigs or Americans, nor for his countrymen in Ireland, but for the exotic people of India—"most for the importance; most for the labour; most for the judgment; most for constancy and perseverance in the pursuit. Others may value them most for the *intention.* In that, surely, they are not mistaken." [2] He persuaded himself to believe that he wanted everything he had done, said, or written, to be forgotten, except this.[3]

He spoke, of course, in the petulance of humiliation. The acquittal of Hastings in 1794, after fourteen years of exhausting prosecution, came to Burke as a personal insult, as well as a national calamity, and during his last years, when griefs and insults weighed upon his self-respect from every side, he found such compensations as were to be had in little gusts of petulance, in spectacular storms of sarcasm and polemic, and in receding flashes of hope—the hope, for example, that his good friend French Laurence would one day expose the acquittal as a fraud and clear his memory "from that load which the East India Company, King, Lords, and Commons, and in a manner the whole British nation (God forgive them), have been pleased to lay as a monument upon my ashes." [4] "The times are bad," he said, in Yeatsian manner, "very bad; —great heart in the worst men; in the rest, miserable dejection." [5] If ever Europe should recover its civilization—for in Burke's bruised pride, Indian delinquents and Jacobins sometimes blurred together as "allies" [6]—he convinced himself it would be useful work to expose what was occurring in India—a "barbarous and inhuman condemnation of whole tribes and nations, and of all the classes they contain." [7] "Remember!" he pleaded with Laurence: "Remember! Remember!" [8]

Burke's writings on India taxed his spirit as profoundly as those on France, and they bulk almost as large. Some of them, like the speech *On Mr. Fox's East-India Bill* (1783), *On the Nabob of Arcot's Debts* (1785), and the four opening speeches at Hastings' trial (1788), reach oratorical heights that few if any Englishmen except Burke himself have equaled, but much also is depreciated by a spirit of dry fatigue, exasperation, and strain. As trial manager and committeeman, he was hedged in by technical decorums; at the same time he confronted the staggering, almost superhuman labor of collecting, digesting, and explicating publicly the texture of vital detail in two decades of Indian history. The sheer claims of outlandish, confused, and unheard-of fact would have reduced a lesser mind to imbecility. In the sixties, as a young man entering Parliament, Burke had "thought himself obliged, by the research of years, to wind himself into the inmost recesses and labyrinths of the Indian detail," [9] and thus when the Hastings debate began, in the eighties, he could talk knowledgeably as few others could (except returned nabobs) of *sezawals* and *choultries, polygars, jaghires,* and *soubahs,* without flinching or pretense. He had the kind of mind, often found in good lawyers, which controls, or can rapidly acquire, an astounding range of information without sinking under it; he was the kind of man who would know in a moment, who could draw into ready and familiar focus, the functions of a *banyan,* the Mohammedan property laws, the Elizabethan origins of the East Indian Company, the circumstances of the last famine, the statistics of Bengal export, the testament of Tamerlane, the unprosecuted peculations of one Mr. Stuart. But to reconstruct such detail in the minds of a cold, and very often hostile, auditory, without the sacrifice of its significance, was a feat for an angel, not for a man. Burke just barely missed. The reversal of his own self-estimate, posterity's preference for his reflections on France, is probably just. But it is also unfortunate. Perhaps more than anything else it has fed the myth of his insularity and *status-quo*ism, when Burke wanted simply to be remembered as a good man, who, with little thought to what it cost him, did his duty by the rest of common humanity.

The Hastings trial (1788–1794), the culmination of his labors, actually defines a kind of second period in his India career in temper and style—a period often disfigured by some of the same excesses which show up in his writings on France during the same years. The first period puts one more in mind of his speeches on America. For example, his speech *On Mr. Fox's East-India Bill* (1783) is most nearly, of all his later pronouncements, like the speech *On Conciliation With America* (1775). It breathes the same innocent and manly reasonableness, the same lofty and cogent taste; it fuses the personal and the formal by the same alchemy of which Burke alone had the secret. It subordinates everything to the statement of a single principle, which it explores from different sides—in this instance, not the beauty of liberty and the wisdom of a generous heart, but the awful duty which attaches to all power. As we said, Burke began his researches on India when he was first studying America and the organization of the empire. By 1772 he had distinguished himself enough to be offered the leading place in a council of three dispatched to India in that year to investigate reports of abuse. He elected to stay in Parliament instead, but he never stopped improving his acquaintance with Indian affairs, personally through correspondence with friends like his "cousin" William Burke, Sir William Jones the translator, and later Sir Philip Francis, and officially, through service on India committees in the Commons. During early debates preceding the act of 1773, whose provisions he thought unwise (and whose unwisdom he had the exasperating pleasure of explaining ten years later),[10] Burke defended the chartered independence of the company against what he judged to be a Tory and court conspiracy to grab its patronage and influence, and to levy on its wealth as a facile compensation for mismanagement in the American colonies. His goal was "keeping the company out of the hands of any court projector, who may think of decorating the crown with the collected spoils of the East."[11] But even at this date his grounds were as much humanitarian as political: such power in illiberal hands would plunder the natives as it had on St. Vincent's, in the West Indies—an incident which Burke termed "massacring (in the true European mode of civilization)."[12]

There are other resemblances with his reflections on America. He urged Parliament not to "consider laws, religion, morality, and the principles of state policy of empires as mere questions of profit and loss"[13]—that is, in the shopkeeping spirit. He observed with pain "the intrusion into this important debate of such company as *quo warranto,* and *mandamus,* and *certiorari;* as if we were on a trial about mayors and aldermen, and capital burgesses; or engaged in a suit concerning the borough of Penryn, or Saltash, or St. Ives, or St. Mawes"[14]—that is, the intrusion of a spirit of pettifoggery. He called for a legislative liberality appropriate to "this grave deliberation of policy and empire." He ridiculed "the optical illusion which makes a brier at our nose of greater magnitude, than an oak at five hundred yards distance."[15] He traced "all the calamities of this country to the single source of our not having had steadily before our eyes a general, comprehensive, well-connected, and well-proportioned view of the whole of our dominions, and a just sense of their true bearings and relations." "But if we make ourselves too little for the sphere of our duty; if, on the contrary, we do not stretch and expand our minds to the compass of their object; be well assured, that everything about us will dwindle by degrees, until at length our concerns are shrunk to the dimensions of our minds." [16] Amidst vehement declamation about private property, corporate franchise, faction, coalition, and whatnot, gentlemen, he noticed, said little about "the interest and well-being of the people of India." [17] And yet, he went on, "if we are not able to contrive some method of governing India *well,* which will not of necessity become the means of governing Great Britain *ill,* a ground is laid for their eternal separation." [18]

Knowing that "distance of place and absence from management, operate as remoteness of time," [19]—that is, operate as history—Burke struggled for a historical means "by which India might be approximated to our understandings, and if possible to our feelings; in order to waken something of sympathy for the unfortunate natives, of which I am afraid we are not perfectly susceptible, whilst we look at this very remote object through a false and cloudy medium." [20] That is, he applied his principle that a people must be governed, if they are to be governed at all, according to their concrete character and circumstances. But this time his task of characterization was incomparably harder: it was no longer a question of understanding and making understood a familial colony like America or Ireland, or even a neighboring nation like France, in which, for all their complications, a community of fundamentals was latent and yoked together the most violent and adverse parties when they little guessed its presence. He confronted in India profound cultural differentiations which hardly anybody in eighteenth-century Europe was prepared to understand. (Whether they are really understood now, felt on the pulses, after a century and a half of development in historiography and communications, is surely doubtful.)

Burke could combat easily enough the provincialism of the smug (although Burke is not above a little playful snobbery, as in, for example, his reference to "Meer Jaffier, Lord Clive's nabob, seated on his musnud").[21] He could remind Parliament that the people of India were not "gangs of savages, like the Guaranies and Chiquitos, who wander on the waste borders of the river of Amazons, or the Plate; but a people for ages civilized and cultivated; cultivated by all the arts of polished life, whilst we were yet in the woods." [22] He could generalize about the dignity of its princes, the antiquity of its priesthood, nobility, laws, learning, and history, and its multitude of cities,

> not exceeded in population and trade by those of the first class in Europe; merchants and bankers, individual houses of whom have once vied in capital with the bank of England; whose credit had often supported a tottering state, and preserved their governments in the midst of war and desolation; millions of ingenious manufacturers and mechanics; millions of the most diligent, and not the least intelligent, tillers of the earth. There, are to be found almost all the religions professed by men, the Braminical, the Mussulman, the Eastern and Western Christian. . . . All this vast mass, composed of so many orders and classes of men, is again infinitely diversified by manners, by religion, by hereditary employment, through all their possible combinations.[23]

That is, he could make the very point he should have made: that all this "renders the handling of India a matter in a high degree critical and delicate. But oh! it has been handled rudely indeed." [24] Occasionally he could indulge himself in the sort of *explicatio morum,* selective, comparative, and practical, in which he excelled—for example, in his discussion of the principle of "locality" in ancient Hindu society. (A sample must be, perhaps unpardonably, long: Burke juggles several principles at one time for long periods, to show their cross-bearings.)

> Their legislator, whoever he was (for who he was is a matter lost in the midst of a most obscure antiquity), had it as a great leading principle of his policy to connect the people with their soil. Accordingly, by one of those anomalies which a larger acquaintance with our species daily discovers, and which perhaps an attentive reflection might explain in the nature of man, this

aboriginal people of India, who are the softest in their manners of any of our race, approaching almost to feminine tenderness, who are formed constitutionally benevolent, and in many particulars made to fill a larger circle of benevolence than our morals take in, who extend their goodwill to the whole animal creation,—these people are, of all nations, the most unalliable to any other part of mankind. . . . No Hindoo can mix at meals even with those on whom he depends for the meat he eats. This circumstance renders it difficult for us to enter with due sympathy into their concerns, or for them to enter into ours, even when we meet on the same ground. . . . None of their high castes, without great danger to his situation, religion, rank, and estimation, can ever pass the sea; and this forbids, for ever, all direct communication between that country and this. . . . We must not think to force them into the narrow circle of our ideas; we must extend ours to take in their system of opinions and rites, and the necessities which result from both: all change on their part is absolutely impracticable. We have more versatility of character and manners, and it is we who must conform. We know what the empire of opinion is in human nature. I had almost said that the law of opinion was human nature itself. . . . The variety of balanced opinions in our minds weakens the force of each. . . . But God forbid we should pass judgment upon people who framed their laws and institutions prior to our insect origin of yesterday. With all the faults of their nature, and errors of their institutions, the institutions, which act so powerfully on their natures, have two material characteristics which entitle them to respect:—first, great force and stability; next, excellent moral and civil effects. . . . They have stood firm on their ancient base—they have cast their roots deep in their native soil; perhaps because they have never spread them anywhere else than in their native soil. Their blood, their opinions, and the soil of their country, make one consistent piece, admitting no mixture, no adulteration, no improvement: accordingly, their religion has made no converts; their dominion has made no conquests; but in proportion as their laws and opinions were concentrated within themselves, and hindered from spreading abroad, they have doubled their force at home. They have existed in spite of Mahomedan and Portuguese bigotry, in spite of Tartarian and Arabian tyranny, in spite of all the fury of successive foreign conquest, in spite of a more formidable foe—the avarice of the

English dominion. . . . It is confirmed by all observation, that where the Hindoo religion has been established, that country has been flourishing. We have seen some patterns remaining to this day.[25]

Burke could make such analyses of what would otherwise be exotic or unintelligible. He made them not, he said, "for the gratification of historical curiosity"; instead, "the contexture is necessary to demonstrate to your lordships the spirit of our Bengal politics": [26] "I have not gone out of my way to bring before you any circumstance relative to the Gentoo religion and manners, further than as they relate to the spirit of our government over them; for though there never was such food for the curiosity of the human mind as is found in the manners of this people, I pass it totally over." [27] It is necessary to remark this purposiveness and selectivity in Burke's portraiture because of Macaulay's half-erroneous praise. Remarking rightly that Burke had "that noble faculty whereby man is able to live in the past, in the future, in the distant, and in the unreal," that "India and its inhabitants were not to him, as to most Englishmen, mere names and abstractions, but a real country and real people," and that he had "just as lively an idea of the insurrection at Benares as of Lord George Gordon's riots," Macaulay then indulged himself in a long picturesque-romantic catalogue of details that tells us more about his own taste than about Burke's: the burning sun, the rich tracery of the mosque, the praying Imaum, the drums, and banners, and gaudy idols, the graceful maiden with the pitcher on her head, and so on.[28] Whereas in truth Burke's neoclassic imagination was more practical and intellectualized. His purpose was not to fascinate, but to familiarize; not to paint thrilling pictures, but to grasp and draw in the actual relations of things; to find the grounds of social and moral community. In this way, reaching out into a world beyond the horizon, Burke could combat the provincialism, indifference, and complacency, which blinded Englishmen at home to the human situation. He could remind them of the human situation which is always present in politics, and which defined both their own limits and their duty to other men whose limits differed in shape.

As in his speech on conciliation with America, Burke contrived picturesque and rhetorical "views," but their aim was to arouse in his auditors a familiar understanding, to recruit their ordinary (and inactive) feelings in support of *the reason of the case*. Take, for example, the famous description of Hyder Ali's invasion and waste of the Carnatic, which, as Hazlitt observed, will "do equally well for poetry or prose." [29] Resolving, "in the gloomy recesses of a mind capacious of such things," [30] to revenge perfidious plots against him by the East India Company, Hyder Ali gathered his armies from every quarter, "and compounding all the materials of fury, havoc, and desolation, into one black cloud, he hung for a while on the declivities of the mountains."

> Whilst the authors of all these evils were idly and stupidly gazing on this menacing meteor, which blackened all their horizon, it suddenly burst, and poured down the whole of its contents upon the plains of the Carnatic.—Then ensued a scene of woe, the like of which no eye had seen, no heart conceived, and which no tongue can adequately tell. All the horrors of war before known or heard of, were mercy to that new havoc. A storm of universal fire blasted every field, consumed every house, destroyed every temple. The miserable inhabitants flying from their flaming villages, in part were slaughtered; others, without regard to sex, to age, to the respect of rank, or sacredness of function, fathers torn from children, husbands from wives, enveloped in a whirlwind of cavalry, and amidst the goading spears of drivers, and the trampling of pursuing horses, were swept into captivity, in an unknown and hostile land. Those who were able to evade this tempest, fled to the walled cities. But escaping from fire, sword, and exile, they fell into the jaws of famine.[31]

A nation "stretched out its hands for food"; hundreds perished in the streets of Madras. For eighteen months the destruction raged, until "when the British armies traversed, as they did, the Carnatic for hundreds of miles in all directions, through the whole line of their march they did not see one man, not one woman, not one child, not one four-footed beast of any description whatever. One dead, uniform silence reigned over the whole region." [32] Such eloquence, however, was only Burke's prelude to a practical comparison. The Carnatic, he said, is barely smaller than England. Figure to yourself, Mr. Speaker . . . the form and fashion of your sweet and cheerful country from Thames to Trent north and south, and from the Irish to the German Sea east and west, emptied and embowelled. . . . Extend your imagination a little farther, and then suppose your ministers taking a survey of this scene of waste and desolation; what would be your thoughts if you should be informed, that they were computing how much had been the amount of the excises, how much the customs, how much the land and malt tax, in order that they should charge (take it in the most favourable light) for public service, upon . . . the whole of what England had yielded in the most exuberant seasons of peace and abundance? What would you call it? To call it tyranny sublimed into madness, would be too faint an image; yet this very madness is the principle upon which the ministers at your right hand have proceeded in their estimate of the revenues of the Carnatic." [33]

Indeed, in his major wish, that is, judged by his own standard of what sooner or later had to be done, Burke could not help failing. The sort of practical approximation of East and West which he valued and supposed to be necessary would have to be the work, in all likelihood, of centuries of mutual criticism and accommodation, under the pressure of great transforming forces. He could not really cross the "gulf," as he called it,[34] which inveterate usage had radicated in both sides with unguessed depth and adhesion, as in some measure, by glimpses, he almost certainly perceived:

We are in general, Sir, so little acquainted with Indian details; the instruments of oppression under which the people suffer are so hard to be understood; and even the very names of the sufferers are so uncouth and strange to our ears, that it is very difficult for our sympathy to fix upon these objects. I am sure that some of us have come down-stairs from the committee-room, with impressions on our minds which to us were the inevitable results of our discoveries, yet if we should venture to express ourselves in the proper language of our sentiments to other gentlemen, not at all prepared to enter into the cause of them, nothing could appear more harsh and dissonant, more violent and unaccountable, than our language and behaviour. All these circumstances are not, I confess, very favourable to the idea of our attempting to govern India at all.[35]

"But," he went on, "there we are; there we are placed by the Sovereign Disposer; and we must do the best we can in our situation. The situation of man is the preceptor of his duty." Against the luxuriant backdrop of Indian mystery and remoteness, Burke's voice rings out in the hardheaded humility, the courageous diffidence of common sense, proceeding from fact to principle, and principle to fact, persevering, unafraid, sympathetic, experimental—and, very often, violently mistaken. His rajahs and zemindaries wear knee pants, shortcoat, and queue; they stand on their dignity, tapping a snuffbox. For the same reason that destined him to fail he was unfair to Hastings who, high-handed enough to be sure, and not always scrupulous about his means, had tried crossing the same gulf in his own person, and had failed in other ways. Asked to guide the company through the fogs of cultural dyspathy, Hastings too had oversimplified, fallen backwards, resorted to extraordinary methods and to force.[36] If Burke failed, however, to escape the hermetic sheath of an eighteenth-century European, he failed while he was attempting to follow a principle; and it can be argued that whenever or if the grounds of intercultural community are ever laid, it will probably be by practical and objective approximations of the kind his wisdom envisioned and tried to further: by compliant realism, tolerance, self-watchfulness, and a will to adopt as much good as can possibly be recognized, no matter what its source nor where it is found.

Once one understands the complexity of Burke's helpless insights into the matter, one goes back to the brilliant acrobatics of a revolutionary deist like Paine and all his (important) talk of universals and nature and reason and rights, with the disappointed, indifferent, perhaps faintly amused respect of a *pater familias* at the circus.

In sheer analytical and descriptive grasp, however, of the East India Company's proceedings, its structure, history, and spirit—insofar as it showed the dark side of its ordinary and English face—Burke was superbly adequate. His reports upon its "ostensible" institutions were scholarly, precise, and packed, but he was at his most brilliant in explicating what he called "the principal, the inward, the real." [37] Starting as an Elizabethan commercial adventure, the Company had succeeded to power after power, until finally, "things took a course very different from their usual order. A new disposition took place, not dreamt of in the theories of speculative politicians, and of which few examples in the least resembling it have been seen in the modern world, none at all in the ancient. . . . It became that thing which was supposed by the Roman law irreconcilable to reason and propriety—*eundem negotiatorem et dominum*. . . . In fact the East-India Company in Asia is a state in the disguise of a merchant. Its whole service is a system of public offices in the disguise of a counting-house." [38]

It came to pass that over an extent of nearly 300,000 square miles, not a man could eat a mouthful of rice without the Company's permission.[39] Yet, Burke observed, the mercantile politicians, unlike the new people in other conquests and colonizations, did not come as an offset of their parent nation; they held political power without the bridle of popular criticism; no door "was left open for the public sense to enter into that society." [40]

The Company in India does not exist as a national colony. In effect and substance, nobody can go thither that does not go in its service. The English in India are nothing but a seminary for the succession of officers. They are a nation of placemen;—they are a commonwealth without a people; they are a state made up wholly of magistrates. . . . The consequence of which is, that being a kingdom of magistrates, what is commonly called the *esprit de corps* is strong in it. The spirit of the body predominates equally in all its parts; by which the members must consider themselves as having a common interest, and that common interest separated both from that of the country which sent them out, and from that of the country in which they act. No control upon them exists.[41]

Its civil service "resembled the military service of the Mahrattas—little pay, but unbounded license to plunder," [42] and throughout the hierarchy, since almost everybody improved himself with minor extortions or embezzlements, practically nobody would inform against the most heinous. The Company was driven by the spirit of monopolistic capitalism at its most exquisite pitch, draining off resources with little view to the happiness or permanent welfare of the local populations. It was a "vehicle of tribute." [43] "England has erected no churches, no hospitals, no palaces, no schools; England has built no bridges, made no highroads, cut no navigations, dug out no reservoirs. Every other conqueror of every other description has left some monument, either of state, or beneficence, behind him. Were we to be driven out of India this day, nothing would remain, to tell that it had been possessed during the inglorious period of our dominion, by anything better than the ourang-outang or the tiger." [44] The situation was aggravated further by the influx of ambitious young people, concerned only to make a quick fortune, and return to the elegant and hospitable retirement, the *mariages de convenance,* and respectable influence of England.

The natives scarcely know what it is to see the grey head of an Englishman. Young men (boys almost) govern there, without society and without sympathy with the natives. They have no more social habits with the people, than if they still resided in England; nor indeed, any species of intercourse but that which is necessary to making a sudden fortune, with a view to a remote settlement. Animated with all the avarice of age, and all the impetuosity of youth, they roll in one after another; wave after wave; and there is nothing before the eyes of the natives but an endless, hopeless prospect of new flights of birds of prey and passage, with appetites continually renewing for a food that is continually wasting. . . . English youth in India drink the intoxicating draught of authority and dominion before their heads are able to bear it, and as they are full grown in fortune long before they are ripe in principle, neither nature nor reason have any opportunity to exert themselves for remedy of the excesses of their premature power. The consequences of their conduct, which in good minds (and many of theirs are probably such) might produce penitence or amendment, are unable to pursue the rapidity of their flight. Their prey is lodged in England; and the cries of India are given to seas and winds to be blown about, in every breaking up of the monsoon, over a remote and unhearing ocean.[45]

The Indian people were demonized by a bureaucratic avarice and "the desperate boldness of a few obscure young men, who having obtained, by ways which they could not comprehend, a power of which they saw neither the purposes nor the limits, tossed about, subverted, and tore to pieces, as if it were in the gambols of a boyish unluckiness and malice, the most established rights, and the most ancient and most revered institutions, of ages and nations." [46] "Our dominion has been a vulgar thing." [47]

If the avaricious servants of the Company, as he painted them, were like bold and cunning boys incorporated for debauchery, their Indian stewards—*banyans*—were somewhere between pimps and blackmailers. The moment a young Englishman arrives in India, Burke said, the intriguing *banyans* pounce upon him: "They have knowledge of the country and its affairs; they have money, they have the arts of making money. The gentleman who comes from England has none of these; he enters into that world as he enters into the world at large, naked. His portion is great simplicity, great indigence, and a strong disposition to relieve himself." [48] In time the nominal master is the half-willing slave of his helpers, and he must have "as many hands as one of the idols in an Indian temple, in order to receive all the bribes." [49]

We know how young men are sent out of this country; we know how happy we are to hear soon that they are no longer a burden to their friends and parents. The banyan knows it too. He supplies the young servant with money. He has him under his power; first, from the necessity of employing such a man; and next (and this is the more important of the two), he has that dreadful power over his master which every creditor has over his debtor. Actions the most abhorrent to his nature he must see done before his face: and thousand and thousand worse are done in his absence, and he dare not complain.[50]

The *esprit de corps* of banyanism migrated to England among its newly initiated nabobs, and settled as an ill-defined but effectual bloc, steadily controlling the power which flows toward the wealthy, toward loan-brokers, patrons, investors, and entrepreneurs. It perpetuated in English life the manners learned in an Asiatic absolutism—low connivance, confederacy, predatory avarice. It threatened to make England a nation of banyans.[51] For hardly a family in England, Burke said, was without monied or friendly relation to the corps, by way of kinship, marriage, obligation, employment, or debt; everybody felt only disgruntled suspicion and resentment of any very serious meddling with the vitals of so interesting an institution. And though the public quickly fired at reports of malversation in India, "they were not equally sensible to the evils, which arose from a system of sacrificing the being of that country to the advantage of this." [52] The system itself tended both to generate and to stabilize the evils. As Laski observed, Burke "saw how a nation might become corrupted by the spoils of other lands. He knew that cruelty abroad is the parent of a later cruelty at home." [53] Burke's classic example was Paul Benfield, the master-artist in "the profession of soucaring," [54] whom he accused of buying a parliamentary interest to secure ministerial protection for his triumphs of Indian fraud.

Throughout his Indian speeches Burke recurred to paradoxical, somehow chiaroscuro images which fuse morbidity and vigor, sexual lust and affected delicacy, as if nothing but paradox could express his tone of bewildered disgust at the spectacle of a rapacious government founded by Englishmen. The speech *On the Nabob of Arcot's Debts* (1785) is a representative example. Burke spoke of the engendering of crime, of corrupt prodigality. The careless and unashamed extortions of directors "animated the strong desires of their servants to this prohibited prolific sport, and it soon produced a swarm of sons and daughters, not in the least degenerated from the virtue of their parents." [55] An affected moderation and purity in the directors was really "pander and bawd to the unbridled debauchery and licentious lewdness of usury and extortion" [56] by money-jobbers like Benfield. Burke scoffed at "the chalice of the fornications of rapine, usury, and oppression, which was held out by the gorgeous Eastern harlot; which so many of the people, so many of the nobles, of this land had drained to the very dregs. Do you think that no reckoning was to follow this lewd debauch? that no payment was to be demanded for this riot of public drunkenness and national prostitution?" [57] By transfer of the image, he transferred also an accusation of collusion with Benfield to the minister Henry Dundas, who, Burke insinuated, brought forth six heavily partial and slanted reports from the Committee of Secrecy intended to forestall a genuine investigation of the facts. It was the technique of "concealment through discovery" which Burke later attributed to Hastings' ingenuity.[58]

> He and delicacy are a rare and singular coalition. He thinks that to divulge our India politics, may be highly dangerous. He! the mover! the chairman! the reporter of the committee of secrecy! he that brought forth in the utmost detail, in several vast printed folios, the most recondite parts of the politics, the military, the revenues of the British empire in India! With six great chopping bastards, each as lusty as an infant Hercules, this delicate creature blushes at the sight of his new bridegroom, assumes a virgin delicacy; or, to use a more fit, as well as a more poetic, comparison, the person so squeamish, so timid, so trembling lest the winds of heaven should visit too roughly, is expanded to broad sunshine, exposed like the sow of imperial augury, lying in the mud with all the prodigies of her fertility about her, as evidence of her delicate amours—*Triginta capitum foetus enixa jacebat, alba solo recubans albi circum ubera nati.*[59]

The images, preponderantly sexual, are not exclusively so: their effect depends essentially upon their qualification by other images or suggestions associated *en passant*. The flavor of the morbid is established when Burke refers to the mysteriously indefinite and fluctuant debt of the Nabob as a "gigantic phantom." "When this gigantic phantom of debt first appeared before a young minister, it naturally would have justified some degree of doubt and apprehension. Such a prodigy would have filled any common man with superstitious fears. He would exorcise that shapeless, nameless form, and by everything sacred would have adjured it to tell by what means a small number of slight individuals, of no consequence or situation . . . could have, in a few years, (as to some, even in a few months,) amassed treasures equal to the revenues of a respectable kingdom?" [60] The paradox is prepared in a stream of allusions to the phantom's "growth" [61] and "plumpness," [62] while continuing references to its being "amongst the deepest mysteries of state," [63] its being "a sort of floating debt," [64] until finally the paradox is established in a new image of vigor: "In short, when you pressed this sensitive plant, it always contracted its dimensions. When the rude hand of inquiry was withdrawn, it expanded in all the luxuriant vigour of its original vegetation." [65] The whole is reinforced and expanded by what at the time appear to be, but are not, discrete sallies—for example, "Let no man hereafter talk of the decaying energies of nature" [66]—until in the total effect, the two poles of the paradox are unified in a virtual proposition: that something unnatural, pretending a delicate supervision but actually prostituting India in concealment, has engendered monsters of illegitimate wealth with disgusting fertility and frequency, and for its own pleasure. More important still, the basic image defines the tone of the speaker and therefore, suffusively, enriches the suggestion of isolated phrases in the speech, indeed the whole of its diction, which would otherwise have a denotative neutrality. Phrases like *seduced creditors,*[67] *the gigantic corruption of this single act,*[68] *drawing out all the juices of the body,*[69] *winking at these abuses,*[70] the *naked possibility,*[71] *little appearance of de-*

*cency,*[72] *appear full of tenderness to that ruined nation,*[73] take on added richness in Burke's argument and define the quality of his persuasion—a Swiftian disgust. "Tyrannous exaction," Burke said, "brings on servile concealment; and that again calls forth tyrannous coercion. They move in a circle, mutually producing and produced; till at length nothing of humanity is left in the government, no trace of integrity, spirit, or manliness in the people, who drag out a precarious and degraded existence." [74] To repeat, however: the chain of imagery, though centrally, is not exclusively sexual, and the paradox of unnatural vigor or generative death—of the unnatural infesting or cohabiting with the natural—is picked up and amplified by other horrid suggestions. For example: in Burke's reference to the Nabob's debt as "the foul, putrid mucus, in which are engendered the whole brood of creeping ascarides, all the endless involutions, the eternal knot, added to a knot of those inexpugnable tape-worms, which devour the nutriment, and eat up the bowels of India." [75] Or again, in a passage like this one, warning against the reactionary effect of such corruption upon English politics:

These abuses, full of their own wild native vigour, will grow and flourish under mere neglect. But where the supreme authority, not content with winking at the rapacity of its inferior instruments, is so shameless and corrupt as openly to give bounties and premiums for disobedience to its laws, when it will not trust to the activity of avarice in the pursuit of its own gains, when it secures public robbery by all the careful jealousy and attention with which it ought to protect property from such violence, the commonwealth then is become totally perverted from its purposes; neither God nor man will long endure it; nor will it long endure itself. In that case, there is an unnatural infection, a pestilential taint fermenting in the constitution of society, which fever and convulsions of some kind or other must throw off; or in which the vital powers, worsted in an unequal struggle, are pushed back upon themselves, and, by a reversal of their whole functions, fester to gangrene, to death; and, instead of what was but just now the delight and boast of the creation, there will be cast out in the face of the sun, a bloated, putrid, noisome carcass, full of stench and poison, an offence, a horror, a lesson to the world.[76]

Burke often sustains a drift of associative imagery or suggestion throughout individual speeches, which, not single in any mean, technical fashion, has about it a kind of clustering or cumulative singleness of effect. It is one of the increasingly distinctive features of his rhetoric as it develops, roughly from about 1780 on (the year of his speech on economical reform), into the sarcasm—the sustained paradox and innuendo—of his last years. As the appreciative Hazlitt was first to observe, Burke's style is the living projection of his sensibility, an intensely personal and associative style in essence, though its steady undercurrent of association is not always visible, breaking only here and there into its characteristic tropes of paradox, pun, allusion, and personification. Once visible, several tropes run together in a larger, not-quite-fused associativeness, which is somehow pyramidal in a strangely inverted fashion: that is, whole speeches, viewed in retrospect, seem like individual tropes, whose bearing upon one another is somehow not-quite-fused. Yet a single spirit, readily identifiable and unique, pervades the whole, qualifying one stand with another, stamping the whole with a characteristic unity. The critic snatches out a luminous phrase, and it putties; he quotes a paragraph, confident of preserving some good thing within it, and it is as useless as an amputated limb. Quoting whole pages is no better. One understands Hazlitt's despair: "to do him justice, it would be necessary to quote all his works; the only specimen of Burke is, *all that he wrote.*" [77] Style is the man indeed. Burke's style, like his thought, drives toward the organic, falling just short of what the organic, by any known theory, is supposed to be, yet in fact being a practical expression of it.

With what might appear on the surface a complete *volte-face* from his conservative principles, and from his defense of the Company's charter during the seventies, Burke argued, in support of Fox's bill, that such corruption had grown within the East India Company insensibly and over so long a period that it was now fixed beyond reformation: [78] that power should be taken out of the Company's hands, no matter what the legal validity of its charter, "on the same principles on which have been made all the just changes and revolutions of government that have taken place since the beginning of the world," [79] that is, on the grounds that the abuse of power is tending to a systematic and inveterate prey upon human rights. Every "species of political dominion," he said, is "a *trust;* and it is of the very essence of every trust to be rendered *accountable;* and even totally to cease, when it substantially varies from the purposes for which alone it could have a lawful existence." [80] For "the rights of *men,* that is to say, the natural rights of mankind, are indeed sacred things; and if any public measure is proved mischievously to affect them, the objection ought to be fatal to that measure. . . . Indeed, this formal recognition, by the sovereign power, of an original right in the subject, can never be subverted." [81] The sufferings of the Indian people before his mind's eye, he ridiculed "those treacherous expedients, called moderate measures," [82] and "that half virtue, which, like the ambiguous animal that flies about in the twilight of a compromise between day and night, is to a just man's eye an odious and disgusting thing. There is no middle point in which the Commons of Great Britain can meet tyranny and oppression." [83] He deprecated the criminal complicity of acquiescence. And he pointed to the hypocritical folly of pretending that abusers would correct their own abuses. Henry Dundas, he said, who proposed a bill to offset Fox's,

> would keep the present government of India in the court of directors; and would, to curb them, provide salutary regulations;—wonderful! That is, he would appoint the old offenders to correct the old offences. . . . He would appoint the wolf as guardian of the sheep; but he has invented a curious muzzle, by which this protecting wolf shall not be able to open his jaws above an inch or two at the utmost. Thus his work is finished. But I tell the right honourable gentleman, that controlled depravity is not innocence; and that it is not the labour of delinquency in chains that will correct abuses.[84]

He noticed that "the laws, which ought to secure the people against the abuse of power, are employed to screen that abuse against the cries of the people," [85] so that "whatever grievance is borne is denied to exist; and all mute despair, and sullen patience, is construed into content and satisfaction." [86] He turned his full contempt upon the idea of:

A compromising, balanced, neutralized, equivocal, colourless, confused report [of injustice]; in which the blame was to be impartially divided between the sufferer and the oppressor; and . . . which, according to the standing manners of Bengal . . . would recommend oblivion as the best remedy; and would end by remarking, that retrospect could have no advantage, and could serve only to irritate and keep alive animosities: and by this kind of equitable, candid, and judge-like proceeding . . . the whole complaint would calmly fade away; the sufferers remain in the possession of their patience, and the tyrant of his plunder.[87]

His Indian tracts, beginning a few years after the American Revolution and continuing well into the French, are a brilliant complement (or, as some may insist, antidote) to the dominant conservatism of his writings on France. They are not really inconsistent with, say, the *Reflections,* but they have a contrary emphasis or drift. The sole question with him, he said, was whether the measure proposed was required by the necessities of India; he would not consent "totally to lose sight of the real wants of the people who are the objects of it, and to hunt after every matter of party squabble that may be started on the several provisions." [88] To be sure, one can find Burke expressing the same "insuperable reluctance in giving my hand to destroy any established institution of government, upon a theory, however plausible it may be"; [89] he insisted upon proving the abuse of the charter significant, habitual, and incorrigible, before he would advise Parliament to touch it; and he further reminded them that since the power vested in the reformer is also a trust, "it is the use we make of the resumed power that must justify or condemn us in the resumption of it." [90] Also, much of his anger with the Company's administration proceeded from his belief that, looking on India as a depthless glut, they had ruthlessly refused to acquiesce in and conserve its established institutions: Hastings had set up "the whole nobility, gentry, and freeholders, to the highest bidder. No preference was given to the ancient proprietors." [91] "All the castles were, one after the other, plundered and destroyed. The native princes were expelled; the hospitals fell to ruin; the reservoirs of water went to decay; the merchants, bankers, and manufacturers disappeared; and sterility, indigence, and depopulation, overspread the face of these once flourishing provinces." [92]

Burke wanted to move gradually, though not slowly, as "one fraud furnishes light to the discovery of another, and so on, until the whole secret of mysterious iniquity bursts upon you in a blaze of detection." [93] But the main force of his argument, unlike that of the *Reflections,* errs on the side of popular protest, humanitarian internationalism, and eagerness, even yearning, for change. If by some freak Burke's angry wish had been granted, if nothing had survived of his work except his pleading "the cause of the natives of India," he would be looked upon now—as he conceived himself to be—as one of the more dedicated, idealistic, and zealous (albeit still Christian, English and unmetaphysical) liberals in an era of liberal upheaval. People might remember his early friendship with Mirabeau instead of his later animus and disgust.[94] Fully allowing that Fox's East-India Bill, whose substance really grew from his own research and reflection,[95] was a bold, novel departure from the beaten track of India government, Burke supported it nevertheless, wholeheartedly, as aiming at "the rescue of the greatest number of the human race that ever were so grievously oppressed, from the greatest tyranny that was ever exercised." [96] He called it "the *Magna Charta* of Hindostan," [97] and he hoped for justification by the future.

Not that Burke can be tuned in upon the febrile frequency of *Ça ira:* his liberalism is Christian, not Jacobin. His views, however, pulled down a storm of reactionary wrath from high places—from the Lords, the Crown, the East India Company itself, and the retinues of each, from all chartered corporations; the defeat of the bill exploded the Fox-North coalition and threw Whigs out of government for the next fifty years. John Morley thinks, since the bill "was indisputably inconsistent with the spirit of his revered Constitution," [98] it deserved defeat. But this is doubtful: the bill may have deserved defeat, but how could it be inconsistent with the spirit of Burke's constitution, that is, his idea of the constitution, if after scrutiny he judged otherwise? It may be inconsistent with one's abstraction of Burke's idea, but that would argue as well for the one-sidedness of the abstraction. Reverent of precedent, Burke was not precedent-ridden; reverent of law, he was contemptuous of legalism. "I have long thought," he wrote in 1795, "that, though we have many persons of parts and of Eloquence and of first rate Capacities for Business of all sorts, that the animal called a *Statesman* was (against the Rule of the Schools),—'a lost kind.' " [99] It cannot be remembered too often that Burke's politics premise responsibility to changing experience, a statesmanlike pursuit of the reality principle, and more important still, that he can be made out to be a conservative only in a locus of specific judgments, not in his ultimate commitments which have reference to a standard conceived as eternal. Nothing eternal can be bound by relative categories like conservative and liberal, constitutional or unconstitutional. For example, justice in human relations (and politics is a branch of human relations) is not any more *a priori* conservative than *a priori* liberal; neither is charity. The *practical* determination of either depends, as Burke said, upon the construction of a vital context, a "situation." For, although justice and charity are eternally the same, the modes of their actualization are as various as situations are possible. *Dieu s'impose, l'homme dispose.* And what in one instance may call for hesitancy and lagging-back, in another instance may exact "the enlargement to comprehend, the spirit to undertake, and the eloquence to support . . . a measure of hazardous benevolence." [100]

For this reason, it is essential to know the context when analyzing Burke's ideas. Nothing he says is wisely to be abstracted from its context without great care and a generous will to know the truth. When he exalts the Anglican establishment in the *Reflections* he writes consciously to an audience who despise it without really knowing what it is about, hysterical Ahabs in quest of a blind vengeance; Burke tries to get at its "objective" fundamentals. On other occasions, he finds himself in opposition to its policies; he disliked "political theologians, and theological politicians." When Burke marvels at the American character he is conscious of addressing English people blinded by resentment and misinformation to the fundamentals which they have in common with Americans; but America as such has no fetish-attraction for him. When he argues for free trade in Ireland, he sees the mighty weight of inertia, prepossession, and self-interest, which stand behind mercantile restraints, and are not soon or easily to be budged; but he is no free-trader forever and in all circumstances. He turns the full energy of his rhetoric against Dissenters when collectively and generally they adopt a subversive politics; but he defends them and argues for their relief and independence when their claims are limited, and in the case of post-revolutionary France, argues for their re-establishment in the sector of France they dominated before the revolution, despite their political affinities. He proposes, and draws up a detailed plan, for the regulation instead of the abolition of the slave trade because at the time he argues (six years before Wilberforce would take up the project) he knows that neither regulation nor abolition is likely, but he tries for what he has most hope and chance of achieving; when Wilberforce proposed abolition in 1789, Burke supported him entirely, arguing that civilization and slavery are incompatible.[101] He attacks the power of monarchy when it is overgrown, and defends the monarchy when it is under radical attack. He cautions his electors that he will abide by his best judgment, when they incline to rough him, but if they grow lazy or indifferent, he warns them that their welfare depends fundamentally upon their being critical, informed, and discriminating. There is no "inconsistency" in this behavior. In the most literal etymology, there is great consistency, an extraordinary capacity, amounting to genius, for holding diverse factors and considerations in mind relative to a state of fluctuant affairs, and for drawing from them a kind of middle in which is to be found the proper or fundamentally right conduct in respect to their actual combined relevance.

Not everybody admires this sort of thing; some will insist upon finding in Burke, what they will also find in his friend Samuel Johnson, an irritating rigor of inconsistency—unannounced shifts of commitment, involutions and returns upon himself, name-calling, judgments philosophic in range but hyperbolic and facile, judgments that, explored and juxtaposed with others, yield little system. Burke qualifies as the spirit prompts, not as a locomoting logic holds to the rails; evading the slow steady grind of thought from proposition to proposition, Burke glides down the wind of his intuition, like a mystic horseman black against the moon and yodelling; where he passed is an odor of brimstone and drifting on the night faint cries of "Certitude, System, Reason!" The more one examines Burke, if one insists upon an epistemological anchorage, the more convinced one is likely to be that Burke is really without principle and stand at all, a gypsy intellect. The tradition of his dishonesty may even become plausible. But it is just such variability, such shiftiness and wandering search, from the anchorage of *mos majorum,* which characterizes his genius. His tacks and shifts are the liberties of one who "will hazard an opinion": "one who wishes to preserve consistency, but who would preserve consistency by varying his means to secure the unity of his end; and, when the equipoise of the vessel in which he sails may be endangered by overloading it upon one side, is desirous of carrying the small weight of his reasons to that which may preserve its equipoise." [102]

## II

One very general impression left in a reader's mind when he lays aside the trial speeches against Hastings is that of an enormous expense of spirit in a waste of zeal. It rises from two tragic defects in Burke's character which disqualified him as a trial lawyer, in the very degree they ennobled him as a special pleader.

To be sure, Burke possessed the hairsplitting acumen that

a trial lawyer needs, the capacious recall and watchful perseverance and ready talent for histrionics. But he was handicapped, first of all, by the very quality that in other respects made his greatness: he blended (or blinded) his person with the case. Burke tried to believe it was intentional. When during the course of the Hastings trial he was formally censured, by the Commons he represented, for accusing Hastings of murder, Burke made a backhanded apology to the Lords and explained the duty of a prosecutor as this:

> If not only I, but the whole body of managers, had made use of any such expression as I made use of, even if the Commons of Great Britain in parliament assembled, if the collective body of parliament, if the voice of Europe had used them; if we had spoken with the tongues of men and angels, you, in the seat of judicature, are not to regard what we say, but what we prove; you are to consider whether the charge is well substantiated, the proof brought out, by legal inference and argument. . . . Your lordships well know, that, when we come before you, you hear a party; that when the accused come before you, you hear a party; that it is for you to doubt and wait till you come to the close, before you decide: that it is for us, the prosecutors, to have decided before we came here. To act as prosecutors, we ought to have no doubt, or hesitation, nothing trembling or quivering in our minds upon the occasion. We ought to be fully convinced of guilt, before we come to you.[103]

Within limits, this is unexceptionable enough. A good trial lawyer may feign an indignation to watch its effects, he may insinuate, surmise, and by many means make a case, because the interior linkages of evidence are not to be grasped *prima facie:* he is allowed to throw his drag-seine in the muddy holes. But also he may be wise to keep a distance between his private character and his role as representative; otherwise the failures of his cleverness return upon himself as accusations. The defeat of his argument becomes a personal defeat, and persuading himself that justice and the heat of his prejudice are one, he is left to sulk. As usual, Burke made an exposition of his own defect. He admitted that his study during eight or nine years of "whole volumes of reports, whole bodies of evidence"—much of which had been ruled out of court—had "brought to my mind such a conviction as will never be torn from my heart but with my life." [104] A self-protective distance, a plebeian disinterest was hardly in his character; he was essentially a man of causes, not of cases, whose conscience was easily stirred by great issues to great convictions. Much of the time during the trial, except for his reverence of legal process, Burke's trouble was similar to that of the best among French revolutionaries whose behavior he so often and brilliantly condemned: his humanity was (literally) at the horizon, and like the horizon it flew before him.[105]

At the beginning, Burke knew that proving anything against Hastings in court (as distinct from proving to oneself) was very nearly impossible (as the trial progressed, as he became more personally involved, his hopes rose to blind him). "Speaking for myself, my business is not to consider what will convict Mr. Hastings (a thing we all know to be impracticable), but what will acquit and justify myself to those few persons, and to those distant times, which may take a concern in these affairs and in the actors in them." [106] He would join battle on principles. The trial would state a kind of minority report in history; it would explicate general principles and bring them into the public eye; it would alarm the criminals in their hiding-places, put an end to the obvious malpractices, chasten and alert the whole nation to its responsibilities; it would air out the whole fetid, involved, and grotesque pagoda of monopolistic capitalism. Burke had first to convince himself, of course, of Hastings' guilt. In 1781 he was "an admirer of [Hastings'] talents, and the farthest in the world from being engaged in a faction against him." [107] Unsure where blame should fall, he was willing to make every allowance possible: "I never will readily hear of laying on one man, that blame which ought to lie on many, if really there should be found any matter of blame at all." [108] By 1785, however, he was wondering how to prove "a *general evil intention,* manifested through a long series and a great variety of acts" [109]—"a corrupt, *habitual* evil intention." [110]

By 1788 Hastings figures in his mind as "the most daring criminal that ever existed." [111] Somehow Hastings grew to be a symbol of everything wrong in India—an Oriental despot, a rapacious money-grubber, "the captain-general of iniquity," [112] a mere "bullock contractor" in the office of a statesman,[113] a Macbeth.[114] Surely this was overshooting, no matter how Burke should try to justify it as a "sympathetic revenge" in behalf of the Indian people.[115]

The second and related defect, which was also a greatness, sprang partly from Burke's own character, partly from the circumstances amid which he was thrown as a trial manager—the necessity of being circumstantial. The remoteness of India, the involutions and gaps in the evidence, the costiveness of witnesses, the powerful bloc supporting Hastings—nothing concurred in favor of proof. Preparing the case in 1785, he admitted privately that "we bring before a bribed tribunal a pre-judged cause." [116] Accepting the situation, then, his technique would be:

> not only to state the fact, but to assign the criminality, to fix the *species* of that criminality, to mark its consequences, to anticipate the defense, and to select such circumstances as lead to presumptions of private corrupt views. By following this method, our resolutions . . . will convey a tolerably clear historical state of the delinquencies, attending rather to the connexion of things than the order of time. They will, on this plan, likewise mark out the enormity of the offence, and point to those particulars which may interest the feelings of men, if any they have left; but without something of that kind I know nothing can be done.[117]

That is, he would deflect argument away from technicalities into moral drama. He would speak to the understanding and conscience.[118] He would judge motives, impose private inferences, argue from presumptions; he would fix in the imaginations of his listeners an impression of the character of British government in India just as he himself sensed it—whether or not it constituted a legal proof. His speeches would therefore be a kind of dramatic art, quite as much as they would be logical exposition. And so they are: the narrative of Nundcomar, the cruel machinations of Debi Sing in the province of Dingagepore, the tale of Hastings and the Begums. One is reminded very much of the quality of portraiture in Gibbon's *Decline and Fall* (they are sketched on a vast canvas with tiny strokes) : but with a basic difference. Gibbon's facts were relatively reliable; Burke's—as he complained again and again—were often dark and half-suppressed in "folds of iniquitous artifice." [119] Gibbon enjoyed the cool privacy of his study; Burke argued in the arena where personalities clash and an audience must be aroused. Gibbon wrote within limits self-imposed; Burke filled the role of prosecutor addressing the House of Lords. Gibbon had a purpose; Burke had a cause. But granted these serious limitations, since nobody was hurt, the gain was enormous, if in no other way than for the statement of Burke's leading principles, and for the living example of the *kind* of courageous internationalism which empire exacts.

One of his sharpest intuitions was the magnitude and gravity of the situation. As early as 1783 he had insisted that, "We are on a conspicuous stage, and the world marks our demeanor," [120] and during the trial he recurred to his belief: "It is not the culprit who is upon trial, it is the House of Commons that is upon its trial, it is the House of Lords that is upon its trial, it is the British nation that is upon its trial before all other nations, before the present generation, and before a long, long posterity." [121] It was perfectly possible, Burke said, after a show of pomp and process for everyone to part "with the most perfect complacency and entire good humour towards one another, while nations, whole suffering nations, are left to beat the empty air with cries of misery and anguish, and to cast forth to an offended heaven the imprecations of disappointment and despair." [122] But there would be a retribution. In the midst of a list of tortures inflicted upon natives by Debi Sing under British authority, Burke remarked that, sooner or later, "crippled and disabled hands will act with resistless power. What is it that they will not pull down, when they are lifted to heaven against their oppressors? Then, what can withstand such hands? Can the power that crushed and destroyed them? Powerful in prayer, let us at least deprecate, and thus endeavour to secure ourselves from, the vengeance which these mashed and disabled hands may pull down upon us. My lords, it is an awful consideration. Let us think of it." [123] Though retribution in history may be long and subtle in arriving, nevertheless it arrives. "We may bite our chains if we will, but we shall be made to know ourselves." [124] "Let us do what we please to put India from our thoughts, we can do nothing to separate it from our public interest and our national reputation. Our attempts to banish this importunate duty will only make it return upon us again and again, and every time in a shape more unpleasant than the former." [125] The idea of Providence working in history, which Hume had neatly dissected and, to his own satisfaction, explained away,[126] never lost its hold upon Burke, who believed that emergent situations in the historical process, though their causal origins may be obscure, always stand under a judgment, a disposing law and intention, with which it is willful disaster not to cooperate.[127] Partly for this reason, he took his own personal role in India reform, especially after he was elected trial manager, as a religious obligation. His lofty zeal is a product of his sense of a duty imposed by his situation.

Any analysis of Burke's leading principles will terminate in his religion, his Christianity: implicit in everything he ever wrote, it reaches its most overt and unequivocal expression during the last fifteen years of his life, and especially in his writings on India. Its lineaments shine through the folds of his prosecutor's rhetoric with unwonted solemnity and frankness. Yet it calls for some explanation. Though Burke considered himself a common lay Anglican, he was very far from an easy translator of dogma into government, and about all one can state with perfect certainty is that the Anglican church leavened his experience.

Someone has said that the quarrel in politics for a long time has been not really between liberals and conservatives, but between empiricists and disciples of the revolutionary tradition. Yet the latter distinction draws false lines quite as much as the first. Perhaps a more practical differentiation would be something like this—a quarrel between those who have imagined the reality of the historical process, in the plenitude of its mysterious contexture, and those who have not. Those who have imagined it are less likely (in the very moment of premising novelty, and the wisdom, if not the duty, of openness) to expect any grandiose transformation in the nature of the process itself, because they have perceived something of the limitations of the present as well as something of its excellence; because they perceive that the novelty which endures is never entirely novel, that while newness is constantly drying out and fading into old possession, a possession older still is constantly having to be renewed. And the process, going on, exacts the same relative status of reciprocal criticism and mutual accommodation as before, imposes *mutatis mutandis* the same duties of conservation and renewal. On these grounds, progress is seen, to use a metaphor of Burke's, as a deposit—as spiralling plateaus of achievement and integration within the process, which do not alter the nature of the process itself. A responsible pleasure in the novel achievements of one's own time is not inconsistent with a Tiresias-like perspective of their limited importance. But all differentiations of this sort are idle—as the historical process itself would seem to be idle, meaningless—without reference to an ahistorical ground. The real quarrel in politics concerns the ahistorical ground to which one should refer. For Burke this ground was provided by ethical values derived from Anglican humanism in its eighteenth-century version. It is on the high ground where ethical values supersede all historical events that Burke's religion edges into his politics and conditions its possibilities.

Christian though he is, only once in the entire canon of his writings is the Christ analyzed as a fountainhead of political principle [128]—at the very close of his speech on the sixth day of the Hastings trial when Burke pleads with the assembled Lords to imitate the bishops in their midst:

> Representatives of that religion which says that their God is love, that the very vital spirit of their institution is charity; a

religion which so much hates oppression, that when the God whom we adore appeared in human form, he did not appear in a form of greatness and majesty, but in sympathy with the lowest of the people,–and thereby made it a firm and ruling principle, that their welfare was the object of all government; since the person, who was the Master of Nature, chose to appear himself in a subordinate situation. These are the considerations which influence them, which animate them, and will animate them, against all oppression; knowing, that He who is called first among them, and first among us all, both of the flock that is fed and of those who feed it, made Himself "the servant of all."[129]

In this instance the Christ is a figure for imitation, one standing for a principle of self-eclipse and ethical sympathy with "the lowest of the people" against "oppression"—that is, a humanitarian who in his conduct exemplifies principles which are the will of God.

Most commonly, however, Burke speaks of the will of God, in eighteenth-century fashion, as identical with the moral law —"one great, immutable, pre-existent law, prior to all our devices, and prior to all our contrivances, paramount to all our ideas and all our sensations, antecedent to our very existence, by which we are knit and connected in the eternal frame of the universe, out of which we cannot stir." [130] This cosmic and existential responsibility binds every man to every man (and to God) and imposes commensurate duty upon every power conventionalized by society in functions, rights, and privileges. It follows that there is no such thing as arbitrary power, such as Hastings claimed that he was forced to assume by Indian customs: that "all power is limited by law, and ought to be guided by discretion and not by arbitrary will:— that all discretion must be referred to the conservation and benefit of those over whom power is exercised; and therefore must be guided by rules of sound political morality." [131]

The individuating feature of the English constitution, Burke believed, was its success in rendering all power, including that of the governors, responsible to its lawful duty, instead of to arbitrary will: more especially through the process of impeachment.

There is but one law for all, namely, that law which governs all law, the law of our Creator, the law of humanity, justice, equity:—the law of nature and of nations. So far as any laws fortify this primeval law, and give it more precision, more energy, more effect by their declarations, such laws enter into the sanctuary, and participate in the sacredness of its character. But the man who quotes as precedents the abuses of tyrants and robbers, pollutes the very fountain of Justice, destroys the foundations of all law, and thereby removes the only safeguard against evil men, whether governors, or governed:—the guard which prevents governors from becoming tyrants, the governed from becoming rebels." [132]

From the same moral law, in his famous *Appeal From the New to the Old Whigs,* Burke had deduced what appear to be, and are usually considered, conservative conclusions:

Taking it for granted that I do not write to the disciples of the Parisian philosophy, I may assume that the awful Author of our being is the Author of our place in the order of existence; and that, having disposed and marshaled us by a divine tactic, not according to our will, but according to His, He has in and by that disposition virtually subjected us to act the part which belongs to the place assigned us. We have obligations to mankind at large which are not in consequence of any special voluntary pact. They arise from the relations of man to man, and the relations of man to God, which relations are not matters of choice. On the contrary, the force of all the pacts which we enter into with any particular person or number of persons amongst mankind depends upon those prior obligations. . . . Parents may not be consenting to their moral relation; but, consenting or not, they are bound to a long train of burdensome duties towards those with whom they have never made a convention of any sort. Children are not consenting to their relation; but their relation, without their actual consent, binds them to its duties; or rather it implies their consent, because the presumed consent of every rational creature is in unison with the predisposd order of things. Men come in that manner into a community with the social state of their parents, endowed with all the benefits, loaded with all the duties of their situation . . . so, without any stipulation on our own part, are we bound by that relation called our country, which comprehends (as it has been well said [by Cicero]) "all the charities of all." [133]

Now men of uncharitable temper may construe the philosophy of the divine tactic as a rationalization of very homely sentiments; they will make it yield bovine conservatism. Burke saw that a man grows up in only one pasture of the world, and delights in its little vistas. Not only is he in that pasture, but in some manner the pasture lives within him, nourishes and forms his sensibility. Or, as Burke explained, on the fourth day of rebuttal during the Hastings trial: "All creatures love their offspring; next to that they love their homes; they have a fondness for the place where they have been bred, for the habitations they have dwelt in, for the stalls in which they have been fed, the pastures they have browsed in, and the wilds in which they have roamed. We all know that the natal soil has a sweetness in it beyond the harmony of verse. This instinct, I say, that binds all creatures to their country, never becomes inert in us, nor ever suffers us to want a memory of it." [134] The line of demarcation, however, between creature comforts and the comforts of being a creature is indistinct. By one of those good-natured generalizations which make up the trade of eighteenth-century politics, Burke concedes this sensibility of the pasture a hardihood whose importance in the divine eyes is not always understandable.

My lords, men are made of two parts, the physical part and the moral. The former he has in common with the brute creation. Like theirs, our corporal pains are very limited and temporary. But the sufferings which touch our moral nature have a wider range, and are infinitely more acute, driving the sufferer sometimes to the extremities of despair and distraction. Man, in his moral nature, becomes, in his progress through life, a creature of prejudice—a creature of opinions—a creature of habits, and of sentiments growing out of them. These form our second nature, as inhabitants of the country and members of the society in which Providence has placed us.[135]

The sweetness of natal soil man and beast enjoy in common, but by the dispensation of Providence, "creaturely prejudice" is man's alone? When his wind is up, Burke can surround the moral law with a wonderful ambiguity. To be sure, one gets something of his meaning. Burke knew that people differ in their opinionatedness, and being a gentleman, he disliked seeing them suffer for what they cannot help. He also disliked overweening, even when it has been refined into condescension. One can hardly admire his sympathy too much. But it seems not absolutely a part of being charitable to men to sacrosanctify their failures, to muster the angels in defense of animal limits. If "place," the basic concept of the philosophy of the divine tactic, means only the home grounds (or even worse, the digestive tract) any philosophy derived from it is likely to be so limited that of course the "moral law" which regulates "place" must seem instead to be its expression. And so materialism considers it.

Two things, however, which are really one, are almost always forgotten by uncharitable critics who mention the passage on the divine tactic—Burke's flexibility, and his sensibility to the historical process. Having loaded "the place assigned us" with duties, having built his feudal credo, he then opens all the windows to air it out: "I admit, indeed, that in morals, as in all things else, difficulties will sometimes occur. Duties will sometimes cross one another. Then questions will arise which of them is to be placed in subordination? which of them may be entirely superseded? . . . Duties, at their extreme bounds, are drawn very fine, so as to become almost evanescent. In that state some shade of doubt will always rest on these questions, when they are pursued with great subtlety." [136] And secondly, "our place in the order of existence" is not necessarily static. To exist is to be alive, and to be alive is to be in process. "Place" may also mean a vital situation, a state of affairs, a context of existential determinants, whose furthest bounds are dark, uncertain. For example: "It has pleased Providence," Burke said, toward the close of the trial, "to place us in such a state [in the year 1794], that we appear every moment to be upon the verge of some great mutations." Nevertheless, he went on: "There is one thing, and one thing only, which defies all mutation; that which existed before the world, and will survive the fabric of the world itself; I mean justice; that justice, which emanating from the Divinity, has a place in the breast of every one of us, given us for our guide with regard to ourselves and with regard to others, and which will stand after this globe is burned to ashes, our advocate or our accuser before the great Judge, when He comes to call upon us for the tenor of a well-spent life." [137]

In this second, less exceptionable, more unequivocal, and Christian sense, "place" is not *a priori* either liberal or conservative. In the distance, one still hears some static: one would like to know more about the "place" in the breast, the conscience. So would Burke, apparently. He is not very agreeable, puts on his Latin armor, and walks in a circle. "The place of every man determines his duty. If you ask, *Quem te Deus esse jussit?* You will be answered when you resolve this other question, *Humana qua parte locatus es in re?*" [138] Something has to be fixed. Burke really means to say that God is fixed, oversees and judges the constant, infinitesimal shiftings of actualization—the "places" of the historical process—which bind a man in whether he likes it or not. No matter how complicated a situation gets, there is always a right way to meet it; and conversely, no action is good or bad without proportion and reference. If one takes the philosophy of the divine tactic on this its Christian, instead of its Hindu side, its political derivations are flexible.

The built-in flaw of Burke's empiricism was in building cases upon the personal encounter with chance or merely circumstantial evidence: for when everything is relevant, nothing can be decided; without a principle of selection, nothing can be ascertained; and the true Gestalt of a case is dissolved in the windy limbo of appearances and impressions. The idea of a moral law, a Logos, judging circumstance, or intending it to go somewhere, is, however, a saving counterbalance, an organizing principle. It frees the intellect while it obligates the will. It allows Burke to distinguish as bovine conservatism is prone not to do, between a technical and a substantial order of morality.[139] It commits his thinking to moral principles in politics without a prejudgment of whether in any given situation they are best achieved by changing or standing still, by rebelling or acquiescing, or, as usual, by some middle course. The same reverence for "moral law" which in his writings on France is the ground of conservative humanism, in his writings on India is made sole and explicit authority for his liberal humanism. Those "obligations to mankind at large which are not in consequence of any special voluntary pact" are the source of his sympathy for the Indian people, even the lowliest.

Nothing seems to have impressed Burke's imagination so strongly in the trial as the spectacle of "men, separated from a remote people by the material bounds and barriers of nature, united by the bond of a social and moral community;—all the Commons of England resenting, as their own, the indignities and cruelties that are offered to all the people of India." [140] It was mysterious and awesome, he told the Lords, but a fact, that "exiled and undone princes, extensive tribes, suffering nations, infinite descriptions of men, different in language, in manners, and in rites—men, separated by the barrier of nature from you, by the providence of God are blended in one common cause, and are now become suppliants at your bar." [141] He impeached Hastings not alone in the name of the Commons, but also in the name of the people of India, of the eternal laws of justice, and of human nature itself.[142] Justice, he said, is the most distinguished attribute of God, and the "highest act of religion, and the highest homage which we can and ought to pay, is an imitation of the Divine perfections as far as such a nature can imitate such perfections . . . by this means alone we can make our homage acceptable to Him." [143] Gratitude should be expressed by virtues, not by mouths,[144] and charity was the only virtue he had ever heard of which "derives from its retirement any part of its lustre; the others require to be spread abroad in the face of day." [145] With such a map of misgovernment before him, he could not keep faith with the legalities of the Company's charter, for in doing so, he would "break the faith, the covenant, the solemn, original indispensable oath, in which I am bound, by the eternal frame and constitution of things, to the whole human race." [146] When Hastings defended his peculations and bribes by saying "that actions in Asia do not bear the same moral qualities which the same actions would bear in Europe," Burke fumed against this "plan of *geographical morality*":

By which the duties of men, in public and in private situations, are not to be governed by their relation to the great Governor of the universe, or by their relation to mankind, but by climates, degrees of longitude, parallels not of life but of latitudes; as if, when you have crossed the equinoctial, all the virtues die, as they say some insects die when they cross the line; as if there were a kind of baptism, like that practiced by seamen, by which they unbaptize themselves of all that they learned in Europe, and after which a new order and system of things commenced.[147]

After reciting, with due flourishes, a long string of cruelties by the *banyan* Debi Sing—iron wedges driven between fingers that had been tightly laced; bloody beatings of men hung upside down, sometimes with whips, sometimes with thorn branches, sometimes with poisonous *bechettea;* girls raped before their parents, wives before their husbands; torches planted in the source of life—at this point, while Mrs. Sheridan fainted in the gallery, Burke complained gravely, holding up a volume of evidence to prove he was not exaggerating: "These, my lords, were sufferings which we feel all in common in India and in England, by the general sympathy of our common nature." [148] He then went on to describe an even worse moral suffering which followed these tortures—the automatic loss of caste. Granted the card-stacking in this particular instance, nevertheless this is the sort of thing one is still likely to admire Burke for in his Indian tracts: the swift, unexpected generalization cutting back through impenetrable masses of detail to a commonplace which nobody had remembered and few will contradict and which astonishes everybody with the simple weight of its meaning. Whether Hastings is culpable, where, and in what degree, ceases to be very important before the plain fact of a human identity which no cultural differences can erase, and a human responsibility which endures despite all the films of illusion which come to conceal it.

The application of a universal moral law to politics is ordinary enough, goodness knows, in the eighteenth century. What is important in Burke is his common sense and imagination. Unwilling to carry over a rigid theoretical system into his politics, Burke is left virtually with (1) a faith in the ultimate brotherhood of men under Providence, but (2) a working commitment to a particular moral and ideational complex derivative from English and Anglican experience. For example, he strove in his measure, to develop a generous candor, a feeling dignity, public spirit, and openness, like that of his friend Lord John Cavendish, who, Burke said, "was of a character that seems as if it were peculiar to this country. He was exactly what we conceive an English nobleman of the old stamp, and one born in better times, or what in our fond fancies we imagine such men to have been and in such time."[149] Therefore, he refers to regulative principles like justice, charity, and liberty under law—all these being the formal causes or interior ideal patterns according to which unfolding circumstances are to be modeled and budgeted by human reason, and which in turn stand in judgment upon defects. He is practical-minded and commonsensical in applying the moral law. He exemplifies a peculiar fusion of religious values and imaginative empiricism which has had a way of reappearing among the English people, from Hooker to Coleridge,[150] from the Cambridge Platonists to Whitehead —a particular mode of entertaining ideal values which, so far from weighing them down with the rigors of a static, perfectionist state, have on the contrary released their thinking for successful and humane compromises within the flux of the actual.

# EVENTS IN THE LIFE OF BURKE

# BIBLIOGRAPHY

# NOTES

# Events in the Life of Burke

1729 Born 12 January in Dublin; son of a middle-class Anglican lawyer and a Roman Catholic mother; continued Anglican throughout his life.

1736–1743 Lived five years with mother's family in village of Ballyduff, and attended Catholic school; in 1741 entered boarding school at Ballitore run by a Quaker, Abraham Shackleton; "read the Bible, morning, noon, and night."

1743–1749 At Trinity College, Dublin; won a scholarship in classics, founded a debating society, and published in a short-lived periodical *The Reformer;* pamphleteered in favor of seating Dr. Lucas, an advocate of independence, in the Irish House of Commons.

1750 At father's insistence, entered law school in London (The Middle Temple), but finding law "not too apt to open and liberalize the mind," drifted toward a literary-journalistic career.

1756 *A Vindication of Natural Society,* an ironic impersonation of the style and ideas of Bolingbroke; married Jane Nugent, daughter of an Irish Catholic doctor and Presbyterian mother; largely depended on Dr. Nugent for support; probably at work on *An Essay Toward an Abridgment of the English History* (published posthumously).

1757 *A Philosophical Inquiry Into the Origin of Our Ideas of the Sublime and the Beautiful,* an epochal work in eighteenth-century criticism, which had been "rolling in his thoughts" since undergraduate days; collaborated with William Burke (family relation uncertain) in publishing *An Account of the European Settlements in America.*

1758 Contracted with Robert Dodsley to edit and write for the *Annual Register,* a yearly review of contemporary history, politics, and literature; contributions uncertain, but probably responsible for issues from 1759 to 1765; kept his editorship secret, and did not resign officially until thirty years later; birth of his son Richard (and of another son, Christopher, who died in infancy).

1761–1765 Short on money but becoming known for encyclopedic learning, became private secretary to William "(Single-speech" Hamilton; during two-year return to Ireland with Hamilton (who was secretary to the Lord Lieutenant), wrote *Tracts on the Popery Laws* (unpublished).

1764 Back in England, became original member of "The Club," along with Johnson and Reynolds, whom he had known several years.

1765 Became private secretary to Marquis of Rockingham, just starting a one-year administration as first minister; made M.P. from the pocket borough of Windover; his first speeches in Commons, on the Stamp Act, "filled the town with wonder."

1768 Borrowed enough money to purchase a country estate at Beaconsfield.

1769 *Observations on a Late Publication Entitled "The Present State of the Nation"*, attacking American and financial policies of Grenville; by now had become leading spokesman and political manager for the Rockingham Whigs.

1770 *Thoughts on the Cause of the Present Discontents,* a major statement of constitutional principles and party government in an attack on Toryism and the court clique of George III.

1771–1775 Acted as agent for the colony of New York; visited France in 1773; speeches on freedom of the press (juries and libel laws, report of Parliamentary debates) and on religious toleration (on the Acts of Uniformity and on the relief of Protestant dissenters).

1774 *Speech on American Taxation,* his first speech to be published; campaigned for M.P. at Bristol, the second-leading commercial center, and was elected.

1775 *Speech on Conciliation With America* and outbreak of war in America.

1776 *Address to the King.*

1777 *A Letter to the Sheriffs of Bristol.*

1780 *Speech at Bristol Previous to the Election;* having lost his Bristol seat (largely because of stand on American war and on Irish trade and religion), was made M.P., with Rockingham's influence, from pocket borough of Malton—the seat which he held for the remainder of his career; year of the Gordon riots, in which his life was endangered; turned to constitutional questions in *A Letter on Parliamentary Reform, Speech on the Duration of Parliaments,* and the great *Speech on the Economical Reformation.*

1781 Appointed to Select Committee of the House to study colonial abuses in India, which he had been studying informally, on his own, for several years.

1782 American war ended; became Paymaster-General in second Rockingham ministry, but resigned when Rockingham died three months later; continued Irish concerns in *A Letter to a Peer of Ireland* and constitutional questions in *Speech on the Representation of the Commons in Parliament.*

1783 Became Paymaster-General once more, for eight months, after Fox-North coalition—his last public office; made his great *Speech on Fox's East India Bill,* a bill for which he was largely responsible.

1784 Death of Johnson; honored with one-year title of Lord Rector of Glasgow University; influence in Parliament starting to decline with the coming to power of Pitt and a new generation.

1785 *Speech on the Nabob of Arcot's Debts,* his last speech written for publication.

1786–1794 Guided impeachment proceedings against Warren Hastings; at opening of trial before the House of Lords in 1788, delivered a four-day oration for the prosecution; remained occupied by the trial off and on during the next eight years.

1789 Outbreak of the French Revolution.

1790 *Reflections on the Revolution in France,* which stirred national controversy, provoked numerous replies, and divided the Whig party.

1791 Made formal, public break with Fox and Sheridan, and was in effect expelled from the Whigs; wrote *An Appeal from the New to the Old Whigs,* defending his consistency and defining the principles of "Old Whigs" who derived from the "Glorious Revolution" of 1688; continued analysis of the French revolution in *A Letter to a Member of the National Assembly* and *Thoughts on French Affairs.*

1792 Death of Reynolds; continued with all issues in *Heads for Consideration on the Present State of Affairs, Sketch of a Negro Code,* Speech on the *Petition of the Unitarian Society,* and *A Letter to Sir Hercules Langrishe on the Subject of the Roman Catholics of Ireland.*

1793 Continued with all affairs in *Remarks on the Policy of the Allies, Observations on the Conduct of the Minority,* and *A Letter to Richard Burke* concerning Ireland.

1794 Made speeches at the Hastings trial, including the closing *Speech In General Reply,* his last appearance in Parliament; unexpected deaths of his son and his brother; retired to Beaconsfield with pensions from the Crown.

1795 Hastings acquitted; wrote defenses of his career in *A Letter to William Elliot, Esq.* and *Letter to a Noble Lord,* a tract on economics in *Thoughts and Details on Scarcity,* and turned to Ireland again in *A Letter to William Smith* and *Second Letter to Sir Hercules Langrishe.*

1795–1797 Wrote four *Letters on a Regicide Peace,* two of them unpublished until after his death.

1797 Wrote *Letter on the Affairs of Ireland;* died 9 July, probably of stomach cancer, and was buried, by his own request, at Beaconsfield.

# Bibliography of Works Cited

For general bibliography, which is exceedingly complicated and unsettled, see Thomas W. Copeland and Milton Shumway Smith, *A Checklist of the Correspondence of Edmund Burke, Arranged in Chronological Order and Indexed Under the Names of 1200 Correspondents,* Cambridge, 1955; Francesco Cordasco, *Edmund Burke: a Handlist of Critical Notices and Studies,* 18th-Century Bibliographical Pamphlets No. 12, Long Island University Press, 1950; *Cambridge Bibliography of English Literature* (4 vols., 1941), II, 632–636; W. T. Lowndes, *Bibliographer's Manual of English Literature* (rev. H. G. Bohn), London, 1858–1864; and *The R. B. Adam Library Relating to Dr. Samuel Johnson and His Era,* 3 vols., 1929–1930.

## I. PRIMARY SOURCES: BURKE


*An Account of the European Settlements in America.* Revised by Edmund Burke. 6th edn., 2 vols., London, 1777.

*Edmund Burke, New York Agent, With His Letters to the New York Assembly and Intimate Correspondence With Charles O'Hara, 1761–1776.* Ed. Ross J. S. Hoffman for the American Philosophical Society. Philadelphia, 1956.

*Burke: Select Works.* Ed. E. J. Payne. 2nd edn., 3 vols., Oxford, 1904.

*Burke's Politics: Selected Writings and Speeches of Edmund Burke on Reform, Revolution, and War.* Ed. Ross J. S. Hoffman and Paul Levaik. New York, 1949.

*Correspondence of Edmund Burke and William Windham With Other Illustrative Letters From the Windham Papers in the British Museum.* Ed. J. P. Gilson for the Roxburghe Club. Cambridge, Eng., 1910.

Crewe, Mrs. "Extracts from Mr. Burke's Table-Talk at Crewe Hall, Written down by Mrs. Crewe," Ed. R. M. Milnes. *Miscellanies of the Philobiblon Society,* Vol. VII, Part 5. London, 1862–1863.

*The Early Life Correspondence and Writings of the Rt. Hon. Edmund Burke LL.D. With a Transcript of the Minute Book of the Debating "Club" Founded by Him in Trinity College Dublin.* Ed. Arthur P. I. Samuels. Introd. and Supplementary Chapters on

Burke's Contributions to the *Reformer* and His Part in the Lucas Controversy by Arthur Warren Samuels. Cambridge, Eng.. 1923.

*Edmund Burke's Speech on Conciliation With America.* Albert S. Cook. Longman's English Classics. New York, 1903.

*A Notebook of Edmund Burke: Poems, Characters, Essays and Other Sketches in the Hands of Edmund and William Burke Now Printed for the First Time in Their Entirety.* Ed. H. V. F. Somerset. Cambridge, Eng., 1957.

*The Works and Correspondence of the Right Honourable Edmund Burke.* Vols. I–II, *Correspondence 1744–1797.* Ed. Charles William (Earl Fitzwilliam) and Sir Richard Bourke. 2nd edn. London: Francis and John Rivington, 1852.

*The Works of the Right Honourable Edmund Burke.* 8 vols. London: Henry G. Bohn, 1854.

## II. SECONDARY SOURCES: BURKE

### *A. Biography and Special Studies*

Bentham, Jeremy. *Defence of Economy Against the Late Mr. Burke.* N.P., 1817.

*Boswell's Life of Johnson.* Ed. George Birkbeck Hill. 6 vols., Oxford, 1887.

Bryant, Donald Cross. *Edmund Burke and His Literary Friends.* Washington University Studies in Language and Literature, New Series. No. 9, St. Louis: December, 1939.

Cone, Carl. "Pamphlet Replies to Burke's Reflections," *Southwestern Social Science Quarterly,* XXVI (June, 1945), 22–34.

Copeland, Thomas W. *Our Eminent Friend Edmund Burke.* New Haven, 1949.

Einaudi, Mario. "The British Background of Burke's Political Philosophy," *Political Science Quarterly,* XLIX (1934), 576–598.

Goodrich, Chauncey A. *Select British Eloquence, Embracing the Best Speeches Entire of the Most Eminent Orators of Great Britain for the Last Two Centuries.* [1852.] Ed. Bower Aly. New York, 1963.

Halliday, W. R. "Burke and the Cavendishes," *English Historical Review.* XLVII (1932), 280–286.

Hamm, Victor M. "Burke and Metaphysics," *New Scholasticism, XVIII* (January, 1944), 3–18.

Hutchins, Robert M. "The Theory of the State: Edmund Burke," *Review of Politics,* V (1943), 139–155.

Mackintosh, James. *Vindiciae Gallicae: Defence of the French Revolution and Its English Admirers Against the Accusations of the Right Hon. Edmund Burke; Including Some Strictures on the Late Production of Mons. De Calonne.* London, 1791.

Magnus, Sir Philip. *Edmund Burke: a Life.* London, 1939.

Millar, M. F. K. "Burke and the Moral Basis of Political Liberty," *Thought,* XVI (1916), 79–101.

Morley, John. *Burke*. "English Men of Letters"; London, 1912.

Murray, The Rev. Robert H. *Edmund Burke: A Biography*. London, 1931.

Paine, Thomas. *Rights of Man*. Vol. I, *The Complete Writings of Thomas Paine*. Ed. Philip S. Foner. New York, 1945.

Priestley, Joseph. *Letters to the Right Honourable Edmund Burke, Occasioned by His "Reflections on the Revolution in France, etc."* 3rd edn. Birmingham, 1791.

Prior, James. *Life of the Right Honourable Edmund Burke*. 5th edn. revised, London, 1854.

Robert, Brother J. "Toleration for Catholics: the Mind of Burke," *Thought*, XIV (1939), 633–643.

Sutherland, L. Stuart. "Edmund Burke and the First Rockingham Ministry," *English Historical Review*, XLVII (1932), 46–70.

Timbs, John. *Anecdote Lives of William Pitt, Earl of Chatham, and Edmund Burke*. London, 1880.

Wecter, Dixon. *Edmund Burke and His Kinsmen: a Study of the Statesman's Financial Integrity and Private Relationships*. University of Colorado Studies in the Humanities, Series B. Vol. I, No. 1, Boulder, 1939.

*B. Histories and General Criticism*

Aris, Reinhold. *History of Political Thought in Germany from 1789 to 1815*. London, 1936.

Arnold, Matthew. "The Function of Criticism at the Present Time," *Essays in Criticism*. 1st Series, London, 1903.

Babbitt, Irving. *Democracy and Leadership*. 2nd edn., Boston, 1925.

Barker, Ernest. *Essays on Government*. 2nd edn., London, 1951.

——— *The Ideas and Ideals of the British Empire*. "Current Problems"; Cambridge, Eng., 1941.

Barzun, Jacques. *Romanticism and the Modern Ego*. Boston, 1943.

Birrell, Augustine. *Obiter Dicta*. 2nd Series, New York, 1887.

Brinton, Crane. *English Political Thought in the Nineteenth Century*. London, 1933.

Brown, Ivor. *English Political Theory*. 2nd edn. revised, London, 1929.

Buckle, Henry Thomas, *Introduction to the History of Civilization in England*. Introd. with notes by John M. Robertson. Revised edn., New York, 1925.

Butler, Geoffrey G. *The Tory Tradition: Bolingbroke, Burke, Disraeli, Salisbury*. London, 1914.

Cecil, Lord Hugh. *Conservatism*. "Home University Library"; London, 1925.

Cobban, Alfred. *Edmund Burke and the Revolt Against the Eighteenth Century: a Study of the Political and Social Thinking of Burke, Wordsworth, Coleridge, and Southey*. London, 1929.

Dowden, Edward. *The French Revolution and English Literature*. New York, 1897.

Graham, William. *English Political Philosophy from Hobbes to Maine*. London, 1899.

Halevy, Elie. *The Growth of Philosophic Radicalism*. Trans. Mary Morris. "Beacon Paperback"; Boston, 1955.

Hazlitt, William. *The Complete Works of William Hazlitt*. Ed. P. P. Howe after the edition of A. R. Waller and Arnold Glover. Vol. VII, "Character of Mr. Burke," *Political Essays;* Vol. VIII, "On Genius and Common Sense," *Table-Talk;* Vol. XI, "Sir James Mackintosh," *The Spirit of the Age;* Vol. XII, "On the Prose-Style of Poets," *The Plain Speaker*. London, 1931.

Hearnshaw, F. J. C. "Edmund Burke," in *The Social and Political Ideas of Some Representative Thinkers of the Revolutionary Era*. Lectures Delivered at the University of London 1929–1930. Ed. Hearnshaw. London, 1931.

Kirk, Russell. *The Conservative Mind from Burke to Santayana*. Chicago, 1953.

Laski, Harold J. *Political Thought in England from Locke to Bentham*. "Home University Library"; London, 1944.

Lecky, William E. H. *A History of England in the Eighteenth Century*, Vol. III, New York, 1882.

Lowell, James Russell. "Rousseau and the Sentimentalists," in *Essays, Poems and Letters*. Ed. Wm. Smith Clark II. New York, 1948.

Martin, Kingsley. *The Rise of French Liberal Thought: a Study of Political Ideas from Bayle to Condorcet*. Ed. J. P. Mayer. 2nd edn. revised, New York, 1954.

Ransom, John Crowe. "Empirics in Politics," *Kenyon Review*, XV (Autumn, 1953), 648–654.

Sabine, George H. *A History of Political Theory*. Revised edn., New York, 1955.

Stephen, Sir Leslie. *History of English Thought in the Eighteenth Century*. 3rd edn., 2 vols., New York, 1949.

Tocqueville, Alexis de. *The Old Regime and the French Revolution*. Trans. Stuart Gilbert. "Anchor edn."; Garden City, 1955.

Vaughan, C. E. *Studies in the History of Political Philosophy Before and After Rousseau*. Vol. II, *From Burke to Mazzini*. Ed. A. G. Little. Manchester, 1925.

Wellek, René. *A History of Modern Criticism: 1750–1950*, 2 vols. completed, New Haven, 1955.

——— *The Rise of English Literary History*. Chapel Hill, 1941.

Whitney, Lois. *Primitivism and the Idea of Progress in English Popular Literature of the Eighteenth Century*. Baltimore, 1934.

Willey, Basil. *The Eighteenth Century Background: Studies on the Idea of Nature in the Thought of the Period*. London, 1940.

——— "Thought," in *The Character of England.* Essays ed. Ernest Barker. Oxford, 1947.

Wilson, Woodrow. *Mere Literature and Other Essays.* Cambridge, Mass., 1896.

## III. OTHER WORKS

Acton, Lord. *Essays on Church and State.* Ed. with introduction by Douglas Woodruff. London, 1952.

Arnold, Matthew. *Culture and Anarchy.* Ed. W. S. Knickerbocker. New York, 1929.

Bacon, Francis. *The Physical and Metaphysical Works of Lord Bacon, Including His "Dignity and Advancement of Learning," in Nine Books; and His "Novum Organum"; or, Precepts for the Interpretation of Nature.* Ed. Joseph Devey. London, 1853.

Becker, Carl. *The Heavenly City of the Eighteenth-Century Philosophers.* New Haven, 1932.

Bentham, Jeremy. *A Fragment on Government and An Introduction to Principles of Morals and Legislation.* Ed. with introduction by Wilfrid Harrison. Oxford, 1948.

Bera, Marc-André. "A. N. Whitehead; un Philosophe de l'Expérience," in *Actualités scientifiques et industrielles.* No. 1056, Paris, 1948.

Black, J. B. *The Art of History: a Study of Four Great Historians of the Eighteenth Century.* New York, 1926.

Burtt, Edwin A. *The Metaphysical Foundations of Modern Physical Science.* Revised edn., New York, 1932.

Butterfield, Herbert. *The Englishman and His History.* "Current Problems"; Cambridge, Eng., 1945.

——— *Man on His Past: the Study of the History of Historical Scholarship.* The Wiles Lecture Given at the Queen's University, Belfast, 1954. Cambridge, Eng., 1955.

Cecil, David. *The Young Melbourne: and the Story of His Marriage With Caroline Lamb.* Indianapolis, 1939.

Coleridge, Samuel Taylor. *Biographia Literaria.* Introd. Arthur Symons. "Everyman's Library"; London, 1934.

——— *Inquiring Spirit.* Selections including unpub. MSS ed. Kathleen Coburn. New York, 1951.

Curtis, L. P. "Gibbon's Paradise Lost," in *The Age of Johnson: Essays Presented to Chauncey Brewster Tinker.* New Haven, 1949.

Gibbon, Edward. *The Autobiographies of Edward Gibbon.* Ed. John Murray. 2nd edn., London, 1897.

——— *Private Letters of Edward Gibbon.* Ed. R. E. Prothero. 2 vols., London, 1896.

*The God That Failed.* Ed. Richard Crossman. Essays by André Gide. Richard Wright, Arthur Koestler, Stephen Spender, Ignazio Silone, Louis Fischer. 2nd "Bantam edn."; New York, 1954.

Godwin, William. *An Enquiry Concerning Political Justice and Its Influence on General Virtue and Happiness.* Ed. with introduction, notes, and variant readings of 1st and 2nd edn. by F. E. L. Priestley. 3rd edn., 3 vols., Toronto, 1946.

Goldsmith, Oliver. *The Works of Oliver Goldsmith.* Ed. Peter Cunningham. Vol. III, New York, 1900.

Hegel, G. W. F. *Lectures on the Philosophy of History.* Trans. J. Sibree. London, 1878.

Hilles, Frederick, W. *The Literary Career of Sir Joshua Reynolds.* New York, 1936.

Hobbes, Thomas. *Leviathan.* "Everyman's Library"; London, 1943.

Home, Henry (Lord Kames). *Elements of Criticism.* Ed. and revised by J. R. Boyd. New York, 1866.

Howe, P. P. *The Life of William Hazlitt.* 2nd edn., New York, 1923.

Hume, David. *Essays and Treatises on Several Subjects.* 2 vols., London, 1784.

Johnson, Samuel. *The Works of Samuel Johnson, LL.D. With an Essay on His Life and Genius by Arthur Murphy.* Vol. II, *Taxation No Tyranny.* 3rd American edn., New York, 1846.

Joyce, Michael. *Edward Gibbon.* London, 1953.

Locke, John. *The Works of John Locke.* Vols. I-III, *An Essay Concerning Human Understanding.* London, 1823.

Macaulay, Thomas Babington. *The Works of Lord Macaulay.* Vol. XV, "Warren Hastings." Ed. Lady Trevelyan for the Jenson Society. N.P., 1907.

Marx, Karl and Friedrich Engels. "Manifesto of the Communist Party," in *Great Books of the Western World.* Ed. Robert M. Hutchins. Vol. L, *Marx.* Chicago, 1955.

Montesquieu, Baron de. *The Spirit of the Laws.* Trans. Thomas Nugent. Revised by J. V. Prichard. Introd. O. W. Holmes. 2 vols., New York, 1900.

Morris, Christopher. *Political Thought in England: Tyndale to Hooker.* "Home University Library"; London, 1953.

Parrington, Vernon L. *Main Currents in American Thought: an Interpretation of American Literature from the Beginnings to 1920.* Vol. II, *The Romantic Revolution in America.* New York, 1930.

Pepper, Stephen. *World Hypotheses: a Study in Evidence.* Berkeley, 1942.

Reynolds, Sir Joshua. *The Life and Discourses of Sir Joshua Reynolds.* Life by Allan Cunningham. 2nd edn., New York, 1873.

——— *Portraits: Character Sketches of Oliver Goldsmith, Samuel Johnson, and David Garrick, Together with Other Manuscripts Discovered Among the Boswell Papers and Now First Published.* Ed. with introduction by F. W. Hilles. New York, 1952.

Santayana, George. *The Works of George Santayana.* Vol. VIII, "English Liberty in America," *Character and Opinion in the United States.* "Triton edn."; New York, 1937.

Whitehead, Alfred North. *Adventures of Ideas.* New York, 1933.

——— *Introduction to Mathematics.* New York, 1948.

——— *The Organization of Thought.* London, 1917.

——— *Science and the Modern World.* New York, 1925.

Wood, Paul Spencer. "Native Elements in English Neo-Classicism," *Modern Philology,* XXIV (1926), 201–208.

Young, G. M. *Gibbon.* New York, 1933.

——— *Last Essays.* London, 1950.

# Notes

*Since there exists no modern standard edition of Burke, I have used the one which I found most convenient:* The Works of the Right Honourable Edmund Burke, *Bohn's British Classics, 8 vols. (London, 1854), cited hereafter by volume and page numbers only.*

## I. The Organic Premise

1. Harold J. Laski, *Political Thought in England from Locke to Bentham* (London, 1944), p. 172.

2. *Ibid.*, pp. 213–214.

3. *Ibid.*, pp. 206–207.

4. Christopher Morris, *Political Thought in England: Tyndale to Hooker* (London, 1953), p. 197.

5. Reinhold Aris, *History of Political Thought in Germany from 1789 to 1815* (London, 1936), p. 270.

6. *The Rambler,* April 1858, quoted in *Essays on Church and State,* ed. Douglas Woodruff (London, 1952). pp. 455–456. Acton probably valued the many passages which suggest an organic grasp of history. For one example among many, it occurred to Burke as early as 1757 that Roman *municipia,* provinces, and colonies in early Britain, though "dissimilar parts," were however, "far from being discordant": "[They] united to make a firm and compact body, the motion of any member of which could only serve to confirm and establish the whole; and when time was given to this structure to coalesce and settle, it was found impossible to break any part of it from the empire.

By degrees the several parts blended and softened into one another" (VI, 220).

7. Add. 5437, Acton Papers, Cambridge Univ. Library, quoted in Herbert Butterfield, *Man on His Past: the Study of the History of Historical Scholarship,* Wiles Lecture (Cambridge, Eng., 1955), p. 70. Cf. Alfred Cobban, *Edmund Burke and the Revolt Against the Eighteenth Century: A Study of the Political and Social Thinking of Burke, Wordsworth, Coleridge, and Southey* (London, 1929), pp. 258–268.

However, on such grounds, one may fix responsibility for "romanticism" upon developments in the general culture of England as well as upon Burke.

Professor Wellek, watching it guide *The Rise of Littrary History* (Chapel Hill, 1941), defines the "historical sense" as "a recognition of the individuality in its historical setting and an appreciation of the historical process into which individualities fit" (p. 48). In aesthetics, theory of language, and history of literature, he finds it characterized by a shift towards an irrational or emotionalistic psychology, the genetic approach working from origins, and the concept of internal, necessary evolution emergent from biological analogies (p. 94). Such "historism," according to Professor Wellek's later *A History of Modern Criticism* (New Haven, 1955) began in England, but (reaching an "impasse" by the end of the century) was taken over, deepened, and refined by German thinkers who better grasped its philosophical problems and potentialities, and in turn worked out modern organicism. The difficulty with his brilliant analysis is that it underplays national differences; it tends to assume the organic is the organic, wherever you find it; but his abstracted likeness conceals a gulf of practical assumption beneath. For example, each pole of an analogy has specific content, and what is implied by the use of an organic analogy depends very much upon the content, which is often national; what is meant by a "national mind," for example, is in good part determined by how one is accustomed to think of the human mind in fact. Burke warned ("Policy of the Allies," III, 456) against losing one's sense of the concrete in the rarefied air of abstract constructs: "our guides, the historians, who are to give us their true interpretation, are . . . often fonder of system than of truth."

The historical sense in England seems to have been a cultural diffusion, something like an aspect of national character very long in forming, not a professional code or a school of thought like history *en philosophe*. The oversimplification of national character is a pitfall for historians of ideas. For example, Cobban, who also paid a passing notice to the philosophic implications of biological analogies, with side glances at German thought, attributed Burke's concept of "growth" in the state to "the influence of Leibnitz's principle, only at the present day being challenged in the sciences, that Nature never makes jumps and nothing happens all at once. With Burke the idea penetrates to political thought" (*Revolt Against the Eighteenth Century,* p. 91). Yet in truth, the *feeling* for continuity and growth in the English commonwealth and "slow change, analogous in its gradualness and unconsciousness to the processes of vegetable nature, or better still to the mutations and conservation of heredity," reached expression in England well before Leibnitz was born—for example, among Elizabethan and Jacobean antiquaries. Butterfield, in *The Englishman and His History* (Cambridge, Eng., 1945) shows how far back the historical sense goes. He quotes from Spelman's *Of the Ancient Government of England:*

"To tell the Government of *England* under the old *Saxon* laws, seemeth a *Utopia* to us present; strange and uncouth; yet can there be no period assign'd, wherein either the frame of those laws was abolished or this of ours entertained; but as Day and Night creep insensibly, one upon the other, so also hath this Alteration grown upon us insensibly, every age altering something, and no age seeing more than what themselves are Actors in, nor thinking it to have been otherwise than as themselves discover it by the present" (Butterfield, p. 36).

Burke, who used and praised Spelman in his youthful abridgment of English history, (I, 414) also borrowed the idea, the phrasing, and the striking day-night image in "Thoughts on the Cause of the Present Discontents" (I, 7-8, 22). A few decades later, Coke was feeling something similar; and even using an "organic" metaphor: "Interroge pristinam generationem (for out of old fields must come the new corn) and diligently search out the judgements of our forefathers: and that for divers reasons . . . we are but of yesterday (and therefore had need of the wisdome of those that were before us) and had been ignorant (if we had not received light and knowledge from our forefathers) and our daies upon the earth are but as a shadow in respect of the old and auncient daies and times past, wherein the lawes have been by the wisdom of the most excellent men, in many successions of ages. by long and continuall experience (the triall of right and truth) fined and refined, which no one man (being of so short a time) albeit hee had in his head the wisdome of all the men in the world, in any one age could never have effected or attained unto" (Butterfield, p. 50).

Whatever the hap of ideas derived from it, a historical sense has continued a lively part of English culture *mutatis mutandis* from early times down to the present moment—for example, in the criticism of T. S. Eliot—and it very much interested Burke to clarify it and keep it alive for his own day. Not before Burke, however, did the historical sense rise to such brilliantly self-conscious expression as specifically part of the national character; perhaps Acton's remark has a virtual truth.

8. Butterfield, *Man on His Past,* p. 18. The list of great or near-great historians whose thought was shaped by Burke is astonishingly long—for example, Macaulay, Savigny, Guizot, Niebuhr, De Tocqueville, Lecky, Stephen.

9. Aris, *Thought in Germany,* p. 309.

10. *Ibid.,* p. 187.

11. *Last Essays* (London, 1950), pp. 107–108.

12. Laski, *Locke to Bentham,* p. 213.

13. *Ibid.,* p. 174.

14. "Thoughts on Scarcity," V, 87.

15. W. E. H. Lecky, *A History of England in the Eighteenth Century* (New York, 1882), III, 228.

16. The number of critics who associate Burke with "the organic" is legion; but very few try to explain what they mean by it. Understandably. "The organic," as it circulates in free usage, is a house of many mansions, a dark house with dark rooms, each with obscure passageways into all the others: one can walk from room to room, straining to see, and never know precisely where one is—except that one is inside a house. C. E. Vaughan is an exception: "Burke," *Studies in the History of Political Philosophy Before and After Rousseau,* ed. A. G. Little (Manchester, 1925), II, 26 ff. He finds in Burke "the whole theory of the State as an organism." Cf. Augustine Birrell, *Obiter Dicta,* 2nd Series (New York, 1887), pp. 188–190; Edward Dowden, *French Revolution and English Literature* (New York, 1897), p. 95; Ivor Brown, *English Political Theory,* 2nd edn. revised (London, 1929), pp. 71, 76; Sir Leslie Stephen, *History of English Thought in the Eighteenth Century,* 3rd edn. (New York, 1949), II, 230; F. J. C. Hearnshaw, "Edmund Burke," *The Social and Political Ideas of Some Representative Thinkers of the Revolutionary Era* (London, 1931), pp. 96–97; Lecky, *England in the Eighteenth Century,* pp. 224, 236. For dissenting or qualifying opinions, see Cobban, *Revolt Against the Eighteenth Century,* pp. 89–93; Lois Whitney, *Primitivism and the Idea of Progress in English Popular Literature of the Eighteenth Century* (Baltimore, 1934), pp. 200–201; Irving Babbitt, "Burke and the Moral Imagination," *Democracy and Leadership* (Cambridge, Mass., 1924), pp. 100–101.

17. Burke to Windham, Oct. 1793, *Correspondence of Edmund Burke and William Windham with Other Illustrative Letters from the Windham Papers in the British Museum,* ed. J. P. Gilson, Roxburghe Club (Cambridge, Eng., 1910), p. 72. Cf. p. 90.

18. "Reflections," II, 366.

19. *Novum Organum,* Bk. II, aphorisms ii–vi.

20. Quoted in E. A. Burtt, *The Metaphysical Foundations of Modern Physical Science* (New York, 1932), p. 221.

21. Henry Home (Lord Kames), *Elements of Criticism,* ed. and rev. J. R. Boyd (New York, 1866), p. 31.

22. *Ibid.,* p. 35. Burke apparently looked upon Kames's work as continuous with his own. When Malone, in 1789, suggested that Burke revise and enlarge *The Sublime and the Beautiful,* in the light of thirty years' experience, Burke answered that the train of his thinking had moved away from aesthetics—"such speculations"—and that, though the subject was new when he wrote, Lord Kames and others had "gone over the same ground" more recently. See James Prior, *Life of the Right Honourable Edmund Burke,* 5th edn. (London, 1854), p. 47; and Donald Cross Bryant, *Edmund Burke and His Literary Friends,* Washington University Studies, New Series, Language and Literature,

No. 9 (December, 1939), p. 234. Kames's using the phrase "organic system" is notable. Most English thinkers at different periods who have been attracted to the organic premise, or interested in it—for example, Hobbes, Coleridge, Whitehead—are unable to accept all the implications that can be made to flow from it without qualification. The "mechanical" is made to persist alongside. Whitehead, for example, described the metaphysical doctrine in *Science and the Modern World* (New York, 1925) as "the theory of organic mechanism" (ch. 5). Similarly, the "artificial animal" of the *Leviathan* is hardly more than emblematic; such hints of organicism as are present are rendered thoroughly mechnical by Hobbes's view of nature and man. Coleridge, though he hates anything smacking of the "mechanical," is not really an exception. His lifelong ambition to reconcile Plato and Aristotle in an indigenously English system amounts to little more, in one light, than his inability to rest in the notions taken in from contemporary German thought (Platonic, organic), his brilliantly felt and obscurely achieved ambition to make them jibe with the commonsensical, practical, and traditionary (Anglican, Aristotelian, and "mechanical-empirical").

23. Quoted in Basil Willey, "Thought," *The Character of England,* ed. Ernest Barker (Oxford, 1947), p. 335.

24. Notes for Speech on Amendment on the Address, Nov. 30, 1774, *Correspondence of the Right Honourable Edmund Burke,* ed. Charles William, Earl Fitzwilliam, and Sir Richard Bourke [1844], Rivington edn. (London, 1852), II, 415–416.

25. "Reflections" II, 307. On the persistence of Nature in his thought, see Willey, *The Eighteenth Century Background: Studies on the Idea of Nature in the Thought of the Period* (London, 1940), pp. 240–252, esp. 243–245.

Burke, like Kames, simply refuses to give up the idea of Nature as a fixed objective harmony in things, always the same; and yet one confronts the paradox that in seeking to conform his thinking with Nature, he turns to History. To follow the "nature" of a case apparently means to Burke to keep in view at one time as many operative factors as the evidence of the case admits or unfolds; at any given moment to allow diverse, and often conflicting factors to express their actuality within the case at hand, with a view to their reconciliation. By such a method, looking backward and forward, without pre-judged design, but holding to what one achieves stage after stage with a kind of prejudice, holding the achieved in stable suspension, acknowledging its first claim, its contingent option—by such a method, one is committed to the progressive definition of a *character* (a concrete "nature") and as new or unconsidered factors are encountered and reconciled, and old factors die out of relevance, of a *character* which sometimes may be said to "grow" in the complexity of its characterization, sometimes merely continues in the essence of what it was.

## II. Burke and America

1. "Thoughts on the Cause of the Present Discontents," I, 307.

2. *Ibid.*, p. 316.

3. *Ibid.*, pp. 337–338

4. Burke to Charles James Fox, Oct. 8, 1777, V. 447 ff.

5. Burke to the Marquis of Rockingham, Aug. 23, 1775, *Fitzwilliam Corr.* I, 281–282.

6. *Ibid.*, p. 282. For an imaginative account of Burke's relations with Bristol, see Ernest Barker, "Burke and His Bristol Constituency," *Essays on Government,* 2nd edn. (Oxford, 1951), ch. 6.,

7. "Observations on a Late Publication, Intituled, 'The Present State of the Nation,'" I, 299.

8. "A Letter to John Farr and John Harris, Esqrs., Sheriffs of the City of Bristol, on the Affairs of America," II, 37–38.

9. David Cecil, *The Young Melbourne: and the Story of His Marriage with Caroline Lamb* (Indianapolis, 1939), pp. 1–18.

10. For example: I, 182–184, 293–299, 415–424; II, 34–42; V, 498–509.

11. "Sheriffs of Bristol," II, 40. In 1780 Burke said: "The distemper of this age is a poverty of spirit and of genius; it is trifling, it is futile, worse than ignorant, superficially taught; with the politics and morals of girls at a boarding-school, rather than of men and statesmen; but it is not yet desperately wicked, or so scandalously venal as in former times." "Speech on a Bill for Shortening the Duration of Parliaments," VI, 140–141. A year before his death in 1797, he was still talking about "the mediocrity of the age I live in"—"A Letter From the Right Honourable Edmund Burke to a Noble Lord . . ." V, 135. Henry Buckle comments: it was indeed "the golden age of successful mediocrity; an age in which little men were favoured, and great men depressed; when Addington was cherished as a statesman, and Beattie pensioned as a philosopher; and when, in all the walks of public life, the first conditions of promotion were, to fawn upon ancient prejudices, and support established abuses." *Introduction to the History of Civilization in England,* introd. J. M. Robertson (New York, 1925), p. 264.

12. To Fox, V. 450. On Johnson's suspicion, see *Boswell's Life of Johnson,* ed. George Birkbeck Hill, 6 vols. (Oxford, 1887), II, 348; III, 45–46.

13. "Speech on American Taxation," I, 430–431.

14. "Sheriffs of Bristol," II, 15.

15. "Speech on Moving His Resolutions for Conciliation with the Colonies," I, 453, 454.

16. "Sheriffs of Bristol," II, 17.

17. *Ibid.* p. 41.

18. "To the Electors of Bristol, on His Being Declared by the Sheriffs Duly Elected One of the Representatives in Parliament for That City," I, 446—cited hereafter as "Conclusion of the Poll."

19. John Morley, *Burke,* English Men of Letters (London, 1912), p. 21.

20. "Sheriffs of Bristol," II, 16.

21. A recent study with new biographical materials is *Edmund Burke, New York Agent, With His Letters to the New York Assembly and Intimate Correspondence with Charles O'Hara, 1761–1776,* ed. Ross J. S. Hoffman, American Philosophical Society (Philadelphia, 1956). This book should kill once and for all any suspicion of Burke's honor during his American agency.

22. "On Conciliation," I, 460.

23. *Ibid.,* p. 456.

24. *Ibid.,* p. 459.

25. *Ibid.,* p. 461.

26. "Observations on a Late Publication," I, 277.

27. "On Conciliation," I, 462.

28. "Present Discontents," I, 336.

29. "On Conciliation," I, 451.

30. "Observations on a Late Publication," I, 261.

31. *Edmund Burke's Speech on Conciliation with America,* ed. Albert S. Cook, Longmans' English Classics (New York, 1903), p. xii.

32. Letters ". . . on the Proposals for Peace with the Regicide Directory of France," No 2, V, 234.

33. "American Taxation," I, 389–390.

34. Wellek, *A History of Modern Criticism: 1750–1950,* p. 111. This development of sympathetic imagination, in Prof. Wellek's analysis, coincided with a "turn to pathos and rhetoric" (p. 114) and an "empiricist logic which ceased to be able to account for abstraction," and as a result Burke could not "distinguish between a work of art and real life"; he implicitly justified efforts of imagination "naturalistic in technique" and "emotionally harassing" (p. 118). A like monster is laid at Johnson's doorstep (p. 79). Prof. Wellek has middle-class tragedy in mind.

35. "An Essay Towards an Abridgment of the English History: in Three Books," VI, 297. On influence of the *Lettres Persanes,* see A.P.I. Samuels, *The Early Life, Correspondence, and Writings of the Rt. Hon. Edmund Burke* . . . (Cambridge, Eng., 1923), pp. 59–61. The four pamphlets *A Free Briton's Advice to the Free Citizens of Dublin* (1748–1749), which appear to be young Burke's, show a clear influence of Montesquieu; reprinted in Samuels, pp. 331–355.

36. "An Appeal From the New to the Old Whigs, in Consequence of Some Late Discussions in Parliament, Relative to the Reflections on the French Revolution," III, 113.

37. "On Conciliation," I, 462.

38. *Ibid.,* p. 472.

39. *Ibid.,* p. 473.

40. "Sheriffs of Bristol," II, 32: ". . . the high spirit of free depend-

encies, animated with the first glow and activity of juvenile heat, and assuming to themselves, as their birthright, some part of that very pride which oppresses them."

41. "On Conciliation," I, 472–473.

42. *Ibid.,* p. 464.

43. Morley, *Burke,* p. 83.

44. "Sheriffs of Bristol," II, 29. On *contextualism,* with which Burke's thinking has some affinity, as distinct from *organicism,* with which his thinking also has some affinity, see Stephen Pepper, *World Hypotheses: a Study in Evidence* (Berkeley, 1942), pp. 232–280.

45. "Sheriffs of Bristol," II, 30.

46. *Ibid.,* p. 31.

47. *Ibid.,* p. 29.

48. Quoted in Stephen, *Thought in the Eighteenth Century,* II, 241.

49. "On Conciliation," I, 479–480.

50. *Ibid.,* p. 464.

51. *Ibid.*

52. *Ibid.,* p. 465.

53. *Ibid.*

54. "Sheriffs of Bristol," II, 33.

55. *Ibid.*

56. "On Conciliation," I, 470.

57. "Taxation No Tyranny," *The Works of Samuel Johnson, LL.D. With an Essay on His Life and Genius by Arthur Murphy,* 3rd American edn. (New York, 1846), II, 437.

58. "On Conciliation," I, 471.

59. *Ibid.,* p. 466.

60. *Ibid.*

61. *Culture and Anarchy,* ed. W. S. Knickerbocker (New York, 1929), pp. 53–54.

62. For an interesting twentieth-century analogy, see *The God That Failed,* ed. Richard Crossman, Bantam Books (New York, 1954), pp. 7–8. Communism has less success in Protestant countries owing to their history of non-conformism.

63. "On Conciliation," I, 466.

64. *Ibid.,* p. 467.

65. *Ibid.*

66. *Burke's Conciliation,* ed. Cook, pp. 121–122.

67. "On Conciliation," I, 468.

68. "American Taxation," I, 431.

69. "Observations on a Late Publication," I, 270–271.

70. "On Conciliation," I, 468.

71. *Ibid.,* pp. 468–469.

72. *Ibid.,* p. 459.

73. *Ibid.,* p. 467.

74. *Ibid.,* p. 476.

75. Purely theoretical statements of the principle, however, are present in Montesquieu's *L'Esprit des Lois.* For example: "The government most conformable to Nature is that which best agrees with the humour and dispositions of the people in whose favour it is established."

76. "On Conciliation," I, 469.

77. "Observations on a Late Publication," I, 277–278.

78. "Present Discontents," I, 311.

79. Burke to the Marquis of Rockingham, Aug. 23, 1775, *Fitzwilliam Corr.,* I, 282.

80. "Present Discontents," I, 311–312.

81. "Observations on a Late Publication," I, 199.

82. "Sheriffs of Bristol," II, 27.

83. For an illuminating historical summary which also brings the idea up to 1945, from a point of view congenial with Burke's, see Butterfield, *The Englishman and His History,* ch. 5, *et passim.* A limitedly "Whig interpretation of history" has grown to the dimensions of a national ethos.

84. "Present Discontents," I, 311–312. On Saxon liberty and law—"monuments of our pristine rudeness"—see "English History," VI, 415–422.

85. "On Conciliation," I, 509.

86. *Ibid.*

87. *Ibid.,* p. 473.

88. *Ibid.,* p. 508.

89. *Ibid.,* pp. 508–509.

90. *Ibid.,* p. 508.

91. "Sheriffs of Bristol," II, 36.

92. See [William Burke] *An Account of the European Settlements in America,* [rev. Edmund Burke] 6th edn. (London, 1777), II, 146–161.

93. "On Conciliation," I, 469.

94. "Sheriffs of Bristol," II, 31–32.

95. "Conclusion of the Poll," I, 448.

96. "Observations on a Late Publication," I, 278.

97. "Two Letters to Gentlemen in the City of Bristol, on the Bills Depending in Parliament Relative to the Trade of Ireland," II, 45.

98. "On Conciliation," I, 509.

99. *Ibid.,* p. 479.

100. "Observations on a Late Publication," I, 258.

101. *Ibid.,* p. 257.

102. "Sheriffs of Bristol," II, 32.

103. "Conclusion of the Poll," I, 447.

104. "Sheriffs of Bristol," II, 29.

105. *Ibid.*

106. "On Conciliation," I, 501–502.

107. "Conclusion of the Poll," I, 447.

108. "On Conciliation," I, 476.

109. "American Taxation," I, 434.

110. G. W. F. Hegel, *Lectures on the Philosophy of History,* trans. J. Sibree (London, 1878), pp. 474–475.

111. "On Conciliation," I, 476. In his discussions of empire, Burke formulates a distinctively English conception whose essentials, very much as he states them, dominated the nineteenth century and have kept intact during the twentieth. See Ernest Barker, *Ideas and Ideals of the British Empire* (Cambridge, Eng., 1941), pp. 8, 36–37, 68–70, *et passim.* However, for the contrary opinion, see Lord Hugh Cecil, *Conservatism* (London, 1925), pp. 62 ff.

For a twentieth-century interpretation of "English liberty" which, very similar to Burke's, also clarifies his latent assumptions, see George Santayana, "English Liberty in America," *Character and Opinion in the United States,* in *The Works of George Santayana,* Triton edn. (New York, 1937), VIII, pp. 108–130. English liberty, a "method, not a goal" (p. 111), requires that one "remain plastic and continually invite amendments, in order to continue broadly adjusted to an infinite moving world" (p. 129). It implies a poetic practicality (p. 114), a sense of duty (p. 120), a cooperativeness (pp. 124–125). Irving Babbitt starts upon a like tack, but, says he, this theory of English liberty is "almost too familiar for restatement"! "Burke and the Moral Imagination" *Democracy and Leadership,* pp. 105–106.

112. *Select British Eloquence* [1852], repr. with introd. by Bower Aly (New York, 1963), p. 215.

113. "On Conciliation," I, 471.

114. "Speech at His Arrival at Bristol," I, 440.

115. "On Conciliation," I, 486.

116. *Ibid.,* p. 484.

117. *Ibid.,* p. 487.

118. *Ibid.,* p. 489.

119. A. N. Whitehead, *The Organization of Thought* (London, 1917), p. 113.

120. "Taxation no Tyranny," *Works,* 3rd Am. edn., II, 430.

121. "On Conciliation," I, 489.

122. "American Taxation," I, 403.

123. *Ibid.*

124. *Ibid.*

125. *Ibid.,* p. 404.

126. "Observations on a Late Publication," I, 270.

127. "Address to the British Colonists in North America," V, 482.

128. "Sheriffs of Bristol," II, 27.

129. *Ibid.,* p. 28.

130. *Ibid.*

131. "American Taxation," I, 434.

132. *Ibid.*, p. 435.
133. "On Conciliation," I, 439.
134. "Sheriffs of Bristol," II, 35–36.
135. "Address to Colonists," V, 484.
136. "Present Discontents," I, 332.
137. "On Shortening Parliaments," VI, 137.
138. "American Taxation," I, 406-409.
139. *Ibid.*, pp. 424–26.
140. *Ibid.*, pp. 426–429.
141. *Ibid.*, p. 390.
142. *Ibid.*, p. 397.
143. *Ibid.*, p. 415.
144. *Ibid.*, p. 390.
145. "On Conciliation," I, 462–463.
146. *Ibid.*, p 463.
147. "Sheriffs of Bristol," II, 13.
148. "On Conciliation," I, 463.
149. *Ibid.*
150. *Ibid.*
151. "American Taxation," I, 435–436.
152. "On Conciliation," I, 506.
153. "Observations on a Late Publication," I, 264.
154. *Ibid.*, p. 247.
155. "American Taxation," I, 407.
156. *Ibid.*, p. 431. Those appealing to rights would include Johnson, Lord Lyttleton, Gov. Pownall, Chatham, and the Americans generally; see Stephen, *Thought in the Eighteenth Century,* II, 239.
157. "Observations on a Late Publication," I, 281.
158. "Sheriffs of Bristol," II, 30.
159. *Ibid.*, p. 26.
160. "On Conciliation," I, 482.
161. "American Taxation," I, 432–433.
162. "Sheriffs of Bristol," II, 34.
163. "On Conciliation," I, 501.
164. *Ibid.*, p. 500.
165. "Observations on a Late Publication," I, 283.
166. "American Taxation," I, 431.
167. Burke to Dr. Robertson, June 10, 1777, *Fitzwilliam Corr.*, I, 340.
168. "New to Old Whigs," III, 31–32.
169. Burke to the Marquis of Rockingham, Nov. 5, 1777, *Fitzwilliam Corr.*, I, 358.
170. "Sheriffs of Bristol," II, 11.
171. *Ibid.*, p. 3.
172. *Ibid.*, p. 4.
173. *Ibid.*, p. 6.
174. *Ibid.*, p. 7.

175. Burke to Richard Champion, March 1776, *Fitzwilliam Corr.*, I, 306.

176. "Sheriffs of Bristol," II, 8.

177. *Ibid.*, p. 9.

178. *Ibid.*, pp. 7–8.

179. *Ibid.*, p. 10.

180. *Ibid.*, p. 5.

181. *Ibid.*, p. 11.

182. *Ibid.*, p. 20.

183. Burke to the Marquis of Rockingham, Feb. 2, 1774, *Fitzwilliam Corr.*, I, 225.

184. "Sheriffs of Bristol," II, 14.

185. Burke to the Marquis of Rockingham, Nov. 5, 1777, *Fitzwilliam Corr.*, I, 357.

186. "Sheriffs of Bristol," II, 19.

187. *Ibid.*, p. 8.

188. *Ibid.*, p. 11.

189. *Ibid.*, p. 17.

190. *Ibid.*

191. Burke to the Marquis of Rockingham, Dec. 20, 1774, *Fitzwilliam Corr.*, I, 258.

192. Burke to the Duke of Richmond, Sept. 26, 1775, *ibid.*, pp. 293–295.

193. Burke to the Marquis of Rockingham, Aug. 23, 1775, *ibid.*, p. 282.

194. "Sheriffs of Bristol," II, 39.

195. *Ibid.*

196. "Sheriffs of Bristol," II, 40. See L. Stuart Sutherland, "Edmund Burke and the First Rockingham Ministry," *English Historical Review, XLVII* (Jan. 1932), 46–70: The representative principles of eighteenth-century Whigs grew not from the prepossessions of the great landed inheritors of the revolutionary settlement of 1688, but were "forced out by the change from power to opposition, a compound of new needs with old loyalties."

197. Sir Philip Magnus, *Edmund Burke: a Life* (London, 1939), pp. 58–59, 91–92, 110, *et passim*. The argument briefly is that by the eighteenth century the "divine right of kings" had become the "divine right of aristocracy"; that Burke was like "a tutelary priest in the presence of a row of sacred images."

198. Burke to the Duke of Richmond, Nov. 17, 1772, *Fitzwilliam Corr.*, I, 190–191.

199. Burke to unknown correspondent, 1771, *ibid.*, p. 166.

200. *Ibid.*

201. "Sheriffs of Bristol," II, 38.

## III. Burke and Ireland

1. *Fitzwilliam Corr.,* II, 435.
2. "Regicide Peace," No. 3, V, 290, Cf. Burke to Windham, Sept. 27, 1789, *Windham Corr.,* p. 21. The French are more "democratical" than Americans.
3. "Speech at the Guildhall, in Bristol, Previous to the Late Election in that City, Upon Certain Points Relative to His Parliamentary Conduct," II, 135.
4. Reported in Prior, *Life,* p. 174.
5. James Mackintosh, *Vindiciae Gallicae: Defence of the French Revolution and Its English Admirers Againt the Accusations of the Right Hon. Edmund Burke: . . .* (London, 1791), p. 137.
6. "To Fox," Oct. 8, 1777, V, 452.
7. "Letter to a Peer of Ireland, on the Penal Laws against Irish Catholics . . . 1782," III, 283.
8. "On Conciliation," I, 458.
9. "Two Letters to Bristol," II, 51.
10. "A Letter to Thomas Burgh, Esq.," V, 509.
11. *Ibid.,* p. 508.
12. "Previous to the Election," II, 137–138.
13. Burke to Anthony Dermott, Aug. 17, 1779, *Fitzwilliam Corr.,* I, 405.
14. "Letter to Sir Charles Bingham, Bart., on the Irish Absentee Tax," V, 440.
15. *Ibid.,* p. 439.
16. *Ibid.,* p. 440.
17. "To Burgh," V, 493.
18. "To Bingham," V, 444.
19. *Ibid.,* p. 442.
20. *Ibid.,* p. 438.
21. *Ibid.*
22. "To Burgh," V, 497.
23. "Two Letters to Bristol," II, 47.
24. *Ibid.,* p. 49.
25. *Ibid.,* p. 54.
26. *Ibid.,* p. 46.
27. *Ibid.,* p. 52.
28. *Ibid.,* p. 53.
29. *Ibid.,* p. 46.
30. *Ibid.,* pp. 51–52.
31. *Ibid.,* pp. 47–48.
32. *Ibid.,* p. 52.
33. "A Second Letter to Sir Hercules Langrishe," VI, 57.
34. "To Fox," Oct. 8, 1777, V, 446.
35. *Ibid.,* p. 449.

36. Burke to Richard Champion, Oct. 9, 1778, *Fitzwilliam Corr.*, I, 379.

37. "To Burgh," V, 498.

38. *Ibid.*, p. 497.

39. "Previous to the Election," II, 136.

40. "To Burgh," V, 504.

41. *Ibid.*, p. 505.

42. "Two Letters to Bristol," II, 43.

43. "Previous to the Election," II, 135.

44. "To Burgh," V, 494–496.

45. *Ibid.*, p. 495.

46. *Ibid.*

47. "Previous to the Election," II, 135.

48. "Two Letters to Bristol," II, 43–44.

49. *Ibid.*, p. 44.

50. *Ibid.*, p. 47.

51. "To Burgh," V, 498.

52. *Ibid.*, p. 497.

53. "Thoughts and Details on Scarcity, Originally Presented to the Right Honourable William Pitt, in the Month of November, 1795," V, 84.

54. *Ibid.*, p. 89.

55. *Ibid.*, p. 83.

56. *Ibid.*, p. 92. Cf. Burke to John Burke, 1777, quoted in Robert M. Hutchins, "The Theory of the State: Edmund Burke," *Review of Politics,* V (April, 1943), 140n. "I am, for one, entirely satisfied that the inequality, which grows out of the *nature of things,* by time, custom, successions, accumulation, permutation, and improvement of property, is much nearer that true equality, which is the foundation of equity and just policy, than anything which can be contrived by the tricks and devices of human skill."

57. *Ibid.*

58. "Regicide Peace," No. 1, V, 216.

59. "Speech on a Motion for Leave to Bring in a Bill to Repeal and Alter Certain Acts Respecting Religious Opinions; May 11, 1792," VI, 114—cited hereafter as "Petition of the Unitarians."

60. "Thoughts on Scarcity," V, 100.

61. *Ibid.*, p. 87.

62. "Reflections on the Revolution in France, and on the Proceedings in Certain Societies in London Relative to That Event: in a Letter Intended to Have Been Sent to a Gentleman in Paris," II, 351–352. Most critics consider Burke's economics an illiberal blind spot; see Cobban, *Revolt Against the Eighteenth Century,* pp. 190–197. Yet, be it noted, Burke expressed unusual sympathy with the plight of the working classes: "[The monks in France] are as usefully employed as if they worked from dawn to dark in the innumerable servile, degrading,

unseemly, unmanly, and often most unwholesome and pestiferous occupations, to which by the social economy so many wretches are inevitably doomed. If it were not generally pernicious to disturb the natural course of things, and to impede, in any degree, the great wheel of circulation which is turned by the strangely-directed labour of these unhappy people, I should be infinitely more inclined forcibly to rescue them from their miserable industry, than violently to disturb the tranquil repose of monastic quietude." "Reflections," p. 431. Cf. "A Vindication of Natural Society . . . by a Late Noble Writer," I, 42.

63. Bryant, *Literary Friends,* p. 248. For Burke's mild boast of his originality, see "To a Noble Lord," V, 124.

64. "Speech on Presenting to the House of Commons (on the 11th February, 1780), a Plan for the Better Security of the Independence of Parliament, and the Economical Reformation of the Civil and Other Establishments," II, 84.

65. "Letter on the Affairs of Ireland, Written in the Year 1797," VI, 89.

66. *Ibid.,* p. 88.

67. "Tracts, Relative to the Laws Against Popery in Ireland," VI, 30.

68. "Petition of the Unitarians," VI, 123–124.

69. "A Letter to Sir H. Langrishe, Bart. M. P. on the Subject of the Roman Catholics of Ireland, and the Propriety of Admitting Them to the Elective Franchise, Consistently With the Principles of the Constitution as Established at the Revolution," III, 309.

70. "Speech on the Second Reading of a Bill for the Relief of Protestant Dissenters," VI, 108.

71. "Tracts on Popery Laws," VI, 34.

72. "Petition of the Unitarians," VI, 116.

73. *Ibid.,* p. 122.

74. *Ibid.,* p. 166.

75. "Letter to Richard Burke, Esq.," VI, 72.

76. "Reflections," II, 370.

77. "Petition of the Unitarians," VI, 115.

78. "Tracts on Popery Laws," VI, 33.

79. *Ibid.,* p. 32.

80. *Ibid.,* pp. 32–33.

81. *Ibid.,* p. 33.

82. "Reflections," II, 421.

83. "Previous to the Election," II, 146.

84. Burke to William Burgh, Feb. 9, 1775, *Fitzwilliam Corr.,* I, 266–267.

85. "To Richard Burke," VI, 73.

86. "Reflections," II, 362.

87. *Ibid.,* p. 370.

88. *Ibid.,* p. 369.

89. "To a Peer of Ireland," III, 292.

90. Joseph Priestley, *Letters to the Right Honourable Edmund Burke, Occasioned by His "Reflections on the Revolution in France, etc.,"* 3rd edn. (Birmingham, 1791), p. viii, *et passim.*

91. "A Letter to the Right Hon. Edmund Perry," V, 488–489.

92. "Regicide Peace," No. 4, V, 425.

93. "Reflections," II, 370.

94. "Speech on the Petition, . . . to be Relieved from Subscription to the Thirty-Nine Articles, as Required by the Acts of Uniformity," VI, 93.

95. "Reflections," II, 368.

96. *Ibid.*, p. 376. Cf., "Speech on a Motion for Leave to Bring in a Bill to Quiet the Possessions of the Subject Against Dormant Claims of the Church," VI, 173.

97. *Ibid.*, p. 367.

98. *Ibid.*, p. 368.

99. *Ibid.*, p. 364.

100. *Ibid.*, p. 365.

101. *Ibid.*, p. 364.

102. *Ibid.*, p. 366.

103. *Ibid.*, p. 430.

104. "Tracts on Popery Laws," VI, 34.

105. *Ibid.*

106. *Ibid.*, p. 32.

107. "Reflections," II, 424.

108. *Ibid.*

109. *Leviathan*, Bk. I, ch. 11.

110. "Regicide Peace," No. 2, V, 245–246.

111. *Ibid.*, p. 245.

112. "To Richard Burke," VI, 67–68.

113. Burke to the Rev. John Erskine, April 1779, *Fitzwilliam Corr.*, I, 392.

114. "To Richard Burke," VI, 72.

115. "Remarks on the Policy of the Allies with Respect to France, Begun in October, 1793," III, 445.

116. "A Letter to William Smith, Esq.," VI, 50.

117. "To Richard Burke," VI, 63.

118. "Previous to the Election," II, 166.

119. "To a Peer of Ireland," III, 296.

120. "Previous to the Election," II, 154–155.

121. "To Edmund Perry," V, 488.

122. "Tracts on Popery Laws," VI, 32.

123. *Ibid.*, p. 18.

124. *Ibid.*, p. 20.

125. "To Richard Burke," VI, 74.

126. "Letters, With Reflections on the Executions of the Rioters, in 1780," V, 518.

127. "Previous to the Election," II, 157.
128. *Ibid.*, p. 144.
129. "Executions of the Rioters," V, 518.
130. "Previous to the Election," II, 144–145.
131. "Thoughts on French Affairs, etc. etc., Written in December, 1791," III, 350.
132. "Tracts on Popery Laws," VI, 27.
133. "To Langrishe," III, 301.
134. *Ibid.*, p. 320.
135. *Ibid.*, p. 321.
136. "To Richard Burke," VI, 70.
137. "Executions of the Rioters," V, 517.
138. "To Langrishe," III, 339.
139. "To a Peer of Ireland," III, 285.
140. "To Langrishe," III, 325–326.
141. "On the Affairs of Ireland," V, 90.
142. "To a Peer of Ireland," III, 289.
143. "Previous to the Election," II, 148.
144. "To Langrishe," III, 336.
145. "Tracts on Popery Laws," VI, 48.
146. "To Langrishe," III, 335.
147. *Ibid.*, p. 305.
148. *Ibid.*, p. 304.
149. "To a Peer of Ireland," III, 287.
150. "To Richard Burke," VI, 62.
151. Morley, *Burke*, p. 24.
152. "To Langrishe," III, 335.
153. "To Richard Burke," VI, 63.
154. "To a Peer of Ireland," III, 294.
155. "To Langrishe," III, 306–307.
156. "To William Smith," VI, 54.
157. "Tracts on Popery Laws," VI, 43.
158. *Ibid.*, p. 30.
159. "On the State of Ireland," *Fitzwilliam Corr.*, II, 179.
160. "Tracts on Popery Laws," VI, 44.
161. *Ibid.*, p. 43.
162. *Ibid.*, p. 29.
163. "To Richard Burke," VI, 67.
164. *Ibid.*
165. "Previous to the Election," II, 165.
166. "To Richard Burke," VI, 69.
167. *Ibid.*, p. 65.
168. *Ibid.*, p. 66.
169. *Ibid.*
170. "To Langrishe," III, 310.
171. *Ibid.*, p. 312.

172. "To Richard Burke," VI, 66.
173. "Previous to the Election," II, 149.
174. "To Richard Burke," VI, 69.
175. "To William Smith," VI, 52.
176. "To Langrishe," III, 313.
177. *Ibid.*
178. "Second Letter to Langrishe," VI, 58.
179. "To William Smith," VI, 53.
180. "Tracts on Popery Laws," VI, 45.
181. "On the State of Ireland," *Fitzwilliam Corr.,* II, 172.
182. "Tracts on Popery Laws," VI, 45–46.
183. See the account of Burke's relations with Thomas Leland and Thomas Campbell in Bryant, *Literary Friends,* pp. 227–232.
184. "Tracts on Popery Laws," VI, 46.
185. "To Richard Burke," VI, 71.
186. "To William Smith," VI, 50.
187. "To Richard Burke," VI, 78.
188. *Ibid.,* pp. 75–76.
189. *Ibid.,* p. 76.
190. *Ibid.,* p. 74.
191. *Ibid.,* p. 79.
192. "Previous to the Election," II, 164–165.
193. "Tracts on Popery Laws," VI, 26.
194. *Ibid.,* p. 24.
195. *Ibid.*
196. *Ibid.*
197. *Ibid.,* p. 22.
198. *Ibid.,* pp. 21–22.
199. *Ibid.,* p. 20.
200. *Ibid.,* pp. 20–21.
201. *Ibid.,* p. 21.
202. *Ibid.,* p. 22.
203. *Ibid.,* p. 21.
204. *Ibid.,* p. 22.
205. *Ibid.*
206. *Ibid.,* p. 24.
207. *Ibid.,* p. 22.
208. *Ibid.,* pp. 22–23.
209. *Ibid.,* p. 19.
210. *Ibid.,* p. 20.
211. "Executions of the Rioters," V, 520.
212. "Reflections," II, 367.
213. "Tracts on Popery Laws," VI, 16.
214. "Previous to the Election," II, 163–164.
215. "Tracts on Popery Laws," VI, 30.
216. "To Richard Burke," VI, 63–64.

217. *Ibid.*, p. 78.
218. "Previous to the Election," II, 163.
219. "Second Letter to Langrishe," VI, 60.
220. "To Richard Burke," VI, 75.
221. "On the State of Ireland," *Fitzwilliam Corr.*, II, 183.
222. "Previous to the Election," II, 164.
223. "To Langrishe," III, 308.
224. "To Fox," Oct. 8, 1777, V, 453.
225. *Fitzwilliam Corr.*, II, 183.
226. "To Langrishe," III, 343–344.
227. *Fitzwilliam Corr.*, II, 183.
228. "Petition of the Unitarians," VI, 117.
229. Burke to Richard Burke, Jun., Sept. 9, 1792, *Fitzwilliam Corr.*, II, 138.
230. "Previous to the Election," II, 162.
231. "A Letter to the Right Honourable Henry Dundas, One of His Majesty's Principal Secretaries of State, With the Sketch of a Negro Code," V, 522.
232. "To a Peer of Ireland," III, 283.
233. *Ibid.*, p. 296.
234. *Fitzwilliam Corr.*, II, 138.
235. *Main Currents in American Thought: an Interpretation of American Literature From the Beginnings to 1920* (New York, 1930), II, 366. Cf. p. 392: Though Emerson "was never tired of praising Burke," yet Burke's political theory was "so fundamentally hostile to Emerson's major convictions—so legalistic in its reverence for government from the grave, so explicit in denial of new-born rights—that it is a fair assumption that Emerson never took the trouble to understand him but was content to enjoy his glowing rhetoric." Who never took the trouble to understand Burke?
236. "Speech on the Motion Made in the House of Commons, the 7th of February, 1771, Relative to the Middlesex Election," VI, 128.
237. "Report, Made on the 30th of April, 1794, from the Committee . . . in Relation to Their Proceedings on the Trial of Warren Hastings, Esquire . . . With Their Observations Thereupon," VI, 476.
238. "Reflections," II, 421.
239. "Tracts on Popery Laws," VI, 19.
240. "On the Negro Code," V, 524.
241. "To Langrishe," III, 332.
242. "Second Letter to Langrishe," VI, 57.

## IV. Burke and Constitutional Reform

1. Burke to Joseph Harford, Sept. 27, 1780, *Fitzwilliam Corr.*, I, 449.
2. "Previous to the Election," II, 136.
3. "To a Noble Lord," V, 116.
4. "A Letter on the Duration of Parliaments, to the Chairman of the

Buckinghamshire Meeting, Held on the 13th of April, 1780, at Aylesbury," VI, 4. Buckle praises other "great measures" of the nineteenth century which Burke anticipated, including his attacks upon laws against forestalling and regrating at market, upon laws against insolvents, upon the law for enlisting soldiers for life, and upon the absolute power of judges in libel cases. *Hist. of Civ.*, pp. 261–262.

5. Burke to Richard Champion, Oct. 9, 1778, *Fitzwilliam Corr.*, I, 378.

6. "To a Peer of Ireland," III, 295.

7. "Speech on a Motion, Made by the Right Hon. Wm. Dowdeswell, for Leave to Bring in a Bill for Explaining the Powers of Juries in Prosecutions for Libels," VI, 164.

8. "Two Letters to Bristol," II, 44.

9. "Previous to the Election," II, 133.

10. Burke to Harford, *Fitzwilliam Corr.*, I, 449.

11. Prior, *Life*, p. 323.

12. "To a Noble Lord," V, 120–121.

13. Burke to Harford, *Fitzwilliam Corr.*, I, 450.

14. "Regicide Peace," No. 3, V, 270.

15. "To a Noble Lord," V, 116. Burke contracted a reforming zeal very young. At eighteen he wrote periodical essays called *The Reformer* (reprinted in Samuels, *Early Life*) to improve the morality of Dubliners by correcting their taste. A classmate thought him "damnd absolute" in argument; Samuels, p. 239.

16. "A Letter to William Elliot, Esq., Occasioned by the Account Given in a Newspaper of the Speech Made in the House of Lords, by the [Duke] of [Norfolk], in the Debate Concerning Lord Fitzwilliam," V, 78.

17. "Reflections," II, 438–439.

18. *Burke's Politics: Selected Writings and Speeches of Edmund Burke on Reform, Revolution and War,* ed. Ross J. S. Hoffman and Paul Levack (New York, 1949), p. xxxi.

19. *Defence of Economy Against the Late Mr. Burke* (n.p., 1817), pp. 12, 13, 28, *et passim.* Bentham considered Burke's "principles" the oratorical sophistries of "the agent and spokesman of *the ruling few*" (p. 47); his appeals for candor, moderation, wisdom, etc., a "fine-spun web, with purity at top and corruption at bottom" (p. 12); his ideal a "government, in which, under the guidance of upstart Machiavelism, titled and confederated imbecility should lord it over King and people, and, behind the screen of secrecy, waste, oppression, and peculation should find themselves for ever at their ease" (p. 38). As convinced as Burke that politics is empirical, Bentham differs in *the mode of mind* regulating his empiricism: the moral order has evaporated from his thought. Burke's principles are essentially humanistic, and imply a union of the intellectual with the moral. Nothing better could illustrate the limitation of empiricism *qua* empiricism—its dependence upon a prior set of values to be pursued. In *An Introduction to the Principles*

*of Morals and Legislation* (1789), Bentham subjects "principles," and other "fictitious entities" equally part of Burke's idiom, to the same iconoclasm (I, xiv, 3 and 10; chs. X, XI). For the irony of his creating a "fictitious entity" of his own in the principle of utilitarianism, as also for brief comparisons with Burke, see Crane Brinton, *English Political Thought in the Nineteenth Century* (London, 1933), pp. 14, 15, 21, 30. For other comparisons, see Elie Halevy, *The Growth of Philosophich Radicalism, Beacon Press* (Boston, 1955), pp. 167–182.

20. *Biographia Literaria,* introd. Arthur Symons, Everyman's edn. (London, 1934), p. 187.

21. Quoted in *Inquiring Spirit,* ed. Kathleen Coburn (New York, 1951), pp. 137–138.

22. *Friend,* I, quoted in Coburn, p. 267.

23. In conversation with Hazlitt; see P. P. Howe, *The Life of William Hazlitt,* 2nd edn. (London, 1923), p. 37. On Coleridge's continuity with Burke in politics, see Cobban, *Revolt Against the Eighteenth Century,* ch. 6; and Russell Kirk, *The Conservative Mind from Burke to Santayana* (*Chicago,* 1953), pp. 115–127.

24. *Table Talk,* April 8, 1833, quoted in Coburn, p. 266.

25. "Petition of the Unitarians," VI, 113–114.

26. "To Langrishe," III, 317–318.

27. Whitney, *Primitivism and Progress,* pp. 193–205.

28. "To a Noble Lord," V. 125, Cf. "To a Peer of Ireland," 287–294, on the education of the Irish Catholic clergy.

29. "Prosecutions for Libels," VI, 160.

30. "Reflections," II, 430.

31. *Ibid.,* p. 362.

32. "On the Acts of Uniformity," VI, 92.

33. "Abridgment of English History," VI, 194.

34. "On the Economical Reform," II, 64.

35. "To a Peer of Ireland," III, 289.

36. "Speech on the First of December, 1783, . . . on Mr. Fox's East-India Bill," II, 176.

37. Burke to Mons. Dupont, Oct., 1789, *Fitzwilliam Corr.,* I, 559; and "A Letter to the Empress of Russia," V, 437.

38. *Ibid.,* p. 563.

39. "On the Economical Reform," II, 83.

40. *Ibid.,* p. 64.

41. "Tracts on Popery Laws," VI, 33.

42. Stephen, *Thought in the Eighteenth Century,* II, 219; Laski, *Locke to Bentham,* p. 173. Thomas W. Copeland lists nineteenth-century eulogies of Burke as man and stylist, for example, by Hazlitt, De-Quincy, Macaulay, Arnold, and Stephen, in *Our Eminent Friend Edmund Burke* (New Haven, 1949), p. 4. The opposite opinion, that Burke was insane, especially during his last years, had formed before he died; see Windham's diary, Nov. 7, 1790, quoted in Magnus, *Life,*

p. 217; and John Timbs, *Anecdote Lives of William Pitt, Earl of Chatham, and Edmund Burke* (London, 1880), pp. 347–348, where Burke's manly and sane decision to ignore the charges is preserved. In 1857 Buckle considers the exaggerations of Burke's rhetoric as evidence of "complete hallucination." All great revolutions tend to increase insanity, he explains—*Hist. of Civ.,* pp. 264–269. Copeland, without tendentious blame, in 1949 coolheadedly considers the possible symptoms of paranoia (pp. 88–90).

For a representative hostility to his conservatism, see William Graham, *English Political Philosophy from Hobbes to Maine* (London, 1899), p. 167: "In every direction he was a reactionary or rather a conservative, in full and entire sympathy with things as they are, with no belief in and no sympathy with progress." And Ivor Brown, *English Political Theory:* "Truly the man was pathetically obsessed with the will to believe" (p. 72). "Burke had no critical power" (p. 73)! "His eye in a fine frenzy rolls" (p. 74), but "his idol—the wealthy, land-owning Whig—was not at all a nice one" (p. 77). The tone of contemptuous hostility is continued to 1943 by Hutchins, *RP,* V, 155: "In discussing the theory of the state Burke developed, then, not so much a philosophy of conservatism, for a philosophy is a reasoned and coherent view of the universe or some aspect of it, as a series of specious arguments, rhetorical flourishes, and quotable lines which Tories of all later generations have hurled at the heads of those who sought social improvement. At the last God, man, and nature conspire, except in Ireland, to keep things as they are."

For a fair-minded, witty statement of the view which, respectful of Burke, distrusts the influence of his "total conservatism"—meaning theological-pragmatic conservatism—and denies its applicability, see John Crowe Ransom, "Empirics in Politics," *Kenyon Review, XV* (Autumn, 1953), 648–654.

43. Eight caricatures from the British Museum are reproduced in Magnus; two others in Copeland. Cf. Timbs, pp. 192–195.

44. "Reflections," II, 395–596.

45. "Burke and the Moral Imagination," *Democracy and Leadership,* pp. 97–116.

46. *Boswell's Life,* ed. Hill, V, 213–214. Cf. William Hazlitt, "Character of Mr. Burke," *Political Essays,* in *The Complete Works of William Hazlitt,* ed. P. P. Howe (London, 1932), VII, 312.

47. The *locus classicus* is *The Prelude,* Bk. VII, lines 512–543. For a general discussion of Wordsworth's political indebtedness to Burke, see Cobban, *Revolt Against the Eighteenth Century,* ch. 5.

48. Burke's ideas pop up in Arnold repeatedly. Representative praise is to be found in "The Function of Criticism at the Present Time," *Essays in Criticism,* 1st Series (London, 1903), pp. 13–15. Burke's politics are "the true philosophy of an epoch of concentration," but he "lived in a world which neither English Liberalism nor English Toryism

is apt to enter;—the world of ideas." Lecky's thought is pervaded by Burke in a similar fashion. A representative appreciation, by no means uncritical, is in *England in the Eighteenth Century,* III, 196–238. Cf. Kirk, *Conservative Mind,* pp. 285–293.

49. For example: Hoffman and Levack, *Burke's Politics,* introd.; M. F. K. Millar, "Burke and the Moral Basis of Political Liberty," *Thought,* XVI (1916), 79–101. Cf. Brother J. Robert, "Toleration for Catholics: the Mind of Burke," *Thought,* XIV (1939), 633–643. However, they are in just reaction to positivist interpreters of Burke—for example, Stephen, Lecky, and Buckle—all of whom consent to ignore Burke's religion completely. Lord Cecil insists that Burke was a Tory all his life. *Conservatism,* p. 40 ff. It is not irrelevant that Lord Acton, as a young man, considered Burke's speeches from 1790–1795 as "the law and the prophets." All that was Protestant, partial, or revolutionary, he claimed, had yielded to a purely Catholic view of history and politics. *Essays on Church and State,* ed. Woodruff, p. 13.

50. "To Richard Burke," VI, 69.

51. Babbitt, *Democracy and Leadership,* pp. 99, 107, 109–110. That is, regretting a strain of anti-intellectualism in Burke, Babbitt nevertheless praises his reference of intellect to an "ethical center" which is "natural" to man; to overshoot it invites nemesis.

52. "Reflections," II, 412.

53. *Ibid.,* pp. 412–413.

54. "Present Discontents," I, 323.

55. "Speech on the Second Reading of a Bill for the Repeal of the Marriage Act," VI, 170–171.

56. "Reflections," II, 410.

57. "From New to Old Whigs," III, 85.

58. "Reflections," II, 323.

59. "On East-India Bill," II, 180.

60. "From New to Old Whigs," III, 85.

61. *Ibid.,* pp. 85–87.

62. "Reflections," II, 365–366.

63. *Ibid.,* p. 396.

64. *Ibid.*

65. "On Shortening Parliaments," VI, 132.

66. *Ibid.,* p. 134.

67. "To Chairman of the Buckinghamshire Meeting," VI, 3. Cf. remarks on a Corn Bill in 1772: "On this occasion I give way to the present Bill, not because I approve of the measure in itself, but because I think it prudent to yield to the spirit of the times. *The people will have it so; and it is not for their representatives to say nay.*" Quoted in Buckle, *Hist. of Civ.,* p. 260n.

68. "Present Discontents," I, 310.

69. "Tracts on Popery Laws," VI, 20.

70. *Ibid.,* p. 29.

71. "To Langrishe," III, 334–335. George H. Sabine quotes this passage with the erroneous implication that Burke was uninterested in any other kind of representation. *A History of Political Theory,* Revised edn. (New York, 1955), p. 610.

72. Burke to a Member of the Bell-Club, Bristol, Oct. 31, 1777, *Fitzwilliam Corr.,* I, 355.

73. "Present Discontents," I, 347.

74. *Ibid.,* p. 348.

75. *Ibid.,* p. 343.

76. *Ibid.,* p. 348.

77. Sabine, pp. 615–617, 652. Not that Sabine makes a direct accusation; but he is tendentious. He selects those aspects of Burke which anticipate Hegel, "whose philosophy embodies systematically all of Burke's scattered principles." The transition from Hegel to fascism is then made (pp. 621–622) in the "idealization of the national state," whose beginnings he had emphasized in Burke. Though full of helpful insights, Sabine is the victim, or makes his reader the victim, of his Occamite razor.

78. "To Langrishe," III, 302.

79. *Ibid.,* p. 304.

80. "On the Economical Reform," II, 121.

81. "To Langrishe," III, 326.

82. "Regicide Peace," No. 1, V, 190.

83. "On the Affairs of Ireland," VI, 83.

84. "Previous to the Election," II, 138. Cf. Barker, "Burke and Bristol," *Essays,* pp. 191–203.

85. "To Langrishe," III, 335.

86. *Ibid.*

87. "To a Peer of Ireland," III, 287.

88. "On Conciliation," I, 488.

89. "Present Discontents," I, 350–351.

90. "Reflections," II, 435.

91. "Speech on a Motion Made . . . to Inquire Into the State of the Representation of the Commons in Parliament," VI, 144–145—cited hereafter as "Reform of the Representation."

92. Burke to Dr. Robertson, June 10, 1777, *Fitzwilliam Corr.,* I, 339.

93. "From New to Old Whigs," III, 113.

94. Kingsley Martin, *The Rise of French Liberal Thought: a Study of Political Ideas From Bayle to Condorcet,* ed. J. P. Mayer (New York, 1954), p. 167. Magnus (*Life,* p. 27) also attributes the Blackstonian idea of "balance" to Burke, as does Sabine (*Hist. of Theory,* p. 608) and Barker, "Burke and the French Revolution," *Essays,* p. 209.

95. "Motion Relative to the Speech From the Throne, *Lunae, 140 Die Junij,* 1784," II, 255–256.

96. "Reform of the Representation," VI, 148.

97. "Present Discontents," I, 332.

98. "Regicide Peace," No. 1, V, 153.

99. Baron de Montesquieu, *The Spirit of the Laws,* trans. Thomas Nugent, rev. J. V. Prichard, introd. O. W. Holmes (New York, 1900), I, 8. Becker says, "Montesquieu was not primarily concerned with the laws as they exist, but with some ideal quality of rightness which, considering all the physical and human circumstances, they ought to have" *The Heavenly City of the Eighteenth-Century Philosophers* (New Haven, 1932), p. 115. That is, he repeats the liberal criticism (see Martin, above, n. 94) begun by Condorcet (Becker, p. 101), that Montesquieu confused what is with what ought to be. Though true in the letter, the criticism is false in spirit; it assumes some sort of oversimple materiality in "what is."

100. Montesquieu, *Spirit of the Laws,* p. xxxv.

101. *Ibid.,* p. 2: "Before there were intelligent beings, they were possible; they had therefore possible relations, and consequently possible laws. Before laws were made, there were relations of possible justice. . . . We must therefore acknowledge relations of justice antecedent to the positive law by which they are established."

102. *Ibid.,* pp. 7–8.

103. *Ibid.,* p. xxxvii.

104. *Ibid.,* p. 7.

105. "Abridgment of English History," VI, 297. For example, in his mechanistic analogies between the "physical world" and the "intelligent world": see pp. 49, 350. On the widespread desire to unite "moral phenomena" into a synthesis analogous with the physical, see Basil Willey, *The Eighteenth Century Background,* p. 137.

106. Stephen, *Thought in the Eighteenth Century,* II, 188.

107. "Reform of the Representation," VI, 148.

108. *Ibid.*

109. "To Chairman of the Buckinghamshire Meeting," VI, 3.

110. "From New to Old Whigs," III, 83.

111. "Reform of the Representation," VI, 149.

112. "From New to Old Whigs," III, 82–83.

113. *Ibid.,* p. 85.

114. "Reform of the Representation," VI, 148.

115. "From New to Old Whigs," III, 83: "This mode of decision where wills may be so nearly equal. . . ."

116. "On Shortening Parliaments," VI, 132.

117. "To Chairman of the Buckinghamshire Meeting," VI, 3.

118. To Harford, Sept. 27, 1780, *Fitzwilliam Corr.,* I, 451.

119. "To Burgh," V, 494.

120. "To a Noble Lord," V, 119.

121. "On Shortening Parliaments," VI, 132.

122. "To a Noble Lord," V, 122.

123. *Ibid.,* p. 120.

124. "Reform of the Representation," VI, 150.

125. "To Chairman of the Buckinghamshire Meeting," VI, 2.

126. "To a Noble Lord," V, 117.

127. "Reform of the Representation," VI, 153. Incidentally, the next sentence of this famous passage quotes Pope's *Epistle to Arbuthnot,* 1. 410: "I will nurse its venerable age, and with lenient arts extend a parent's breath."

128. Cobban, *Revolt Against the Eighteenth Century,* p. 90.

129. "To William Elliot," V. 78. Burke used the analogies consciously; see the curious passage where he jokes about his use of them in a letter to Windham, Nov. 29, 1795, *Windham Corr.,* pp. 184–185. "I renounce, abjure and detest all the heretical pravity of my Metaphors. . . . I give up my foolish Roots, and Trunks and branches and all their vain foliage. I give them cheerfully to warm your stoves. 'Has, Vulcane, dicat *Sylvas* tibi Villicus Aemon'!

For the future I shall stick to my profession. We Lawyers do not always make the best hand of a Metaphor. I have burned my fingers with them."

130. J. B. Black, *The Art of History: a Study of Four Great Historians of the Eighteenth Century* (New York, 1926), pp. 167–169.

131. Michael Joyce, *Edward Gibbon* (London, 1953), p. 134.

132. *Hist. of Crit.,* I, 65, 110, *et passim;* and *The Rise of Literary History,* pp. 48, 94, *et passim.*

133. "Regicide Peace," No. 1, V, 153.

134. Prior, *Life,* p. 38. Cf. *Boswell's Life,* ed. Hill, I, 471–472. By 1796, however, Burke was referring to "the excellent queries of the excellent Berkeley." "Regicide Peace," No. 4, V, 372. Perhaps he came to feel a latent likeness with the great Irish Christian philosopher, and anti-materialist. Abstraction was a rallying-issue in English philosophy after Bacon, and the contempt for quiddities and *entia rationis* attaches, in Berkeley, to Newtonian concepts of *matter* and *motion,* just as, in Burke, it attaches to other Enlightenment "fallacies of misplaced concreteness" in politics—for example, *Raison* and *natural rights.*

135. *Burke's Politics,* ed. Hoffman, p. xxix.

136. "Reform of the Representation," VI, 153.

137. *Ibid.,* p. 145.

138. *Ibid.,* p. 146.

139. "Reflections," II, 332.

140. "Reform of the Representation," VI, 149.

141. *Ibid.* For an extended discussion of the role of expediency and right in Burke's thought, see Vaughan, "Burke," *Political Philosophy Before and After Rousseau,* III, 3–12, 36–37, 43–45, 59–63.

142. "Present Discontents," I, 376.

143. For example, "Tracts on Popery Laws," VI, 21.

144. "On Shortening Parliaments," VI, 134.

145. "Prosecutions for Libels," VI, 161.

146. *Ibid.,* p. 160.

147. *Ibid.*

148. "Reflections," II, 307.

149. "There is in the commerce of life, as in Art, a sagacity which is far from being contradictory to right reason, and is superior to any occasional exercise of that faculty; which supersedes it; and does not wait for the slow progress of deduction, but goes at once, by what appears a kind of intuition, to the conclusion." "Discourse XIII," *The Life and Discourses of Sir Joshua Reynolds,* 2nd edn. (New York, 1873), p. 229. The semantics of *sagacity,* a favorite word of Burke's, might be interesting. Hobbes, for example, uses it (*Leviathan,* Bk. I, ch. 3) to signify purposive thought as distinct from daydreaming or the stream of consciousness: "a hunting out of the causes of some effect, present or past, or of the effects of some present or past cause." *Sagacity* ranges among the linked "imaginations" of the mind with an intention or design. His eye is on the Latin etymology (*sagacitas,* mental acuteness, keenness of sense; esp. keenness of scent in a hunting dog, fr. *sagire,* to feel acutely, to perceive). But *right reason* (Bk. I, ch. 5) is an arithmetical addition or subtraction of "parcels." In Locke (*Essay Concerning Human Understanding,* Bk. IV, ch. xvii, sec. 2) *reason* is made to include *sagacity*—which "finds out"—together with *illation* or inference, which traces logical connections. Reynolds' use of *sagacity* keeps but reapplies the root meaning of "keenly snuffing out a conclusion; taking in, by a kind of basic aesthetic experience, of a spread of relations which seem real and unified but of which we have no explicit cognition," as distinct from "the slow progress of deduction." Hazlitt, who quotes the passage from Reynolds appreciatively, renames the sagacity *common sense,* and adds: "Mr. Burke, by whom the foregoing train of thinking was probably suggested, has insisted on the same thing, and made rather a perverse use of it in several parts of the Reflections on the French Revolution." "On Genius and Common Sense," *Table-Talk,* in *Works,* ed. Howe, VIII, 32–33. Hazlitt refers to Burke's apology for "old prejudices" and "inbred sentiments" which for the English public embody their civilized patrimony. For example: "Many of our men of speculation, instead of exploding general prejudices, employ their sagacity to discover the latent wisdom which prevails in them . . . they find what they seek." "Reflections," II, 359. *Sagacity* connects with the 18th-century English development of the concept of the mind as a bundle of organized associations and reasonings, habitually on call, and then of "imagination" as more reliable than "reason" because it draws upon the whole of past experience.

150. "To Chairman of the Buckinghamshire Meeting." VI, 2.

151. *Ibid.,* p. 3.

152. *Ibid.,* p. 4.

153. Bryant, *Literary Friends,* p. 243.

154. *Ibid.,* p. 257.

155. *Private Letters of Edward Gibbon,* ed. R. E. Prothero (London,

1896), II, 251. Cf. I, 240, Burke is "a water-mill of words and images." And *The Autobiographies of Edward Gibbon,* ed. John Murray (London, 1897), p. 320n.

156. *Boswell's Life,* ed. Hill, II, 260.

157. Bryant, p. 156.

158. *Boswell's Life,* ed. Hill, II, 450.

159. *Ibid.,* V, 213.

160. Burke to Richard Burke, Jun., and T. King, Feb. 1773, *Fitzwilliam Corr.,* I, 212.

161. "Thoughts on French Affairs," III, 372.

162. "Reform of the Representation," VI, 148.

163. "Tracts on Popery Laws," VI, 24.

164. "Reform of the Representation," VI, 145.

165. Stephen, *Thought in the Eighteenth Century,* II, 220. For a discussion of Burke's "practical imagination" not inconsistent with my own, see Edward Dowden, *French Revolution,* pp. 96–104. Cf. Lecky, *Hist. of Eng.,* III, 199–201; and Woodrow Wilson, *Mere Literature and Other Essays* (Cambridge, Mass., 1896), pp. 128–129, 157–160.

166. "Reform of the Representation," VI, 146–147.

167. *Ibid.,* p. 147.

168. "Reflections," II, 368.

169. "To Richard Burke," VI, 80.

170. A. N. Whitehead, *Adventures of Ideas* (New York, 1933), p. 50, speaking of the utilitarian's phrase "the greatest happiness of the greatest number."

171. Stephen, II, 230.

172. *Ibid.,* p. 231. Cf. Barker, "French Revolution," *Essays,* p. 223: Prescription is "the historic process behind any system of institutions, which forms their connecting cement."

173. "From New to Old Whigs," III, 79–80.

174. *Ibid.,* p. 82.

175. III, 340.

176. "To William Elliot," V, 77.

177. "Reflections," II, 307.

178. *Ibid.,* p. 295.

179. "Regicide Peace," No. 3, V, 154.

180. Laski also suggests the seminal influence of Hume upon Burke (as well as upon Bentham): *Locke to Bentham,* pp. 122–123. Cf. Sabine, *Hist. of Theory,* pp. 606–607, 612; Cobban, *Revolt Against the Eighteenth Century,* pp. 78–80, 253–254; Bryant, *Literary Friends,* pp. 221–225.

181. "Enquiry Concerning Human Understanding," *Essays and Treatises on Several Subjects,* II (London, 1784), Sec. IV, pt. 2.

182. *Ibid.,* Sec. VII, pt. 1.

183. *Ibid.,* Sec. VIII, pt. 2.

184. *An Essay Concerning Human Understanding,* in *The Works of John Locke,* III (London, 1823), Bk. II, ch. xxi, secs. 2, 3.

185. *Ibid.,* I: Introd., secs. 6, 7.

186. "Regicide Peace" No. 1, V, 153.

187. "A Philosophical Inquiry Into the Origin of Our Ideas of the Sublime and Beautiful, with an Introductory Discourse Concerning Taste, and Several Other Additions," I, 143.

188. Burke to Richard Shackleton, July 12, 1746, *Fitzwilliam Corr.,* I, 11.

189. Burke to Shackleton, March 21, 1746–47, *ibid.,* p. 12.

190. The title was apparently suggested by Francis Hutcheson's *Inquiry Into the Origin of Our Ideas of Beauty and Virtue:* see Prior, *Life,* p. 37; and Samuels, *Early Life,* p. 212. Burke mentions Locke (I, 70, 155, 171) and Newton (pp. 143, 161). On the debt to Hume, see Bryant, *Literary Friends,* pp. 221–222. Cf. Victor Hamm, "Burke and Metaphysics," *New Scholasticism,* XVIII (Jan. 1944), 5–8. Burke's preface is a cogent epitome of the empirical method carried into belles-lettres.

191. "On the Economical Reform," II, 101.

192. "Reflections," II, 439.

193. *Ibid.,* p. 334.

194. *Ibid.,* p. 440.

195. *Ibid.,* p. 463.

196. *Ibid.,* pp. 316–317.

197. *Ibid.,* pp. 295–296.

198. "Present Discontents," I, 331.

199. "To a Noble Lord," V, 120.

200. "Present Discontents," I, 368.

201. *Ibid.,* p. 346. Contrary to Sabine (*Hist. of Theory,* p. 614) who says that Burke, mopping up after Hume, cleared away "the pretense that social institutions depend on reason or nature."

202. "On the Economical Reform," II, 123.

203. *Ibid.,* p. 58.

204. *Ibid.,* p. 56.

205. *Ibid.,* p. 68.

206. *Ibid.,* p. 58.

207. *Ibid.,* p. 69.

208. *Ibid.,* p. 56.

209. *Ibid.,* p. 87.

210. *Ibid.,* p. 94.

211. *Ibid.,* p. 121.

212. *Ibid.,* p. 91.

213. *Ibid.,* p. 90.

214. *Ibid.,* p. 82.

215. *Ibid.,* p. 83.

216. *Ibid.,* p. 106. Burke abolished, however, the sinecure of the Board of Trade, on which Gibbon sat. Reverencing it, he said, as an Academy of Belles-lettres, he thought it a needless expense as government; it was a crow's nest in which nightingales were imprisoned. Magnus, *Life,* p. 100. Gibbon was delighted by the speech: *Autobiographies,* ed. Murray, pp. 320n, 321.

217. *Ibid.,* p. 101.

218. *Ibid.,* p. 102.

219. "To a Noble Lord," V, 122.

220. "On the Economical Reform," II, 120.

221. "Reflections," II, 439.

222. "On the Economical Reform," II, 65.

223. "Report to Inspect the Lords' Journals," VI, 471.

224. "On Shortening Parliaments," VI, 133.

225. "On the Economical Reform," II, 56.

226. *Ibid.,* p. 122.

227. "To a Noble Lord," V, 122.

228. "On the Economical Reform," II, 64.

229. *Ibid.,* p. 65.

230. *Ibid.*

231. "On the Economical Reform," II, 105.

232. *Ibid.,* p. 95.

## V. Burke and The French Revolution

1. Burke to Lord Charlemont, Aug. 9, 1789, quoted in Prior, *Life,* p. 295.

2. Burke to Mons. Dupont, Oct. 1789, *Fitzwilliam Corr.,* I, 557.

3. *Ibid.,* p. 558.

4. Prior, *Life,* p. 310. Barker suggests that it was "undertaken at two different times and in two different sections, with the result of some repetition and a double covering of the same ground." "French Revolution," *Essays,* p. 212. In a letter to Windham, Oct. 27, 1790, *Windham Corr.,* p. 22, Burke says: "In the infinite variety of matter contained in my general Subject I may have made some mistakes, and I wrote sometimes in circumstances not favourable to accuracy. I wrote from the Memory of what I had read: and was not able always to get the documents from whence I had been supplied, when I wished to verifye my facts with precision. But I hope my errors will be found to be rather mistakes than misrepresentations."

5. "Reflections," II, 381.

6. *Ibid.,* p. 409.

7. "Observations on a Late Publication," I, 230.

8. "Reflections," II, 382, 384, *et passim.*

9. "Regicide Peace," No. 2, V, 258–259.

10. "From New to Old Whigs," III, 13.

11. "Regicide Peace," No. 2, VI, 260. De Tocqueville, comparing pre-

and post-revolutionary France, confirms Burke's prediction in its broad outlines. The Revolution issued in a government even more autocratic and centralized than the *ancien régime;* "facilities to despotism . . . were hunted for among the wreckage of the old order and duly salvaged," just as "some rivers after going underground re-emerge at another point, in new surroundings." *The Old Regime and the French Revolution* [1856], trans. Stuart Gilbert (New York, 1955), pp. ix–xii, 209, *et passim.* De Tocqueville echoes Burke at point after point, yet for some strange reason damns him with faint praise (p. 2).

12. "Reflections," II, 418; cf. p. 403.
13. *Ibid.*, p. 406.
14. *Ibid.*, p. 434. Actually he says the design is too big for one work, and he must reserve till another time much of his analysis of British principles. *An Appeal from the New to the Old Whigs* (1791) is a thematic completion.
15. *Ibid.*, pp. 308–309.
16. "Regicide Peace," No. 2, V, 253.
17. *Ibid.*, No. 1, p. 214.
18. *Ibid.*, No. 2, pp. 253–254.
19. "A Letter to a Member of the National Assembly; in Answer to Some Objections to His Book on French Affairs," II, 554.
20. "Regicide Peace," No. 2, V, 254–255.
21. *Ibid.*, No. 1, p. 214.
22. *Ibid.*, p. 215.
23. *Ibid.*, pp. 213–214.
24. *Ibid.*, No. 2, p. 255.
25. "Reflections," II, 439–440.
26. Burke to Dupont, Oct., 1789, *Fitzwilliam Corr.*, I, 561.
27. "Reflections," II, 398.
28. *Ibid.*, p. 309.
29. *Ibid.*, pp. 454–455.
30. *Ibid.*, p. 467.
31. *Ibid.*, p. 387.
32. *Ibid.*, p. 429.
33. *Ibid.*, p. 432.
34. *Ibid.*, p. 428.
35. *Ibid.*, pp. 432–433.
36. *Ibid.*, p. 428.
37. *Ibid.*, p. 429.
38. "Regicide Peace," No. 3, V, 313. In this particular passage, Burke is talking not about superstition, but about the "love of lucre," both, however, "general energies."
39. "Reflections," II, 430.
40. *Ibid.*, pp. 429–432.
41. *Ibid.*, p. 476.
42. "To a Noble Lord," V, 148.

43. "To William Smith," VI, 52.

44. "Thoughts on French Affairs," III, 364.

45. "Reflections," II, 322.

46. *Ibid.,* p. 348.

47. Burke to Philip Francis, Feb. 20, 1790, *Fitzwilliam Corr.,* I, 574.

48. "Reflections," II, 348–349.

49. *Ibid.,* p. 322. De Tocqueville concludes the same, even upon the origin of French egalitarianism. *Old Regime,* ch. 11.

50. "Regicide Peace," No. 1, V, 208.

51. "Reflections," II, 350.

52. *Ibid.,* pp. 405–406.

53. "Regicide Peace," No. 4, V, 397.

54. Thomas Paine, *Rights of Man* [1791], in *The Complete Writings of Thomas Paine,* ed. Philip S. Foner (New York, 1945), I, 260. Dowden conceived an answer to this famous quibble: Burke "did not believe that plucking away the plumage was the best way of restoring the dying bird to vigor and enabling it to fly." *French Revolution.* p. 122.

55. Prior, *Life,* p. 315.

56. *Ibid.,* p. 316.

57. *Ibid.,* p. 317.

58. *Vindiciae Gallicae,* p. 201. Cf. Paine, I, 272. Paine, of course, was the main symbol of antagonism in Burke's own eyes; and Paine's arguments, attributed to "they," are the ones quoted in *An Appeal From the New to the Old Whigs.*

59. *Letters to Burke,* p. 6. Cf. Paine, I, 258–259, 268, *et passim:* Burke's book is a "dramatic performance" full of "tragic paintings" and "the spouting rant of high-toned declamation."

60. *Vindiciae Gallicae,* p. 102. So Paine argues (p. 256) that Burke is unable to see that a revolt may take place against the despotism of principle, when there lies no charge of despotism against men. In private Burke conceded that the Anglican clergy of his day was "very much degenerated, not as Individuals, but as a Corps from loss of Decorum in Conduct." Mrs. Crewe, "Extracts From Mr. Burke's Table-Talk, *at* Crewe Hall," ed. R. M. Milnes, in *Miscellanies of the Philobiblon Society* (London, 1862–63), VII, 9.

61. "Reflections," II, 283.

62. *Ibid.,* p. 282.

63. *Vindiciae Gallicae,* p. 99n.

64. *Letters to Burke,* p. 112. Notice the blurred distinction between reform and revolution.

65. Transformed, of course, into the class struggle. The polar opposition of *feudal* and *enlightened* becomes the historic enmity of the revolutionary bourgeoisie to the feudalism which generated it, and which it destroys. As the bourgeoisie generates new classes and new conditions of oppression, it becomes *mutatis mutandis* the social equivalent of its old enemy, and must be opposed and destroyed by men with

the final light, generated from within, the revolutionary proletariat—*Manifesto of the Communist Party,* ch. I. Marx and Engels, like Bentham, would see in Burke only "speculative cobwebs, embroidered with flowers of rhetoric, steeped in the dew of sickly sentiment" (III, 1, c); yet curiously enough, one of Burke's strong points is what Marx claimed for the Communists—that is, the ability to "express in general terms actual relations springing from an existing . . . historical movement going on under our very eyes" (II).

66. "Reflections," II, 351.

67. "On the Economical Reform," II, 83.

68. "Reflections," II, 511.

69. *Ibid.,* p. 308.

70. *Ibid.,* p. 517. In 1773, the year Burke visited Paris, the Montgolfier brothers went up in hot-air balloons.

71. *Autobiographies,* ed. Murray, p. 342n. One can easily forget, however, Gibbon's own scholarly interest in the "medieval"; one of his last projects was a scheme to edit and publish English medieval chronicles: G. M. Young, *Gibbon* (New York, 1933), pp. 176–177.

72. *Letters of Gibbon,* ed. Prothero, II, 237, 251. The most brilliantly suggestive account of Gibbon's view of the Revolution is Young, chs. 16–17. For a general comparison of Burke's and Gibbon's political assumptions, see L. P. Curtis, "Gibbon's Paradise Lost," in *The Age of Johnson: Essays Presented to Chauncey Brewster Tinker* (New Haven, 1949), pp. 73–90. For Reynolds' interesting attempt to support Burke, as well as to sustain irony, see the fragmentary "Discourse XVI" in *Portraits,* ed. F. W. Hilles (New York, 1952).

73. "Reflections," II, 427.

74. *Ibid.,* p. 428.

75. Birrell, *Obiter Dicta,* p. 193.

76. Burke to Ragonaut Row, 1782?, *Fitzwilliam Corr.,* I, 507.

77. "Policy of the Allies," III, 456.

78. "Abridgment of English History," VI, 295.

79. *Ibid.,* p. 366.

80. *Ibid.,* p. 406.

81. "Reflections," II, 334–335.

82. *Ibid.,* p. 412.

83. "From New to Old Whigs," III, 77.

84. "Reflections," II, 333.

85. "From New to Old Whigs," III 77.

86. "Reflections," II, 413–414.

87. "From New to Old Whigs," III, 3.

88. "Reflections," II, 299.

89. James Russell Lowell, "Rousseau and the Sentimentalists," in *Essays, Poems and Letters,* ed. Wm. Smith Clark II, Odyssey Series [gen. ed. Robert Schafer] (New York, 1948), p. 112. Cf. Barker, "French Revolution," *Essays,* p. 224.

90. "Regicide Peace," No. 3, V 271–272.

91. "To a Member of the National Assembly," II, 539.

92. *Ibid.*, p. 541.

93. *Ibid.*, p. 536.

94. *Ibid.*, p. 540. There are several studies of Burke and Rousseau. For a brief and suggestive critical comparison, see Jacques Barzun, *Romanticism and the Modern Ego* (Boston, 1943), pp. 22, 41–44, *et passim*. For a brief and suggestive critical contrast, see Babbitt, *Democracy and Leadership*, chs. 2, 3. Best of all, see Cobban, *Revolt Against the Eighteenth Century*, pp. 134–135, 235–236, 251–252, 255–256.

95. *Ibid.*, p. 541.

96. *Ibid.*, pp. 534–535.

97. *Ibid.*, p. 537.

98. *Ibid.*, pp. 540–541.

99. *Ibid.*, p. 538.

100. "Reflections," II, 441–442.

101. "To a Member of the National Assembly," II, 535–536. Cf. Mrs. Crewe, "Table-Talk," *Misc. of Phil. Soc.*, VII, 36: Burke expressed disgust for "the new fashioned feelings introduced into the World by Rousseau, Sterne etc. and said this had produced much trash for circulating Libraries."

102. "Regicide Peace," No. 3, V, 272.

103. "Reflections," II, 441.

104. "Regicide Peace," No. 1, V, 209.

105. "To a Member of the National Assembly," II, 540.

106. "Reflections," II, 333–334.

107. *Ibid.*, pp. 358–359.

108. *Ibid.*, p. 359.

109. *Ibid.*, p. 358.

110. *Ibid.*, p. 349.

111. *Ibid.*, p. 454.

112. *Ibid.*, p. 359. Cf. Barker, "French Revolution," *Essays*, p. 223; by prejudice Burke means "the historic feeling which forms the support of institutions, and constitutes a vitalizing sentiment active on their behalf." Cf. Mrs. Crewe (above, n. 101), p. 62: Customs "are chiefly cherished in Provinces far from Capitals. They are the standing Wisdom of a Country, though frequently Preposterous on a first view of them."

113. *Ibid.*

114. *Ibid.*, pp. 358–359.

115. *Ibid.*, p. 367.

116. "Regicide Peace," No. 1, V, 212.

117. *Ibid.*, p. 208.

118. A. N. Whitehead, *Introduction to Mathematics* (New York, 1948), p. 42.

119. "From New to Old Whigs," III, 12–13.

120. To Dupont, Oct. 1789, *Fitzwilliam Corr.*, I, 562.

121. *Ibid.,* p. 563.
122. *Ibid.,* p. 564.
123. *Ibid.,* pp. 564–565.
124. "Reform of the Representation," VI, 147.
125. "Reflections," II, 358.
126. *Ibid.,* pp. 334–335.
127. "From New to Old Whigs," III, 55.
128. "Regicide Peace," No. 1, V, 152.
129. Babbitt, *Democracy and Leadership,* pp. 111–112.
130. "Regicide Peace," No. 4, V, 397.
131. *Ibid.,* pp. 355–356.
132. "Preface to the Address of M. Brissot to His Constituents, Translated by the Late William Burke, Esq., 1794," III, 526.
133. I, 1 f.
134. William Godwin, *An Enquiry Concerning Political Justice and Its Influence on General Virtue and Happiness,* ed. F. E. L. Priestley (Toronto, 1946), I, 13n. In dissent from Burkian principles, Godwin nevertheless thought Burke to have "very few equals" in "the long record of human genius" (II, 545n).
135. "Thoughts on French Affairs," III, 366.
136. "Reflections," II, 388.
137. "Regicide Peace," No. 1, V, 230.
138. "To a Member of the National Assembly," II, 549.
139. "Regicide Peace," No. 2, V, 243.
140. *Ibid.,* p. 231.
141. *Ibid.,* No. 1, p. 222. According to Reinhold Aris, Adam Müller hailed Burke as "The last prophet who had descended on this disenchanted world." *Thought in Germany,* p. 308.
142. *Ibid.,* No. 4, p. 359.
143. *Ibid.,* No. 3, p. 324.
144. *Ibid.,* No. 4, p. 410.
145. "To William Elliot," V, 81.
146. "Regicide Peace," No. 1, V, 155.
147. *Ibid.,* No. 3 pp. 304–305.
148. "Reflections," II, 492.
149. "To a Noble Lord," V, 141.
150. "Regicide Peace," No. 2, V, 231.
151. *Ibid.,* p. 232.
152. "Heads for Consideration on the Present State of Affairs, Written in November, 1792," III, 409.
153. "Regicide Peace," No. 2, V, 235.
154. "To a Member of the National Assembly," II, 553. At the same period, with a very different temperament, and with different purposes and sympathies, Blake is railing against "Newton's sleep." The comparison is not so impossible as it first may seem; struggling to affirm timeless truths, both are struggling to free themselves of something stuffy, insipid,

even satanic, in one sector of the intellectual life of their time. Each, of course would regard the other as infected. The closest comparison is with earlier humanists like Swift or Fielding who felt that reason had been narrowed and shrunk to a mere mathematical spectre. A like feeling would motivate idealist attempts to spiritualize reason, to purify it of the pale cast of the laboratory.

155. "Policy of the Allies," III, 444.

156. "Thoughts on French Affairs," III, 374.

157. "To a Noble Lord," V, 142.

158. "Regicide Peace," No. 1, V, 209.

159. "Policy of Allies," III, 419.

160. *Ibid.*, p. 418.

161. *Ibid.*, p. 420.

162. *Ibid.*

163. "Thoughts on French Affairs," III, 356–357: ". . . like a battery in which the stroke of any one ball produces no great effect, but the amount of continual repetition is decisive. Let us only suffer any person to tell us his story, morning and evening, but for one twelvemonth, and he will become our master." Cf. "Observations on the Conduct of the Minority," III, 493–494.

164. *Ibid.*, p. 376. Cf. "Regicide Peace," No. 1, V, 190–191.

165. "Regicide Peace," No. 4, V, 418–420.

166. *Ibid.*, No. 1, V, 224.

167. "Thoughts on French Affairs," III, 386.

168. "To a Member of the National Assembly," II, 541–542.

169. "Regicide Peace," No. 1, V, 209.

170. "Policy of Allies," III, 433.

171. *Ibid.*, p. 457.

172. "Regicide Peace," No. 1, V, 205.

173. *Ibid.*, No. 4, p. 401.

174. *Ibid.*, No. 2, pp. 255–256.

175. *Ibid.*, No. 1, p. 200; cf. pp. 165–182, 191.

176. *Ibid.*, p. 158.

177. Prior, *Life*, p 349. On the general unconcern in England, see Carl Cone, "Pamphlet Replies to Burke's *Reflections*," *The Southwestern Social Science Quarterly*, XXVI (June, 1945), 22, *et passim.*

178. *Ibid.*, p. 369.

179. *Ibid.*, p. 407.

180. "Sir James Mackintosh," *The Spirit of the Age: or Contemporary Portraits*, in *Works*, ed. Howe, XI, 102.

181. *Vindiciae Gallicae*, p. 55.

182. *Ibid.*, pp. 55–56.

183. *Ibid.*, p. ii.

184. "Policy of Allies," III, 456.

185. For Burke's famous prediction of a Napoleon-like dictator, see "Reflections," II, 489.

186. For example, Martin, *Rise of French Liberalism,* ch. 11; Becker, *Heavenly City,* p. 102 f.
187. "Policy of Allies," III, 438. Cf. "Regicide Peace," No. 2, V, 235–236.
188. "Regicide Peace," No. 1, V, 157.
189. *Ibid.,* No. 2, p. 243.
190. *Ibid.,* No. 1, p. 228.
191. "To a Member of the National Assembly," II, 542–543.
192. "Thoughts on French Affairs," III, 358.
193. "Regicide Peace," No. 1, V, 164–165.
194. "Thoughts on French Affairs," III, 350.
195. "Regicide Peace," No. 4, V, 412.
196. *Ibid.,* No. 2, p. 256.
197. *Ibid.,* No. 1, p. 205.
198. *Ibid.,* No. 4, p. 418.
199. "From New to Old Whigs," II, 98–99.
200. "Regicide Peace," No. 2, V, 245.
201. *Ibid.,* p. 247.
202. "Preface to Brissot's Address," III, 524.
203. "Thoughts on French Affairs," III, 367.
204. "Regicide Peace," No. 2, V, 246.
205. "To William Elliot," V, 75.
206. "Regicide Peace," No. 3, V, 283.
207. "To a Noble Lord," V, 136.
208. "To William Elliot," V, 78–79.
209. "To a Noble Lord," V, 136.
210. "To William Elliot," V, 76.
211. *Ibid.,* pp. 81–82.
212. "Reflections," II, 284.
213. "To William Elliot," V, 79.
214. *Ibid.,* p. 80.
215. *Ibid.,* p. 77.
216. *Ibid.,* p. 79.
217. *Ibid.,* p. 82.
218. "From New to Old Whigs," III, 14.
219. "Regicide Peace," No. 1, V, 191.
220. "To a Member of the National Assembly," II, 522–523.
221. "From New to Old Whigs," II, 115.
222. "Thoughts on French Affairs," III, 393.
223. "From New to Old Whigs," II, 15.
224. "Policy of Allies," III, 417.
225. *Ibid.,* p. 421.
226. *Ibid.,* p. 419.
227. "To a Member of the National Assembly," II, 520.
228. "Regicide Peace," No. 4, V, 396–397.
229. *Ibid.,* No. 1, p. 229.

230. "Policy of the Allies," III, 442.
231. *Ibid.*, p. 443.
232. "Regicide Peace," No. 1, p. 208.
233. *Ibid.*, No. 4, V, 429.
234. *Ibid.*, p. 428.
235. "Reflections," II, 514.
236. "Regicide Peace," No. 1, V, 208.
237. *Ibid.*, No. 3, p. 234.
238. *Ibid.*, No. 1, p. 168.
239. *Ibid.*, No. 4, p. 393.
240. *Ibid.*, No. 1, p. 161.
241. *Ibid.*, p. 169.
242. "To a Noble Lord," V, 140.
243. "Regicide Peace," No. 1, V, 184–185.
244. *Ibid.*, No. 3, p. 268.
245. "Preface to Brissot's Address," III, 516.
246. *Ibid.*, p. 521.
247. "Regicide Peace," No. 4, V, 397.
248. "To a Noble Lord," V, 139.
249. "To a Member of the National Assembly," II, 536–537.
250. "The Sublime and the Beautiful," I, 186. (Italics mine.)
251. "Regicide Peace," V, 400.

## VI. Burke and India

1. Birrell, *Obiter Dicta,* pp. 151–152.
2. "To a Noble Lord," V, 124.
3. Burke to Dr. Laurence, July 28, 1796, VIII, 492.
4. Burke to Dr. Laurence, Feb. 10, 1797, *ibid.*, p. 503.
5. Burke to the Rev. Dr. Hussey, Nov. 28, 1795, *Fitzwilliam Corr.*, II, 302.
6. Burke to Philip Francis, Feb. 20, 1790, *ibid.*, I, 575.
7. Burke to Dr. Laurence, July 28, 1796, VIII, 493.
8. *Ibid.* Cf. letter to Laurence, Feb. 10, 1797, p. 504.
9. "On East-India Bill," II, 175.
10. "Ninth Report From the Select Committee (of the House of Commons) Appointed to Take Into Consideration the State of the Administration of Justice in the Provinces of Bengal, Bahar, and Orissa, and to Report tht Same. . . ," IV, 3–29.
11. Burke to the Marquis of Rockingham, Nov. 23, 1772, *Fitzwilliam Corr.*, I, 193.
12. Burke to the Marquis of Rockingham, Oct. 29, 1772, *ibid.*, p. 177. For a discussion of other, less flattering motives in his concern (the ambitions of his brother), see Dixon Wecter, *Edmund Burke and His Kinsmen,* Univ. of Colorado Studies in the Humanities, I (Boulder: Feb. 1939), 49–75. Burke's integrity is vindicated, his blind family loyalties regretted (p. 107).

13. "Speeches on the Impeachment of Warren Hastings," 2nd Day of Reply, May 30, 1794, VIII, 50.
14. "On East-India Bill," II, 174.
15. "Nabob of Arcot's Debts," III, 125.
16. *Ibid.,* pp. 125–126.
17. "On East-India Bill," II, 174.
18. *Ibid.,* pp. 175–176.
19. Burke to a Prussian Gentleman, 1772, VIII, 453.
20. "On East-India Bill," II, 183.
21. "Warren Hastings," 4th Day, Feb. 16, 1788, VII, 61.
22. "On East-India Bill," II, 181–182.
23. *Ibid.,* p. 182.
24. *Ibid.,* pp. 182–183.
25. "Warren Hastings," 3rd Day, Feb. 15, 1788, VII, 43–47.
26. *Ibid.,* 4th Day, Feb. 16, 1788, p. 65.
27. *Ibid.* 3rd Day, p. 49.
28. "Warren Hastings" [Oct. 1841], in *The Works of Lord Macaulay,* ed. Lady Trevelyan, Jenson Society edn. (n.p., 1907), XV, 301–302. Morley takes issue with Macaulay on the same point, but opposes in return not Burke's practical imagination, but his philosophic reverence for all old and settled order. *Burke,* pp. 129–132.
29. "On the Prose-Style of Poets," *The Plain Speaker,* in *Works,* ed. Howe, XII, 13.
30. "Nabob of Arcot's Debts," III, 159.
31. *Ibid.,* p. 160.
32. *Ibid.,* p. 161.
33. *Ibid.,* pp. 161–162.
34. "Warren Hastings," 3rd Day, Feb. 15, 1788, VII, 43.
35. "On East-India Bill," II, 196–197.
36. For a convenient *aperçu* of Hastings' real behavior alongside Burke's charges, see Robert H. Murray, *Edmund Burke: a Biography* (Oxford, 1931), pp. 320–346.
37. "Warren Hastings," 3rd Day, Feb. 15, 1788, VII, 24. Cf. pp. 36, 41.
38. *Ibid.,* p. 23.
39. "On East-India Bill," II, 181.
40. "Ninth Report," IV, 7.
41. "Warren Hastings," 3rd Day, Feb. 15, 1788, VII, 26.
42. *Ibid.,* p. 28.
43. "Ninth Report," IV, 51.
44. "On the East-India Bill," II, 195.
45. *Ibid.,* pp. 194–195.
46. *Ibid.,* p. 222.
47. "Warren Hastings," 4th Day, Feb. 16, 1788, VII, 58.
48. *Ibid.,* 3rd Day, Feb. 15, 1788, p. 33.
49. *Ibid.,* 5th Day, Feb. 17, 1788, p. 135.
50. *Ibid.,* 3rd Day, p. 34.

51. *Ibid.*, 1st Day of Reply, May 28, 1794, p. 489.
52. "Ninth Report," IV, 64.
53. Laski, *Locke to Bentham,* p. 181.
54. "Nabob of Arcot's Debts," III, 146.
55. *Ibid.*, pp. 138–139.
56. *Ibid.*, p. 175.
57. *Ibid.*, p. 187.
58. "Warren Hastings," on the 6th Charge, Bribery and Corruption, May 7, 1789, VII, 413.
59. "Nabob of Arcot's Debts," III, 194–195.
60. *Ibid.*, pp. 131–132.
61. *Ibid.*, pp. 153, 158.
62. *Ibid.*, p. 155.
63. *Ibid.*, p. 154.
64. *Ibid.*, p. 155.
65. *Ibid.*
66. *Ibid.*, p. 150.
67. *Ibid.*, p. 152.
68. *Ibid.*, p. 150.
69. *Ibid.*, p. 151.
70. *Ibid.*, p. 127.
71. *Ibid.*, p. 126.
72. *Ibid.*, p. 174.
73. *Ibid.*, p. 183.
74. *Ibid.*, p. 176.
75. *Ibid.*, p. 173.
76. *Ibid.*, p. 194.
77. "Character of Mr. Burke" [1807], *Political Essays,* in *Works,* ed. Howe, VIII, 301.
78. "On East-India Bill," II, 233.
79. *Ibid.*, p. 236.
80. *Ibid.*, p. 178.
81. *Ibid.*, p. 176.
82. *Ibid.*, p. 232.
83. "Warren Hastings," 1st Day of Reply, May 28, 1794, VII, 457.
84. "On East-India Bill," II, 236–237.
85. "Warren Hastings," 4th Day, Feb. 16, 1788, VII, 103.
86. *Ibid.*, 5th Day, Feb. 17, 1788, p. 192.
87. *Ibid.*, p. 193.
88. "On East-India Bill," II, 243.
89. *Ibid.*, p. 180.
90. *Ibid.*, p. 179.
91. *Ibid.*, p. 221.
92. *Ibid.*, p. 218.
93. "Nabob of Arcot's Debts," III, 146.
94. The best account of the friendship is in Bryant, *Literary Friends,*

pp. 305–306. On their later relations, see Prior, *Life,* pp. 243, 482; and "Warren Hastings," 9th Day of Reply, June 16, 1794, VIII, 440–441.

95. Morley, *Burke,* p. 102; Murray, *Edmund Burke,* p. 307, who refers to documents; Magnus, *Life,* p. 135. But see Prior, *Life,* pp. 227–231.

96. "On East-India Bill," II, 246.

97. *Ibid.,* p. 179.

98. *Burke,* p. 108.

99. Burke to Woodford, Nov. 29, 1795, *Windham Corr.,* p. 182.

100. "On East-India Bill," II, 246.

101. Magnus, *Life,* pp. 184–185.

102. "Reflections," II, 518.

103. "Warren Hastings," 6th Charge, Bribery and Corruption, May 5, 1789, VII, 348–349.

104. *Ibid.,* p. 354.

105. Cf. "To a Noble Lord," V, 142.

106. Burke to Philip Francis, Dec. 10, 1785, *Fitzwilliam Corr.,* I, 525.

107. Burke to Sir Thomas Rumbold, March 23, 1781, *ibid.,* p. 461.

108. *Ibid.,* p. 463.

109. To Francis, Dec. 10, 1785, *ibid.,* p. 524.

110. *Ibid.,* p. 525.

111. "Warren Hastings," 3rd Day, Feb. 15, 1788, VII, 36.

112. *Ibid.,* p. 15.

113. *Ibid.,* 1st Day of Reply, May 28, 1794, p. 501.

114. *Ibid.,* 3rd Day of Reply, June 3, 1794, VIII, 56.

115. *Ibid.,* 1st Day of Reply, May 28, 1794, VII, 471.

116. To Francis, Dec. 10, 1785, *Fitzwilliam Corr.,* I, 523.

117. *Ibid.,* p. 526.

118. "Nabob of Arcot's Debts," III, 172.

119. "Warren Hastings," 6th Charge, Bribery and Corruption, April 21, 1789, VII, 297.

120. "On East-India Bill," II, 174.

121. "Warren Hastings," 1st Day of Reply, May 28, 1794, VII, 456.

122. *Ibid.*

123. *Ibid.,* 5th Day, Feb. 17, 1788, p. 187.

124. *Ibid.,* 4th Day, Feb. 16, 1788, p. 101.

125. "Nabob of Arcot's Debts," III, 196.

126. For example, see the ironical "Of the Original Contract" in *Essays and Treatises on Several Subjects* (London, 1784), I, 472 ff.

127. For example, "the rules of prudence . . . are formed upon the known march of the ordinary providence of God." "Regicide Peace," No. 2, V, 236. Cf. Barker, "French Revolution," *Essays,* pp. 231–232. Dowden compares Bishop Butler: *French Revolution,* pp. 108–109. In 1785 Burke considered Butler's *Analogy* "the most satisfactory answer to the objections of philosophic skeptics": Hamm, *New Schol.,* XVIII, 16n. Cf. Mrs. Crewe, "Table-Talk," *Misc. of Phil. Soc.,* VII, 55: "among others, Butler's *Analogy* is greatly in my estimation." For a discussion

of the contrasting influences of Hume and Butler upon Burke's thought, see Mario Einaudi, "The British Background of Burke's Political Philosophy," *Political Science Quarterly,* XLIX (Dec. 1934), 581 ff. However, Lord Acton says (*Home and Foreign Review,* Jan. 1863, p. 253, quoted in *Essays,* ed. Woodruff, pp. 427–428): "The essence of Whiggism is the acknowledgment of the supremacy of the divine will . . . the absolute exclusion from politics of that arbitrary element which asserts itself in Toryism by denying the claims of principle, and in Radicalism by rejecting the authority of fact. It upholds the laws of the country; but it clings to their spirit, not to the temporary forms by which that spirit is expressed or secured. In this way Selden shared in the Great Rebellion, Somers justified the Revolution, and Burke defended the constitutional idea in the American and the Revolutionary wars." Cf. Ransom, *Kenyon Review,* XV, 648–650.

128. However, there are incidental references—for example, like that to the Prince of Peace, "Reflections," II, 345.

129. "Warren Hastings," 6th Day, Feb. 19, 1788, VII, 230–231.

130. *Ibid.,* 4th Day, February 16, 1788, p. 99.

131. *Ibid.,* 2nd Day of Reply, May 30, 1794, VIII, 2–3.

132. *Ibid.,* 1st Day of Reply, May 28, 1794, VII, 504. Barker conceives that in its fundamentals Burke's political philosophy is Thomistic; he suggests analogies (but not identifications) with Suarez and other theologians of the Counter-Reformation: "French Revolution," *Essays,* pp. 218n, 224–225. Cf. Millar, *Thought,* XVI, 79 ff.; and Hamm, *New Schol.,* XVIII, 17–18, *et passim.* All are speculating. A more likely speculation may seem to be that of Morris, *Tyndale to Hooker,* pp. 197–198: "Burke diverged from Locke by going back to another side of Hooker. If Locke was influenced by Hooker's belief in natural law, in reason, and in the necessity for consent, Burke was to return to Hooker's sense of history, to his belief that tradition and authority were reasonable, that men cannot dispense with government, and that constitutions are organic things."

133. III, 79–80. Hutchins (*RP,* V, 150) concludes: "The will of God forbids all change, for the will of God has placed men where they are found at birth." Another half-truth by a partisan critic.

134. June 5, 1794, VIII, 141–142. Ransom says (*Kenyon Rev.,* XV, 652); "[Burke's] is an empirical faith, the religious counterpart of falling in love with what is nearest to you and most domesticated yet most wonderful." Cf. Reynolds' speculations on "prejudice," obviously inspired by Burke: "Prejudice Is the Wisdom of the Supreme and the chief engine of Political Wisdom—it is a ray of the divine Wisdom which when catchd by Man approaches nearer to divinity . . . can any thing be more benevolent more consistent with divine wisdom than giving us that disposition to like and prefer and esteem that the most beautifull that we are most accustom'd to. . . . I have endeavored to distinguish

between those the different kinds of Prejudices, those narrow ones which we have from a partial and confined view, and which are to be eradicated, and the more enlarged which is the Wisdom of the creator." F. W. Hilles, *The Literary Career of Sir Joshua Reynolds* (New York, 1936), pp. 227–228.

135. *Ibid.,* 7th Day of Reply, p. 274.

136. "From New to Old Whigs," III, 81.

137. "Warren Hastings," 8th Day of Reply, June 14, 1794, VIII, 439–440.

138. "From New to Old Whigs," III, 80.

139. "Warren Hastings," 4th Day, Feb. 16, 1788, VII, 94.

140. *Ibid.,* 6th Day, Feb. 19, 1788, p. 229.

141. *Ibid.,* 3rd Day, Feb. 15, 1788, p. 16.

142. *Ibid.,* 6th Day, p. 231.

143. *Ibid.,* 6th Charge, Bribery and Corruption, April 21, 1789, p. 232.

144. *Ibid.,* p. 233.

145. *Ibid.,* April 25, 1789, p. 320.

146. "On East-India Bill," II, 220.

147. "Warren Hastings," 4th Day, Feb. 16, 1788, VII, 93–94.

148. *Ibid.,* 5th Day, Feb. 17, 1788, p. 191.

149. Burke to [ ], Dec. 28, 1796, quoted in W. R. Halliday, "Burke and the Cavendishes," *English Historical Review,* XLVII (April, 1932), 284. Cf. Mrs. Crewe, "Table-Talk," *Misc. of Phil. Soc.,* VII, 49: Having "thought it for a long time past an ignorant Age," Burke considered "our forefathers as deeper Thinkers than ourselves, because they set an higher Value on good sense than knowledge in various Sciences, and this good sense was derived very often from as much study and more knowledge, though of another sort."

150. For a suggestive synopsis, tying together Hooker, the Cambridge Platonists, Burke, and Coleridge, see Willey, *"Thought,"* in *The Character of England,* pp. 321–339. All these great men are, of course, practicing Anglicans. On the characteristic Englishness of Whitehead, as well as on the "Anglo-Saxon religiosity" essential in his thinking, see the lucid sketch by Marc-André Bera, "A. N. Whitehead: un Philosophe de l'Experience," *Actualités scientifiques et industrielles,* No. 1056 (Paris, 1948), pp. 3–54. The main points of M. Bera's study apply equally well to the men above: Whitehead is a philosopher of experience, a philosopher of the concrete, instinctively empirical (p. 26), poetic (p. 20), practical (p. 38), moderating (p. 35), and hostile to neat systemization (pp. 16, 32). He is a reforming conservative, p. 35), with a respect for the sense of the English public (p. 36), a dramatic sense of history (p. 37), and a high valuation of liberty (p. 34). He is essentially theocentric (pp. 46 ff., esp. p. 48), but at the same time dedicated to the endless, reciprocal confrontation of general principle with irreducible fact (pp. 34, 38). His Englishness is "une méthode de pensée,"

"une forme de l'esprit" (p. 31), derived in good part from his having received the empirical tradition, and in turn having maintained and expanded it (p. 39).

A number of other English "thinkers" from Sir Thomas Elyot to Wordsworth exemplify similar characteristics. As M. Bera says: "Quand les philosophes ne sont pas des savants, ce sont des artistes, des historiens, ou de simples gens de lettres, mais jamais ce ne sont des philosophes de profession. . . . Ce sont des autodidactes, des self-made men" (pp. 6–7).

Among Burke's contemporaneous friends, one might call attention to —of course, the gigantic figure of Johnson, but also to lesser lights like Reynolds. The *Discourses* is in spirit and at key points a startlingly close analogue and companion piece to Burke; the rumor that Burke wrote them, now discredited, is understandable; see Hilles, *Literary Career of Reynolds,* pp. 136–141, *et passim.* They accord in the phrasing of key single ideas like *principle* and *sagacity* (XIII), *prudence* (XII), distrust of methodical theory (VII, XII), and reprehension of excesses (VIII), as also in larger motivations like the premium on tradition as assimilative experience which enables (not defeats) progress, the interest in psychology, and a generous, open-minded nationalism, with its peculiar English blend of benevolence, practicality, and sophistication, and its emphasis on effecting the happiness of individuals by a continuity of diffused values (IX). "Nature" (meaning very loosely to Reynolds, neo-Platonic types) in later discourses, for example XII, is not a strait-laced intellectual scheme, but something subtle and inexhaustibly various at work in the particular, which is beyond the retention of memory and must be resorted to again and again. Here, as in Burke, is a flexible "empiricist's" notion of an ideal order of permanence only to be known in conjunction with the mazes of novelty and accident, and whose knowledge, in Reynold's phrase, is "perfect freedom."

One may also adduce Goldsmith, despite his strain of *philosophie.* Burke's taste is comparable to that of his friend, whom he turns to account (cf. "To a Noble Lord, V, 142, "Their humanity is at the horizon—and, like the horizon, it always flies before them," and *The Traveller,* lines 24–28). That is, conscious of a great literary past in England, especially of "the divine *Shakespear*" (Samuels, *Early Life,* p. 301), and with a special appreciation for writers of the Queen Anne age, "like stars lost in each other's brightness," Burke like Goldsmith turned his disgust upon the "false refinement, which diffuses a languor, and breathes a frivolous air over everything," which is "our present weakness in that oldest and most excellent branch of philosophy, poetical learning, and particularly in what regards the theatre." "Hints for an Essay on the Drama," VI, 177; see Mrs. Crewe, "Table-Talk," *Misc. of Phil. Soc.,* VII, 14, 36, 49. Cf. Goldsmith's *Enquiry Into the Present State of Polite Learning in Europe,* chs. 11–12. Goldsmith's *Enquiry,* early and rude as it is, should be compared with Burke and English thinking in general in its protest against abstraction, system-making, and rejection of the medieval past, especially among Frenchmen; its plea for "taste" and virtual identification of "taste" and "common sense"; its assumption that "learning" is transient and cannot flourish till "slow gradations of improvement have naturalized it to the soil," that is, its premium upon live, continuous tradition, diffused throughout a stable society; its calling for a national literary criticism, and its assumption that the English character is a perennial spring of (literary) value which ought to be cherished and cultivated in the familiar. Also, something of a wild, sweet, and serene Irish lyricism links the two expatriates and admirers of Montesquieu.

Cf. Paul Spencer Wood, "Native Elements in English Neo-Classicism," *MP,* XXIV (1926), 201–208; and Wilson, *Mere Literature,* pp. 157–160.

# Index